Why Bright Kids Get Poor Grades and What You Can Do about It

A Six-Step Program for Parents and Teachers

3rd Edition

Dr. Sylvia Rimm

Great Potential Press™

Why Bright Kids Get Poor Grades and What You Can Do about It
A Six-Step Program for Parents and Teachers, **3rd Edition**

Edited by: Jennifer Ault
Interior Design: The Printed Page
Cover Design: Julee Hutchison

Published by
Great Potential Press, Inc.
P.O. Box 5057
Scottsdale, AZ 85261
www.giftedbooks.com

Printed and Bound in the United States of America

12 11 10 09 08   5 4 3 2 1

Library of Congress Cataloging-in-Publication Data

Rimm, Sylvia B.,
  Why bright kids get poor grades and what you can do about it : a six-step program for parents and teachers / Sylvia Rimm. -- 3rd ed.
        p. cm.
  Includes bibliographical references and index.
  ISBN-13: 978-0-910707-87-9
  ISBN-10: 0-910707-87-1
1. Underachiever--United States. 2. Academic achievement--United States. 3. Personality and academic achievement. I. Title.
  LC4691.R57 2008
  371.95'6—dc22
                              2008014748

About the Author

Sylvia Rimm, Ph.D., is a best-selling author of many books on parenting and has appeared regularly on NBC's *Today* show. As director of the Family Achievement Clinic in Cleveland, Ohio, and as a clinical professor at Case Western Reserve University School of Medicine, Dr. Rimm is a foremost expert on how to raise children in an environment that encourages learning and achievement.

Dr. Rimm writes a parenting column, syndicated through Creators Syndicate, and she has served for many years on the Board of Directors of the National Association for Gifted Children (NAGC). She received her master's and doctoral degrees in educational psychology from the University of Wisconsin-Madison. A mother of four, Dr. Rimm lives in Ohio with her husband.

Also by Dr. Sylvia Rimm

- *Education of the Gifted and Talented* (with Gary A. Davis) (5th ed.)
- *Exploring Feelings: Discussion Book for Gifted Kids Have Feelings Too*
- *Gifted Kids Have Feelings Too—And Other Not-So-Fictitious Stories for and about Teenagers*
- *Growing Up Too Fast: The Rimm Report on the Secret World of America's Middle Schoolers*
- *How Jane Won: 55 Successful Women Share How They Grew from Ordinary Girls to Extraordinary Women*
- *How to Parent So Children Will Learn*
- *Keys to Parenting the Gifted Child*
- *Raising Preschoolers*
- *Rescuing the Emotional Lives of Overweight Children*
- *Rimm's Parenting for Achievement: Training Course*
- *See Jane Win® for Girls: A Smart Girl's Guide to Success*
- *See Jane Win®: The Rimm Report on How 1,000 Girls Became Successful Women*
- *Sylvia Rimm on Raising Kids*
- *Underachievement Syndrome: Causes and Cures*

Dedication

To my husband, Buck, and my children and grandchildren:
Ilonna, Joe, Miriam, Benjamin, Abraham,
David, Janet, Daniel, Rachel,
Eric, Allison, Hannah, Isaac,
Sara, Alan, Samuel, and Davida

Contents

List of Figures

Acknowledgments

First, I wish to acknowledge my own family for providing the basic, day-to-day trial and error learning that helped make this book possible. I especially want to thank my husband, Buck, my partner in parenting, from whom and with whom I have learned so much. Family appreciation extends to my parents and my children, as well as my siblings, in-laws, nieces, and nephews.

The therapists and clients, both parents and children, at Family Achievement Clinic provided the next most important source of information and experience. Therapy brings the psychologist very close to the personal lives of many, and I have often felt so intensely committed that it was almost as if many of these children were my own. Their parents' problems were my problems. I want to extend to those parents and children my appreciation for their confidence as I carefully and, I hope, sensitively used their lives to build a theory and a model in the expectation that I could also help others. My appreciation also goes to all those therapists who helped me to develop my clinic and my model, but especially Frances Culbertson, Michael Cornale, and Jeanne Behrend.

When I enter a school, I always feel a special warmth that reminds me that good things are happening in the building. Schools and education are a real love for me, so I wish to acknowledge the many teachers and administrators who contributed to my love of learning, to my commitment to education, and to so many ideas and practical suggestions in this book. I want to remind them of how important they are to our children and ask for their continued help in building knowledge for reversing Underachievement Syndrome.

NBC's *Today* show producers, Patricia Luchsinger and Janet Schiller, receive a special thank-you for introducing me to millions of parent viewers who continue to correspond with me regularly. Thanks to Katie Couric, Matt Lauer, Al Roker, and Ann Curry, whose delightful interviews help me to answer parents' needs.

There are many people who assisted me in the writing of this book. A special thank-you goes to Gary A. Davis for many extremely helpful suggestions for the first edition of my book. My staff, Marilyn Knackert,

Joanne Riedl, Tammy Weisser, Christy Oestreich, and Lori Butler, merit my deepest appreciation for their contributions to the typing and editing of the manuscript. Finally, I would like to acknowledge Peter Ginna for his excellent editorial work on the second edition and Jim Webb and Jennifer Ault of Great Potential Press for their contributions to this third edition of *Why Bright Kids Get Poor Grades and What You Can Do about It*.

Preface

This third edition of *Why Bright Kids Get Poor Grades* celebrates approximately 30 years of developing and using the Trifocal Model to reverse Underachievement Syndrome for capable children who are not working to their abilities in school. As of this writing, 135,000 copies of the book have been sold. The framework for the model was first published in 1986 and was titled *Underachievement Syndrome: Causes and Cures*. In 1989, a *Guidebook for Implementing the Trifocal Underachievement Program for Schools* was supplemented. In 1995, after I became a consulting correspondent to NBC's *Today* show and host of "Family Talk with Sylvia Rimm" on public radio, Crown Publishers published an update and second edition of the original book using the present name.

For this third edition, I've updated the book again. While this new edition continues to provide the same principles that have reversed underachievement for thousands of children, I've added sections that reflect information that has been gleaned from my clinical experiences, my research and that of others, and the successful experiences of other educators and parents. New sections on gender issues, perfectionism, differentiated curriculum, resilience, peer pressures, and the affiliation-achievement balance have been included. I have also added additional suggestions for children with attention disorders, organizational problems, dual exceptionalities, and processing speed and listening skill deficits.

As always, teachers and parents alike will find my book readable and practical. They will identify patterns from their own childhoods that may have contributed to or distracted from their own motivation, and they will become able to identify these patterns in the students in their classrooms and the children in their homes.

As a psychologist who has worked directly with families and educators, I find that whenever I give a presentation or workshop, at least one—and sometimes more than one—teacher or parent takes me aside privately to thank me for making a difference for their child or student. Also, letters and emails arrive from grown children or their parents updating me on achievement progress. My sample is biased in that successful, happy people are more likely to want to report results to me. I know that I wasn't able to help all of the children that I've attempted to assist. Those whom I've failed were most often sidetracked by drug dependence or addiction.

My favorite letter comes from a young man whom I worked with in Wisconsin when he was in fourth and fifth grade. He was a sad, lonely, and disorganized underachiever with little confidence and poor social skills. He was creative and imaginative but felt alienated from his father, brother, and classmates. His grades were terrible. His IQ and achievement test scores were above average but not in the gifted range. It was difficult to know what potential he had, and there was much work to do with his family, his school, and his social and emotional skills. I chose this letter because this young man recalled so well the kinds of messages that I've given to thousands of other children. The letter demonstrates that reversing underachievement is more than just about achievement, but about leading a fulfilled life. I hope that you, too, will enjoy his letter:

Dear Dr. Rimm,

I recently saw you on the Today *show and just had to write you. You were my psychologist back when I was in grade school. I went to school in Wisconsin back in the early '80s. You helped me through my underachievement issues that plagued my academic and social success. I owe most of the success that I now enjoy to you. You helped instill in me the confidence that I desperately needed to break free from my shell and allow myself to grow. I remember that you told me never to be afraid of getting the wrong answer because that is how we learn. I remember you told me to continue to explore my creativity through writing and acting because that is how I would truly find my strengths. I remember how you taught me to manage my life strategically because this would help my confusion and random, inconsistent behavior. Finally, I remember that you told me to never be afraid to express myself no matter what others thought.*

Dr. Rimm, in many ways, you have been there for me over the past 15 years because of what you taught me. I never became a famous writer and I have never starred on Broadway, but I will soon have a degree from the University of Wisconsin—Madison and attend law school. I have considered myself a leader since high school. I have held leadership roles in every single organization I have been involved with over the past 10 years. I have been blessed with some of the best friends anyone could ask for—good, strong relationships that you helped me identify, seek out, and keep. I now consider my parents and brother my best friends and closest confidants, and I face the world with an uncompromising confidence that I will make a difference. Thank you, Dr. Rimm, for giving me the tools to make my dreams come true.

I have been working in the trenches together with parents and teachers to successfully reverse underachievement for countless children. My Trifocal Model targets children, their parents, and their teachers to reverse Underachievement Syndrome. I developed this model at my Family Achievement Clinic in Wisconsin and used it at Family Achievement Clinics at Metro Health Medical Center, Cleveland Clinic, and now at my own Family Achievement Clinics in Ohio and Wisconsin. My Trifocal Model is also used in many schools and counseling centers. It is a practical model based on real-life problems.

We know that parents want to parent well and that teachers want to teach well. Yet despite those excellent intentions, problems are accidentally perpetuated because of the confusion of children's behavior or because conflicting life events often pressure adults into responding to children in ways that reinforce their nonproductive patterns. If some of the scenarios described in my book make you feel uncomfortable or guilty, remember that even excellent parents and teachers make mistakes. There are no perfect parents or teachers. Please remind yourself of all of the right and good things that you've done as you search for the techniques to improve the problem areas.

This book is for the parents who value achievement in their children and for the teachers who are challenged to motivate all students. My purpose is to assist parents and teachers in guiding the many children and adolescents who want so much to be bright and important but who have not learned that the path to achievement and personal control of their learning includes commitment, perseverance, and resilience.

Part 1 of this book describes the symptoms and causes of Underachievement Syndrome. Part 2 documents the practical techniques that can be used successfully by parents, teachers, and clinic personnel. You, as parents and teachers, will undoubtedly invent additional techniques to implement the basic steps of the model.

My experience has also led me to formulate what I call Rimm's Laws of Achievement. I will refer to these principles throughout the book and will explain them more fully in Chapter 14, but I put them here at the beginning because they are the basic underlying principles of successful teaching and parenting.

Yes, Underachievement Syndrome is epidemic. It continues to enter innumerable classrooms and homes. But with your help and knowledge, we can motivate and inspire children to achieve, feel good about themselves, and improve our society, which needs their contributions. I hope that you will use my book to reverse Underachievement Syndrome in your classroom or in your home.

Rimm's Laws of Achievement

Rimm's Law #1: Children are more likely to be achievers if their parents join together to give the same clear and positive message about school effort and expectations.

Rimm's Law #2: Children learn appropriate behaviors more easily if they have effective models to imitate.

Rimm's Law #3: What adults say to each other about children within their hearing dramatically affects children's behaviors and self-perceptions.

Rimm's Law #4: Overreactions by parents or teachers to children's successes and failures lead them to feel either intense pressure to succeed or despair and discouragement in dealing with failure.

Rimm's Law #5: Children feel more tension when they are worrying about their work than when they are doing that work.

Rimm's Law #6: Children develop self-confidence and resilience through struggle.

Rimm's Law #7: Deprivation and excess frequently exhibit the same symptoms.

Rimm's Law #8: Children develop confidence and an internal sense of control if they are given power in gradually increasing increments as they show maturity and responsibility.

Rimm's Law #9: Children become oppositional if one adult allies with them against a parent or a teacher, making them more powerful than an adult.

Rimm's Law #10: Adults should avoid confrontations with children unless they are reasonably sure that they can control the outcomes.

Rimm's Law #11: Children will become achievers only if they learn to function in competition.

Rimm's Law #12: Children will continue to achieve if they usually see the relationship between the learning process and its outcomes.

How to Get the Most Out of This Book

This book can help you if you are a parent, a teacher, or another adult who is trying to understand your children's (or students') or your own childhood patterns of underachievement.

Part 1 of this book concentrates on the causes of underachievement. The quizzes before each chapter permit a brief evaluation that can help determine how the factors described in the chapter have affected your children, students, or yourself. If your score on the quiz is high, be sure to read the chapter thoroughly. If it's low, you may prefer only to skim the material for preventative purposes.

Within Part 1 of the book are some Parent Pointers and Teacher Tips, which are indicated by notes in the margins. These will help you to initiate some changes even before you get to Part 2, which describes in detail practical techniques for reversing Underachievement Syndrome.

Part 2 of the book includes step-by-step recommendations for parents and teachers. Because there are a variety of underachieving patterns, you may wish to read this section with a highlighting pen in hand. If your child's other parent or parents wish to read your copy of the book, suggest that they use other colors for highlighting. Although the resulting text may become colorful, the color coding can be used to concentrate on specific steps for all of the important adults in your child's life to take.

Don't be overwhelmed by the quantity of recommendations in this book. No child will need all of the changes listed in these pages. You need only to select those that apply to your children or students.

If you prefer other media, there are tests, videos, CDs, and DVDs available that can help you communicate and implement these methods. My user-friendly website, www.sylviarimm.com, can provide you with additional information.

Please don't hesitate to communicate with me if you have further questions. You may write to me at my website, although you may need to be patient in waiting for responses. Eventually, though, I do answer every question. I've made every effort to make the reversal of your children's or students' underachievement an interactive experience.

Part 1

Why Bright Kids Get Poor Grades

Ask yourself the following questions before you read Chapter 1. (If you're a teacher, read "this student" for "my child.")

1. Does my child forget to do homework assignments?

2. Does my child give up easily?

3. Does my child avoid competitive activities unless he/she is almost sure to win?

4. Does my child start working late on homework each night?

5. Does my child watch two or more hours of TV (or play two or more hours of video games) on school nights?

Score 1 point for each "yes" response, and total the points. Scores are explained below.

Total Points

4–5:	My child has characteristics that indicate a very serious underachievement problem.
2–3:	My child has characteristics that indicate a fairly serious underachievement problem.
1:	My child has characteristics that indicate only minor underachievement problems.
0:	My child has no characteristics of Underachievement Syndrome.

Read this chapter to understand the characteristics of underachievers.

Chapter 1
What Is Underachievement?

Our nation continually searches for better ways to educate its children. National and international studies routinely report depressing statistics about U.S. children's lack of basic skills, inadequate knowledge of science, below-average skills in mathematics, inept critical thinking, and poor problem-solving abilities, as well as their lack of readiness for post-high school education and the workforce. The U.S. Department of Education conducted a study, ending in 2001, which reported that only 53% of students who enter a four-year institution actually earn a bachelor's degree.[1]

These problems have been blamed on such villains as television, movies, violent computer and video games, the economy, the breakdown of the family, large classes, the Internet, not enough class time, shortages of funds, and poor discipline. Education professionals complicate the discussion by use of such inside jargon as "cultural deprivation," "learning disabilities," "tracking," "test bias," "no child left behind," "Title One," and "inclusion." Children are diagnosed with disorders such as Learning Disability, Executive Dysfunction difficulties, Attention Deficit Hyperactivity Disorder, Asperger's Syndrome, Bipolar Disorder, Overanxious Disorder, and Depressive Reaction.[2] The endless controversy can be bewildering to most parents who may not also be educators, as well as for educators who truly want to teach children.

All of these debates about why American children don't learn as well as they should ignore a very basic issue. Even if we add time to the school day, give new titles to federal funding, increase teacher salaries, reduce class size, fund education for children with special needs, and change tests to reflect differences in cultural environments and learning styles, we are still not facing a central problem in our schools.

Millions of children who have no actual diagnosable disorder that would affect learning—children with average, above-average, and even gifted intellectual abilities, including those from homes where education is valued—are simply not performing up to their capabilities.[3] These children may be very creative or verbally or mathematically precocious, yet despite their abilities, they do not perform well in school. Social and emotional factors are the culprits, and psychological strategies must be used to prevent and reverse their underachievement.

Underachievers sit in virtually every classroom and live in many families. They waste educational resources, try the patience of even the best teachers, manipulate their families toward chaos, and destroy their own confidence and sense of personal control.

The problem is disconcertingly widespread. When I appeared for a five-minute interview on NBC's *Today* show covering the topic of bright, underachieving children, that one segment attracted more than 20,000 phone calls and thousands of letters from distressed parents from all over the country (see Figure 1.1). It seems that I had hit a raw nerve for tens of thousands of families who recognized the symptoms of Underachievement Syndrome in their children.

Figure 1.1. Excerpts from *Today* Show Viewers' Letters

New York:
My youngest son is a freshman at SUNY Oswego College and is going through a very difficult time. He is at an emotional low and has called us for help. We're not sure what to do for him.

North Carolina:
My son, an eleventh grader, is a gifted student and having a lot of problems this year. I'm afraid he is throwing away all of his chances for the future.

Florida:
Zachary is five years old and in kindergarten. He's been reading since he was two years of age. However, I am concerned with his behavior. He gives up very easily. Sometimes he'll throw a pencil. Zachary also demands attention and excessive praise, which is not easy to deliver to one child in a class of 27 children.

Tennessee:
My son, Kevin, was told he would be in the school's Academic Olympics. Since he isn't doing his work, his teacher is considering sending someone else in his place. Kevin cried about it because he wants very much to be a part of this. He claims that he tries, but he just cannot seem to get assignments turned in.

Iowa:
Our son is definitely experiencing all of the problems you mentioned. Jarrod is 16 and tested in the 90th percentile on all of his basic skills tests, but he's getting D's and F's in every academic subject. He had to repeat sophomore English because he just would not turn in assignments. He doesn't do homework at all.

Texas:
I have a college student who was a National Merit Scholar who is on scholastic probation because she hasn't a clue about what studying entails. The process is foreign to her since she floated through high school. She is quite devastated, and we really don't know how to teach her to study.

> **Pennsylvania:**
> My daughter is 18, got a 1340 on her SATs, and is getting C's and D-'s in her post-graduate year.
> **Idaho:**
> I am interested in where I can read more about the topic of gifted kids who don't hand in papers, stop going to classes in college, etc. Sounds like you have met my son, recently readmitted to Middlebury College (VT) for his "last chance."

What is Underachievement Syndrome, and what causes it? There is no gene for underachievement, no neurological or biological explanation for inadequate school performance by capable children. Nor can we find in the educational institution a particular cause for underachievement, for there are many children with similar abilities who achieve well in the same classrooms. Instead, underachieving children seem not to have learned the process of achievement—in fact, they have *learned* to underachieve.

Underachievers usually begin as apparently bright and often very verbal preschoolers, but at some point, their enthusiasm for learning and their satisfactory school performance change—gradually for some, suddenly and dramatically for others. The change in their achievement patterns can easily be seen by comparing their year-to-year achievement test scores. Percentile scores are stable while children are in an achieving mode, but they decline steadily when children enter the underachieving mode. But there are other more apparent indicators as well. The most obvious warning is the direct communication from teachers that these children are not working to their abilities. Parents also notice their children's disinterest and detachment from the school learning process.

What are the characteristics of children with Underachievement Syndrome? Underachievers tend to be disorganized. They dawdle, forget homework, lose assignments, and misplace books. They daydream, don't listen, look out the window, or talk too much to other children. They have poor study skills—or none at all. They consider themselves to have studied if they've briefly read the material while lying on their beds watching TV or listening to music.

Some underachievers are slow and perfectionistic; they may say that if they finish their work, it will probably be wrong anyway. On the other hand, some will complete their work quickly but are much more concerned about finishing the assignment than about doing quality work. Their papers have so many careless errors in them that one wonders if they gave any thought to the assignment at all.

Some underachieving children are lonely and withdrawn. They don't seem to want any friends. They may cry, whine, and complain, or they may be teased and tormented by their peers. Others are bossy and lose their tempers easily. Some are aggressive and may start playground fights. If underachievers show any interest in school, it is related to their social life or sports. They may find one subject or a teacher they like, but in general, they describe school as boring.

Some never read books, while others immerse themselves in reading as an escape. They especially like to read when they are supposed to be doing homework or household chores. Television, computers, or video games may serve as alternative escapes, and conveniently, these children rarely hear their parents calling when they are staring at the TV or computer screen or playing video games.

Some underachievers are literal and concrete in their thinking and apparently cannot solve abstract problems at all, while others display very creative and unusual thinking. The creative underachievers may have many unusual ideas, but they rarely bring their ideas to closure. They seem unable to complete what they begin. Some creative underachievers immerse themselves so completely in a chosen project that they attend to little else, and they fall behind in all of their other school responsibilities.

Despite these variations in the characteristics of underachievers, they do have one very important trait in common: *Underachievers are unconsciously manipulative*, some less obviously than others. They may overtly attempt to manipulate parent against parent, teacher against parent, parent against teacher, or friend against friend. Covertly, they may manipulate parents to do much of their homework for them or teachers to postpone deadlines or give them more assistance or less challenging assignments.

What do underachievers say about their school problems? They have innumerable defenses. School is boring when they are young, irrelevant when they are older. The boredom or irrelevance is constant and tends to be unrelated to the actual assignments. They blame their poor grades, which they say don't matter, on "terrible teachers." They think that drama, sports, music, or having a social life is more important than schoolwork. "Who wants to be a geek anyway?" they retort. They sometimes claim that they don't have the ability to do better, and their intelligence or ability test scores must be wrong. They call achievement their parents' goal, not theirs, and blame their problems on unfair comparisons with sisters or brothers or unfair pressures by their parents. They excuse themselves from making an effort by saying that they'd rather not do the work at all than do it less than perfectly. Sometimes they complain that they're putting themselves under too much pressure and probably shouldn't expect so much of themselves.

Underlying these children's poor study habits, weak skills, disorganization, and defensiveness is a feeling of a lack of personal control over their educational success. Underachievers don't really believe that they can achieve their goals even if they work harder. They may readily acknowledge that their lack of effort is the cause of the problem, and they are likely to admit that they would need to make considerably more effort to achieve their high goals. Even then, however, they're not certain that they could achieve them. Effort might make a small difference, but small differences are not enough and not worth the investment and risk.

These children set their goals either too high or too low, and as a result, they guarantee failure. They want to be millionaires, professional football players, inventors of computer games, rock stars, Olympic gymnasts, or presidents, and they have magical ideas about the effort necessary to arrive at these unrealistic goals. They may say such things as, "If my mother would only let me work on the computer for as long as I wanted, I could eventually earn a six-figure salary," or, "If my parents would let me practice the guitar instead of wasting my time on math, I would be successful." They have not yet discovered what the word *work* actually means. They understand it as having a romantic and mystical air that is closer to fun and action than to the persevering effort that is required for achievement. They cannot build firm self-confidence because they have not learned a real sense of effort.

Children cannot build confidence by accomplishing only easy tasks. They already know that anyone can accomplish these tasks. It is when children accept the risk of struggle and find that they can accomplish that which they didn't think was possible that they begin to build self-confidence. It is from actual achievement that one develops a strong self-concept. Underachievers deny themselves the opportunity to build confidence because they direct their energies toward avoiding the relationship between process and outcome, between effort and achievement.

Ours is a competitive society, and families and schools are competitive. Underachievers have highly competitive feelings, but they may not be obvious. They aspire to be winners and are poor losers. If they don't believe they can win, they may quit before they begin, or they may select only those experiences in which they are certain of victory. They are competitive, internally pressured children who have not learned to cope with defeat.

It is not possible to be productive in our society or in our schools until one learns to cope with competition, and this requires understanding that winning and losing are always temporary. It is a fallacy for parents and teachers to believe that they can create home and school environments in which children can always succeed. Indeed, even if they could create this kind of environment, it would be an overprotective and therefore unhealthy one for children. Children who learn to lose without being devastated and use failure experiences to grow will achieve in the classroom and in society. Children who can lose without feeling like losers discover resilience—the key to positive growth. Our goals should not be schools without failure—only schools without children who *feel* like failures.

Even as schools try to make classrooms more collaborative, they cannot extinguish the basic competitive motivation that pervades society. Children should certainly learn to cooperate, but they must also learn to win graciously and lose courageously.

The concept of competition is too often considered a negative one. Perhaps it would be easier for parents and teachers to accept competition if we applied the term *resilience* to surviving or coping with competition. In my research on the childhoods of more than 1,000 successful women, the most positive experience that these women listed most frequently was winning in competition.[4] Winning is exhilarating and encourages achievement. However, bouncing back from small losses builds resilience and the strength of character that all children will require in their adult lives.[5]

Regardless of how parents or teachers personally feel about competition, children continuously compare their performance to that of other children at home and at school; thus, learning to compete effectively is central to achievement in school. Underachievers have not internalized this basic competitive message. Instead, they manipulate their families and school environments in fear of failure. They learn to avoid competition unless they can win, and in the process, they miss important skills. As their underachievement cycle continues, they feel less and less capable. Their fear of failure increases. Their sense of efficacy decreases. They and their parents feel helpless and hopeless as the gap between where they are and where they should be widens menacingly. The cycle continues downward in a spiral that perpetuates the problem. Underachievement Syndrome adversely affects the child and often the entire family. It feeds on itself and grows until something or someone either deliberately or spontaneously intervenes to reverse the cycle.

In unplanned interventions, teachers, friends, mentors, or other important people may be the catalysts that help underachievers reverse their problem. In some cases, these other individuals serve as models for underachievers. In others, it is their support that is most critical. Because underachievers often have the potential for high achievement, they may take great leaps in the skills that they develop for their new roles. Examples of underachievers turned "superachievers" are the unimpressive classmates one remembers from high school who return to their 10-year high school reunions with high-level college degrees or impressive careers. They are confident and successful, and we wonder how someone who appeared to lack high ability could accomplish so much. They are often called *late bloomers.*

Unfortunately, only a small percentage of late bloomers emerge from their latent states to develop their talents. Most continue their downward cycle to become high school and college dropouts. If they manage to remain in school until graduation, they show only marginal achievement and have little interest in learning. They join the workforce of underachievers and lead lives in which they drastically underuse their abilities—to their own frustration and to society's loss. Their lifestyles take on "easy way out" patterns, or they move through adulthood realizing that they should have lived differently but feel helpless to change.

You, as parents and teachers, can do something about underachievement. You will be able to do this better if you learn why bright kids get poor grades. Additionally, you can accomplish more if you work with each other. If you suspect that you have an underachiever in your family or in your classroom, this book will help you to recognize and deal with your underachiever's problems.

First, try to identify your type of underachiever. Then look further for the family and/or school pattern that may have shaped the underachievement style. Finally, try those recommendations that will help you to reverse the underachievement cycle at home and at school. Be realistic; it is usually easier to identify your underachiever and the family/school pattern than to change them, so plan for patience and perseverance. You may not be able to (or wish to) change every error you uncover, but even small improvements will be gratifying. A sense of achievement for your children and for underachievers in your classroom will build their self-confidence. Children who don't seem to care about school and grades can be motivated to learn and achieve by parents and teachers who understand the underlying causes of their problems. Underachievers can master the skills that will enable them to cope with competition in our society and, therefore, can be free to experience the joy of self-motivated learning and accomplishment.

What Do Underachievers Look Like?

Underachievers come in many varieties, and although they are truly individual, they often fit into prototypical categories. In real life, the prototypes are not pure in any one child but are blended. However, the descriptions in this chapter will help you to determine if your child or student has Underachievement Syndrome. Figure 1.2 can help you to visualize your child's prototypical category.

Figure 1.2. The Inner Circle of Achievers

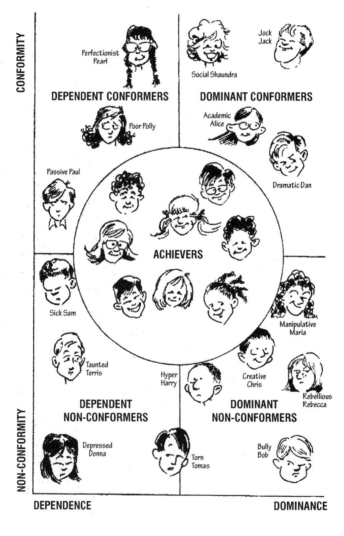

If you're not sure that your child is an underachiever, think about the last parent-teacher conference you attended. Consider your child as you see him or her at home. Compare your child with the children that are described in the next section. If some of these descriptions remind you of your child at home or of students in your classroom, it is likely that they have Underachievement Syndrome.

Categories of Underachievement

Perfectionist Pearl

> Neat, tidy papers. Neat, tidy desk.
> Perfectionist Pearl always does her best.
> Handwriting's A, Spelling's okay,
> But Pearl can't get her work done today.

Today, second-grade teacher Mrs. Jones has assigned an original story. The other children started 20 minutes ago, but Pearl doesn't have a word down on her paper, not even a title. Finally, she raises her hand timidly. "Mrs. Jones," she whines, "I just don't know what to write about." Mrs. Jones is perplexed. Why is Pearl, who is so bright, who completes workbook pages so perfectly, and who uses impeccable grammar, unable to think of a topic for a one-page story? Mrs. Jones makes several suggestions, and Pearl listens quietly. Tears glaze her eyes, and she explains, "Mrs. Jones, I don't see how I can write a story if I can't find a perfect topic!"

Pearl's problems have just begun. In third grade, she may still be a very fine student. As long as her work assignments are concrete and specific, she performs well. However, when she needs to think abstractly, come to conclusions based on reasoning, originate her own ideas, or take a small risk, she is paralyzed by fear of failure. Her grades and confidence will really begin to decline in middle school. Gifted Pearl, who began school at the top, moves steadily toward classroom mediocrity.

At home, Pearl's room is neat. She is obedient. She causes no problems. She is the perfect child until adolescence. Adolescence brings a strange rebellion. Anger, eating disorders, and feelings of depression appear. Pearl searches for ways to control a small part of her life perfectly, because for Pearl, the alternative to perfection is failure. She sets impossibly high standards for herself and feels helpless in her search for success.

Poor Polly

This sad child finds a sympathetic ear among parents, teachers, and eventually her teenage friends. She claims that schoolwork is difficult and her peers don't accept her, and she is afraid to try new experiences. She seems to thrive on anticipating negative outcomes and on persuading adults in her environment to reassure her about her intelligence, her social skills, or her self-confidence. Parents and teachers, who do much of the early reassuring, comment on Polly's low self-esteem but don't realize that by giving so much attention to her avoidance techniques, they are preventing her from developing confidence.

This continuous attention to Polly's negative anticipations causes two problems. First, the frequent, sincere, and kind attention teaches Polly that self-doubt and feeling sorry for herself are effective ways to elicit assurances of support and love. Second, the attention often protects her from attempting risk-taking activities that would help build her self-confidence. Although solicitous adults are truly attempting to provide kind assistance to her, that assistance prevents the growth of self-confidence and encourages the avoidance behaviors that maintain Polly's underachievement.

Most important, parents and teachers tend to describe these kinds of children as immature. Recommendations to enter school a year later, retain them, or get tutoring are typical. However, this can result in these children being held back unnecessarily, and they are usually expected to do less than what they are capable of to avoid putting them under too much pressure.

Passive Paul

Paul slouches at his desk. He yawns, daydreams, meanders through math. His assignments are rarely complete and, if they are, never completed well. He raises his hand to ask questions, but not to answer them. When called upon, he gives non-responses, such as, "I don't know," "I'm not sure," "I don't understand," or, "I forgot." He is a likable, pleasant, good kid who just doesn't get his work done but never seems to worry about it. "He can't seem to concentrate," the teacher says. "Perhaps Paul needs medication." His parents wonder if he has an attention disorder.

"I'm doing much better now, Mom," Paul says with confidence.

"Yes, I have all of my homework done," he says, bending the truth reassuringly.

"Gee, I'm sorry I got that F; Ill do better next time," he tearfully apologizes. "My mind just wanders."

Paul's homework is rarely done. Books and assignments don't come home for study, and grades continue downward in a never-ending plunge toward failure.

Unmoved and unmoving, Paul passively withdraws to the television screen. He is immobile and unresponsive when his mother calls him to his homework. He stares intently at the TV as her normally quiet tone escalates. He blinks his eyes as Mother's shouts pervade the room. Finally, when Mother screams in desperation, he apologizes for not hearing and asks what she'd like him to do. When she suggests homework, he lies assuringly, telling her that his homework is all complete, and retreats to the screen in further absorption.

Mother, frustrated and despondent, is reassured by Dad that Paul must certainly have done his homework, so why not let him watch TV? Thus, they, too, settle comfortably in front of the screen until the next teacher conference.

Sick Sam

Mom: Sammy, are you up yet? Time to wake up. Time for school.

Sam: (Silence)

Mom: (5 minutes later) Sammy, it's past time to get up. You'll miss the bus.

Sam: (Weakly) Mom...

Mom: Yes, dear, what is it?

Sam: Mom, I don't feel so good...got a bellyache.

Mom: Sammy, your stomach hurts again? Maybe you shouldn't have eaten that pizza. Try to get up and walk around a little. You might feel better.

Sam: (More weakly) But Mom, it hurts so much I can't move!

Mom: All right. I guess you'd better stay in bed. Go back to sleep. It must be your allergy.

Sam spends the morning in his bed, but by 11:00, he's up and feels much better. Mom cooks him a nice, wholesome lunch and keeps him company as they sit at the kitchen table. They chat and giggle, and she assures him that he's a wonderful, talented boy, and if he could only stay well, she's sure he could be an A student. Sam agrees and laments on how hard it is to keep up with schoolwork because he's missed so much school. He protests to Mom, "It just doesn't seem fair that the teachers pile on all that make-up work. How do they expect me to ever catch up?" Mom sympathizes and assures Sam that she'll talk to his teachers about the problem. "Don't worry, Sammy," she comforts. "Just stay well. Why don't you go in the living room now and relax and watch television?" And Sam does.

At 2:00, the telephone rings. The principal, Mrs. Smart, is on the line. She expresses concern about Sam's frequent absences. Mother details Sammy's maladies, his allergies, his asthma attacks, and his digestive problems. Mrs. Smart explains to Sammy's mother how these illnesses could be caused by tension. She suggests finding out the reasons for Sam's pressures. Sam smirks to himself as he snuggles under the blanket, watching his favorite TV show, and listens to his mom's response.

"Mrs. Smart," she blusters, "if those teachers would just stop giving Sammy so much homework, maybe he could relax a little and feel better." Although Mom sounds convincing on the telephone, she can't help but wonder to herself if Sammy is really sick.

Taunted Terris

> Terris is a fag,
> Terris is gay,
> Push him down, beat him up,
> Don't let him play!

Notice Terris on the playground. He wanders alone, watches the ball game, and maybe talks to other kids, but he usually leaves the group after being teased or taunted.

Terris is overweight. He may or may not be gay. Indeed, he hasn't thought much about sex with either girls or boys. The boys, however, continue to tease. He says he doesn't have any friends, but he really doesn't want any. After school each day, he sits at the kitchen table with his mother, whining and complaining about the mean kids at school. Mom seems to understand and wishes that the teachers would protect poor Terris or that the kids wouldn't be so mean.

Dad says that Terris needs to learn to play baseball. He tries to teach the boy sports but ends each attempt with angry scolding. The ritual is also punctuated by Terris' return to Mom with complaints that "Dad doesn't understand me." A mom-and-dad brouhaha terminates most father-and-son activities. Dad gives up, and Mom wonders why her husband doesn't do better with her son. She feels sure that Terris' real problems are caused by Dad, the school, or the other kids.

In school, Terris doesn't finish assignments. He works slowly, daydreams, and sometimes brings his work home to finish with Mom's help. He works at the kitchen table so that Mom may alternate stirring the soup with doing fourth-grade math. Terris may manage to do a few problems on his own, but he doesn't really see how he can do any work without his mother. When she's not home, he doesn't even start. "Why try?" he thinks to himself. He needs help. Mom must tell him what to do. Big sister should protect him from the kids at school. Why do the kids pick on him all the time? Why is he so weak and small? Why can't he do anything on his own?

"Don't give up, Terris. Try the computer." And Terris does. Terris loves the computer, and the keyboard doesn't require social conversation. Terris can control the computer. It responds predictably. Everyone knows that Terris is terrific with the computer, and although all agree that he is somewhat weird, Terris is at last a hero! His assignments continue uncompleted unless they are related to his computer skills.

Depressed Donna

Donna's childhood and adolescent sadness is typically the result of a more extreme form of any of the dependent patterns described above. Depression can also come about when dominant children feel that they have lost power. The main characteristic of depressed children is a feeling of inefficacy. Passive children who have escaped so much from stress or effort may feel depressed at their extreme inadequacy, and perfectionists who see no way to accomplish perfect goals may feel equally depressed. Children who feel in control only when they dominate their environment may feel depressed or out of control if they can't persuade parents, teachers, or friends of their point of view. Whatever the specific causes of depression may be, the symptoms are similar. Sadness, tears, frequent sleeping or sleeplessness, binge eating or non-eating, inactivity, and preoccupation with sad themes or suicide are all symptoms that can alert parents to their children's cries for help.

Depressed adolescents often don't sleep at night. They watch TV, play video games, or talk to friends through their computer modems. They finally fall asleep in the wee hours of the morning and are too tired to get up for school. They sleep or doze through most of the day, only to return from school to immediately nap. Nighttime arrives. The entire household is asleep, but Donna can't sleep again. She calls herself a "night person." Unfortunately, there is no "middle of the night" school for her to attend.

Depressed children should receive professional help; they have reached a stage beyond which parents or teachers alone can treat them. Identifying the symptoms and recommending help are important tasks for both parents and teachers, because symptoms may show up at home or school, but not necessarily in both environments.

Torn Tomas

Today is Tuesday. Tomas was at his father's house last night. He looks a little sleepy and a bit more rumpled than yesterday. Wednesday will be another bad day, but Thursday and Friday will be better. Next week, Tomas will also have two sleepy days, but we're not certain which days. The two visitation days vary from week to week.

Other things change for Tomas, too:

At Dad's house, the family has fun; at Mom's house, he has to do homework and chores.

At Dad's house, he does his homework in front of the TV; at Mom's house, he has to work at his desk in his room.

At Dad's house, he can stay up with his dad and Dad's girlfriend until he gets tired; at Mom's house, his bedtime is 8:30.

At Dad's house, he takes exciting vacation trips; at Mom's house, it's boring.

At Dad's house, no one makes him study; at Mom's house, he listens to nonstop sermons on the importance of schoolwork.

Dad often calls Mom. They argue on the telephone. Tomas hates it when they ask him where he wants to be for Christmas. If he chooses Dad, the gifts will be bigger but Mom will be sad. If he chooses Mom, Dad says he won't be mad, but inside, Tomas knows that he will be angry. Tomas wishes he didn't have to choose.

Tomas loves his mother and father, and every night, he prays that they'll get back together. If they don't, he wonders if maybe he ought to move in with Dad. After all, when he grows up, he wants to be a man like his dad and have fun. There isn't much sense in *study, study, study* anyway. Just when Tomas thinks he has things all figured out and is about to say to Mom that he'd like to move for a while, he finds her in the kitchen crying. She says she's so lonely and wishes that Tomas would be happy at her house. Then Tomas is sad and feels sorry for her, and he knows that he can't leave her. He assures her that he'll try to be good and to help her. He shuffles up to his room, slouches at his desk, and stares distantly at his math book, wondering if other kids feel as mixed up as he does.

Jock Jack, Social Shaundra, and Dramatic Dan

Captain of the football team, blue-ribbon swimmer, first-chair trumpet soloist, star of the school play, or chairperson of student council—Jack, Shaundra, and Dan share similar characteristics. They thrive in competitive activities and are personable and socially adept as well. They are natural athletes, charismatic actors, talented musicians, or excellent leaders.

These kids seem to be propelled toward success. As high school seniors, they give their parents great joy. At the athletic, music, or drama awards banquet, parents and children alike feel pride as they experience the thrill of receiving awards for excellent contributions to the team, drama club, band, or student council. Why is this a problem? Actually, it may not be, but one needs to look carefully, because the senior high awards banquet may represent the peak achievement of these young people's careers.

Why are Jack, Shaundra, and Dan underachievers? These teens who are the pride of their teams and their families may have reached the high point of their lives at that senior banquet, despite the special talent and competitive spirit that has served them so well. If you look carefully at their activity selections, you may discover that they participate only in activities in which they are winners. They select sports if they will be captains, drama if they will be stars, band if they will play first chair, and social activities if they can be leaders. Although they actually have excellent scholastic potential (*They must be bright—how else could they learn all of the lines for the play?*), they claim that schoolwork has never provided a satisfactory competitive challenge. However, it may actually have provided *too much* competitive challenge. Their drive to win, encouraged first by their parents and then internalized, automatically eliminated activities in which they could not attain first place. They became just average students because they did not see themselves as winners in academics.

Now as they graduate to life after high school, they may join a traveling drama troupe, organize a musical group, or go to college to play football, but they will discover that hundreds of stars are competing with them and that they are no longer outstanding. Worse, their history of academic underachievement has narrowed their career options. They will wander and search. If they are fortunate, they may find a community, a career field, or a school environment in which they can again be stars—big fish in little ponds. If they do find such havens, they may be successful; if they do not find a niche that accepts their leadership, they flounder and dissipate their many undeveloped talents. They will always remember how high school represented the best years of their lives.

Academic Alice

Alice is extraordinarily gifted, with an IQ of 150. She learned spontaneously to read when she was three years old. She did double-digit addition in her head by age four. Her extensive vocabulary and high-level reasoning captivated and entertained adult friends and relatives. "Surely she's a genius," they declared.

A 4.0 grade point average, honors classes, and first-place ranking in her small-town graduating class of 200 established Alice as an achiever. At graduation ceremonies, she received awards, honors, and scholarships. There was no doubt about Alice's bright future. She was university bound and planned a career in medicine.

Alice has shown no signs of Underachievement Syndrome. How did she get into this book? Let's look further. She's a freshman now at a prestigious Eastern university, taking her pre-med classes—chemistry, calculus, biology, and English literature. There are between 400 and 500 students in each of her lectures, and many of them also ranked first in their graduating classes. Some have had two years of chemistry, calculus, and advanced biology before they entered college. Alice wonders, "How do they know so much? They seem so much brighter than I. How can I compete?" Her fears are confirmed with her first exam grade, which is a B instead of the usual and expected A.

"Why do I feel so depressed?" she wonders. "After all, a B is a good grade, and there's plenty of time to bring it up to an A." Alice resolves to study harder. She spends many hours preparing for the second exam. However, she finds it difficult to concentrate on the course content. She feels tense at the thought of the test and is obsessed with worries of how she will perform. Nevertheless, she is reasonably confident that she has mastered the information until the morning of the exam. As she stares at the first question, the words blur. She feels nauseous. She can't remember ever seeing that concept. Could she have missed it entirely? "Relax, Alice," she tells herself as she skips down the page to look at the other questions. Some she feels confident about; others she knows she has studied but is not sure of the answers.

Fifteen minutes have passed, and Alice hasn't marked a single answer on her paper. "Can anyone see how nervous I am?" she wonders. "So this is test anxiety," she concludes, and then determinedly begins responding in the best way that she can. But she runs out of time with five more questions to go. "Darn!" She slumps in her chair. "That's probably a B again. Oh, well. I guess in college I'm a B student."

Five days later, the test grades are returned. She has a C—the first C in her entire school history. She expected an A or at least a B+. How can she tell Mom about this? How can she get into medical school? Maybe she isn't as bright as they told her. Her friends are getting A's—what's happened? She'll study harder next time. The material is so complex. It seems so irrelevant. "How will calculus make me a good physician?" she asks herself. "What a stupid way to select doctors! Why am I here? Should I quit? Should I change my major? My parents will be so disappointed; they'll never understand. How can I have become such a failure? Failure…failure…failure…."

What happens to Alice as the tension builds? There are certainly many possible outcomes, some positive and some negative, depending on how creatively she handles her dilemma. She may adjust to the tension and bring her grades back up to A's. She may learn to live as a B student and continue her medical direction. She may find that she's an A student in psychology or literature and that she prefers an entirely different career than the one she originally selected. There are also less favorable outcomes—dropping out of college, depression, and in a few cases, that most distressing final solution, suicide.

Alice was an achiever, but her Underachievement Syndrome came late in her education. Young adulthood is a difficult time to deal with competition and with one's first losing experiences. Alice feels alone with her problem.

Manipulative Maria

Maria: Ms. Smith, you know that D you gave me in math? Do you suppose you could up it just a little? I'm afraid to go home.

I've never had a D before. My father will kill me! I promise I'll work harder next quarter.

Ms. Smith: (Thoughtfully) *Maria seems so worried and frightened. I wonder if her father will beat her. She did promise to do better next quarter. I guess I could give her one more chance.* (To Maria) Well, I guess I could change it to C if you're sure you'll get all of your homework done next quarter.

Maria: I promise! Thank you so much, Ms. Smith! I really do appreciate your kindness. Yes, I will try harder. Gee, you really saved me!

The next quarter, Maria does a repeat performance. Can her father really be so mean? As a matter of fact, however, Maria twists Dad around her little finger, too. Although occasionally he or Mom catch onto her, they rather enjoy her charming persuasiveness and can't really say no to her. She is a good, sweet kid who is helpful and obliging, and it just may be, they admit, that they spoil her a bit. She's always had lots of toys and clothes, and no, they really can't think of anything she's wanted that she hasn't received. Maria's requests for possessions are endless, and her specific need for designer labels is becoming outrageous.

Maria's social life at school is a significant priority for her compared to her study habits. She chatters incessantly and buzzes around the playground from friend to friend. Despite her apparent conversational ease and sophisticated appearance, her friendship circle is unstable. Her peers avoid close alignments to protect themselves from being overwhelmed and manipulated.

Ms. Smith wonders why Maria is so insecure. It must be that her parents are mean, she reasons.

Mom wonders why Maria is so insecure. It must be that the other kids are jealous, she believes.

Dad wonders why Maria is so insecure. It may be that school is too demanding, he concludes.

They all resolve to provide Maria with extra affection to compensate for her poor self-concept. Maria manipulates on.

Creative Chris

"School is boring. What's the purpose in teaching me to read and do workbook pages at this simplistic level when I'm capable of reading far above it?" Chris challenges his third-grade teacher. She can tell he's going to be a problem. She must keep him busy. She assigns more work-book pages. Chris schemes and plans. "How can I avoid all this dull stuff?" He slows his work. He daydreams. He creates reasons why he should not have so many assignments. He brings his rationale home to Mom and persuades her to go to school to argue for him. She becomes his advocate. He is now excused from his assignments. He can read a library book instead, but he must stay out of trouble. This wasn't exactly what Chris or Mom had in mind for academic challenge, but it seems better than busywork.

Chris reads extensively and continually. When there are chores assigned at home, Chris is reading. When the teacher explains math, Chris hears only half of the lesson because the book on his lap absorbs the other half of his attention. His literature teacher expects eight book reports each year. Chris reads 30 books but does not complete a single report.

"Chris," Mom queries, "you enjoy reading so much, why won't you write those book reports?"

"Because, Mom," Chris retorts, "I shouldn't waste good reading time writing the obvious. My teacher knows I've read the books. I see no reason to give her written proof."

"Yes, I guess that does make sense," Mom acknowledges.

By sixth grade, Chris and his teachers are in full battle. Chris will not do his assignments. His teachers insist on giving him poor grades. Chris argues that he knows the work and can pass every test, and he does. His exam grades are B's and C's without any effort. His teacher averages these with F's for his missing assignments, and so his report card shows C's and D's.

As Chris's psychologist, I ask, "Chris, can you explain why you're doing so poorly in school when you are so capable and so interested in learning?"

"I could get A's if I made the effort. I just don't care about grades," he defends himself.

"Chris, are you sure you could get A's if you put forth the effort?" I question further.

A silence follows. "No, I guess I'm not sure—probably only B's. I start to listen to the teacher explain the math, and it seems so easy and boring, so I get back into my book. Then I guess I must miss some small explana-tion so that when I look at my homework assignment, I'm not sure I understand it. I feel too dumb to ask questions because maybe the teacher explained it while I was reading, so I just don't do the math. By now, I sup-pose there are quite a few gaps, so maybe I could only get a B. I usually get a C with no work, so why should I bother? Even when I do make the effort, the teacher doesn't notice. I guess C's are good enough. Its more important to learn and be creative than to get good grades anyway."

And Mom agrees. Chris is just too gifted and creative for typical schools.

In addition to Chris's vast reading experiences, he writes poetry and short stories. He adds unique comments to classroom discussions and delights in drawing original cartoons. However, he is determined not to conform, and so he receives little academic credit for his creative contributions. By high school, Chris prides himself on his unique dress, his unique music, and his unique friends. The very same drugs he swore in middle school he would never, ever be dumb enough to try add to the uniqueness of his social experiences. His mother says, "He has always marched to the beat of a different drummer."

Rebellious Rebecca

Rebecca's bedroom door is locked. She has closed herself off from her parents. She no longer wants to hear their scolding, their reprimands, or their continuous criticisms. In her determinedly messy bedroom, her phone, stereo, and journal writing are outlets for the anger that she feels toward her parents, her teachers, the counselor, and the rest of the whole adult world. Sometimes she gets depressed and feels alone, as though she has no goals or purpose. Her friends, her smoking, and her drinking may help her to push away her feeling of emptiness temporarily. She doesn't know what she's *for*, but knows for certain what she's *against*. She labels her parents' way of life as narrow, empty, and hypocritical. "You should see the way they really are," she complains to the shrink to whom they've sent her.

In school, her once-consistently good grades vacillate between A's and F's. She tells the guidance counselor that school is irrelevant and asks, "Why should I bother studying English grammar since I'll never use it anyway?" She definitely sees no purpose in going on to college. She works well for the teachers she likes, but she proclaims, "I can't get along with Mrs. Smith, the Spanish teacher, because she doesn't like me no matter what I do. So there isn't much sense in studying Spanish." The number of teachers that Rebecca dislikes increases each year.

At the last dance, Rebecca seemed drunk or high. She was with Social Sam, the student council president. They are a nice couple and seem so right for each other. Why do her parents feel uncomfortable about their relationship? Rebecca says that she has finally found someone who really loves her. By her junior year, she is pregnant. That may be followed by marriage, single parenting, or just as likely, abortion. The smoking, drinking, drugs, and sleeping around alternately feel to her like expressions of her individuality and her desperation. Her Underachievement Syndrome seems minor in the constellation of much more difficult problems.

Hyperactive Harry

Harry is disorganized, sloppy, and has nonstop high energy. In school, he's out of his seat, continually touching, tapping, or slapping other children. His schoolwork is not completed. Some papers may make it home; others mysteriously disappear into a messy school desk, messy locker, or messy bookbag. He listens to his teacher sporadically and tunes out instructions, rules, and threats and warnings. Mysteriously, he clearly hears praise and rewards and messages that relate to food or recess time. His handwriting is illegible, and his math problems are sloppily incomplete. Inconsistency pervades. Grades vary between A's and F's, and there are no obvious explanations for the variations. Harry's teacher has recommended that he be given medication for hyperactivity, for surely something is terribly wrong.

At home, Harry's room is in chaos. Last week's underwear is tucked between the mattress and the box spring, and bread crusts from last month, yesterday, and yesteryear are crunched up among his books, toys, and papers on the shelves. His behavior is equally chaotic. Sometimes he disappears down the street without a word and reappears hours later with apologies to Mom, who is frantic with fear. She blends scolding with loving as she puts her arm around him with affection but furiously threatens to ground him for a month. Life settles down for an hour or so, and then he's gone again, only to return to the same ceremonial scolding and hugging. During meals, he converts a normal chair into a one-legged rocker and never leaves a meal without at least four separate sets of reprimands. His activity pattern at home is continuous—continuous change, continuous mess, continuous noise, and continuous turmoil.

"Dear, it seems so quiet today. Where's Harry?"

"Yes, it is so nice and quiet. Harry's at Grandma's."

"Ah, yes!"

Bully Bob

Bob's temper tantrums have controlled the family since the "terrible twos." Bob has learned that he can get exactly what he wants instantly if he lays on the floor and kicks his feet or holds his breath until he is blue. Candy at the supermarket, his sister's toys, or going to town with Mom are all at his command if he protests loudly enough. So he does. Dad tells Mom that she's spoiling their son. She insists that Dad is just too hard on little Bobby and that Dad needs to be more understanding. So Dad tries.

By age seven, when Bob's shouting isn't effective enough, he tries throwing things, just pillows and soft items at first, but then a jar or a dish. That shows Mom and Dad that he's serious. Crashing vases are intimidating. The family learns to exercise care so that Bob won't become angry; thus, he doesn't have to resort to throwing often. Verbal threats keep his parents and siblings under his control. Homework? Studying? Why should Bob do his schoolwork? Who's going to make him do that boring math anyway? Certainly not his parents. Why should he care if he gets poor grades? He knows that he can do that easy stuff without all the studying. Why do teachers give so many assignments? To no one's surprise, Bob's grades are poor.

Bob does have one complaint. He says that the kids don't like him, they're always picking on him, and he has no friends. Teachers on the playground break up Bob's fights almost daily. He loses his temper if the guys don't play his way, and he throws the bat if he strikes out. "The ref should have called a ball!" he shouts angrily. When the kids call him *bully*, he retorts, "They started it. They just don't like me!"

How to Determine if Your Child Has Underachievement Syndrome

The children I've described may be familiar. They may resemble some that you know. More likely, the child that you suspect to be an underachiever is a blend of several of these descriptions. For example, Rebellious Rebecca is often the adolescent stage of the child Manipulative Maria. The characteristics of Sick Sam and Taunted Terris may be blended in one child. In addition, many Passive Pauls and Perfectionist Pearls may be more or less extreme than those described here.

You may find that your child exhibits some of the habits or behaviors described, but you are uncertain as to whether these indicate a problem. It is true that achieving and happy children sometimes show many of the same characteristics as do underachievers. The main differences are in the degree to which they show the characteristics. All children—all people—achieve less than they are capable of some of the time. It is when underachievement becomes a habitual way of responding in school that it should become a serious concern.

Ask yourself the following questions before you read Chapter 2. (If you're a teacher, read "this student" for "my child.")

1. Was my child the center of an unusual amount of attention for the first three years of his/her life?

2. Were my child's parents divorced before he/she was a teenager?

3. Did my child have many health problems as a preschooler?

4. Does my child have a same-gender sibling who is less than three years younger or older than he/she?

5. Does my child want a lot of one-to-one attention?

Score 1 point for each "yes" response, and total the points. Scores are explained below.

Total Points

4–5:   My child encountered very serious risks for underachievement.

2–3:   My child encountered fairly serious risks for under-achievement.

1:   My child encountered only minor risks for under-achievement.

0:   My child has no obvious risk factors that would lead to underachievement.

Read this chapter to learn about risk factors that may initiate Underachievement Syndrome.

Chapter 2
Early Risks

Psychologists and educators argue endlessly about the nature/nurture basis of intelligence—the extent to which genetics and environment contribute to cognitive ability. However, there is nothing in the psychological or educational literature that suggests that underachievement is inherited. There is no genetic theory to explain why many children who have obviously high ability do not perform well in school. Therefore, in identifying the causes of underachievement, we must look toward learned behaviors.

Children learn to underachieve, and the habits may be initiated very early—before they enter school. Their first teachers may be parents, grandparents, siblings, childcare providers, or important others who are part of their lives during infancy and early childhood. The behaviors that are likely to result in underachievement are not viewed as problems during those early years. Sometimes they originate because of a particular set of circumstances for a specific child in the family, while in other cases, they stem from the general child-rearing approaches of the parents. In the first circumstance, only one of the siblings may be adversely affected; under the latter conditions, several or all of the children may be affected, although not necessarily to the same extent.

Let's look at those early risks for later problems. Pre-school environments that predispose children to Underachievement Syndrome fall into several categories, including the unwelcomed child, the overwelcomed child, early health problems, gender issues, particular sibling combinations, specific marital problems, and giftedness. Each will be explained separately. Although none necessarily result in underachieving children, these environments increase the likelihood of underachievement.

The Too Soon Child

We have long recognized that the unwelcomed or rejected child is likely to have adjustment or emotional problems. However, we can't ignore the continually increasing numbers of children born to mothers who are only adolescents themselves or to fathers who have no wish to be involved in parenting. Some are married; some are not. Even if they initially welcome the new baby, they often tire of the responsibility that has interfered with their own normal adolescent development.

Even when there is love for the child, there may not be the maturity and consistency necessary for appropriate parenting. The child often leads the parents rather than vice versa. Limits may be set by continuous yelling and spanking, and there is little inspiration for learning. The structure that facilitates learning in the early years may not even exist. Reading or playing with children may be replaced by television and turmoil. Parents who work all day may not have the energy, motivation, or dedication to teach their children at night. If these children find a good environment in a daycare center or with a grandparent, that environment may actually be more conducive to achievement than the culturally-deprived environment that they may experience with their own parent(s).

The Overwelcome Child

Parents are rarely admonished for overwhelming their children with too much attention. Even though some may suggest that parents shouldn't spoil their children, it is more in vogue to recommend that parents not worry about their excessive demonstrations of love. Present folklore holds that one can't love a child too much. Although it is true that extraordinary love in itself is not harmful, excessive attention can be a risk for later underachievement and emotional problems. Many children in the present generation could be categorized as *overwelcomed*.

These paraphrased statements provided by parents of underachievers are examples of overwelcome children who are at risk:

> We waited so long for Allison. We knew she'd be the perfect child. My pregnancy was difficult. I had three previous miscarriages. We were so thankful that she was healthy and alive. She became the center of all our thinking. Grandparents, aunts, and uncles all helped us admire and care for her because she was the first grandchild in our family.

> We had tried for 10 years to have our own child. Then we waited three more years before all of the adoption papers were accepted. When we saw Latoya, we were immediately in love. We knew she would be more precious than even a birth child could be.

I wanted so much to make Amon perfectly happy. When he whimpered, I was there to comfort him and hold him, rock him, or feed him. I changed his diaper almost before he tinkled. I wanted to be sure he wouldn't develop diaper rash. I was so happy to be a mother. I left my career and decided to devote all my days to helping Amon develop into whatever his potential would allow.

Luke couldn't sleep, so we took turns rocking him until he would finally fall asleep in our arms. We couldn't leave him with babysitters because he would cry until we returned. It was almost as if he knew how much we loved him.

I read about the research on early infant stimulation, and I was determined to encourage Brady's abilities. I would climb into the playpen with him to talk to him and to teach him how to play with his infant toys. I would never let him play alone.

Erin was premature and spent her first four weeks in a hospital incubator. When we finally got her home, I was devoted to caring for her. She almost never cried because I perceived her needs even before she began to feel uncomfortable. She was a perfect baby.

My husband and I had such difficult childhoods. Our parents were poor, and we had so many brothers and sisters that few of our material or affectional needs were met. As we looked at our son Juan, we made a commitment together to provide him with both the affection and material possessions that we both felt were lacking in our own childhoods. We have much, and we wanted to give our all to that beautiful new baby.

The inherent danger that comes with this extraordinary commitment to the new infant is that it previews other parental behaviors, including overindulgence and overprotectiveness. The child for whom all is accomplished before any effort is exerted is not required to take initiative. These parents may couple this intense investment of self with unrealistically high expectations because the success of their new infant becomes an extension of their own personal aspirations. Almost from birth, the infant is viewed by the parents as the long-awaited answer that gives meaning to their own lives and to their own senses of fulfillment.

Of course, new babies should be welcomed and loved. Parents surely must make extensive commitments to the wonderful beings that they have created. It is only the exaggeration and the extreme of personal parent investment that may steal from the children their own sense of efficacy and competence. Doting parents confer on their children extensive power to manipulate their adult world before they have the knowledge, wisdom, and maturity to wield such power. These children learn very early how to get important people to do their bidding. They expect their needs to be gratified instantly by others, and they literally become addicted to continuous and immediate adult attention. They are not permitted to struggle to accomplish the personal challenges of early childhood.

Early Health Problems

Allergies, asthma, congenital birth defects, or physical or mental handicaps may lead to the sort of intense relationship and commitment by one or both parents (usually the mother) to infants or preschool children that could potentially have a debilitating effect on the children's development of self-sufficiency.

These children's temporary requirements may place so many obligations on the parents that they are required to forgo their own personal, social, intellectual, or career interests in order to minister exclusively to the overwhelming needs of their children. They thus invest themselves almost totally in the children and make their *raison d'être* the alleviation of their children's pain, the development of their full potential, or their adjustment to the non-handicapped world. The kinds of commitments that parents of these children make are reflected in the following paraphrased statements:

> Jennifer was hospitalized 12 times in her first four years of life. She had surgery five times to enable her to walk. Then there were other emergencies—pneumonia twice and a routine tonsillectomy, which became complicated. Nothing seemed simple for Jenny. Several times I believed that we might lose her. My husband managed the rest of the children, or they stayed with my sister, but I was near Jennifer during all of her illnesses. I spent many nights in hospital chairs suffering almost as much as Jenny suffered, dedicating those years to keeping her from death's door. Now, when I see her in such good health, I feel comforted to know that my efforts were worthwhile, and I only

want to help her catch up with her schoolwork and adjust better socially.

Our pediatrician shocked us completely when he revealed to us that our beautiful baby had Down Syndrome. My husband and I struggled with the decision as to whether to place him in an institution or keep him at home. After as much research and deliberation as time would allow, we decided that it would be best for our son to develop in a normal family setting. As I rocked my infant in my arms, I determined in my own mind that I loved him as much as I could a normal child, and I would dedicate my life to helping him achieve all that he could, despite his limitations.

Cody had continuous food allergy problems, and I monitored his diet carefully. I breast-fed him until he was two and a half years old because there was so little he could eat. At age three, he began having asthma attacks. I slept in his room so that I could be near him if he wanted me. Bob, my husband, said he was too dependent, spoiled, and babied. However, I felt that Bob was much too impatient with Cody and was pressuring him to grow up too soon. Bob thought that he should be a jock, but Cody was just too small and sickly for sports. It seemed that Bob did not want me to mother Cody, although that was exactly what I wished to do. I loved my new mother role, and Cody really needed me.

Cases such as these all begin with a child's unusual physiological or psychological needs and a loving parent responding totally to the child. However, as the parents narrow their own lives and withdraw from their own goals, sacrificing themselves in an attempt to save their children, the children's wants supersede all else. The relationships become symbiotic and mutually dependent. Although the children's biological and educational requirements are met, their feelings of well-being are tied to immediate gratification and positive feedback from the parents. In turn, the parents measure their own personal successes almost totally by the health and learning gains of their children.

Initially, the relationship is synergistic and mutually beneficial. The children's gains go beyond what physicians predict. The parents' satisfactions exceed what they had expected, and they feel that their great commitment is well-rewarded. The preschool years are dominated by sacrifice and hard-earned success. This pattern may continue into the early school years or as long as the handicapped children's demands can be met on a reasonable and tolerable basis. But sooner or later, the children must be weaned from this dependence or the relationships become pathologically parasitic. The sacrificing parents grow weary of the extensive commitment and now view these same children as hopelessly demanding, rebellious, and no longer within their control. Further, they have constricted their own lives to the extent that they have lost many potential opportunities for personal growth, and they may have strained their marriages beyond repair.

Although the parents now see the importance of initiating new goals that foster more independence, they remain limited by the demands of their manipulating special children and their own guilt. They remind themselves frequently of the commitment that they made to their infants, but they question how long they must continue these encompassing obligations. Both parents, if they are still married, often comment on how caring for these children has become all-consuming and how the children dominate the family. Sometimes the need for attention continues even after the handicaps or illnesses have disappeared.

Gender Issues

Biological differences and gender stereotypes affect student underachievement. For example, in the case of mathematics, it was assumed for many years that girls were biologically less capable than boys. Girls underachieved dramatically based on that assumption. Advanced mathematics classes used to host almost all boys, and girls avoided these classes based on the belief that they were incapable of skill in higher mathematics. Now, girls' math test scores are not significantly different than those of boys, and even in the area of extreme talent, girls are making great progress. In a 1980 study, Benbow and Stanley found a ratio of 13 boys to 1 girl for students under age 14 who achieved over 700 on SAT math tests.[1] By 1997, the ratio had improved to 4 boys to 1 girl,[2] and by 2005, it changed further to 2.8 boys to 1 girl.[3] Because this ratio has changed dramatically over time, it is likely to continue to change further, and it is unlikely that girls' lesser performance is due to biological differences.

That said, boys have been found to have better spatial abilities, and spatial abilities do predict higher math ability. Preschool boys also tend to play more with toys that may promote spatial ability during the early years when brain growth is rapid. We're not certain whether that differential interest is related to biological differences or to the gender-stereotyped play interests of boys and girls. Regardless, research finds that spatial ability can be improved through training.[4] Time and research alone will help differentiate between the impact of biology and environment on gender differences, but changes in math for girls are already dramatic.

There are other gender differences that affect early achievement motivation, or the lack thereof. For example, our elementary classrooms are led mainly by female teachers. In my research about the childhoods of successful women, the women frequently shared stories of how they absolutely loved their grade-school teachers and often wanted to be exactly like them. My favorite example is that of an MIT professor who in first grade wanted to be a first-grade teacher; in second grade, a second-grade teacher; in third grade, a third-grade teacher, and so on, until finally she decided to become a college professor. Another favorite story was shared by a successful and happy elementary school teacher who loved her own teachers so much that she copied their handwriting each year. Undoubtedly, that close identification of girls with their teachers positively encourages their early achievement.

Boys surely learn much from female teachers and do indeed often fall in love with their early teachers. However, they are less likely to identify with them because of gender and thus unconsciously are less likely to consider their education as a masculine enterprise unless their fathers are very strong educational advocates. Mothers, rather than fathers, often take the lead in communicating with teachers, particularly in the early years, again emphasizing the femininity of the educational enterprise to their children and giving girls a head start in school compared to boys.

On the not-so-positive side, the perfectionist tendencies that more girls exhibit than boys may be related to those same strong attempts to please teachers. While perfectionist characteristics in elementary school are helpful for early learning of basic skills, they can decrease creativity and risk-taking. They can also result in procrastination and under-achievement later in life if they cause children to become too rigid and self-critical.

In a study of adjustment to kindergarten for children with different temperament extremes, Rimm-Kaufman found that bold boys tended to speak up frequently at circle time in kindergarten, while bold girls very quickly changed their behaviors by speaking up less.[5] After six weeks, the bold girls' verbal contributions had decreased to the extent that they resembled the many fewer contributions of the shy girls, while the bold boys continued to speak up and also had more behavior problems. The girls were much more compliant to teacher requests. Teacher attitude may have mediated this, as Rimm-Kaufman noted that teachers' comments about bold boys tended to reflect a "boys will be boys" conclusion, while bold girls were discussed by teachers as potentially becoming problem children.

A gender issue that seems to affect boys more negatively than girls is related to the speed and legibility of handwriting. These are tied together because when children's handwriting is illegible, they are often asked to slow down, and when they write too slowly (and neatly), they are typically encouraged to speed up. In the early elementary grades, children commonly assume that the first one done is the smartest, and the last one done isn't very smart at all.[6] This problem of struggling with hand-eye coordination as it affects handwriting may, as with spatial ability, find its origin in preschoolers' gender differential play interests. More girls than boys enjoy coloring, writing, and crafts that develop the small muscles used in writing. Furthermore, the very same boys who struggle with handwriting, or what I refer to as *pencil anxiety*, are often the boys whose small muscle coordination related to Legos and screwdrivers is not problematic. It's not that these boys haven't participated in activities that develop their small muscle coordination; it's that they haven't participated enough in activities that will develop the specific coordination that enables them to write.

Gender issues continue into middle school and high school when peer pressures begin to have more impact. When there is anti-intellectual peer pressure, that pressure is often mitigated for students who are involved in sports. Thus for tweens and teens, involvement in sports helps elevate them to popularity, whether or not they are good students. Since somewhat more boys than girls continue to be involved in sports, there is also less peer pressure on boys to underachieve than on girls.

Girls more often feel as though they risk their popularity by getting A's on their report cards. The following statement was made by a sixth-grade girl and is a perfect example of the pressure that many bright girls face: "I'd like to all get A's for myself and also to please my parents and teachers, but if I did, the popular kids would exclude me, and it would probably even take away my friends."[7]

Girls continue also to face unconscious bias by teachers and employers. When information is attributed to a male or female, whether it is college essays, job applications, portfolios, or tenure reviews, documents associated with males consistently receive higher ratings by evaluators than the very same information with female names attached.[8]

More boys have Autism spectrum disorders, learning disabilities, attention disorders, and behavior problems, and all of these pose disadvantages for achievement and risks for underachievement.

In summary, gender continues to be an issue in underachievement in our classrooms today. Sometimes girls are favored, and other times boys are. Teachers who are gender sensitive are more likely to encourage achievement in all children.

Particular Sibling Combinations

Birth order and sibling rivalry affect all children. For example, studies have found relationships between birth order and IQ scores, as well as birth order and achievement.[9] Other studies describe typical characteristics of oldest children, middle children, and the "baby of the family" position. Beginning with Cain and Abel, history and literature frequently document cases of extreme sibling rivalry.

There are specific sibling combinations that predispose children toward underachievement. These particular combinations are inherently more competitive than usual, and one or more of the siblings are disadvantaged by this competition. Many families learn to minimize sibling rivalry or at least assist siblings in dealing with their irrational competitiveness. However, in these special combinations, the parenting job is extremely challenging.[10]

The combinations that seem unusually difficult include: very close-aged, same-gender siblings; siblings of an extremely gifted child; a large family of children with one who is considerably younger; and siblings of a child with extreme physical or mental health problems. Let's look at some examples of each of these combinations.

> Our boys are only 11 months apart. Because they are so close in age, we made a special effort to give them the same privileges and responsibilities. They share their room, toys, and clothes. Despite the similarities in the way we treat them, the younger of the two always complains that we are unfair. The boys argue intensely and seem almost to hate each other.

In the case in which two close-aged, same-gender siblings are treated similarly, both children are likely to feel more competitive pressure. Because they are expected to act the same, the age difference typically puts stress on the younger one to keep up with the older one, often causing the younger one to feel inadequate. The older one may also feel some frustration because he does not receive special privileges that go with age.

Because the older sibling usually outperforms the younger, he will appear confident unless his superior ability is threatened. This child then may become defensive. Both siblings are also likely to compete for a close relationship with the same-gender or most powerful parent. Recognizing individuality by acknowledging privileges of age and differences in interests and abilities tends to relieve some of the competitive pressures. However, parents can expect to feel frustration as they try to deal with two competitive brothers or two hostile sisters who *should* be such good company for each other.

> Our older daughter is extraordinarily gifted. She's cooperative, pleasant, and a high-achieving student. Her younger brother has an equally high IQ, but we have never managed to get him to achieve well in school. He learned everything quickly but was sloppy, careless, and oppositional from first grade on.

When the first child exhibits unusual talent, she is likely to be the recipient of special parent and school attention, unusual educational opportunities, and a multitude of honors and awards. This child becomes the pacesetter for the siblings who follow. High standards are set, and younger siblings believe that in order to earn equal recognition, they must achieve a similar level of success. Even if they are very capable, they are likely to view such an accomplishment as quite impossible. Because they want to establish an individual and respectable place in the family, and because they view themselves as unlikely to compete successfully, they select a different and sometimes opposite direction for achievement and attention.

If the family can support the younger child's unique intellectual or artistic activities, he may develop both competence and confidence. However, if the oldest sibling's accomplishments are significant, it is often difficult to convince younger children of their own talent. In such cases, they may resort to non-accomplishment for attention seeking. Their failures and behavior problems may become their route to family recognition. These may not be highly rewarding for them, but they believe that they have no alternative because they can find no other effective way to get family consideration. They attain equal time by manipulating family members to attend to their problems, thus setting an underachieving cycle in motion.

Another option available to a second child, who may also be a middle child, is social success. If the intellectually gifted or achievement-oriented first child is not particularly competent socially, middle children may compete by being friendly, likable, and brilliantly social, like Heather:

> Heather is our social butterfly, but we can't seem to motivate her to do any work. Aaron, her oldest brother, is really into science, but he is a loner. Pammy, the baby of the family, is an excellent reader, a good musician, and a serious student. Heather seems too preoccupied with her friends to consider school important. Parties continue endlessly, but study never really begins, regardless of how much we emphasize the importance of schoolwork.

Unfortunately, referring to children as either the "social," "athletic," or "artistic" child may cause them to assume that they can't be high achievers in the intellectual arena. It may also have the impact of causing the achieving child to feel that he or she can't be social or athletic. In effect, it can accelerate the in-family competition.

It's best to respect individual differences and interests but explain to children that they can also have a *whole smart family,* and all children can have reasonable social and creative lives as well. Emphasizing that they don't have to be best in the family to be good at something may be a discussion that requires some repetition.

The sibling combination in which the youngest is called "the baby of the family" may initiate a special style of Underachievement Syndrome. The youngest child is by no means always an underachiever. As a matter of fact, research on eminence finds youngest children to be second only to oldest children as achievers.[11] However, if youngest children are either overindulged or overempowered by older siblings, they will be in the very same situation as the overwelcome child, discussed earlier.

Older children may treat their younger siblings almost as toy dolls and do so much for them that they are prevented from developing their own ideas and activities. In this case, they become dependent on positive feedback from older siblings, and they may become fearful of assuming responsibilities or initiating creative activities. The younger children see little likelihood of becoming as competent and successful as their older siblings, and besides, it is much easier to get any help they need from the collection of big people around them.

How can these children develop self-confidence if they do not attempt challenging tasks? Fear of failure and a habit of taking the path of least resistance prevent them from trying to achieve in the classroom. Anya is an example:

> Anya is five years younger than her brother Brant and six years younger than her sister Natalie. Anya has always been coddled and spoiled by her older brother and sister. Although we all acknowledge that Anya probably always gets exactly what she wants and manages to evade household chores and responsibilities, everyone adores her. School is easy for her. Although she's very bright, her grades are poor, and teachers always tell us that she's working far below her ability.

The sibling of a handicapped or physically ill child may indeed learn kindness but may also have unusual competitive difficulties. For example, Kim's parents described her behavior problem:

> We can never seem to satisfy Kim. She always claims that Lee, her brother, has more privileges than she. Lee has been sick most of his life and has so many other problems that, of course, we do special things to help him. Kim is healthy, popular, and bright, and she does get almost everything she asks for, but if we say no to her about anything, she loses her temper and blames Lee for her problems. Despite her good abilities, her schoolwork is disastrous.

Kim's problems are analogous to those of the siblings of the unusually gifted child. Lee's continuous illness, surgery, and hospital stays have provided him with constant sympathy from parents and relatives. Although Kim can surely see Lee's real physical suffering, she is also aware of the special encouragement, support, and praise that only he receives.

How is this unfair competition? There is really nothing positive that Kim can do that will bring her the extensive and loving attention that Lee receives. Thus, Kim's continual unreasonable demands on her parents reflect competition for attention equal to that which her brother receives. Because Lee's health problems require so much solicitude, there will be no end to Kim's demands. As her parents become more frustrated and angry with Kim's unpleasant and inconsiderate actions and express this in the form of reprimands, her oppositional behavior increases, and her parents find that there is little positive behavior to praise.

Kim's complaints become accurate descriptions of her problem. Her parents become unfair and antagonistic toward her, and neither she nor they quite understand how family life became so unpleasant. Kim's

Underachievement Syndrome is thus a result of her efforts to attract her parents' attention.

Specific Parenting Relationships

A broken marriage or out-of-wedlock birth creates a situation in which children may develop a very close one-to-one relationship with their mother, which may predispose them to Underachievement Syndrome. A mother in either of these circumstances usually faces a highly stressful situation. If she is alone without a husband, she often feels as though it's just her and her child against the world. If her marriage has ended, she may also feel rejected. She is likely to question her lifestyle and, sometimes, whether life is worth living at all. At this vulnerable time in her life, the mother may decide, at least temporarily, that her children are her only purpose for living. As she dedicates herself to the children's needs, she may, as in the case of overwelcomed children, do too much for them, thus preventing these children from taking initiative.

Alternatively, the mother may try to fill the void created by her now-absent spouse or by the boyfriend who is no longer a part of her life, and as such, she may treat one of her children—usually the oldest—almost as a partner, thus giving him too much power. The child learns to expect this power and is not willing to give it up to conform to the requirements of peers or school.

Other risks for single parents are their dependence on surrogate parents during working hours, although this is also a risk for dual-career parents who are married but who choose to have a relative or friend care for their children while they work. In these situations, grandparents are often called upon for child care. Grandparenting on a regular basis is often comparable to overwelcoming children. Grandparents are more likely than parents to give too much attention, do too much, and buy too much for children. The children learn to relate to adults in either a too-dependent or too-powerfully manipulative way.

Children in such adult settings tend to develop verbal abilities early and express themselves well orally. They may emulate adult power with their adult-like vocabularies and reasoning styles. Parents and grandparents then perpetuate the cycle by treating these children as they see them—like little adults—which only gives the children more power. Conversely, the children may be so used to being coddled by their grandparents that they may look for adult help and attention when even minimum effort is required.

Parents who rely on their children's grandparents for child care may feel caught in both a social and financial bind when they can find no alternative to bringing up the children in a world of two generations of parents. They may hesitate to ask their own parents to change for fear of hurting their feelings in the midst of the appreciation that they feel for the help. Conversely, they may disagree and argue with their parents frequently about child rearing, which then leaves the children confused by the opposition between caregivers.

Marriages that have a pervasive oppositional style may also cause children to develop Underachievement Syndrome. In such marriages, the parents may disagree on most everything, and the topic of child-rearing techniques is no exception. The children in such families are continually surrounded by power struggles. As the parents struggle for power, they pull and tug at their children, who vacillate between them. These children may pick a favorite parent but usually try to please both. If you can visualize one parent tugging at one arm of a child while the other pulls the other arm in the opposite direction, you can sympathize with these children, who may feel literally suspended in midair. They cannot move in either direction, but neither can they move forward.

The oppositional nature of such a marriage, or of a divorce if parents continue to battle, is likely to set off Underachievement Syndrome for children of any age. Even as late as senior high school, formerly excellent students may suddenly change their achievement direction. This may be triggered by the sense that they can no longer please either of their parents or by their concern for pleasing the parent with whom they are no longer living. Divorce can accelerate underachieving patterns and can even be a cause of that underachievement. The more antagonistic the divorce, the more traumatic the breakup for the child.

> Ariel was always a high achiever. She was the only girl of three children. She was her mother's ally during her parents' bitter and angry pre-divorce period. Her mother shared confidences about her father and older brothers that empowered her almost as an adult partner. Her mother was also the main communicator about school responsibilities. After the divorce, Ariel's father took a new interest in maintaining his relationship with her and shared with his daughter some of his negative views about his controlling former wife. Immediately, Ariel became disrespectful toward her mother. Although this girl's underachievement didn't begin immediately, the risk of it increased dramatically.

The Gifted Child

It has been reported that 20% of high school dropouts are gifted.[12] Why are gifted children so vulnerable to underachievement? Their susceptibility stems both from their early childhood home environment and from their school experiences. My clinical experiences with gifted children strongly support an important early environmental influence on the children's giftedness. All of the gifted children that I have seen at my Family Achievement Clinic, regardless of their socioeconomic background, had at least one adult who made a major time commitment to enriching the children's early years. This does not rule out a genetic contribution but only underlines the importance of early enrichment for intellectual development.[13]

Within that early enrichment process are the same risks that are involved in other close one-to-one relationships: the child will become too dependent on an adult relationship, or the child will become too powerful because of the authority granted by the adult. For the gifted child, there are added risks. A large vocabulary, witty comments, apparently mature reasoning, or musical or other talent all attract more than the typical attention of surrounding adults. Parents frequently assume that their gifted children have mature wisdom that corresponds with their adult-like conversation. Parents, grandparents, friends, teachers, and even strangers continually applaud the children's unusual abilities. The children not only thrive on the audiences' encouragement, but they become addicted to it.

There are two situations that frequently occur in gifted children's early school experiences: typical work is not challenging, or the children find that teachers, principals, and parents take action to provide a special individualized program for their needs. The first situation discourages these children's initiative because the academic environment requires no effort and is indeed boring. The second flatters them into believing that their special talents are extraordinary enough to permit them to change an adult-managed system. This is impressive power for a five- or six-year-old—even one who is known as "the brain" among peers.

In summary, the risk for these gifted children results from both attention addiction and too much power. They may learn to expect both uninterrupted applause and complete freedom of choice in their education, but neither is continually possible, regardless of their talent. They are basically enthroned early, and relative to the special attention and power they've received, later school years feel like a dethroning.[14]

Conclusion: Dependence and Dominance

Although there are many high-risk conditions in early childhood learning that can initiate Underachievement Syndrome, obviously *not all children exposed to them will become underachievers.* The same pressures internalized by these children may lead either to extreme motivation or to underachievement. School environments and later parenting techniques may eliminate the problems or worsen them. However, the early childhood situations caused by both circumstances and well-intentioned parenting mistakes frequently have the effect of destroying parenting leadership. Instead, the children learn rituals of either unusual dependence on or dominance over adults. Some children learn patterns that combine both dependence and dominance.

During the preschool years, neither pattern typically causes parents many problems. They become accustomed to the dependent or the dominant relationship. Occasionally they may label their dependent children as somewhat immature, but they assume that the children will outgrow the problem. They may also acknowledge that their too-dominant children are a little bit spoiled; however, they have reasonable confidence that their children's problems will be resolved by their entrance to school. They believe that teachers and the school structure will help the children to adjust.

Daycare centers or preschools sometimes identify these problems early. The dependent children may be recommended for an extra year of school before kindergarten, and the dominant children may, even in preschool, be labeled as behavior problems or as showing signs of Attention Deficit Hyperactivity Disorder (ADHD). For the most part, however, the problems are only viewed as minor.

The risks that direct children toward dependency and dominance are only risks, not absolute predictors of behavior. Although patterns begin early, they are not engraved in stone or unalterable. However, these patterns begin to feel natural to children and parents alike.

Dependent and dominant children practice their control patterns in relating to adults for several years before they enter school. These patterns work well for them, and they know no others. They carry them into the classroom and expect to relate to teachers and peers in the same ways that have been effective at home. Early teachers are able to modify these controlling patterns; however, the more extreme the dependency or dominance, the more difficult the modification. Further, the dependency pattern is often masked as insecurity, immaturity, passivity, or a learning disability. Dominance may be exhibited as giftedness, creativity, or—not so positively—as a behavior or emotional problem. Sometimes, the dominant pattern may not show itself in the early elementary grades because the child may feel fulfilled by the excitement and power of school achievement. Even if some teachers manage these children well in school, the underlying patterns may only lie dormant until the school environment becomes more competitive and the children can no longer feel dominant in their classroom environments.

Ask yourself the following questions before you read Chapter 3. (If you're a teacher, read "this student" for "my child" or "this child.")

1. Is the mother or father in this child's family perfectionistic?

2. Does my child tend to ignore his/her mother, father, or teacher when they make requests?

3. Did the mother or father in this child's family not like school?

4. Is the mother or father in this child's family unhappy in his/her career?

5. Is the mother or father in this child's family disorganized?

6. Do the mother and father in this child's family have very different approaches to child rearing?

7. Is one parent in this child's family a more rigid disciplinarian than the other?

8. Do my child's grandparents live nearby and overindulge him/her?

Score 1 point for each "yes" response, and total the points. Scores are explained below.

Total Points

4–8: My child has very serious problems related to imitation of family patterns.

3–4: My child has fairly serious problems related to imitation of family patterns.

1–2: My child has minor problems related to imitation of family patterns.

0: My child has no apparent problems related to imitation of family patterns.

Read this chapter to understand how your child or student may be unconsciously imitating problem parental attitudes or behaviors.

Chapter 3
Parents as Role Models

C hildren may learn to underachieve by copying their parents—even if their parents are achievers. Unconscious copying begins between ages two and three by a psychological process known as *identification*. Children copy one or both parents, or sometimes grandparents or older siblings. If you can remember your children walking around in a parent's shoes pretending that they were that parent, then you've seen the identification process. Rocking a doll, "talking" on the telephone that isn't connected, "driving" a bicycle to "work," or pretending to vacuum are all typical identification activities that no doubt you have observed in your own children or the children of others.

Identification with an effective and achieving same-gender parent encourages (but does not guarantee) achievement in a child. Indeed, identification research clearly supports the significance of children's identification with good parent models as an important family factor in high achievement, and the lack of that identification, or the identification with a poor parent model, increases the chances of under-achievement. **If you and your spouse view your own lives as interesting and successful and model an equitable and respectful spousal relationship, you will provide optimal role models for both male and female children and thus increase the likelihood of good educational achievement.**

Parent Pointer

Classic research by Mussen and Rutherford[1] and Hetherington and Frankie[2] indicate that the parent model that children choose for identification and imitation depends largely on a combination of three variables: (1) similarities between the parent and child, (2) nurturance, and (3) power.

The first variable is related to the similarities that the children see between themselves and a parent. High similarity between mother and daughter and between father and son strongly support same-gender parent identification if the nurturance and power of the parents are equal. However, striking similarities in appearance, abilities, interests, or personality between sons and mothers or daughters and fathers contribute to cross-gender parent identification and the imitation of the opposite-gender parent.

The nurturance variable simply implies that children tend to identify with and copy the behavior of the parent that they perceives as being warm and loving. The parent may not be particularly warm and loving in general, but there may be a special relationship between the parent and one or more children in the family. If that parent is an achiever, the children may adopt a similar achieving attitude.

The power influence on identification refers to parents' power over their children's lives. Sometimes a parent may appear to be powerful to outsiders because he or she makes decisions about politics or finances or holds a prestigious position in the workforce. However, the children may or may not perceive that parent as powerful depending upon how much impact the parent's decisions have on the children's interests, needs, and discipline. Because power is an important variable that affects identification and because routine observation of power in a family, even your own family, may be misleading, power patterns will be discussed in more detail later in this chapter.

In observing who your children or your students are copying, it is important to be sensitive to all three variables—similarity, nurturance, and power. Identification with a parent may not be constant. It can be different when children are younger than when they grow up. Birth order may affect children's identification patterns. Role model identification may actually change several times and can include grandparents, older siblings, or other persons at home, at school, and in the community. Peers may also become role models, and later, television and movies may produce both real and fictional role models. Despite the multitude of available models, parents are very often the most powerful and effective role models for their own children.

Positive and Negative Models

Fathers and mothers who feel good about their accomplishments are positive models for their children. They value education and hard work and receive intrinsic as well as extrinsic rewards for their efforts. They respect and value each other, and their children see them as supporting partners in a noncompetitive marriage enterprise. They help each other to grow separately, and they share in building a life together, which includes achievement-oriented family activity. Neither parent is all-powerful, and their lives fit together like pieces of an interlocking puzzle to make a total family picture. They have a sense of progress as a family unit, a respect for the value of education, and a family solidarity that is readily emulated.

So much for the ideal. We know that love, virtue, and achievement rarely continue as flawlessly as this idyllic picture. Problematic patterns also occur, sometimes deliberately, but more likely without the family's being aware of them. Unfortunately, parents, at varying times in their adult development and married lives, may act in ways that provide models for underachievement. Recognizing these patterns of behavior is the first step toward correcting them and thus beginning the reversal of children's underachievement.

Remember: as parents, you are a model for your children only part of the time—but all of the time that you're with them. In other words, the productive work that you do in your job and the loving words that you pronounce to your spouse in private are unobserved by your children. However, the tired sighs at the end of the day or the angry demands made of your spouse are heard very clearly. **Your first task is to become more aware of the times and ways in which your children see you.** This may feel a bit like playacting, but the little people you are influencing can see you only when you are on your home stage.

Examine the following potentially harmful model scenarios to see if they seem familiar. You or your spouse may feel some guilt if you see yourselves as negative models who will harm your children's achievement. However, by recognizing problem behaviors, you can change them. The changes you make may not be all that difficult and may actually make you feel better about yourself. If you're married, these changes may even improve the marriage.

I Didn't Like School Either

School is not a positive experience for all children, and you, as a parent or teacher, may indeed have some bad memories of your own childhood education. In your efforts to empathize with your struggling children, you may think it helpful to share with them your unfortunate memories. You may describe the amusing times you outsmarted your teacher, the pathos of your boredom, your criticism of the inadequate education in your school, or the problems caused by your own underachievement. Although confiding these stories of the past may help you and your children feel closer, it also conveys messages of expectation. A gifted, high-energy six-year-old who had just completed his second day in first grade summed it up succinctly: "My grandpa hated school, my dad hated school, and I hate school." Obviously, his family influence and his identification with his father did not contribute positively to his attitude about learning. This boy's negative statements, if repeated in the classroom, would certainly antagonize even the most devoted teachers, and although he was extremely intelligent, he would certainly have been destined for underachievement had the family not changed their inappropriate patterns of communication.

Telling your children about the similarities between yourself and them enhances identification. However, be sure to emphasize the parts that provide a positive model. Save the remaining, more problematic details for later, when they have established their personal identities as achievers. **If you've already told your children all, try to undo the damage by emphasizing your positive accomplishments and indicating that you hope they won't repeat the errors that truly complicated your life and made it more difficult.**

Because children listen more to what you say about yourself than to your lectures, cut down on the latter and give only positive views of the former. There is no advantage to either you or your children in exaggerating your history as an underachieving troublemaker. Though it may seem good material for family humor, if your son or daughter tries to surpass your tricks, it will not help him or her, and this is what you care about.

The Disorganized Home

Disorganization is a typical characteristic of underachievers. Sometimes, although not always, they learn this disorganization from one or more parent models. Some parents pride themselves on their disorganized lifestyle; others fall into disorganization out of despair. The young mother with three children in diapers and two in school may have given up trying to keep order in her home and may settle for soap-opera escape. The father with two jobs, three children, and four parents to support may be floundering for a framework to sustain his busy work schedule.

Families sometimes choose a frenzied lifestyle for their children—for example, one that includes ballet, piano, tennis, baseball, scouts, and half a dozen other activities. The parents' frantic taxiing of children and themselves between involvements leaves little time for structure or clear expectations and responsibilities. Overload is fairly characteristic of our current generation of parents and children.

Some people say that they prefer disorder. They defend their preference in the name of creativity. It is true that creative people feel comfortable with some ambiguity, but true creativity makes meaning and order out of chaos. Finding orderly patterns and explanations in places where no organization or explanations previously existed is characteristic of creativity. People who are successful in their jobs and have made personal contributions actually do organize chaos. Whether in the arts, business, or science, their product represents organization of concepts.

I am not advocating rigidity for children, but moderate structure and flexibility is a reasonable compromise. **Children must have some organization; they need structure and routine so that they can understand their limits and explore the space between.** They must adapt to the organized lifestyle of a school program that requires orderly desks, reasonably neat assignments, homework deadlines, and rules of discipline. Adaptation to some routine is accomplished more easily if it is reflected in their home environment by parents with whom they identify. **Flexibility, within structure, seems to work best.**

Passive-Aggressive Parenting

The following scene may be familiar: Father is lying comfortably on the couch, relaxed *Z*'s emerging from his lips. His passive position does not automatically emit a sense of power. Mother stands nearby and in anger and frustration demands (for the tenth time), "Would you please fix the screen door?" Father does not move. The *Z*'s continue to emerge. Mother leaves the room muttering and sputtering. Father is passive, but he is also powerful. He is very much in charge of the situation, and he is an unfortunate model for his son or daughter.

Note the following conversations with LeShawn, a fourth-grade underachiever, and Martina, a young woman about to leave for college despite multiple years of underachievement:

LeShawn

> Dr. Rimm: LeShawn, who do you think you're most the same as, your mom or your dad?
>
> LeShawn: (Without hesitation) My dad.
>
> Dr. Rimm: How are you the same as your dad, LeShawn?
>
> LeShawn: When my mom calls my dad to do something around the house, he doesn't answer, and when my mom calls me to do my homework, I don't answer either.

Martina

> Dr. Rimm: Martina, who do you consider yourself most the same as, your mom or your dad?
>
> Martina: Definitely my dad. He's less organized, although he knows where everything is. I have my things spread all over the floor, but I know where everything is, too. Mom yells at Dad to straighten things up; he doesn't. Mom yells at me, too, but I like it this way.

Passive-aggressive behavior is characteristic of many underachievers. "I forgot," "I don't know," and "I have no homework" are all forms of passive-aggressive behavior. These children are powerful without appearing to be, but parents and teachers are powerless. What can you say to the children who solemnly admit that they've forgotten? Perhaps you think that they may have a learning disability. So ask them about sports statistics. What powerful selective memories they seem to have!

The situations described above could be the fault of either the wife or the husband. It may indeed be true that the wife cannot get the husband to do chores or organize himself around the house, or it may be that nagging wives are always on their husbands' cases. Regardless of where the blame falls, if this behavior is typical in the family, it is a poor model for the children.

It is not males alone who model passive-aggressive behavior toward their partners. Females, too, do their share, and because it is powerful behavior, either male or female children may imitate it. The most typical female passive-aggressive behavior evolves when a change is being made to a traditional style of family midway through the marriage. In this family, a feminist wife fights against gender stereotyping by using passive-aggressive approaches to avoid taking responsibilities that she considers stereotyped. For example, if her husband would like to have dinner at 6:00, it is never ready until 6:30; or if he has asked specifically that she buy a particular food he enjoys, she always accidentally forgets to buy it. When the frustrated husband comments on her lack of effort to please him, she shrugs and mumbles some reasonable-sounding excuse, like, "I was busy," "I forgot," "Why didn't you buy it?" or, "Then why don't you get dinner ready? You're as able as I am." And so the battle continues.

Passive-aggressive behavior never improves relationships, and just as harmfully, it provides children with an obvious model of underachievement that can be difficult to modify. Furthermore, it is frequently passed from one generation to the next as an acceptable mode of behavior. One father asked me this question: "Do you mean that if I just volunteer to do things around the house without my wife nagging me, it might make a difference in my son's schoolwork?"

You can guess the response. **Direct communication and fair negotiations do much to eliminate passive-aggressive role models.**

Overworked Parents

If passive, lazy, or disorganized parents are inappropriate models, then surely hardworking, industrious parents must be positive role models. Not necessarily. Overworked fathers and mothers who come home exhausted, who complain about the stresses of their jobs, the unfairness of their salaries, or the unjustness of their bosses are modeling negative attitudes about the world of work. Furthermore, if one partner complains that the other partner works too much, or if either finds no time for play or pleasure, they are modeling an image of work as an area to be avoided by children.

In elementary school, these children will only complain about all of the hard work that their teachers ("bosses") give them. By adolescence, they censure their parents as doing nothing but working and insist that it certainly is not the lifestyle that they wish to emulate. An almost certain way to prevent a son from respecting his father is for his mother to complain during his entire childhood about how she hates his father's career or how that career has taken him away from the family. If either parent has returned to school for an advanced degree and complains continually about study overload, or if a partner denigrates college as a waste of time for the other partner, it is very likely that the children will also learn to be negative about their school experiences.

How can hardworking parents manage to change that model for their children when the requirements of their careers consume so much family time? (More suggestions for help in this matter will be given in Chapter 10.) Here's an example from my own busy lifestyle:

When I returned home from my typical 10-hour day to my teenager impatiently waiting for one or both of her parents, I (usually) gathered up all of my energy and my positive recollections of the day and greeted Sara with, "Sara, you just won't believe what an interesting day I had today!" I continued with a description of the latest child I'd helped (no names given, of course), and we shared insights into our cases. I say *our* cases because Sara had learned to share with me her own psychological insights on friends and the children she babysat for or tutored. I was sometimes astonished at her insights into her teenage friends. Sara would say about psychology that she was born into it.

It never really mattered to me if Sara decided to become a psychologist, but I did want her to know how satisfying I found my work to be. An interesting and unexpected side effect was that I felt much less tired and much more satisfied at the end of each day. It had accidentally become a rather good habit.

If this daughter-like-mother story sounds familiar, it may only be a reminder of the old-style country doctor whose son traveled with him as he visited his patients. It wasn't unusual at all for a son to follow in his father's footsteps and choose medicine as a career that he had learned to respect. In Sara's words, he was born into it.

Post-Divorce Parents

Divorce has a special impact on child identification. Both the period prior to and after the divorce present modeling and identification dilemmas for parents and children. The pre-divorce problems are an extension and exaggeration of the oppositional relationship that may have taken place earlier in the marriage. For example, if a boy identifies with an aggressive father and, after divorce, the father remains in a powerful position and furthermore is obviously disrespectful to his ex-wife, the boy may copy his father and also become belligerent toward his mother. He will be, at least temporarily, a behavior problem at home and school, imitating the aggressive style of his father, whom he views as his role model. The actual behavior may vary considerably, depending on the age of the child, the modeled father, and the child's prior experience. Even so, outsiders will view the son as being belligerent toward what appears to be the wronged parent.

If the son has identified with a passive-aggressive mother, he may continue in this style until he finds a different male model or until his mother becomes more assertive. If he accepts his father's behavior as negative, as described by his mother, then he may, when asked, indicate that he is more like his mother. In this case, he prefers to deny any similarity to a father who has been described as "the bad guy."

In one family, where the father had been particularly obnoxious prior to the divorce, each of two boys separately indicated that he was more like their mother—although each concluded that his brother was like their father. It was obvious that neither cherished the image of a lazy, inconsiderate, alcoholic dad as an appropriate model.

For a girl who identifies with her mother, the identification is likely to continue after the divorce and will largely reflect the kind of adjustment to the divorce that her mother makes. The girl may, however, feel a sense of rejection by her father if her mother describes her own feelings of rejection to her daughter. If the daughter does feel rejection, her anger may be addressed toward her mother, whom she may see as the cause of her feelings of rejection. She may be anxious to be with her father to protect herself from being rejected. In order to regain his attention, she may become very rebellious toward her mother.

Each parent, in anger at the other parent, and in an effort to keep the children's love, may have what such parents describe as "an honest, open discussion with the children." Oldest children are the main recipients of these intimate but biased views of their other parent. This unusual parental intimacy can cause children to feel as powerful as adults, to consider themselves equal to either or both parents, and to temporarily feel almost like partners to the parents. Once adultized, these children no longer accept child status. Here's a case example:

> Eleven-year-old Molly vacillated between rebellion and depression. Her mother had a too-perfect boyfriend, she said. Why didn't they consider her ideas before they made plans for an evening, and why did she always have to go along with them? Molly's mother had gone through two divorces, and both fathers had been described as "bad guys" to Molly at one time or another. Molly's favorite memories were of the time she and her mother lived alone when she was six years old. Actually, those were days of custody disputes, and then it was Mother and Molly against Molly's father.

After divorce, there can be other difficult effects of identification patterns. If the parents live near each other and share custody fairly equally, the children are likely to continue identifying with the same parent that they identified with previously. However, if children visit a parent only two to four times a month, that parent, most often the father, typically takes the role of providing fun and games for the children because he does not see them frequently. He is determined to make the meeting enjoyable. He takes them out to dinner, movies, and baseball games. In one boy's words, "Visitation is like a hotel." That visitation parent often has changed his or her style of parenting, and children may view his underlying message as not considering school achievement to be as important as he did before the divorce.

Fun and games may seem fine, but for children who identify with this father, their model is not one of achievement. The children never see their father in a working role, but they always see their mother in a working role, often overloaded. If they are not required to do school-work during visitation, the children may also think that their father does not see education as important. Mother, with whom they live during the school week, expects them to do homework. Is it surprising that they continuously fight with their mother about their school responsibilities?

Of course, if both parents deal with the post-divorce period con-structively, they can clarify the messages that their children receive. Dad can communicate to his children his schoolwork expectations and his interest in the children's achievement and study habits. He can also insist that the children be respectful toward their mother. If parents are aware of the messages that they are communicating and if they are sufficiently concerned about the children to forgo their own power struggles, they can make a dramatic difference in those children's achievement.

In one case in which an achievement message from father to son was clarified, on the few occasions when the son regressed to his old rebel-lion-toward-mother behavior, it took only a brief telephone call from Father to remind his son of his study obligations. It is important that both Mother and Father agree on the same educational message and that the parent with whom the child identifies makes a strong effort to rein-force that message by interest and example.

In another case, a rebellious, angry teenager made a complete rever-sal in attitude and achievement when his father made it clear to him that his mother was exactly right in her expectations of him. Furthermore, this boy, who had rebelled against reading, took to thoroughly enjoying books after his dad gave him a set of his favorite books from his own childhood as a Christmas gift.

When children witness multiple separations and divorces, the mes-sages become even more confusing. Here's an example:

David, a gifted fourth grader with an IQ of 135, was under-achieving. A series of important adults in his life were confusing his academic direction. First, there was his birth father, with whom he never actually lived but visited fairly regularly. Second, there was the man his mother married shortly after David's birth, who took on the fathering role during David's preschool years until he was in second grade. Third, there was a father-to-be, the man that his mother was going out with after her divorce from Father #2. Finally, there was his mother, who had stayed constant during his life.

David was an only child and was receiving conflicting school-related messages from all four adults. Father #1, his birth father, whom David visited approximately once a month, believed that David should study hard and get good grades. However, all of the other adults in David's life put Father #1 down, and so he was considered a "bad guy." Father #2 was David's identification figure. David visited with him two or three times a week. Although this father felt that school was important, he also gave David the message that he was satisfied as long as David earned average grades. David was easily meeting this father's too-low expectations. Father #3 was not giving specific school messages yet. Mother realized that David was underachieving and tried to encourage him. However, she was anxious not to put too much school pressure on him, which really communicated to David that perhaps he could work just a little harder.

The key people here were obviously the initial two fathers. The first, whom David was taught not to respect, was giving the appropriate school message. David was hearing and following the advice of the second father, whose message was truly one of underachievement. It was easy enough for David to follow Father #2's lead, but he was developing some very poor study habits in the process and not bothering to learn some critical skills. When the situation was clarified, all adults were willing to give consistent messages, and with a little perseverance on everyone's part, David raised his school expectations and his achievement.

Prior to or after a divorce, **consistent school-related messages by all important adults are critical to children's school achievement. Those adults should pay attention to their own behavior, as well as their words.** Continual power struggles between parents through their children are likely to result in children's not knowing how to please both parents and in their taking the path of least resistance. They easily become underachievers. This issue increases in importance in our society, where half of the children are no longer brought up in what is known as a traditional two-parent family—specifically, the same two parents that they began with.[3]

Cross-Gender Identification

Cross-gender identification takes place when boys identify with their mothers or girls with their fathers. How does this affect school achievement?

The cross-gender identification of daughters with their fathers is typically not harmful to school achievement or social adjustment. Children are much more accepting of assertive females than they are of effeminate males. Today, when girls are active in sports, they are rarely called tomboys, as they were in earlier generations. In one classic study of female mathematicians, the author found that the more creative mathematicians were oldest daughters who identified with their fathers.[4] Many successful women credit their fathers as their role models.[5] As long as fathers give a pro-academic message to their daughters, the daughters who identify with them are not likely to have school- or career-related problems.

Conversely, if a girl identifies with a father who portrays a tough, anti-school image, then that girl may develop school-related and/or social problems. She is likely to be the girl who wears the oldest torn jeans and the dirtiest sweatshirt, uses tough language, and plays with the boys. She may be determined to do no schoolwork at all. This pattern is relatively easy to change if it is identified early. However, as in most cases of Underachievement Syndrome, the pattern is resistant to change if not discovered until high school. By then, her alternative dress, tough demeanor, and cigarette smoking may classify her as a "loser," and it will indeed be difficult to convince her that school has any purpose at all. If her parents are supportive, **the early change can be made by the** **father deliberately giving a positive school message and showing an interest in his daughter's learning.** This will improve her school attitude and skills. An effort to literally clean up the girl's act in terms of slightly **more appropriate dress and attempts to teach softened language will ease her acceptance into the world**, and she will be more comfortably accepted socially.

If a boy identifies with his mother, it may have a negative impact on his school achievement and is likely to cause at least some temporary problems. Boys in this position tend to exhibit fewer male-stereotyped behaviors and more typical female interests. If his school environment supports a macho image of males and an emphasis on team sports and physical prowess—as it often does—the boy is less likely to be accepted by his peers.

During the preschool and kindergarten years, this causes no problems. Feelings of rejection typically surface, however, between grades two and six. The impact of this developmental period on children's behavior is readily obvious when viewing the typical elementary school playground at recess. Most girls are playing with other girls, jumping rope, swinging, or just talking to each other. Most boys are playing more rough-and-tumble kinds of games and sports. The boy who does not participate or does not appear sufficiently masculine to other boys may be labeled by these boys as "gay" or some similar term of ridicule for appearing effeminate. On the other hand, because girls see him as obviously not one of them, he remains an outsider in their eyes as well.

Being seen by children of both genders as an outsider makes the mother-identifying boy feel isolated and lonely. In his wish for friends, he may fall into a trap of inviting teasing or ridicule as a substitute for a more positive relationship that he doesn't feel capable of attaining. Alternatively, you may see him walking the playground alone, unless he has been fortunate enough to befriend a few others with similar interests who will prevent the loneliness. One fifth-grade boy communicated to me his sense of being different in the following way:

> If you could look down at our playground from an airplane, you would understand what I mean. The boys are playing baseball, and the girls are jumping rope or on the swings. You would find me with two friends just walking around the playground, talking. We're not part of any group or game. We're just different.

That sense of being different, of not being acceptable, at least temporarily, usually has a depressing effect on achievement. Perhaps the sense of feeling socially estranged causes these children to feel stressed and disorganized. They tend to not carry through on their academic assignments or hand in homework, and they seem to find special difficulty with mathematics and writing. Their self-esteem is low, and they feel unaccepted by their peers.

There are other reasons why boys who identify with their mothers become underachievers. These boys fall into two patterns of identification, although the two categories often overlap. One group of boys who identify with their mothers are very dependent. Their identification begins in that very close one-to-one relationship that originates with an early divorce, a father frequently away from home, or an early illness that causes the child to become accustomed to a one-to-one dependent lifestyle with Mother. Mother-dependence results in school underachievement, passivity, and low self-esteem. Sometimes, this dependent pattern results in what appears to be learning disabilities.

The second type of mother-identifying boy is found in an oppositional marriage, in which the mother behaves aggressively or passive-aggressively toward the father to avoid the father's control. This second type can also be found in a single-parent household if the mother shows hostility toward the boy's father or toward men in general. The boy emulates this pattern by not doing the schoolwork expected of him by his father and by his school, thereby also challenging his father's power and authority in general. Mothers are frequently unaware that they are modeling this anti-authority message. These boys may become angry and violent during their teenage years and are particularly angry about and unaccepting of the men that their mothers remarry, if indeed they do.

Identification with their mothers may cause other emotional problems for boys, such as insecurity about their own masculinity. However, many boys change their identification patterns as they mature. They may follow their father's model or copy male teachers, older brothers, neighbors, or other significant males. Adolescent boys, in their desperation to establish their sense of masculinity, may adopt a rebellious peer group or gang as their models for masculinity. The gang becomes their family, permitting them to feel masculine and to fight authority. Unfortunately, the mother who protected her son no longer has much power over the direction he takes, and the son, by adolescence, often feels a love-hate relationship with his mother—hate, because he likely has an unconscious fear about being considered a "momma's boy" or too feminine, like his mother; love, because he does genuinely love her.

If boys identify partially with both parents, it does not seem to cause social or emotional problems. It seems important for boys (but not for girls) to have some—although not necessarily total—identification with male figures.

Some of the problems related to cross-gender identification are related to the gender stereotypes that continue in our society; some are more directly related to achievement. As society becomes more tolerant of gender differences, boys' identification problems may diminish. **Certainly, classroom teachers and parents can help children be more understanding of individual differences.** However, the other types of behavior problems—dependence on a parent, passive aggression, rebellious behavior, and nonvaluing of school—will continue to cause achievement problems.

Parent Pointer

Teacher Tips

Parent Rivalry

Although child development books frequently describe sibling rivalry in families, parenting books seldom discuss the subject of parent rivalry. However, this is a phenomenon which can be found in many families, and parents themselves seldom admit or address the issue. In this situation, one parent unconsciously sabotages or destroys the other parent's power. The saboteur typically does not view his or her own actions as damaging to the partner or the children, but instead sees them as appropriate to being a good parent. Parent rivalry for the children's love is usually only attributed to divorced parents, when in fact it also frequently takes place more subtly in two-parent homes.

In competitive situations, there are winners and losers. In this case, the losing parent appears less powerful to the child. Therefore, the child is less likely to identify with a powerless model. The sabotage rituals in this rivalry cast one parent in the role of "good" or "smart" parent, and by comparison, the second parent is seen in less complimentary terms, mainly "bad" or "dumb." Thus, I call these sabotage rituals *Ogre and Dummy Games*. They may be directed toward the mother or the father, and they may be played out separately or in conjunction with one another.

One important and damaging effect of these rituals is that they reduce the chances that the children will identify with the same-gender parent. However, even if young children do identify with that parent, by adolescence, they will typically compete with him or her. Another sad effect of these rituals is that they make the one described as the "ogre" or "dummy" feel inadequate as a parent and like the "odd man out" in the family dynamic.

Ritual 1: Father Is an Ogre

In this family ritual, the father is viewed by outsiders as successful and powerful, the mother as kind and caring. However, a closer view of the home life often shows a father who wears a big "No" on his forehead—that is, he firmly prohibits many of the activities that the children wish to pursue. However, the children learn to bypass his authority by appealing to their kind, understanding mother. Mom either manages to convince Dad to change his initial decision or surreptitiously permits the children to carry out their desired activities anyway.

Children quickly learn the necessary manipulative maneuvers. The ritual becomes more extreme as the children grow older, because Dad begins to recognize his lack of power over his family. He becomes more authoritarian as he tries to cope with his own sense of powerlessness. In response to his increasing authoritarianism, Mom feels even more obliged to shelter and defend her children. In her desperation, she invents new approaches to sabotaging her husband's power in the belief that she is doing the best thing for her children. She quite literally forces her husband to become an ogre.

Because they see their mother as powerful, girls in this family are likely to be achievement oriented; however, boys tend to underachieve. They see no effective model in their father, who appears both mean and powerless despite all his hard work. They may fear and resent him, and they are unlikely to wish to emulate him.

When we look at the history of this marriage, Father usually serves as the main breadwinner and makes all major decisions. Mother was attracted to this pattern initially and enjoyed it until the children were born. Although Mom may work part-time outside of the home, she is not likely to pursue a meaningful career. She defines her main role as being in charge of the children and other household tasks. At first, Dad has the final word over the children. However, Mom's feelings of powerlessness and her investment in the children cause her to personally decide that, in fact, she should be the children's protector and guide.

The scenario looks like this: Julian, as a little guy, is into a bit of mischief. When Dad finds him playing with some of his tools, he makes it very clear, in a booming voice, that those tools are his and that Julian is never to touch them. Mom assures Dad that Julian is just curious, and he should not get so angry over so small a problem. The next day, Julian is coincidentally playing with the same tools. Now Dad is livid. He has just scolded Julian and has been ignored, and so he scolds louder. Mom watches in agony as Dad roars. Julian is sent off to his room screaming and crying.

Scene two takes place in Julian's bedroom. Mom is holding him comfortingly in her arms and reassuringly explains, "It's all right, Dear. Daddy didn't mean to lose his temper. He just doesn't understand you. You're such a good boy. I know you were just curious."

Thus begins a long line of sabotages that Mom thinks of as necessary protection for her child from her husband's accelerating wrath. She wishes he wouldn't lose his temper so easily and that he would be more understanding of his children. But over the years, the father-son relationship worsens. Father rarely talks to his son, and Julian feels no respect for his father—only an awesome fear and a determination to never grow up to be as mean as he.

The father-son relationship becomes very competitive. The boy directs considerable anger toward a father he knows only by the descriptions and interpretations of his mother. By the time he's 16, the ogre game has solidified into a ritual.

In the following example, it's homecoming weekend at Julian's high school, and Julian has arranged for a date and pre-dance dinner. Naturally, he's short of money. He isn't really worried because he's always short of money. He simply needs to go through a three-scene script to get the necessary funds.

Scene 1: Julian Prepares Mom (Kind Mom)

Julian: (Confident and assured) Mom, could I borrow $75 for the Saturday-night Homecoming dinner and dance? I'll pay you back next week.

Mom: Sorry, Dear. You know that's Dad's decision. Just ask him. I'd like you to go, but I'm not sure Dad will.

Julian: But Mom, you know that Dad will just say I should have saved it up.

Mom: Well, Julian, I'm sorry. You'll just have to ask him anyway.

Scene 2: Julian Asks Dad (The Ogre)

Julian: (Hesitant, speaking quickly as if to get it over with) Dad, could I please borrow $75 for Homecoming? I promise I'll pay it back with interest. I'm just a little short because I didn't realize that dinner would be quite so expensive, and I'm going to get a job soon and then I'll have money.

Dad: (In customary booming voice) Absolutely not! You're just lazy. Why don't you do some work? You get an allowance. You'd better save your money next time. (Returns to TV or computer in typical disgust with his son.)

(Julian retreats silently, head down, relieved to have completed the unpleasant chore.)

Scene 3: Julian Collects (Wonderful Mom)

Julian: (Head is still down with a tear suitably placed on his cheek) Mom, Dad just doesn't understand me. (*He knows this for sure because Mom has told him so for 16 years.*) Even though I said I'd pay him back, he wouldn't give me any money. He wouldn't even talk to me. What's wrong with him?

Mom: (Withdraws money from apron pocket and gives it to Julian with a kind smile) It's all right, Dear. Here's $90—a little more than you need. Have a wonderful time, but don't tell Dad. Could you have your pictures taken at Marianna's house? You know, Julian, your dad doesn't understand teenagers.

Julian: (Hugs mom briefly) You're awesome, Mom! Thanks a lot!

What has this kind, sweet mom done? She has made her husband into an ogre—and a powerless one at that. Why would Julian want to be like his dad? What son would look up to a mean father who doesn't even have his wife's respect?

When Julian was little, he said that he was more like his mom. As he got older and it became uncomfortable for him to acknowledge similarity to his mother, he preferred to think that he was like neither of his parents. "I don't really know who I'm like," he says. As a matter of fact, he doesn't really know what he wants to do, where he wants to go to school, or what he'd like to major in. He just can't seem to find any direction. But that's all right; Mom will probably help!

There are of course variations in the ways in which Mom "tries to help" but inadvertently makes Father into an ogre. For example, she points out to her son that Dad works too hard, and she doesn't see any reason for him to devote so much of their family life to work. However, the underlying message to her son is "Don't be like Dad—don't work so hard. Life without all that work is more meaningful." The son's application of this concept and his response to his parents by the time he gets to high school, or possibly earlier, is "I don't see why I need to do this work at school. There's so much more to life than just schoolwork."

Mom, does it sound familiar? Have you given your son that message? Unfortunately, he no longer listens, even to you, when you now tell him to do his homework.

Here's another variation of the same ogre sabotage ritual:

Dad would like his son to take challenging courses and would like to encourage him in the direction of his own career. Mom protests that their son has the right to choose his own courses, his own career, and to do his own thing. Furthermore, she puts down her husband's career as one that requires too much travel, too much time away from home, too much arguing, or doesn't produce enough salary. Her indirect messages to her son are: Don't be like your father, and don't do the things that he recommends.

The words of this mother's adolescent son come out as "I want to do my own thing." He's not sure what that is, but he doesn't want to be told what it is; he wants to find out for himself. He knows for sure what he's against: his father, his father's career, his father's course choices, and his father's whole world. He must choose something that is different in order to establish his uniqueness.

There is a vacuum. The son says that he must experience living. He can't take advice from anyone (except from those who are also doing their own thing—peers or celebrities). So he grows long hair or shaves his head, experiments with drugs or violence, or joins a religious cult. If he is not permitted to please the people he loves, then he must find some other person or group that accepts and notices him.

By this time, Mom is not happy either, yet she has unwittingly denied her son an ideal model—the man she loved and chose to marry, her successful husband, his successful father. She made her husband into the man against whom her son must rebel instead of a model from whom he could learn, and now neither Mom nor Dad understands their son.

Ritual 2: Mother Is an Ogre

Equal time for females! Here's the way in which the husband makes his wife into an ogre. This ritual creates both underachieving boys and girls. It includes a kind, sweet husband who would be viewed by most women outside of the family as perfect. He's generous, loving, warm, and even likes to discuss feelings. He enjoys his parenting role and considers himself a good, fair father.

This man rarely loses his temper and frequently discusses differences of opinion with his children. They know that they can count on him to talk things over and to understand them. It never occurs to him that competition exists between him and his wife. He feels like a good father and can't imagine why his wife is so controlling. If this image seems familiar, it is because the "Mother Is an Ogre" ritual is frequently portrayed in family sitcoms on television. Even popular, critically-approved family shows can have a dramatic negative effect on families.

Of course, there must be some discipline in the home. Children must be guided. Because Dad is the "good guy," he permits his wife to be in charge of the rules for the children. He doesn't care much for rule making, and Mom clearly sees the need for guidelines for her children.

So she establishes the rules. Now here's the catch: she makes the rules, and he breaks the rules, or at least cleverly guides his children to discover the loopholes in her rules. An example follows:

Scene 1

Children are supposed to do their homework before they watch television. Mom and Dad agree to this rule. The rule is made at a family meeting on Sunday, in which Mom insists on the rule mainly against the wills of father and children. Now it's Monday. Mom walks into the living room to find Matthew watching Monday night football.

Mom: Matthew, have you done your homework?

Matthew: (No response)

Mom: Matthew, have you done your homework yet? Matthew, remember the new rule we made at last night's meeting?

Matthew: Yeah…just a minute. This is an important play.

Mom: (Leaves the room and returns in a few minutes) Matthew, is the play over yet? You have to do your homework.

Matthew: (Looking up briefly) Dad said I could do it after the game. This is a championship game.

Mom: (Leaves room discouraged) *Dad said, Dad said,* so what can I do?

Scene 2

The game is over. Dad and Matthew are sitting on the sofa chatting about the game.

Mom: Matthew, you said you'd do your homework right after the game. (To her husband) Dear, remember the rule we set up yesterday at the family meeting?

Matthew: Dad and I are just talking. We hardly ever have time to talk. I'll do it in a few minutes.

Dad: (To Mom) Dear, this should be an exception. Matt will do his work in a few minutes. We were just having a good talk about the game. (*It's not enough to watch the game. One must also talk about it afterward.*)

Mom: (Leaves room feeling powerless, muttering under her breath) Some rule!

Scene 3

Mom: (Enters the room, no longer patient, feeling angry, and screeching in a loud, tense voice) Matthew, you'd better do your homework! You'll fail your course. It's 10:00. You can't talk all night....

Matthew: Mom, what are you yelling about? I'll get it done. It's too late to concentrate now. I thought I'd go to sleep and get up early and do it in the morning. (In an angry rebellious tone) Don't worry about it. It's my homework, and I'll get it done! You don't even trust me.

Dad: (To his wife) It's okay, Dear. There's no reason to lose your temper. Matthew will do it in the morning. He'll get it done, and it will go much faster after a good night's sleep. (To Matthew in patient voice) Good night, Son. Have a good night's rest. Be sure to do your work in the morning.

Matthew goes off to bed thinking that his mother is really a nag and resolving to do his work in the morning. Dad settles down in front of the TV wondering how his wife became such a shrew. Mother sits down with him in front of the TV feeling drained, angry at herself for losing her temper, wishing she could get her husband to help her, and wondering why she can't get the kids to listen.

She knows for sure that Matthew won't do his homework. When the alarm goes off in the morning, he'll go back to sleep. Even after the snooze alarm goes off twice and she calls to him three or four times, he will barely be able to pull himself out of bed, and when he whizzes down to just miss the bus, Dad will offer him a ride to school on his way to work. She feels exasperated. She knows that she will attend the next parent-teacher conference without her husband and again hear the teacher say, "Matthew is such a bright boy. If he could only use his brains to do his work instead of figuring out ways to avoid it, he'd be a great student." Matthew becomes a bright, underachieving mystery to his teacher, to his mother, and, much later, to his father as well.

The "Mother Is an Ogre" game fosters Underachievement Syndrome in girls as well. Girls in these families underachieve because they see their mothers both as powerless and as ogres—certainly not as appropriate models. They would prefer to be Daddy's little girls and effortlessly please Daddy. The boys in this family are happy to identify with their father. They like being powerful and kind. Unfortunately, the message they receive from Dad does not encourage achievement. It is a passive-aggressive message to ignore Mom, to ignore teachers, and to ignore rules. It is a message to do their own thing and to procrastinate until they feel ready. However, the readiness rarely comes.

Ritual 3: Daddy Is a Dummy

This ritual is a slight modification of the ogre play and is found mainly in homes where mothers are psychologists, educators, social workers, or have taken parenting classes. Their husbands, on the other hand, may be doctors, engineers, or truck drivers, and have not taken parenting courses. The main difference, of course, is that Mom has learned the "right" way to bring up the children, and Dad hasn't. Therefore, Mom decides that it's her responsibility to give Dad directions on how to raise the children correctly:

> Mother knows for sure that boys need their daddies as appropriate male role models, so she explains this to her husband. He is delighted. He has visions of him and his son going off on fishing trips together and watching football games every Sunday. Initially, he is told that he must play with his little boy to get the good positive relationship started. So he does. He coos to him, he feeds him, and he even changes his diapers. Sons are fun! So far, things seem to be working out well. Father is delighted and pleased that his wife knows all about child psychology. He can rely on her knowledge to guide him in his parenting role.

> Somewhere around age two, the problem begins. Dad is in charge for the day, and he finds Lamar exploring and destroying his books and papers. His work is in a shambles. Dad loses his cool. He picks up his little boy, scolds him, and puts him in his crib screaming and crying. Mom enters to find the living room strewn with papers, Dad distraught, and her angelic son screaming desperately in his crib. She begins step one of her "first aid psychology" by immediately taking Lamar out of his crib, comforting his hurts, and explaining that everything will be all right and that poor Daddy just lost his temper.

> Lamar is calmed down, so Mom moves to step two, which is to explain to Dad a better way to handle this kind of dilemma in the future. She indicates that he must explain to his son the

appropriate behavior and refrain at all times from scolding Lamar because punishment is harmful to his self-concept and will cause his son to resent him. She also reminds her husband about the advantages of positive reinforcement. Dad listens patiently as he applies his own first aid to his strewn and crumpled papers that cover the floor. He wonders why he lost his temper, and he feels terrible about possibly damaging his son. He is most willing to try again and resolves to use only positive reinforcement, although he's not sure how he would have done that in this situation. But his wife took the parenting courses, and she should know.

Dad tries again and again. Each time, he seems to lose control and ends up damaging his son's self-concept. Maybe, he thinks, women are just better at bringing up children. If he could only put off playing with Lamar until the boy is a manageable size, then he could probably do better. Perhaps he'll go back to school and get another degree, or he could certainly devote more time to his work in the evenings. If he worked on Saturdays, that surely would improve his opportunities for promotion, and he could earn more money, and in the long run, he probably could do more for his son.

Dad's conclusion: I'll work hard now and play with Lamar when he's older.

Mom's conclusion: I wish my husband wouldn't have to work so much, but he doesn't handle Lamar very well anyway, so at least I can get the boy back on the right track.

Lamar's conclusion: Daddy's never home. All Daddy does is work. I sure don't want to be like Daddy.

At about this time, the "Daddy Is a Dummy" tune reverts to the "Father Is an Ogre" melody, and the song is played out as it was in the first orchestration.

Ritual 4: Mother Is the Mouse of the House

The ritual in which mothers are dummies, which results in rebellious adolescent daughters, begins a conspiratorial relationship between the father and daughter. It's a special alliance that pairs Dad and his perfect little girl with each other but, by definition, puts Mom in the role of being "not too bright" or somehow "out of it":

67

During early childhood, Daddy never needs to say no to Lela. She has a special way of winding him around her little finger. Mother admires the relationship, but from early on, she doesn't quite understand it, nor is she really a part of it. Father and daughter go off hand in hand, looking with wonder at each other. Everyone agrees that Lela is perfect.

Preadolescence arrives, and Mother notes a subtle—and some-times not so subtle—battle taking place between her daughter and herself. She isn't exactly sure why, but Lela can't seem to take the slightest bit of criticism from her. As a matter of fact, if Mother says "black," Lela says "white," and vice versa. Lela often goes to Dad because she is having trouble with Mom. He medi-ates, smoothes things over, and helps Lela to feel better while she snuggles in his lap and complains about how controlling her mother has become.

Lela enters middle school, shows signs of maturing physically, and Dad suddenly begins to worry about his perfect daughter. He remembers clearly when he was a teenage boy. Danger lurks in the corridors, in the lavatories, at school dances, and at preteen parties.

So Dad begins his tirade of cautions about cigarettes, alcohol, drugs, and most of all, boys. He must protect his perfect child from the evils of growing up, but Lela asks, "Don't you trust me?" Dad answers that he trusts her, but he's not sure about the rest of the world. He decides that it's time for rules.

Rules mean "no's." Lela has never really received a "no" from her father, and those no's feel terrible. She appeals to Mom. She asks Mom if Dad is going through a mid-life crisis or something. Coincidentally, he may be, but more important than that, Mom sees her first opportunity to build a closeness with her daughter. She assumes that they're getting closer because Lela is maturing. Now there's a new alliance—mother and daughter against Dad. When that works, Lela is happy. When it doesn't, she returns to Dad. Back and forth, Lela learns to manipulate. She even knows the special categories of requests for each of her parents: clothes and curfew exemptions for Mom; sports and travel for Dad.

Now Lela is in high school. Her parents are worried. They sud-denly realize that it's time for a united front. Mom and Dad are now on the same team, and Lela stands alone against them. They're saying no more frequently, and even when she performs her best manipulations, she cannot change their minds. She feels desperate. She thinks that neither of them understands her. She can't get them to let her do all of the things that she wants to do. She needs help. So she reaches out to her peers. She finds some friends who are having similar problems with their parents. They help her to understand that some parents just aren't "with it." Lela now has her own team. Together they will prove that they can oppose their parents. Lela tries smoking. All of the rebellious friends that she has gravitated toward smoke.

Now Mom and Dad are really anxious. Lela's in with the losers, and they have found cigarettes in her room. How can they trust her? Mom tries to talk to her, but that hardly ever works. Dad tries to communicate their concerns. That's a little better but not really effective because he wants her to stop smoking and change friends. She won't. She says she has to be her own person, and her parents must stop controlling her. Lela's parents don't agree with her. They believe that they should be stricter. They set curfews, and Lela climbs out the window. Now she's smoking pot. They think she's sleeping with a pothead.

Her parents found this out because Mom reads Lela's journal, which she leaves out on her desk. They also know from the same journal that Lela hates her parents. She's disrespectful, uses foul language, ignores their rules, and her formerly A and B grades have dropped to D's and F's. She skips classes, argues with her parents, and her most frequent words are "Stop trying to control me!" In truth, her parents can no longer control Lela, and they can't understand what happened to the sweet little girl that they remember.

Her parents bring Lela to a clinic. She doesn't want to come. She plops herself down in the chair, determined that the psychologist will not help her, and says in a disdainful voice, "My mother is stupid. You'd think she was born a hundred years ago."

"And your father?" the psychologist asks.

"He's not much better…well, maybe a little better. Neither of them know how to live. I really can't stand them. I can't wait until I get out of the house. I'm counting the days."

The rebellious daughter, who had too much power as a small child and whose father unwittingly encouraged her to compete with her mother, feels rejected, unloved, and out of control. These girls take various paths, but they all signal the same sense of lack of power, which they feel mainly because they were given too much power as children. Some girls assuage their feelings of rejection by parents in a pattern of promiscuous sexual relationships. They say that their parents (especially their fathers) do not love them, and they must have love. When such a girl is in a man's arms, she mistakenly believes that he loves her, and it feels good. When he leaves her for the next one, she feels rejected and embittered and easily accepts the next invitation that feels like love.

Other girls express rebellions silently. Bulimia, anorexia nervosa, depression, and suicide attempts are powerful ways of expressing feelings of loss of control. These illnesses leave parents feeling helpless and blaming each other. They put adolescents or young adults in control of their parents but not in control of themselves. The wink of the eye between Daddy and his little girl that puts Mother down as the "Mouse of the House" will later become the preadolescent daughter's roll of her eyes at her mother. When Father says no as well, this daughter feels rejected by both Mother and Father, and she is likely to go from bed to bed in search of love to substitute for the rejection she now feels.

Some rebellious teenagers find aunts, uncles, grandparents, or friends' parents who will side with them against their parents and include them in ogre and dummy games. They may complain to relatives that their parents love each other but don't love them. They search for the comfort of having their father side with them against their mother again, but by this time, both Mom and Dad have given up. Innocent, well-meaning other adults now feel sorry for the rebellious adolescents, take them into their homes, and unwittingly help alienate them from their parents— sometimes forever.

Combinations of the Rituals

In some families in which husband and wife are almost always embattled, all four sabotage rituals can take place simultaneously. Although the parents recognize their own marriage problems, they typically do not identify the sabotage effects on their children. However, the children's school achievement and behavioral patterns will reflect the battling parent with whom they've identified. In embattled families, there are winners and losers, aggressors and passive-aggressors. Sometimes, if the family is highly combative, all of the children are losers, although they may express their losing differently.

The most common example of an oppositional family in which the children of both genders lose is the one in which the daughter is Daddy's little girl who becomes Rebellious Rebecca, and one in which the son, who identifies with his solicitous and kind mother's passive-aggressive behavior, becomes Passive Paul. In embattled families with two same-gender children, one child typically takes the role of one parent, leaving the other sibling the role of the opposite parent. One sibling will appear to be more aggressive, the other passive or, more likely, passive-aggressive. Some sibling examples:

> Trevor, an older son, identified with his mother. His father was not home very much in his early years because he was concentrating on building his career. Jordan, the younger boy, chose Dad as his model. Jordan and Dad were hard workers. Jordan was glad to get out and help his dad, while Trevor, protected by his mother, preferred to stay inside to read or watch TV. By the time the marriage fell apart, the boys were grown. The father was a successful administrator; the mother was unhappy and felt rejected. Jordan was a successful businessman, but Trevor dropped out of school, couldn't hold a job, and was severely depressed.

> In a second family, Felicia, the oldest daughter, was Daddy's little girl. She began as an excellent student and was musically talented. Cherise, her youngest sister, identified with Mom. Cherise was an excellent student, too, and had equal musical talent. In adolescence, Felicia took on the Rebellious Rebecca pattern. Her grades dropped, and her interest in music waned. Cherise continued with her efforts as an excellent student and a fine musician. The father in this family died in a car accident when the girls were in college. The mother carried on independently and successfully and coped extraordinarily well with the disaster. The oldest daughter, who had identified with her father, struggled through multiple marriages and career changes. The younger daughter, however, continued successfully in more stable relationships and a good career.

For families in which there are multiple children, the identification with oppositional parents becomes more complex. The children are forced to take sides because there are clearly two opposing teams. Children who must fight one of their parents often generalize the battle to fighting all authority. Because their customary approach is one of battle, they do not permit themselves to achieve at school. At some point, they feel that they must take a determined anti-school, anti-authority position. It is at this point that their underachievement begins.

One basic underlying cause of Underachievement Syndrome is power struggle within the family. The degree and methods of power struggle will heavily influence the achievement patterns of the children. Teachers can, nevertheless, make a difference for these children, even though the patterns have been initiated at home.

It is worth emphasizing there is much more at stake than poor grades for the children for whom ogre and dummy rituals are being played out. If Mother is angry at men or continually tries to make her son into a better man than her husband, she teaches her son to compete with her husband intensely. This may lead to depression, anger, and even violence.

Furthermore, as the boy attempts both to surpass his father in his mother's eyes and to become a man as well, especially during adolescence, he may turn his anger against his mother. Although he will often not understand the extreme anger he feels, it is surely devastating to his mother, who has invested herself so intensely.

If Father is angry at his wife's control or mediates the relationship between his daughter and his wife and sabotages his wife's power, he unwittingly creates a powerful adolescent that he may no longer be able to control or even guide. He'll become frustrated, and his daughter will feel rejected. This begins the daughter's promiscuous search for as close and exclusive a relationship with a man as she had with her father when her mother was unwittingly left out of the family picture.

Keep in mind that ogre and dummy rituals occur occasionally for all families. For younger children, it is only when there is a continued pattern of these rituals that problems arise. However, during normal adolescence, young people attempt to define their roles on the route to adulthood. Even a single incident of sabotage by one parent will encourage them to test the other parent disrespectfully. It takes only a little more parent sabotage to push the teenager toward oppositional defiant behavior, which can become very difficult to redirect.

Whether underachievement, anger, violence, or promiscuity is the result, the search for too much power easily leads to alcohol and drugs, which of course only empowers the user temporarily. **When men and women in our society learn to value each other's differences in** **positive ways, and when partners are not at war with each other, there will be more achieving, positive, and mentally healthy children.**

Ask yourself the following questions about dependency and dominance before you read Chapter 4. (If you're a teacher, read "this student" for "my child" or "this child.")

1. Do other children seem to pick on my child?

2. Is the mother or father in this child's family overprotective?

3. Does my child need lots of parent help with homework?

4. Does my child often play "class clown"?

5. Does my child cry, whine, or complain a lot?

Score 1 point for each "yes" response, and total the points. Scores are explained below.

Total Points

4–5:   My child has very serious dependency problems.

2–3:   My child has fairly serious dependency problems.

1:   My child has only minor dependency problems.

0:   My child has no dependency problems.

6. Does my child brag a lot when he/she does something well?

7. Does my child often disobey his/her mother, father, or teacher?

8. Does my child blame others or find excuses?

9. Does my child often convince a parent or teacher to change his/her mind?

10. Does my child get one parent (or teacher) to say yes after the other parent (or teacher) says no?

Score 1 point for each "yes" response, and total the points for this section. Scores are explained below.

Total Points

4–5:   My child has very serious dominance problems.

2–3:   My child has fairly serious dominance problems.

1:   My child has only minor dominance problems.

0:   My child has no dominance problems.

Read this chapter to determine if your child is a dependent or dominant underachiever.

Chapter 4
Dependency and Dominance

Parents are rarely certified in child rearing. Their framework for raising children may be influenced by information that they find in books, in magazine articles, on the Internet, or through parenting courses, but the strongest influence will be their own evaluation of how they were raised by their parents.

By the time you, as parents, first stare with awe at the magnificent new being that you have created, you may have already spent countless hours considering how to parent your child. As you and your partner review your own childhoods, you may conclude that they were basically good and that you would like to provide your children with a similar family environment. However, if either you or your partner sees your childhood as having been inadequate, you will no doubt consider at length the many ways that you can be a better parent and help your children avoid the traumatic experiences or feelings of inadequacy that you may have experienced.

Sometimes you discuss your thoughts with the other parent. More often, you think about your plans for your children on your own. As you ponder your own early years and project your emotional experiences into the life of the infant in your arms, you hope that you will be able to "do it right" with this child for whom you feel so much love and commitment. It is almost as if you are a part of this child that you have created.

Counteridentification

The process by which you identify with or "see yourself in" your children is known as *counteridentification*. Counteridentification appears to have both positive and negative impacts on children's achievement. When you counteridentify with your children, you invest yourself in their activities and empathetically share their efforts, successes, and failures. The potential for positive contributions to your children's achievement comes mainly from your investment of time and sharing of skills. In one classic study of the childhood characteristics of talented mathematicians, pianists, and swimmers, those individuals related that a parent, and sometimes both parents, provided an early and influential model.[1] It is reasonable to conclude that, for the individuals in the study, there existed a high degree of counteridentification by the parent.

A familiar, less positive example of counteridentification is the vociferous father arguing desperately with the referee at the Little League baseball game as if it were he who had been unfairly called "out." Another example is the mother who becomes unusually upset when her daughter loses her first boyfriend. It seems almost as if the mother were experiencing her own personal pain and rejection.

Most parents counteridentify with at least one of their children, and as such, it is not the process itself that causes problems. However, when counteridentification causes the parents to do so much for their children that the children are not given sufficient independence to develop their own initiative, or when the parents begin to give the children so much power that the children feel as though they must always be in control, then counteridentification is likely to lead to Underachievement Syndrome.

There is a broad range of ways for parents to foster appropriate independence in children. It is only the extremes that they should avoid. However, as parents reflect on the child-rearing techniques that were used on them as children, they may falsely conclude that if they raise their own children in the opposite extreme of the way in which they were raised, then their children will be happier than they were. So in their attempts to parent their children differently, they may err by going too far in the opposite direction. For example, parents who were brought up with few material possessions are frequently determined to give their children everything. They receive vicarious joy from showering their children with toys and clothes. If parents were brought up with strict discipline, they may exaggerate their efforts by providing too much freedom to their children. If parents believe that they received too few compliments from their own parents, they may lavish praise upon their children in order to build strong self-confidence. The list goes on, but in each case, the counteridentifying parents who go to the opposite extreme, rather than using moderation in their child-rearing techniques, cause problems for their children.

Furthermore, parents generally remember very little about how they were raised as small children. What they remember most is their adolescence, and that may not be the best time to recall when guiding their own small children.

Sometimes counteridentifying parents guide their children in ways that fulfill their own childhood wishes. For example, the talented music major who never fully realized her career in music may be determined to help her daughter develop her musical talents, almost regardless of the child's own interests or abilities. The engineer who wished that he could have been a football player and fondly remembers his football days in high school sees his son's talent early and encourages him to train toward being a professional football player.

If these parents don't pressure their children too much, and if they don't do too much for them, these counteridenti-fications may provide positive guidance. However, extreme pressure may again cause underachievement problems for children. Understanding the ways in which counteridentification causes problems for children can help you modify your parenting techniques appropriately.

Parent
Pointer

Fostering Dependency

When counteridentification encourages parents to do too much for their children, it fosters dependency. Dependency caused by counter-identification can be described in three scenarios. I call the first "Smothering Mothering":

> Amy is a talented art student. Amy's mother was an art major in college and was also very talented. She did not graduate from college but decided to get married and have a family instead. Mom provided Amy with plenty of art materials and ample positive modeling, even as a preschooler. She enrolled Amy in a preschool art class at the local art museum and admired her talent as soon as it showed itself, which according to Mom was almost as soon as Amy could hold a crayon.

> Amy is enthusiastic about her art and proud of her talent. She begins to win school art contests, and mother and daughter are delighted. They work together on each contest, with Mom enthusiastically contributing ideas and suggestions and Amy excitedly incorporating them into her creations. As Amy wins more and more competitions, she senses pressure to continue to win. Mom, who counteridentifies with Amy, thoroughly enjoys her daughter's glory and projects her own unfulfilled wishes for an art career onto Amy.

> The experience of triumph creates a strong pressure in Amy to continue to excel and to gain recognition, even without

external pressure from Mom. However, as Mom and teachers alike project a great future for Amy, she feels even more pressure to be extraordinary. Mom tries not to put pressure on Amy because she easily empathizes with Amy's feelings of stress. They collaborate on Amy's artwork, but eventually, Amy begins to worry that she might not be able to win an art contest without Mom's ideas and help. Now she is distressed and confused.

The next contest is important. Amy explains to Mom that she must do this painting alone. She is ready to begin, but she can't seem to think of a good idea. She tries for several days, but nothing comes to mind except a bewildering fear that perhaps she can't originate ideas without her mother. Mom tries not to interfere but is also anxious because Amy has not yet started her work. Perhaps, Mom concludes, she could just give Amy some hints and then Amy could complete the artwork on her own. Amy accepts the hints and pretends to herself that the ideas were mostly her own anyway. She works on her painting for a little while, but something about it is wrong. Perhaps Mom could help with just a few suggestions. Mom gives those, Amy now feels much more satisfied with her painting, and she enters it into the contest. Hurray! Another blue ribbon for Amy (and her mother). However, this time, Amy really is not sure whether it is she or her mother who has earned the blue ribbon.

The succeeding contests find Amy more hesitant and more dependent on her mother for suggestions, less confident in her own ability, and even less creative. She has become a talented technician, but not a creative artist.

Underachievement? Yes. Mom's counteridentification with Amy has caused her to do too much for her daughter. In the process, Mom has stolen from Amy her confidence and her creativity, and neither of them quite understands why Amy's early talent has not developed beyond mere mechanical art ability and why, despite that talent, Amy lacks confidence in her art.

The second scenario can be called "Bothering Fathering":

Jeffrey is definitely intellectually gifted; his IQ is around 150. He could read before he entered school and understood fractions and decimals by second grade. Despite his clumsy handwriting, he earned A's, but only through fourth grade. In fifth grade, there was a change. Jeff wasn't sure exactly what had happened, but he knew that the work was becoming more complex. The writing was becoming more tedious. At times, he made mistakes. Sometimes he would get only a B. He decided not to bring his B papers home. His mother and father were so proud of all of his A's.

Jeff thought that maybe if he worked more slowly, he could do perfect work, particularly in math. He seemed to be making too many careless errors, so he slowed down. He slowed down so much, though, that he wasn't finishing his assignments in school and had to bring his papers home as homework.

One day he didn't understand his math at all, so he asked his father to explain it. His father was an engineer, and he explained the material to Jeff rather quickly. Jeff thought he understood, but he wasn't quite sure, and he wanted to be certain to have his homework all right. So Dad explained it again. This time, Dad sat down with Jeff, and they worked on math together. Dad was patient and kind. Jeff got all his work done, and he and Dad shared that nice feeling of companionship.

The next night, more homework came home, and Jeff and his father spent more time together. Jeff worked slowly and meticulously. He found it harder and harder to keep up with his classmates, although his grades continued to be mainly A's. Dad spent more and more time helping Jeff with his homework. It was difficult to be patient now. He was worried.

Dad certainly didn't want his brilliant son to bring home poor grades, nor could he understand why Jeff worked so slowly and wanted so much help. For Jeff, what had started as the pleasant companionship of his father had fast become a crutch upon which the boy had learned to lean—and one that he now doubted he could do without. Jeff's Underachievement Syndrome did not show on his perfect report card, but his well-meaning father was increasing Jeff's dependence and lack of confidence nightly.

Jeff was exceptionally bright, and it took little effort to reverse his dependent underachieving pattern. However, this is atypical. Concerned parents who do homework for their children begin a dependency pattern that may be very difficult to reverse.

Strangely enough, the homework dependency pattern often begins in the primary grades on the advice of well-intentioned teachers. At an early conference, teachers may caution parents that their children are falling further behind and need help with homework. The children soon discover that whatever work they don't complete in class can be taken home, where Mom or Dad will give them undivided attention and assistance.

More work comes home. Parents spend more time with the children. Sometimes Dad gets upset that Mom is spending so much time with the homework. Mom and Dad argue about whether the kids need all of this help. The children insist that they don't understand the work and will not write a letter or a number on their paper without Mom's kind supervision. In school, children like this may be labeled learning disabled (LD) because their achievement falls behind that which would be predicted by their IQ scores and because they work effectively only in one-to-one relationships. Here's another case example:

> During a therapy session, Jamel, a third grader, asked for help with almost every word when reading a personality test. The therapist explained to him that she was going for a cup of coffee, and while she was gone, he should write down the words that he couldn't figure out. Five minutes later, she returned to find that Jamel had completed the inventory without writing down a single word. He said that he had "worked out" all of the words.

> In the process of reversing Jamel's homework dependency, his mother needed to sit patiently downstairs and listen to the boy crying for help from his room for an entire week before he agreed to do the homework by himself. Now Jamel not only does his homework on his own, but he brings home much less work because he finishes most of assignments in class.

Most homework-dependent children who rely on their mothers for help do their homework in the kitchen, where Mom can stir the soup while hovering over her children's math problems. Father-dependent homework locations are more likely to be in the dining room or den, not too far from the television set.

The third scenario can be called "Poor Child, Poor Child" and represents the most extreme form of dependency. These are overprotected children whose mothers wash their hair when they're in eighth grade, help bathe them when they're in sixth grade, or rock them after school when they're in first grade because Mother fears that school makes them tense and anxious. These children get their laundry picked up from the floor, washed, and placed neatly in their drawers as if by magic. They come home from school and complain about the hard day they've had, about the kids who are mean to them, the teacher who is unfair, or the principal who picks on them. After the cookie-supported description of problems, they retire to the television set, where, they explain to Mom, they must relax from their tense day at school. They are too tired to do homework. They can't help with the dishes because they worked too hard all day. They breathe a sigh of relief after a five-minute effort at most anything.

These dependent children confuse their parents and teachers by their very real symptoms of tension—bed-wetting, nail biting, repeated yawning, sighing, wheezing, stomachaches, headaches, and tears. Parents and teachers continually ask themselves if they are pushing these children too hard or expecting too much from them. What has actually happened is that so much has been done for these children that they have never experienced any real effort. **All work feels difficult to children who have never learned to carry through even simple tasks independently.** These children have not earned the satisfaction that comes from investing energy in an activity. Furthermore, because all work feels difficult to them, they constantly worry that they will fail and not be able to accomplish even simple tasks that their peers seem able to do.

Worry about not being able to master a task replaces the activity itself; thus, symptoms of tension appear. Rimm's Law #5—Children feel more tension when they are worrying about their work than when they are doing that work—helps parents to understand the reasons for these symptoms of tension.

One of my favorite examples is my own childhood experience of standing before the kitchen sink looking at the stack of dishes that needed to be washed. "I'll never finish," I thought, and I complained to my mom about the enormous job ahead. She ignored my complaint and simply said, "Do them." I did, and the job seemed endless the first time. By the tenth time, I wondered why I had complained; it was a 10-minute job. Suppose my mother had felt sorry for me and done the dishes instead?

Dependent children are aware that they are not keeping up with their peers in the classroom. They do not have the confidence to complete schoolwork without assistance, which causes stress, but when they actually become absorbed in the task, the symptoms of tension disappear. Any adult can identify with the feeling of being overwhelmed when faced with multiple tasks. However, we know from experience that these symptoms will diminish as we begin to accomplish those tasks.

Dependent children continually seek approval, guidance, help, support, and love. Teachers commonly view these symptoms as indicators of lack of love, attention, and approval at home. They may ask parents to: (a) not put pressure on these children, and (b) be sure to give them more affection and attention. This is exactly the wrong communication to give these parents, who have put so little pressure on these children and are already lavishing them with love and attention.

The Freudian legacy has given us the notion that such dependency symptoms of insecurity and tension represent deprivation. In fact, they often indicate an *excess* of attention and assistance. This is what I mean by Rimm's Law #7: Deprivation and excess frequently exhibit the same symptoms. These dependent children are often addicted to attention, affection, and assurances of love. They want more attention continuously, although they are already being given much in the classroom or at home. This paradox makes it difficult for teachers and parents to determine effective approaches to the identification and treatment of these children.

Fostering Dominance

Counteridentifying adults who feel that their own parents did not give them enough freedom may err in the direction of giving their children too much freedom or control. These parents assume that there is an inherent quality within their children that will light the way for them. They believe if they give their children sufficient freedom, the children will somehow sense their own direction. The parents see their role as one of facilitating or permitting appropriate independent growth. Further, they consider themselves to be kind, caring, and sensitive.

When their children look to them for guidance or direction, they are told to make their own choices. Instead of leading, these parents follow their children's direction. When these children push their parent's rules to determine which behaviors are allowed and which are not, they find no clear limits. Instead, the limits vary with the manipulative ability of the children and with the particular mood of the particular parent. The children may also be given the message to "be creative," which they interpret as meaning "be different." In the school setting, they may assume that they need not do what teachers require if they don't find it sufficiently interesting. They expect to make all of the choices.

These children have become so accustomed to controlling their parents that their habitual way of interacting with peers and other adults is to attempt to control them. This extreme habit of control or dominance usually causes behavior and learning problems for children. Sometimes only a fine line separates the kind of problematic control that is called bossiness, compulsivity, competitiveness, or bullying from the more positive forms of dominance known as independence, leadership, political astuteness, and creativity. Some case studies will illustrate how counteridentification can cause problematic degrees of dominance:

> Three-and-a-half-year-old Sonora, an only child, came to Family Achievement Clinic because her parents were asked that she not return to a Montessori preschool, where the teacher described her as having very disruptive tantrums when she wasn't allowed to do what she wanted to do. Tantrums were also taking place at home, especially when Sonora's mother raised her voice to scold the girl. Mom explained that Sonora was so bright that she had always discussed issues with her as if she were an adult. In addition, Dad described a signal that he gave his wife to calm down if she was raising her voice to Sonora.
>
> Because Sonora was a very bright child, it was easy to make the mistake of giving her adult power too soon. Sonora was in control at home and generalized her need to be both center stage and in charge to her preschool class.

In Sonora's case, her mother's counteridentification caused her mother to use an adult conversation style with her early. Sonora simply assumed that same style. Dad overempowered Sonora by signaling to his wife to temper her interactions with their daughter, although he only intended to be helpful. This small signal gave Sonora power over her mother. Fortunately, it is dramatically easy to reverse this kind of problem in preschoolers by teaching parents how to support each other, as well as how to set consistent limits. After Sonora's parents began using these techniques, Sonora was able to become a comfortable, secure child.

Creative parents who were frustrated in their own school experiences may counteridentify with their children and give them too much power in the name of creativity. They admire and reward their children for imaginative ideas, different kinds of thinking, questioning behavior, and generally unusual ways of acting. They proudly point out that their children "march to the beat of a different drummer." Because creativity is a positive quality that certainly should be cultivated, this would not appear to cause any difficulty. But it may, because these children become determined to do only creative work in the classroom and use creativity as an excuse to select only the work they prefer. For example, Creative Chris will write his own stories or plays, participate in drama, and experiment in science or math. However, he refuses to do any workbook, drill, or memory work and insists that it is not reasonable to do such boring or irrelevant busywork.

When first grader Chris puts his hands in a large jar of paste to investigate the concept of displacement, his teacher gets upset at his disorderly conduct. Chris argues that the teacher is preventing his experimentations, and his mother urges the teacher to value his creative exploration.

Fourth grader Chris insists that he sees no reason to learn mathematics facts because he's already selected his career as a fireman, and he only needs to learn the chemistry of extinguishing fires.

Sixth grader Christine argues that she is not worried about her F in science because she received an A in music, and that is her career choice. When adults raise the question of readiness for other careers and point out the competitiveness of performing professionally, Christine argues that she will work hard in music, and if one works hard enough in an area, success is sure to come.

Tenth grader Christine claims that she no longer measures her success by grades and has now set social skills as her number-one priority. Because she intends to excel in social life, Christine has decided to transfer her creativity to that domain and is indeed very successful. She wears the most unusual clothes and hosts the most original parties.

High school graduate Chris rejects a scholarship to an excellent college because he is determined to apply his creativity to an experimental drama group or a traveling rock band, each of which will probably survive for six months or less.

Creative Chris and Creative Christine have received messages to be original, unusual, creative, and different and to attract attention for their uniqueness. They select creative areas of expertise that will vary with their ages and interests. They use these areas of expertise as excuses not to do the routine tasks expected of them, thereby avoiding tasks that involve real challenge or the possibility of failure. As a matter of fact, even in their areas of expertise, they may not demonstrate the perseverance, discipline, and attention to detail required in successful creative enterprises. They may actually fail classes in their specialty areas because they have power struggles with their teachers and will not accept criticism. They claim that others should not be able to judge their creative products, and they refuse to paint, photograph, act, or write in the ways that teachers coach them. They fear that the outcomes won't be their own creative products.

Such students are creative but not positively productive. They are powerful in calling attention to their creativity; however, their creativity is so entwined with opposition to adults that their sense of identity comes to depend on who and what they oppose. By high school, they oppose most of the teachers, as well as their parents. In their search for uniqueness, they often feel extremely lonely. They find it difficult to acknowledge that anyone, even creative friends, could be creative enough to understand their feelings. Also by this time, drugs become very tempting to some highly creative kids in the hope that the altered state produced by those drugs will permit them extraordinarily creative experiences.

Dominant children may relate to other people as if those others were marionettes. The children's expertise, satisfaction, and confidence often depend on pulling the attached strings. They manipulate parents, teachers, and peers, and they are especially talented at manipulating key people against each other to their own advantage. They learn early to blame teachers for their school problems and convince their parents of the accuracy of the blame. They may also manipulate the very same teachers against their parents. They are experts at getting one parent to ally on their side against the other parent. They thrive in homes where ogre and dummy games are played because their manipulations are initiated, encouraged, and supported by these rituals. Grandparents, aunts, and uncles become vulnerable to their manipulations when these children learn that grandparents may say yes when parents say no.

These children also manipulate peers routinely and feel frustrated, angry, unloved, and rejected when friends do not do what they wish. They guarantee disappointment in friendships by defining friendship as a completely controlling relationship. The "victims" of these friendships will say that they feel "owned" or like "pawns," a relationship that the dominant manipulator views as "faithfulness." Friendships are not easy for dominant children because they feel secure only when they completely control their peers.

Manipulative Mark, a preschooler, goes into the store with his mother and asks her to buy him the very same toy that Father has recently denied him. Manipulative Maria, a second grader, persuades her father to let her have a banana split, although Mother told her she couldn't have dessert because she didn't eat her vegetables. As a middle school student, Manipulative Mark persuades his teacher to extend the deadline for a school project because he is working on an extraordinarily enormous one, but when he finally turns in his half-completed project two weeks late, he explains that his mother was too busy working to drive him to the library.

Manipulative Maria, a high school student, refused to accept the "no, later," that her father gave her when she asked to go to the store. He expected her to do her homework first. She managed to get her older sister to drive her to the store and returned to find her father highly displeased with her behavior. He was furious and sent her to her room. She was equally angry and refused to go. He pushed her toward the room, and she pushed him back. She later told a counselor that her father was weak and that she liked pushing him around. She also said that she got along well with her mother but poorly with her father.

Manipulative Maria's mother said that she couldn't control her daughter at all, and Dad said he could only do so sometimes. Both parents had said yes too often to this girl when she was little, and neither parent dared say no very often now. When they tried, Maria was an expert at manipulating her mother to change her father's decision. Maria was very much in charge of her parents and planned to stay that way. Any sudden effort by her parents to set rules would likely move Maria toward becoming Rebellious Rebecca. She would undoubtedly call them irrational and controlling and then use that as an excuse for doing what she wanted without their permission.

Sometimes parents teach oppositional skills simultaneously with engendering too much power. Parents who do this usually view their own past school experiences as unpleasant or inappropriate. Therefore, as they look back to their own childhoods, they not only feel that they were unsuccessful at the school game, but they are also convinced that teachers and principals taught them wrong and ran the schools poorly. They are determined that their children will have better educational experiences and are intent on ensuring that teachers don't make the same mistakes with their children as were made with them. The message to fight the school is given early and often—sometimes subtly and sometimes not so subtly, sometimes for appropriate reasons and sometimes quite inappropriately. Thus, these parents extend the power of their children even beyond its already excessive level to include what Mom or

Dad can accomplish for them in the fury of arguments with teachers or counselors or principals. Indeed, for these oppositional children, fighting authority and establishing what they are against become the bases of building their self-concepts.

Oppositional children find much support for their determined nonconformity. This nonconformity and their oppositional attitudes fit well into ogre and dummy games at home. "Good" Mom sets them against "mean" Dad and isolates them from him. "Nice guy" Dad protects them against "mean, disciplining" Mom. The children sense the battle and take sides with the parent who most often gives them what they want. Then they enlist that parent's help against their teachers. They often compete with teachers in front of the class and frequently win. Sometimes they can even get other children's parents on their side. The final victory is when Mrs. Lopez gets fired because she can't control Damien or the class. These children control peers and parents by bursts of temper or by actually fighting, but more often by debate, argument, and "lawyering."

It seems that almost every rule sets off a battle cry, and the children's parent(s) ally themselves with their children—until adolescence. At this point, parents almost certainly become the enemy, unless they say yes to absolutely everything. Parents are now "authority," and these young people, who have become Rebellious Rebeccas and Roberts, join forces with other anti-school youths, potheads, stoners, gangs, rebels, anti-war, anti-school, anti-government, anti-poverty, or anti-anything groups.

Needless to say, some "anti" groups are bad, and some obviously have real value. That isn't the issue. The issue is that the critical component of the group is that its members are united by what they oppose, not by what they support. They define themselves by what they are against, what they can beat down, and what they are angry about. These young people may go through years of adolescence and young adulthood bitter at the world because it does not respond to their personal efforts or the wishes of their group. Their identity formation is slowed by the effects of their extreme rebellion, depression, and anger. They believe that they should have considerable power, yet they feel powerless. If the cause of their opposition disappears, they feel purposeless.

Fortunately, some of these young people do build positive identities out of the ashes left by their wars. But the battling is destructive nonetheless, and it takes its toll on them, their schools, their families, and society. Their adolescent identity crises may last into their twenties and thirties, and for some, the crisis never seems to be resolved.

There are many psychologists who believe that rebellion is a necessary style of adolescence. Some pushing of limits and defiance surely represent normal adolescence. Extreme and continually defiant behaviors, however, are not normal adolescence. They are mainly nonproductive, with too high a price to pay. These behaviors delay the developmental task of establishing identity. It is mainly a response to too much power given to children too early. "If children were meant to run our homes, God would have created them bigger...."[2]

Summary

Parents and teachers often feel frustration because they can't seem to break these patterns of dependence or dominance. In fact, they reinforce the patterns because they listen too literally to what children say to them. Children and even adolescents tell parents what they are feeling and about their needs of the day or the week. They rarely project realistically for the months—and certainly not the years—ahead. In order for adults to meet the needs of underachievers, they should assume leadership and the power to guide. Although they should certainly listen to these children's words, they need to interpret them in ways that are productive for the children in the long term, even if this causes some temporary discomfort.

Parents require some personal confidence in their own interpretation of their children's future. It is important for adults not to empower children so much that no power is left for those who should guide them. If they listen to children's messages and reframe their views to give them more appropriate direction, children will accept adult leadership and develop the skills and confidence that will provide choices for them as they establish their own identities.

Adults do much of their parenting and teaching intuitively. Intuition works well if they've been parented and taught well and if they are positive, learning, and achieving. However, for adults who do not see their early family life or school life as having been productive, their intuitive sense may lead them astray. For children exhibiting dependency and dominance, counterintuitive responses may indeed be more effective. After all, intuitive responses have already proven ineffective.

Children should have help when they need it, and parents should be sensitive to their feelings. Children should also be encouraged to develop independence and creativity. It is only the extremes that lead to dependency and dominance. When children complain, whine, or are continually negative, or when they request help more frequently than they need it, they are showing symptoms of too-dependent relationships. If they are creative only for the purpose of opposing, or if they insist on wielding power without respect for the rights of others, they are too dominant. These extremes will result in underachievement at some level. Their underachievement is a collection of symptoms.

Although the main emphasis in this book is only on underachievement, these children will also cause other family and relationship problems. Underachievement Syndrome can be cured, and children's dependency or extreme dominance can also be modified to help them live more satisfying and productive lives.

Identification and counteridentification provide the means by which children learn to relate to their personal environments. If children learn to relate in a way that causes them too much dependence, they will lack a sense of confidence and control. On the other hand, if they learn to dominate their environment, they will function only where they excel or are in power. Some children may vacillate between these two extremes of power and tend to feel like either winners or losers. Achievers must learn persistence. Achievers must be problem solvers. Achieving permits the joy of winning and the agony of losing but requires that individuals be able to emerge from those losses without seeing themselves as losers. All children fail at one time or another. It is how they cope with failure experiences that distinguishes achievers from underachievers.

Ask yourself these questions before you read Chapter 5. (If you're a teacher, read "this student" for "my child.")

1. Is my child bored with school?

2. Does my child seem to ask for more teacher help than most children?

3. Does my child tend not to finish class assignments in school?

4. Does my child disrupt the class by talking too much?

5. Does my child complain that schoolwork is too easy?

6. Is socializing the most important part of school for my child?

7. Does my child's class emphasize competition in almost everything?

8. Does my child's class attempt to eliminate all competition?

Score 1 point for each "yes" response, and total the points. Scores are explained below.

Total Points

5–8:	There are probably very serious problems within the classroom.
3–4:	There are probably fairly serious problems within the classroom.
1–2:	There are only minor problems within the classroom.
0:	There are no apparent problems in the classroom.

Read this chapter to discover what classroom risks can cause under-achievement.

Chapter 5
School Causes of Underachievement Syndrome

Schools and teachers can make dramatic differences in children's achievement. Although teachers may follow a variety of philosophies of education successfully, there are some classroom environments that are extremely problematic for underachieving children. Some environments exacerbate and maintain Underachievement Syndrome, while others help to prevent and reverse it. Sometimes, school circumstances are actually the initiating and main causes of the syndrome.

There is a wide range of appropriate styles for teaching children. Avoiding the extremes and maintaining a firm, positive classroom atmosphere are productive guidelines for all teachers. Some specific examples of undesirable, harmful teaching styles can provide insights for both teachers and parents.

Structure

Teachers Loose Louise and Rigid Roger provide opposite but equally counterproductive learning environments in their classrooms. Loosely organized classrooms that provide no structure cause underachievers, who may already lack organizational skills, to flounder. They do not discipline themselves, and they habitually push limits. They get out of their seats continuously, wander aimlessly, don't complete tasks, and get themselves into trouble. Children with attention deficit disorders, especially those with hyperactivity or unfocused high energy, accomplish little in unstructured settings. They are easily distracted by the movement and noise level of the class. Teachers often assume that these children must be given freedom to move around. Actually, high-energy children can be expected to sit firmly in their seats until they have completed their assignments as long as they have appropriate outlets for their energy at other times.

Also, children who depend on one-to-one attention will be at the teacher's desk repeatedly to get help or to ask questions if there are no clear guidelines in the classroom. I recall observing one high-energy child in a loosely structured first-grade classroom and finding him continually out of his seat. The longest time he stayed on one task was 70 seconds. A dependent child that I observed in a third-grade classroom went for teacher or peer help 22 times in 30 minutes. In such classrooms, teachers constantly interrupt reading groups to shush children working at their desks, and there is a general sense of too much sound, movement, and turmoil. These teachers tend to scold frequently, although their repeated reprimands actually serve to increase the noise level.

Teachers have little control in such classrooms. In these settings, dominant children become more powerful and successfully challenge their teachers: "You can't make me do this work; my father's on the school board" or, "I can't do my work because the class is too noisy. Why don't you make it quieter?" This last comment, while probably true, only contributes to the tumult. Even children who have no history of previous discipline problems will act out in disorganized classrooms and may well begin to exhibit behavior problems.

Rigid Roger presides over an equally poor environment for learning. High-energy children may actually function better in this class, provided that Rigid Roger does not overuse punishment. But if these children are frequently reprimanded, the reprimands may become a form of adult attention, and for these attention-dependent children, any attention is better than none. Consequently, they get into further trouble.

Dominant creative or oppositional defiant children struggle for power with rigid teachers. These children see strict control as a call to battle that they are determined to answer. Dominant students will correct and embarrass teachers in front of the class whenever possible. They will argue with them about rules, not hand in assignments that they claim are irrelevant, announce that teachers are unfair to the boys (or the girls), question them for the sake of questioning, and manipulate power struggles among teachers, parents, and principals. Often the teachers' only way to control these children is with grades. However, these children usually prefer to fail rather than acknowledge themselves as losers to teachers. In their battles with rigid teachers, dominant students may feel that conformity would cause them to lose status with their classmates. They continue to refuse to do assigned lessons, regardless of threats or grades.

In the struggle for power between Rigid Rogers and dominant children with Underachievement Syndrome, neither emerge victorious. Here's a case example:

Talicia, a seventh grader with an IQ in the gifted range and especially strong math ability, explained to me about her F in math. She said that she understood the concepts and actually did well on her tests. However, her teacher insisted on some very specific formats for writing her name, date, and alignment of the math problems. He reduced the grade when students did not follow these directions. Talicia pointed out how unfair these directions were and proceeded to explain how she always tended to forget one or more directions. The result was that her grade was always reduced.

In addition, Talicia saw no reason to do all of the busywork required, so she only handed in the assignments that she considered reasonable and refused to do the easy ones when she understood the work. As a matter of fact, she did have very good mastery of the subject, and it was a more exciting challenge to see if she could outpower the teacher. She was determined not to conform to his rigid standards.

In Talicia's situation, her math scores declined only for a year. A much more flexible teacher the following year inspired this gifted girl to return to her former achieving status.

Competition

As I've said before, underachievers do not cope with competition well. They are poor losers and may not even become involved in an activity unless they're almost certain that they will win. They hardly ever admit their problem and sometimes don't even understand it. They get angry and quit, or they pout, whine, find excuses, and give up. They tend to see things in a competitive framework but fear failure because they want so desperately to win. In a highly competitive classroom, their losses are that much more evident.

The more frequently these children see themselves as losers, the less they try. Even the children who have begun to reverse Underachievement Syndrome will be threatened by excessive competition.

Teacher Competitive Cassandra is encouraged to maintain a high level of competition in her classroom because of the positive feedback that she receives from achieving children. These children thrive and perform at their best with competitive challenge. Underachievers are typically not fully aware of the effect of competition on their performance. They will only comment on disliking the class and the students who surpass them.

Of course, there should be some competition in the classroom. Individual and group contests and games that vary from subject to subject help all children to deal with winning and losing. Some practices, however, should absolutely be avoided: the open announcement of individual grades, public criticism of individual children's poor work, announcements of surprise when a child performs well who usually doesn't, and the invidious comparison of class papers. Here's an example of how a teacher's emphasis on competition can go too far:

> Despite an IQ in the superior range, five-year-old Emily was an underachiever whose behavior was encouraged very early by her kindergarten classroom environment. Emily had been a spontaneous and enthusiastic child in her nursery school class, where her teacher had described her as very bright and happily adjusted. But in kindergarten, Emily did not like to go to school. Her kindergarten teacher described her school performance as poor. Emily rarely completed her work, did not seem happy, and tended not to participate in class activities. Classroom observation revealed the competitive environment that gave Emily her sense of failure and caused her to hold back in class.
>
> In this class, the children sat on the floor around the chalkboard for their letter-printing lesson. The teacher announced the letter to be printed, and some children enthusiastically raised their hands. After the selected child printed the letter on the chalkboard, the teacher asked the children if it was printed well. In chorus, they exclaimed an enthusiastic "Yes" if it was, and a punishing "No" if it was poorly executed. The teacher would agree or disagree with the children, pointing out the good qualities or the problems related to the printing of the letter.
>
> When Emily, with her hand barely raised, was selected to perform, the inadequate execution of her letter brought the "no's" that she had come to expect. Furthermore, the in-seat handwriting exercise that followed was carefully monitored by the teacher, who commented on each child's performance.
>
> It was not surprising to observe Emily's very slow performance and her unsuccessful efforts at the perfection that she could not achieve. In this highly competitive kindergarten class, Emily was already being

taught that she could not succeed in a classroom environment. Fortunately, in first grade, Emily was placed with a supportive teacher who fostered a less competitive environment where Emily again developed confidence and enthusiasm. Her Underachievement Syndrome was reversed by a good school year.[1]

Underachievers' responses to large junior high or middle schools clearly illustrate these students' adverse reactions to competition. Frequently, children who were performing well in elementary school begin their underachievement in the larger school setting. When they compare their own performance to that of so many other students, they evaluate themselves as incompetent. They stop making efforts. There may be too few success roles and too many failure roles in a large school environment—for example, only a small percentage of children can make the basketball team or the drama club play. Because our society is highly competitive, it is important for underachievers to learn to function in competition. In the highly competitive classroom or school, the underachiever simply does not have a fair chance.

Labeling

When a child is achieving poorly in school, teachers and parents frequently request help. The child obviously has a need for something different. That *something different* may come in the form of special classes or special assistance from a trained professional. Of course, the extra help costs money. Federal and state governments can sometimes provide such resources, but in order to maintain accountability, funding is attached to certain prescribed conditions. The child must be assessed and labeled in order to receive the necessary funding. These labels vary considerably and are usually abbreviated with initials. For example, there is learning disabled (LD), emotionally disturbed (ED), behaviorally disabled (BD), Attention Deficit Hyperactivity Disorder (ADHD), Asperger's Disorder (AD), or Oppositional Defiant Disorder (ODD).

In this labeling process, there are some real risks. Even with school inclusion guidelines, the labels affect self-expectations, as well as teacher expectations, and in some cases, they cause peer rejection, which may lead to further problems.

Brad had been labeled BD and LD and was placed in a special class for most of his years in elementary school. He hated the label and wanted desperately to be just like other students. He lost his temper frequently in school, did not carry through on assignments, and interacted poorly with peers. Each year was a little worse than the previous one, although teachers and parents made continued efforts to meet his special needs.

Finally, in an effort to reduce the stigma and help Brad adjust, he was included in his regular class for 85% of the day. Brad's assignments were shortened to help him cope with the material, and he was encouraged to complete his homework in order to stay in the regular classes. Although his improvement was not entirely consistent and smooth, within one year, he was relating better with peers, feeling more confident, and completing much more schoolwork. His reading and math skills improved measurably. Brad continued to get some help for his learning disability, but he was able to function far better in the regular classroom when the labels were dropped and he was removed from special classes.

Labeling also affects teachers' expectations in ways that can in turn affect achievement. Rosenthal and Jacobsen's book *Pygmalion in the Classroom*, as well as further research inspired by that book, found strong support for the effect of teacher expectations on actual teacher behavior directed toward a child.[2] An LD label, which influences teacher expectations, may have a dramatic effect on a child's achievement and self-concept. Estimates vary on the degree of the teacher expectancy effect, but a 15% decrease in grades has been considered an average impact. Obviously, if 15% is average, then in some cases, teacher expectations may have a much greater impact than that. Negative labeling of any kind—minority stereotypes, educational categories, or grade expectations—may cause problems.

Carla, a Hispanic student, entered college with reasonable expectations of success. Although she had been a poor student in elementary school, hard work in senior high school showed her that she could do well. Her high school grades were very good, and she felt excited about the challenge of college.

Based on an English entrance examination, Carla's college placed her in a small remedial English class. Most students in the class were on probation, and the English teacher assumed that Carla, too, was a poor student. When Carla came for help, it was because she worried that perhaps she did not have the ability she had only recently come to believe she had. The expectations communicated to her in the English class threatened her precariously-held, positive assumptions about her own abilities. Fortunately, another teacher had confidence in Carla's ability and convinced her that she was indeed a very capable student and that it would take only a small compensatory effort to learn some skills that she had missed earlier in her education.

It was her cultural minority status together with some very real educational gaps that caused Carla to be seen as a negative stereotype. After her confidence was restored, Carla easily learned the necessary English skills and graduated from college as a very successful student.[3]

The second case of teacher expectations is related to the LD (learning disabled) label:

Jeff's teachers sat around the conference table puzzling about this eighth-grade boy. He had been labeled learning disabled, yet no one was quite sure about him. His IQ score was 121, but there was considerable scatter among his separate scores—some were very high, others were below average. Excerpts from a teacher discussion sounded like this:

"Do you suppose I should grade him on a pass/fail criterion because he's learning disabled?"

"I'd like to drop him out of band because of his learning disability."

"He's disruptive and prevents other students from learning."

"He's doing a fine job in math. I don't see any real problem. How can he do so well if he's LD?"

"I know he's LD, but today he got a perfect score on a reading comprehension test. I thought he might have cheated, so I asked him to take the test again."

"My concern in social studies is that he doesn't get his homework in. He tells me unusual stories of why he hasn't done it, and I don't know whether to believe him or not. He seems sincere and his excuses are imaginative, but he can't perform."

"His grades are poor. His homework is sporadic. We don't know if he's bright or slow, and we're not even sure when he's telling the truth. What do we do with Jeff? He's been labeled LD, a behavior problem, a manipulative child, a careless student, and a storyteller. He doesn't fit into this school program, so he must be LD."[4]

Here is a situation that probably happens more frequently than the above—a teacher determined to convince a set of parents that their child is not gifted:

Amber's IQ score was 138. Her mother did not know the score at the time of this incident, nor did her teacher. Amber was a fourth-grade student who had been a very successful, mostly A student through third grade. She was, however, very quiet in class and rarely volunteered during discussion. Her mother thought that Amber might benefit from more advanced reading material, and so early that year, she met with the teacher to make her suggestion. The teacher seemed somewhat defensive and said that she believed Amber was sufficiently challenged and that her mother was putting pressure on her.

The remainder of the year was somewhat of a disaster for Amber. Not only did her grades go to B's and C's to prove her teacher's point, but the teacher confronted Amber with her own conclusion—that she wasn't really as smart as her mother thought. Amber worked very hard that year, but she really never found a solution to improving her grades. By the end of the year, both Amber and her mother felt frustrated and somewhat frightened.

Amber's mother brought her to our clinic and, in an apologetic and tense frame of mind, asked if Amber could be tested to determine what schoolwork should be expected of her. The IQ scores were consistently high. Amber's individual achievement tests supported the findings that her skill levels were far beyond grade level. She was quiet and lacking in self-confidence by the time she came to the clinic, and her achievement would have undoubtedly continued to decline in later years had her mother not challenged the teacher's limiting label.

Stories like this are all too common and occur particularly frequently among the many teachers who are hostile toward gifted educational programs.

Any label that unrealistically narrows prospects for performance by a child may be damaging. The resulting peer pressures and lowered parent and teacher expectations may have permanent debilitating effects on children's school performance. Although there are some circumstances in which such designations are absolutely necessary to obtain educational support, I urge you to consider all of the potential negative consequences before assigning any kind of label to a child.

Negative Attention

As previously noted, children who underachieve are often dependent on attention. Their early childhood home pattern has been one of excessive attention and of either dependent or dominant manipulations. They are accustomed to relating to people in attention-getting ways. They thrive in one-to-one learning situations but adjust poorly in classroom environments where they feel attention deprived. They may show the symptoms of attention deficit disorders even when they have no biochemical problems. They search out ways to gain attention. If the right kind of attention comes easily, they will achieve, but many of these children find it easier to gain negative attention.

Teachers Solicitous Sally and Negative Nellie give negative attention freely and thus unintentionally maintain underachieving behavior. Solicitous Sally is the trickier of the two to identify because she is typically a very good and devoted teacher. She is, however, so sensitive to children's expressions of feelings that she overreacts to their hurts and calls for help. She does this in a caring way without ever realizing that she is reinforcing an underachieving pattern by helping them too much or by providing too much sympathy.

> Keisha, a third grader of average ability, was in the lowest reading group in her class. There was no identifiable learning disability or any distinguishable reason why she should be reading one and one-half years below grade level. She was a quiet, shy child and had learned to depend on her mother's help for daily schoolwork. After I explained to her mother how to encourage her independence at home, I observed the girl in school. In the classroom, she was also quiet and never raised her hand to volunteer questions or answers. I asked her teacher if Keisha requested more help than most children, to which she responded no. She further explained that after giving the class directions on an assignment, she would always go to Keisha's desk because she was sure that Keisha required special help. Keisha had learned to make the same assumption and waited for

her teacher to arrive before she began working on her own. By providing daily attention to Keisha's helplessness, both mother and teacher inadvertently undercut the girl's confidence. Both were solicitous and kind, but neither realized the self-fulfilling prophecy that they were communicating. **Changed expectations, the encouragement of independence, and some accelerated tutoring quickly brought Keisha's work to above-grade level, where it has remained.** She has become a much more confident and independent child.

The second trap that Solicitous Sally may fall into is misinterpreting children's symptoms of pressure:

First grader Jessica showed tears in her eyes if she didn't seem to understand directions immediately. Also, she wouldn't finish her work and broke out crying if the teacher made corrections on her paper. Solicitous Sally did not want to put stress on Jessica, so she tried most delicately to avoid giving her too much work or correcting her errors. However, regardless of what Sally tried, Jessica seemed stressed. She fell further behind her classmates.

At the first teacher conference, Sally explained to Jessica's parents that either Jessica just wasn't mature enough to handle first-grade work or it was too difficult for her. Test scores for Jessica indicated that she had high average ability, so her apparent stress could not be explained. In further discussion with her parents, I discovered that Jessica was a long-awaited child and the only child for the first five years of her life. Jessica was adored and adorned. Her wishes were always catered to, and her cries for help immediately brought a responsive parent. If tasks were difficult for her at home, her parents completed them for her. They dashed to her aid when they noted the least indication of stress. Jessica expected this same kind of response at school. After an explanation of the cause of her problems, her parents were quick to change their approach, and they saw an almost immediate change in their daughter.

Solicitous Sally, however, was more difficult to convince because she was truly afraid of hurting the feelings of so sensitive a child. It took about three months of teacher perseverance, with several supportive phone calls from the psychologist, before the teacher acknowledged with relief that she could indeed see a difference in Jessica. She previously had been absolutely convinced that the child was being put under too much pressure at home, when exactly the opposite was the case. Actually, Jessica was so unaccustomed to effort that almost any work would have caused her stress. Rimm's Law #7—Deprivation and excess frequently exhibit the same symptoms—applies here: **Jessica's symptoms of tension were indications of insufficient experience with pressure rather than too much pressure**.

Another example of inappropriate sympathy is the case of second grader Alonzo:

> In Alonzo's family, there had been a recent divorce and other problems. Initially, Solicitous Sally's concern about the child's stress was appropriate. She explained to Alonzo that if he needed to talk about some problems, she would be glad to help him. Each morning started with a quiet distress story and tears and individual attention before school started. It took several class hours before Alonzo could put aside his problems and get on with his schoolwork.

> Solicitous Sally felt sorry for Alonzo for a long time before the psychologist's intervention. Sally changed her daily routine. **By giving Alonzo a sticker for each happy morning start, she brought him back to being a bubbly, happy child.**

Of course, divorce is always a traumatic event for children, and they should have the opportunity to talk about their feelings. However, it is important that sympathetic attention not become a reward for sad feelings. Overreactions by teachers cause children to sense that they are expected to feel, think, and act sad, and so they actually do. As the behavior continues, they get further and further behind in their studies, and they feel less and less adequate academically. They worry more, and the school anxiety becomes confounded with their family concerns. Symptoms of stress become the basis for their attention from adults. They are frequently sad and cry easily. Their manipulations are not intentional but spontaneous.

A kind teacher should give a message of brief sympathy but should also communicate confidence that the child is able to handle difficult problems. This permits children to develop the strength that builds confidence and will eventually help them surmount obstacles and deal with other life problems.

In summary, Solicitous Sallys are typically wonderful and kind people. **Their sensitivity and empathy are positive if not carried to an extreme.** It is always difficult to determine the fine line between caring and caring too much, but **the message that one must go on with life despite problems is critical for achievement and for living fulfilling lives.**

Most of Negative Nellie's problems are more obvious, and you may have heard or read about them in parenting or psychology classes. However, they continue to require emphasis because negativism remains a problem in many classrooms and is related to underachievement, behavior problems, and poor social relationships. Negativism is difficult for teachers to avoid, and teachers may not be aware of the frequency with which negative attention causes general classroom problems.

The most obvious form of negative attention is continued and repeated reminders by the teacher to quiet down or pay attention. Generally, the frequency and volume of the reminders increase in direct relationship to the increasing noisiness of the children. It is tempting to believe that the reminders actually reinforce the poor behavior.

Although I have observed many classrooms, this kind of chaos usually exists in classrooms where there are new or substitute teachers who have not yet learned to control the general class atmosphere. Therefore, I don't think that this kind of negative attention is a major concern. Other kinds are less obvious but more serious.

When a child misbehaves, teachers typically reprimand the child aloud in front of the class. It is simply more difficult to communicate reprimands or punishment contingencies quietly. Yet both research and practical experience indicate that public reprimands increase the negative behaviors. Although both public and private reprimands are forms of attention, the peer attention that students get from public reprimands motivates them to increase their misbehavior.

In elementary school, an additional problem plagues the child who is frequently reprimanded by the teacher. He becomes the "bad boy" of the class, and the other children don't want to be friends with him. This, of course, gives him another reason to misbehave as a means of drawing attention. When the child and the teacher are alerted to the problem of how the behavior is affecting friendships and **the teacher arranges a quiet signal with the child, behavior and peer relations improve.** In a real sense, the negative attention has been converted to positive attention, and teacher and student are now allied on the same team. Perhaps it is not surprising that the child's behavior improves.

You can probably grasp the problem of the "bad boy" in the classroom if you think back to your own elementary school days. In my school, it was Blair. He was in my class for five years. He chewed his pencils, wouldn't stay in his seat, and didn't get his work done. His desk was always placed near the teacher's or in the front of the room, and he had a regular route between the classroom and the principal's office. Nobody liked Blair. We wouldn't have dared to be friends with him. Blair was poison!

The child who does not complete his work during the school day is usually encouraged not to do so by negative attention. Some specific case examples illustrate a few cautions:

Ricardo hardly ever completed his math before recess. The class penalty for incomplete work was to remain in the classroom during recess. This was effective for the other children, and rarely did anyone other than Ricardo have to stay. But for two reasons, this punishment was ineffective for Ricardo.

First, Ricardo enjoyed the personal help and attention he received while the other children were outside. Second, Ricardo was often teased by the other children during recess anyway. Thus, staying in the classroom during recess was a strong reinforcing shelter for Ricardo. He continued to not complete his math until the penalties were changed.

Jackson, an intellectually gifted fourth grader, never finished his work in school. He told me, "If I finish my work too fast, my teacher will criticize me and tell me I've done a bad job. If I work slowly, she only comes around and reminds me to get to work." In Jackson's case, both responses were negative attentions, but he selected the behavior that was easiest and caused him the least stress.

Boredom

The word regarding school that we hear most frequently from underachievers is *boring*. **The word *boring* needs to be interpreted differently, depending on its use by a particular child.** For some children, it means that the work is too hard; for others, it means that it is too easy. It may also mean "I'm afraid to compete" or "the teacher should do it my way" or "I have a power struggle with the teacher" or "I don't like this subject" or "I'd rather be socializing or playing baseball or

Parent Pointer

watching TV." For a few children, it means that the work is actually uninteresting.

Of course, there are some Boring Barbara and Boring Bob teachers. There are, I hope, only a small percentage of teachers who do not take the initiative to make their classroom activities varied and stimulating. Those teachers have an adverse effect on all students, both achievers and under-achievers. However, when students use the word *boring* as an excuse for underachievement, monotonous teachers are obviously not the problem. These students' descriptions of classes as boring would continue regardless of the subject matter, content, or method of teaching.

The most frequent kind of boredom, referring to material that's too easy or too difficult, causes a genuine problem for underachievers and may even be the origin of their underachievement. **Material that is too difficult is an obvious reason for underachievement.** If children are expected to learn content for which they are not prepared, they may feel justifiably defeated and give up. This occurs most frequently for children who have uneven abilities and thus find some subjects relatively easy while others are truly difficult. The teacher usually assumes that these children are able to handle all tasks well because they give the impression of being very capable. Unfortunately, **children who feel defeated in one skill area easily extend that avoidance style to other subjects in which they are quite capable.**

Children whose families move, and thus must change schools frequently, can easily find themselves continuously behind their peers because of school differences. Each new school may be only a little ahead of what the children have learned in basic skills compared to their former schools, but the feelings of incompetence that come with their always finding schoolwork too difficult may create a sense of defeat that initiates Underachievement Syndrome.

Schoolwork that is too easy can cause another dilemma. It is a frequent cause of Underachievement Syndrome for intellectually gifted children. Gifted children who enter first grade often know most of the material to be covered in that grade, and they are legitimately and consistently bored during their entire first years of school. Some of these children (more boys than girls) develop behavior problems. Others (more girls than boys) may appreciate the positive attention that comes from perfect work and may thoroughly enjoy their early and easy school years. Unfortunately, they learn that schoolwork is effortless. In fifth grade or ninth grade or college, when the curriculum becomes challenging for the first time, they find that they have not learned to study or persevere. They have never experienced getting less than A grades either. They may label school as boring because of that new sense of effort that they must now make or the feelings of failure that come with B's and C's. The source of their problem dates back to the lack of challenge earlier in their school life.

Some interesting cases of intellectually gifted children serve as examples:

Greg, a bright five-year-old, entered kindergarten reading at approximately a third-grade level. His mother was hesitant to mention his reading ability to the teacher because she did not wish to be viewed as an interfering parent.

At first-quarter conference time, the main topic was Greg's misbehavior. His parents were so disturbed by these reports that they again postponed discussing his reading skill. Greg continued to have behavior problems during the entire year, and by spring, the teacher was ready to recommend retention. In addition to his problem behavior, Greg had failed his reading readiness test! It was at this last conference that Greg's shocked parents finally announced to his teacher that their son had been reading all year.

Greg later explained that when taking tests, he felt that it was necessary to circle two responses in test items in which a letter or shape looked exactly like the inverted form of the original letter. Of course, this misinterpretation had caused the failing test grade. A new evaluation of his reading skill found him to have progressed to a fifth-grade reading level. Perhaps it is not surprising that bored Greg became a behavior problem.

Certainly the teacher can be faulted for not identifying Greg's skill early, but parents, too, have a responsibility for communication. In Greg's case, his reading ability was so good that no reasonable teacher would have interpreted such information as parent interference.

Uneven or inconsistent acceleration may cause a similar problem for gifted children. For example, Chantrelle was accelerated one year in math by working independently. As a matter of fact, she was so bright that she completed sixth-grade math in six weeks. However, when she moved to another school district, there was no provision for acceleration, and so she repeated sixth-grade math. In another case, Eric, a first grader, was allowed to read with a second-grade class because that was his appropriate level. When he moved to another district the following year, that school would not permit him to work at two different grade levels, and so he had to read the second-grade material again. These two children, who had already demonstrated that they learned more swiftly than others, were forced to repeat material. Naturally, they were bored.

In some cases, the forced repetition takes place within the same district and even within the same school. It may occur if one teacher views acceleration as appropriate and a second teacher refuses to make exceptions. It may also happen when a school changes from a policy of reading groups to whole-class reading instruction. The children whom these policies hold back, and their parents, are likely to be outraged, which puts both in an oppositional relationship with the school.

This opposition can easily be generalized to other subjects and grades; *boring* is typically the label that these children decide to use to describe almost everything in school. They are certainly at least partially justified. Research has found that intellectually gifted children have typically learned between 35% and 50% of basic skills materials before entering elementary grades,[5] and similar observations continue to be made. Here's a case example:

> Terrell, a very bright fifth grader who was having a major problem with math, described his underachievement trap to me in this way. He said that he would listen as the teacher began his explanation of the material, but as the teacher continued to explain, he felt bored because he already understood and didn't really need to listen anymore. His mind wandered, and he would think about other things. Finally, the teacher would give the assignment, and Terrell would begin his work. Later, he would get to a part he didn't quite understand. Because he hadn't listened, he didn't know whether the teacher had explained this material or not, and he was afraid to ask for help.
>
> Terrell's options weren't good: He could bluff his work, not do it at all, do it with many mistakes, or admit that he wasn't listening. He alternated among the first three options, but he wouldn't dare admit that he required help. Although he recognized his own trap, he got further and further behind in math. The skills gaps were preventing his understanding of the material, and because he needed to "save face," he wouldn't explain the problem to his teacher or his parents. Mainly, he avoided the

confrontation by not completing his assignments, and he continued to maintain that math was easy and boring.

Children must learn early that there is a relationship between effort and outcome. This recognition creates the sense of internal control that differentiates achievers from underachievers. If schoolwork is too hard, their efforts do not lead to successful outcomes, but only to failures. If work is too easy, they learn that it takes very little effort to succeed. Either notion is inappropriate and can foster underachievement. **Teachers should be alert to the skill levels of their students in order to provide the required help or the necessary challenge.** There is no guarantee that we can prevent children from describing school as boring, but at least teachers can ensure an appropriate match between effort and outcome.

Peer Pressure

By the middle grades, peer pressure to be popular often becomes a priority.[6] In a recent survey of more than 5,000 students in grades three through eight, popularity ranked highest among their worries, tied only with fears of terrorism.[7] By as early as *third grade,* 15% of the students indicated that they worried a lot about being popular with the opposite sex, and the percentage of students with worries increases with each grade.

Being smart enough was much lower among the stated worries, although feeling above average in intelligence mediated anxieties about being popular, pretty enough, confident, having nice clothes, and being thin enough. Rating oneself as far above average in intelligence was a less effective mediator for these worries than feeling only above average.

In focus groups, middle-grade students frequently state that they feel conflicted about working hard in school for fear that it puts them into an unpopular "nerd" category. Parents and teachers are often shocked to hear of students who deliberately don't turn in homework or refuse to study for tests because they prefer average grades. A discerning adult can often prevent this from becoming a pattern, but once initiated, underachieving to appear "cool" can take on a life of its own. When underachievement becomes a habit, it destroys self-efficacy. If students mature and decide that it can be cool to earn good grades, win scholastic awards, and be accepted into excellent colleges, they can likely accomplish more than they probably ever earlier believed possible.

IV

Part 2

What You Can Do about It

Chapter 6
Parenting toward Achievement

Parenting toward achievement and good parenting are two ways of describing the same process. Most parents would agree that what they want most for their children is good health, happiness, and a sense of self-worth. Although many children will indicate that they are happy underachieving and have no wish to change their attitudes or behaviors, after having reversed their patterns, achieving better grades, and displaying more positive behaviors, they find that they prefer their lives of accomplishment and hard work, and they indicate their preference for the new patterns of behavior.

School achievement, life accomplishment, and the resulting self-confidence and self-sufficiency are outcomes that all parents wish for their children. Parents are aware that more doors of opportunity will be open to children who achieve in school. Of course, there are also other things that parents value. Many are anxious for their children to be socially accepted; some want them to be active in sports, the arts, drama, or a specific talent area; some parents wish to emphasize creativity or kindness—the list could go on indefinitely. However, because the focus of my book is on preventing and reversing Underachievement Syndrome, this chapter will provide some general parenting guidelines that emphasize achievement goals.

Modeling Achievement

Rimm's Law #2 is: Children learn appropriate behaviors more easily if they have effective models to imitate. This is a critical element of parenting toward achievement. Not only should parents themselves be achievers, but **they must share with their children realistic and positive views of achievement.** Children should observe in their parents the relationship between effort and outcome. They should understand that parents sometimes fail and feel disappointment. However, they must also see their parents survive failure to succeed again. They should experience parent discouragement and elation, and they need to be able to see the intrinsic and extrinsic rewards that come with their parents' efforts. They must also see both creativity and reasonable conformity in their parents. There should be some balance of the positive and negative in their views of their parents as role models. If the parents are achievers, this balance probably exists, but sometimes parents unintentionally give their children a biased and negative perspective on their work.

Parents should also design an "achiever image" of their partners. In doing this, there are some common pitfalls of which both husbands and wives should be aware. Don't continuously complain about your partner's absence due to work, even though you may be concerned that the children are being deprived of his or her parenting. Don't describe each other's careers as bad or blame your partner's loss of temper on stress from the job. Be sure not to attribute family problems to your partner's boss or blame his or her work for marital or economic problems. **Instead, explain to your children the life satisfactions and financial benefits of your partner's hard work.** You can be honest about the parts of your partner's career that you don't like, but it's important to emphasize the positive components and explain why Mom or Dad has chosen a challenging career.

In some circumstances, it may seem either extremely difficult or even trivial to build up a partner's career. However, there are strong parallels between your own and your partner's achievement at work and your children's achievement orientation in school. Parents who engage in continual tirades about their own or their partner's awful careers should be prepared to hear similar attitudes about school from their children. When their children reach adolescence, parents are likely to find the comments quite intolerable. They sound like this:

- "I don't see why I have to do all this schoolwork. I need time for fun."

- "I'm not anything like my dad, and I'd never choose a career like his."

- "I don't know what I want to do or be—something where I don't have to work all the time."

- "The poor grades aren't my fault. That teacher is a terrible grader, and she expects too much."

- "I don't want a career like my mother's; she has no time for the family."

For every negative message that parents give about their own or their partner's career, they will hear a similar one from their children about school because school is the child's "workplace." Sometimes it is indeed impossible to avoid negativism and pessimism; however, if parents can learn to provide a more positive and balanced view of their work, they can certainly expect more positive attitudes about school achievement from their children.

If Mother does not work outside of the home, Father needs to be sensitive to how he describes his wife's work. A common problem husbands have is that they tend to devalue their wives' non-career contributions. Comments such as "Didn't you do anything today?" or "All you ever do is run around and shop (as the family sits down to a delicious home-cooked dinner in their Mother-cleaned home in their Mother-laundered clothes)" label the unsalaried homemakers' contributions as insignificant.

Volunteer activities, which take effort, leadership, creativity, and responsibility and are important to the community or to the children, are often described by Father as aimless social activities. If Mother decides to return to school for further education, Father may describe that education as busywork or point out that Mother's schooling is interfering with the family's meals and activities. This tells the kids that Mother's education is nonessential and nonvalued. If Mother begins a career later in life because she has waited for the children to grow up, she may have a salary disadvantage related to her late start, her lesser training and experience, her geographic limitations, or the generally lower salaries paid to women. Some men minimize the financial contribution women make, as well as the lesser status of their jobs. Sometimes men even feel threatened by their wives' new successes.

The danger of this kind of commentary from Father is that it devalues Mother in the children's eyes and disempowers her. Frequently, it is she who has the primary responsibility for disciplining the children, communicating with schools, and providing educational guidance to the children. Because she has been disempowered by her partner, she is also rendered powerless to guide and discipline the children. Although Father has never directly told his children not to obey their mother, and he actually may be quite explicit about obedience, he has, in fact, modeled disrespect without being aware of the seriousness of his communication. Not only has he devalued his wife, he has also underrated all that she represents: empathetic and loving care for children, concern with education and learning, and the tremendous initiative it takes to combine education or work with homemaking. His children will view their mother, at least partially, through his description and his valuing (or devaluing) of her accomplishments. Boys will ignore and put down their mother and will underachieve. Girls will compete and argue with her and will also underachieve. **Any father who expects his children to respect their mother needs to explicitly describe his respect for his wife's efforts, contributions, satisfactions, and commitments to the community and to education.**

Parent Pointer

Although there are fewer stay-at-home husbands in our society, there are more now than ever before. A man who does not work outside of the home tends to be at risk for being put down by neighbors and other adults. **It is even more critical that his working wife makes clear her perceptions of his accomplishments.** Because of the gender-stereotypical roles of fathers and mothers, mothers, who may feel some guilt at devoting less time to parenting, may find themselves criticizing their partners' parenting within the hearing of their children. This disables and disempowers the father, who is devoted to parenting, in the same way that the mother can be devalued in the traditional household.

Parent Pointer

Modeling achievement and describing it in your partner make a critical difference in your children's motivation to achieve. If this sounds idealistic or impossible, listen to what your children are saying about school. You will hear that they are watching and listening to you and have received your messages about your work and your partner's work. If you expect them to change their efforts and attitudes, you will want to change your modeling. A fringe benefit of positive modeling will be your own more positive appreciation of your work.

Power and Control

Parents are in charge of their children. Children feel secure following their parents' leadership, provided that they have become accustomed to that mode. Although they are likely to sporadically push limits to determine the extent of their freedom, they will respect the word *no* when it is given firmly and fairly.

Children who have not learned to accept limitations in childhood will certainly not accept them in adolescence. Visualize the letter *V* as a model for guiding children. When children are small, they begin at the bottom of the *V* with limited freedom and narrow structure. As they mature and are able to handle more freedom responsibly, the limiting walls of the V spread out, giving them continually more freedom while still maintaining definite limits. During adolescence, as they move to the top of the V, they become capable of considerable independent decision making and judgment but should continue to recognize that there are adults guiding them. They are thus ready for moving out of the V into young adulthood, independence, and personal decision making.

Now reverse that V so that it looks like this: Λ. Children brought up at the base of this figure are given much freedom and many choices. They become accustomed to independent decision making before they are able to handle that freedom responsibly. As they move toward adolescence, parents become concerned that their children may misuse this freedom, and they worry about the dangers that arise in school and the community. Tobacco, alcohol, drugs, and promiscuous sex are perceived as threats from which their children must be protected, so the parents begin to set limits. Freedom is now taken away.

Adolescents who had much control as children now feel over-controlled by their parents, and their statements echo their feelings of restriction. "My parents are controlling me," they complain. They push limits and reflexively oppose and rebel. Worried parents then over-punish and narrow the limits further, resulting in even more rebellion. An angry adolescent, with accompanying underachievement, can quickly turn a happy home into a hostile home. Relative to the freedom and power that these children once had, they feel powerless. Once freedom is given, it is not easily taken away. **The V-shaped path of guidance is much smoother and more comfortable for adolescents and parents alike.**

Expecting adult decision making from children provides power without wisdom. It leads to a struggle for the power that parents gave too early and try to recover too late. The resulting conflict may force adolescents to rebel too stubbornly, parents to respond too negatively, and both to lose the positive home atmosphere that can be so valuable in guiding children.

Giving Clear, Positive Messages

Parenting by positive expectations can be extraordinarily successful in guiding children, both in school and out. If high achievement, positive attitudes, and constructive behavior are expected and reinforced by parents, they will become internalized by children, and the need for punishment will usually be negligible. How do some parents guide their children so well without punishment, while others seem to use it so frequently?

Reasonable Praise

Studies of the lives of eminent and successful people show that there was always at least one parent or significant adult who believed in them as children.[1] Parents and educators have learned to recognize the importance of children's self-esteem in their accomplishments. In order for children to build self-esteem, they require some positive feedback in the form of praise from the adults who surround them. In effect, praise conveys adult values to children.

Although some praise is very good for children, too much praise can cause children to become dependent on it. Because praise conveys values to children, overpraise may actually convey values that can be internalized as pressures. Praise words such as "perfect," "brilliant," "genius," "gorgeous," "smartest," and "extraordinary," if used continuously with children, are likely to be internalized as impossible expectations by the time these children reach adolescence. However, words such as "good thinking," "hardworking," "smart," "talented," "persevering," and "attractive" convey values that will motivate without pressuring. Of course, occasional overpraise is not harmful, but many children have shared with me stories of the pressure of parent expectations that they feel when their parents have really only wanted to encourage them.

Children who rarely receive praise will also be in trouble. They believe that the world expects little of them. Of course, the children who hear only put-downs—such as "lazy," "dumb," "stupid," and "klutzy"— are likely to have the most serious problems. They feel unworthy and inadequate on a daily basis.

The most valued resource that parents have to offer is their own attention. Children normally prefer positive attention, but frequently, they develop bad habits in order to elicit any kind of attention. In other words, they learn ways that are effective for getting attention, whether or not these habits are good for their own growth and development. If attention to problem behaviors monopolizes the time during which children interact with parents, there is little time left for attention to the positive. These children soon lose confidence in their ability to attain that positive notice and never really form the habit of working toward positive parent expectations. More than one discouraged parent has reported that they can rarely find behavior in their children that is worthy of praise. In these cases, a negative or punishing cycle predominates, and it becomes extremely difficult to motivate these children toward constructive behavior—namely achievement.

Consistency between Parents

Clear and consistent messages, agreed upon by both parents (or three or four parents) and transmitted to the child, are essential. Parents should agree, for example, on such underlying values as: (1) the priority of study, learning, school, work, and responsibility, (2) respect for individuality, (3) respect for adults, and (4) recognition of the balance of reasonable amounts of recreation and fun, all of which seem to underlie a positive and achievement-oriented atmosphere. Rimm's Law #1—Children are more likely to be achievers if their parents join together to give the same clear and positive message about school effort and expectations—summarizes the importance of a united front.

This sounds much easier to do than it actually is. Problems of consistency and clarity originate in many places. Any parent may be inconsistent from time to time—that is, parents may change their expectations depending on which neighbor they talked to last, or their own changing mood, or personal pressures acting on them. Parents may not always give clear messages because they may be busy and therefore do not take the time to be clear, because they haven't thought through the message, or because they are not sure themselves how they feel about it.

Here's an example. Mother tells her son how pleased she is to see him working so hard on his science project. She then walks out into the fresh spring air and sees her son's friends playing baseball. Feeling guilty about her son missing the fun, she goes back into the house and suggests that maybe it's time for him to take a break and not push himself so hard. The message given to her son has been changed from the value of hard work to the value of play. This could become even more complicated if both parents send different messages to the boy: Mom praises her son's hard work, but Dad suggests that he not miss the game with his friends and that maybe he's taking his science too seriously.

These complications can be compounded after a divorce or remarriage, and when there are three or four parents, the problem can escalate exponentially. Of course, the more dissimilar the messages are, the more confusing the directions for the children.

Torn Tomas, seen in Chapter 1, is a victim of opposite messages given after a divorce. However, even within an intact marriage, parent expectations may contradict each other, and there are almost always contradictions in situations where there are three or four parents. If parents are truly concerned about their children, they must try to communicate similar messages, or the children will find it impossible to please their parents and to internalize clear directions for positive behaviors. A 17-year-old described his "Torn Tomas" feelings in this way:

> Luis' parents had been married for 20 years, and although they often disagreed and argued, Luis now sensed the severity of their problems. He felt that his father was trying very hard to please his mother. Although his mother that said she was trying to improve their marriage, Luis felt himself being subtly manipulated to side with her against his dad. He recalled a recent incident in which he had asked his parents if he could drive the car to school. His father had said no. His mother came to his defense and persuaded Dad to change his mind. Dad conceded and left for work. Mom then criticized the boy for not being more assertive toward his father. Luis left the house in disgust, squealing the tires as he turned out of the driveway. Yes, he wanted the car. No, he didn't expect his mom to talk for him. No, he didn't plan to start talking back to his father, even if his mom and dad were having problems. His head ached with desperation. How could he please them both? How could he avoid being manipulated by one against the other? How could he prevent the marriage from deteriorating further? He went through his entire school day in turmoil without hearing what teachers or friends were saying. School seemed irrelevant compared to his seemingly insurmountable problem—learning to deal with two people he loved, each of whom was calling him to battle against the other.

Adolescent children can describe their feelings and learn to talk about strategies for handling contradictory messages. Younger children feel torn apart by the sense of not being able to move forward in the fear that one of their parents will certainly be displeased. They simply say that they don't care anymore. They're angry and confused.

One parent may feel that it's "honest and open" to confide in the children about the other parent. Often, parents who do this miss the intimacy of a spouse or other adult, and they feel closer to their children than anyone else at the time. This is what traps them into adultizing the children too soon. The children, on the other hand, feel empowered by the intimacy, so they readily accept it. When mothers tell their sons and daughters that their father is immoral and childish, or when fathers tell their children that their mother is too goody-goody and controlling, the children feel that they have new, more mature insights into adults. They feel at liberty to call their father a "jerk" or their mother a "witch." The parent has unintentionally taught the children to compete with the other parent.

When one parent hears those disrespectful words leveled at the other, he or she may say nothing. But even if these parents tell the children to be more respectful, they may believe the disrespectful words to be accurate. The mother says to herself, "He *is* a jerk," and the father says to himself, "She *is* a witch." The parents do not realize that they've virtually planted these words and instead assume that their children are mature enough to have formed an opinion that coincides with their own. The disrespect continues, and these children, with their adult power, will soon begin to feel comfortable calling their teachers jerks and witches. They will ultimately turn their anger toward the very parents who unintentionally gave them initial permission to be disrespectful.

When parents concur, even subtly, with their children's disrespect toward another adult, they give a clear message to be oppositional and defiant. When parents say nothing, neither disagreeing with nor reframing the children's statements, the children assume that the parent concurs. Rimm's Law #9—Children become oppositional if one adult allies with them against a parent or a teacher, making them more powerful than that adult—summarizes this concept.

How can you reframe your behavior to give a clear message of respect to your children? The mother who feels rejected and angry at her husband's wish for separation can tell her son and daughter that she feels terrible. She can explain that it is difficult for her to understand their father's behavior, but she doesn't want this problem to make them feel unloved by their father. The father who has felt controlled by his wife or former wife can point out to his children how effectively their mother guides them and how this proves her love and concern.

Of course, parents shouldn't tell their kids that they like their spouses' behavior when they actually hate it. That would be dishonest and hypocritical, and kids can see through the lies.

Consistency within a Parent

An example of inconsistency within a parent occurs with a "yes-no" message. The confusion typically takes place with parents who are determined to be rational with their children. They assert that it is wrong to scold children without explaining the reason for the reprimand, and they are certain that their children understand them.

These parents begin very early, attempting the impossible feat of explaining in detail to high-energy two-year-olds exactly why they shouldn't be putting a toy into an electrical outlet. Although the children may be bright and may even have excellent two-year-old vocabularies, their reasoning ability is far below the abstract level that Mother assumes. Their attention spans are brief and certainly do not match the time that Mom or Dad invests in explanations. The children can tell from the parents' tone of voice that they may have done something wrong, but they still feel loved. The parent may even punctuate the reasonable statements with a hug or two. Assured that they are loved, these children return to their play and the fun game of inserting their toy into the electrical outlet. Mom or Dad tries again.

As the children get older and increase the naughty behaviors that have brought them kind voices and hugs, parents become impatient. They lose their tempers, scold, shriek, and sometimes even shake or spank. However, because their intent is to be rational, they feel pangs of guilt after their temporary loss of control. So they apologize to the children for losing their temper or spanking them, and they explain why they, the parents, are misbehaving.

At this point, the children don't really know whether their parent approves or disapproves of their behavior. However, they do learn that what they have done has brought an inordinate amount of valued warmth and attention. Reasonably enough, they increase the kind of undesirable behavior that produces this attention. Punishments are punctuated by hugs and affection, and the children, persuaded by a strong, basic wish for love, may increase the troublesome behavior in a self-perpetuating, accelerating, negative ritual.

Parent Pointer **Every Attention Deficit Hyperactive child whose parents have visited our clinic for help has come from a home environment in which at least one parent gave frequent "yes-no" messages.** It may be that the high-energy child's difficult behavior prompted the parents' confused messages. However, it appears more likely that the conflicting messages diffused the focus of attention for the children so that they developed a habit of pushing limits to attract love and attention from a parent. They accidentally discovered that troublesome behaviors provide the warmth they seek. They learned unclear limits for what is unacceptable. Unpleasant consequences merged with pleasant ones and permitted them to impulsively attempt whatever attracts their parents' attention.

Sometimes the children adapt the parents' contradictory pattern as their own and find it effective. As they get older, they learn to quickly apologize for their own misdeeds and shorten the time between scolding and affection. These children learn that almost any behavior (for example, ignoring chores, rudeness, or poor schoolwork) is acceptable. They can become facile manipulators both at home and at school. The same manipulative ritual learned at home is transferred to the classroom. For example, after each test for which they fail to study, they have an excuse and an apology that the teacher initially believes. The dynamics of the situation confuse parents, teachers, and of course, the children themselves.

Children who are products of these mixed "yes-no" messages increase their misbehavior and manipulations until they cause themselves and others serious problems. They become experts at irresponsible behavior and at avoiding the negative consequences.

"Beat the System" Messages

Adult occupational and financial commitments may not appear, at first glance, to be related to Underachievement Syndrome. However, they play an important role in communicating messages of responsibility in school. School is "the system" for children, and if they view their parent model as trying to "beat the system" by trying to avoid work, they will emulate that parent by also trying to "beat the system" and avoid working in school.

A gifted high school student that I worked with was charming, bright, and creative in many ways, and also an expert at avoiding doing his assignments. During a counseling session, he bragged about just getting by, as if he had turned it into a game. During the same counseling session, his father explained how he was cleverly collecting unemployment benefits, despite possible opportunities directed toward resetting his career goals. Dad's justifications and rationalizations sounded familiar—they were the same excuses I had just heard from his son! If getting by is viewed as a parent's value, it is translated by children into getting by in school. It is clearly a counterproductive message to children instead of the communication of expectations that guides achievement.

Referential Speaking

I use the term *referential speaking* to describe conversation between adults about children within the hearing of those children. Parents frequently speak about their children as if the children are not listening and with little regard for the effects that the conversation may have. If your children hear you talking about them, you can be sure that they will be listening and paying attention. Parents converse in this way to each other, grandparents, other relatives, teachers, neighbors, and even to other siblings. Referential speaking is neither bad nor good, but it has the potential for having a dramatic impact, whether negative or positive, on children, and it may well be a significant cause of many children's problems. It is a means by which parents inadvertently impart values to their children. At worst, it may label them and limit their feelings of personal control over their behaviors.

Referential speaking is so spontaneous that most parents may not be aware of its impact on their children. I would caution you to be very discriminating about what you say to other adults when children are near. Parents tend to engage in referential speaking more frequently with very young children. **You should realize that even very young children tune in immediately to adult conversations that refer to them.**

Parent Pointer

If you refer positively to behaviors such as kindness, consideration, hard work, independence, or effort, you'll encourage your children to continue such behaviors. These descriptions are reinforcing. Discussing your children's accomplishments and achievements is also effective for fostering their achievement orientation. However, too-frequent comments on accomplishment, high grades, and awards may cause your children to feel too much pressure to achieve. For example, bragging to Grandma about an excellent report card will communicate that you value high grades, which is appropriate. But if the bragging involves descriptions of a continuous straight-A record, children may feel that they must meet that impossible standard consistently. Parents may wonder why their children feel too much pressure, when in fact their only direct messages to the children were to do their best. The answer, of course, is that the children were listening when their parents gave referential messages of their expectations to important others in their lives.

The most damaging referential messages are the negative communications, and these take place frequently in many homes. Here are a few excerpts from typical parent-to-neighbor messages:

- "Peter is so disorganized that even his teacher can't help him with his problems."

- "Devina is so shy that I can't get her to talk to any adults."

- "Stephen just doesn't seem to care about anything but sports."

- "Selena hasn't cleaned her room for weeks. She's just sloppy, and I can't seem to get her to take her home responsibilities seriously."

- "Nick insists on doing everything his way, and I've given up fighting him."

- "Carly binges so much; she can't seem to control her eating."

- "Jermain is just clumsy no matter how hard he tries."

- "Aaron is so mean to his baby sister."

These negative comments cause children to assume that they can't control their negative characteristics or behaviors.

A very common and most damaging referential message between parents is a parent's despairing "hello" as his or her partner arrives home from work or travel. The first parent's tirade on the terrible day often includes how impossible the children were, dramatizing the parent's despair and inability to discipline the children. This tirade will only serve to encourage the children's domination over a weak parent. It would be better for the parent to tell the partner about the children's accomplishments. They would then greet Mom or Dad determined to prove how good they can be.

Telephone calls between partners when one of them is traveling or working late have the same powerful effect. Parents should not communicate their feelings of helplessness (even when they do feel helpless) when children might be listening. It has a guaranteed adverse effect on children's behavior. Sometimes too much openness can be damaging.

One of the most difficult to control forms of referential speaking typically comes from adults other than parents. It is the reference to appearance and beauty—much valued attributes in our society. The beautiful child receives frequent admiration, with comments typically directed to the parents about the child within the child's earshot. This continuous message of beauty, particularly if it is acknowledged by the parent or is originated by parents and relatives, may easily lead the child to feel pressure relative to his or her appearance.

Physically beautiful children do not necessarily grow up to be physically beautiful adolescents or adults. Dealing with society's emphasis on good looks is frustrating for the majority of people who don't fit the guidelines of celebrity glamour. Beautiful children who steadily absorb referential descriptions of their appearance are encumbered with an impossible burden that in adolescence may lead to the threshold of eating disorders, perfectionism, and an obsession with fashion and shopping. For these children, school and an interest in accomplishments or career achievements fall far behind in the list of priorities.

Referential conversation among adults is spontaneous and normal. Parents enjoy talking about their children to other adults who show an interest. Unfortunately, it is too easy to engage in adult conversation as if the little folks playing nearby seem too busy to hear the discussion. Just recall these words of your grandparents: "Little pitchers have big ears."

Competition—Winning and Losing

The ability to function in competition is central to achievement. Underachievers have not learned the techniques of competing. Although they may win happily, they have not learned to recover after losses. They lose their tempers, sulk, quit, or don't take the risk of playing unless they are certain to win. Parents should teach their children how to cope in competition because functioning in a competitive environment is synonymous with achieving.

Gail Sheehy, in her book *Pathfinders*, discusses differences among adults in handling their own developmental crises. In comparing adults who viewed themselves as successful and who led reasonably fulfilled lives versus those who saw their lives dominated by frustration and failure, she concluded that the main difference between the two groups was the way in which the successful adults dealt with their failures. "Pathfinders," the term she used for the more satisfied adults, experienced just as many failures as did the others. However, they were able to use those failures to grow and move forward. On the other hand, those who were less satisfied came to identify themselves as failures and remained in their less-than-satisfactory life positions.[2]

Children establish similar patterns. Those who are creative and success-oriented achievers view their failures and losses as learning experiences.[3] When failure occurs, they identify the problems, remedy the deficiencies, reset their goals, and grow from the experience. Failure is only a temporary setback, and they learn to attribute their failure to lack of effort, the unusual difficulty of a task, or perhaps the extraordinary skill of other competitors. As coping strategies, they may laugh at their errors, determine to work harder, and/or redesign their achievement goals. Most important, they see themselves as falling short of a goal, not falling short as people.

Other children take a more self-destructive path, which leads to underachievement. With failure, they become failure oriented.[4] They come to view school as a competitive game that they are incapable of winning, so they logically decide that there is little purpose in playing. They learn to give up easily and to get by with minimal effort. Their skill deficits increase, and these children become underachievers who have little or no confidence in their ability to successfully function in the school game.

To help their children cope with losses, parents should first examine their own competitive style; children may have learned maladaptive responses to failure at home. For example, parents may show an attitude of quitting too quickly if a problem gets difficult, of avoiding any type of competition, or of habitually blaming external sources for their own shortcomings or lack of effort. Parents' restructuring of their attitudes and expectations, therefore, may be the first priority for helping children who are not achieving well in school.

Children should be taught to identify creative responses for their losses or failures. For example, they should recognize that normal people—even very talented ones—cannot be "Number 1" in everything, but that every person has areas in which he or she is talented.

Children should not feel insecure or threatened by an occasional setback, nor should they receive too much sympathy. If your children experience a loss, discussing it may need to wait until after the emotional tension is reduced in order to avoid their defensive responses. You can't expect rational perception or logical thinking during the stress period immediately following an upsetting defeat. A dialogue, rather than a lecture, may better help children understand that: (1) they cannot always win, (2) disappointment does not mean that they are failures, (3) this particular experience simply was not as successful as they had hoped it would be, (4) everyone would like to be smarter (or better, or faster, etc.), and especially (5) the main goal is to play the game at their best performance level, regardless of their competitive ranking. Effort counts.

You should send a clear and direct message to your children about the central role that school learning plays in their lives. Indeed, if children are to succeed academically in a way that capitalizes on all of their abilities and optimally prepares them for higher education, then the learning game should be played above all others. If you stress that winning—regardless of the game—is all-important, then winning at tennis, on the swim team, or in popularity contests may become too crucial to your children. Young adults in their twenties or thirties whose peak life achievements were election to senior class president or starring on the high school varsity basketball team probably feel unfulfilled by adult standards. Their competitive strivings helped them perform at their best, but in areas that were peripheral. Of course, high school should not be all drudgery. However, students should be aiming at higher education and achieving long-term goals, and their academic education should never be secondary to socializing or athletics.

On the other hand, sports teams provide some wonderful opportunities to teach children about competition. The world of sports mirrors how one needs to play the game of school. The good athletes stay in and play their best, even when that game is lost. They discipline themselves. They practice with grueling regularity the necessary skills for their sport. Education, as well as later life accomplishments and creative contributions in the arts, sciences, business, and government, are hard ballgames. The competition is keen, and there is no place for quitters. It is the way in which children play the game of school and life that makes them achievers or underachievers.

Although children must learn to function in competition, and especially to emerge from failures and losses, they should also become involved in noncompetitive activities that are intrinsically reinforcing—interests that they enjoy for personal and not competitive satisfaction. If all of a child's activities are tied to recognition or competition, he or she may be unprepared for relaxation. Children who have not learned to enjoy noncompetitive activities will feel bored and depressed when they are not moving toward a goal. Intrinsically-motivated, noncompetitive activities provide an important diversion that makes competition meaningful. Furthermore, they provide relief from the stress of both winning and losing. In addition to goals for achievement, children must value personal and family goals that are noncompetitive.

Organization

Disorganization is a frequent symptom of Underachievement Syndrome. Most underachievers appear to be purposely disorganized. For some, the disorganization shows itself in messy desks, messy papers, and messy rooms. Others seem unable to plan their time and thus hand in assignments late or not at all. Still others seem unable to organize their talking and thinking, and although they are vocal, their conversation changes continuously from one topic to another.

Concomitant with the disorganization patterns are statements that are not entirely honest, such as "I forgot," "I didn't know I had any homework," "I didn't know today was the deadline," or "I thought I had already completed the assignment." Although some students will admit that such statements are excuses, others will insist that they are honest and accurate. They seem like declarations of opposition to organization and commitments to nonconformity.

Two parenting styles seem to foster disorganization patterns. One kind of parent advocates a disorganized lifestyle. These parents value disorganization as synonymous with freedom and creativity and assert that they prefer it over order. Thus, their children emulate the parents and simply never learn organizational techniques. Disorganization feels natural, right, and creative, and it remains for the whole family a preferred approach to daily life. Extreme disorganization, however, is harmful to achieving in school.

The second parenting style is much more common and more difficult to identify. In this family situation, one parent uses disorganization as a passive-aggressive power play in an oppositional marriage. Typically, one parent is a perfectionist or very structured and apparently the more powerful parent. The second parent, who feels controlled by the first and thus powerless, cannot assertively or rationally deal with this feeling of powerlessness, so this parent uses passive-aggressive techniques, such as forgetting things, not preparing things on time, not accomplishing requested tasks, and ignoring responsibilities. Children may emulate the passive-aggressive parent in opposing or ignoring the more demanding, more structured parent. Disorganization in schoolwork becomes a powerful weapon for these children.

Living with a small amount of chaos or tolerance of ambiguity seems healthy and may contribute to creativity and a noncompulsive lifestyle. On the other hand, reasonable structure and organization are necessary for accomplishment, and it appears again that moderation is more effective than extremism. Parents should take the initiative to model and teach reasonable organizational techniques for dealing with home and school responsibilities.

Try talking aloud about your own organization to heighten your children's awareness of organizational techniques. When parents develop a communication system that enhances effective cooperation in the household chores and responsibilities, children are more likely to follow through with their parents' requests. It's important for parents to agree on how to organize. **Sometimes communication of tasks through notes and checklists is an approach that feels comfortable for both adults and children.**

It's also important to identify the part(s) of organization that your child is lacking. Many parents and teachers complain about children's organizational skills, and many kids admit that organizational skills cause them problems in school. Although disorganization is identified as a culprit, parents, teachers, and children themselves are unclear about what is specifically wrong. By examining the elements of organizational skills, it will be easier to identify and improve the skills that children need help with. Figure 6.1 shows nine main elements of organizational skills. This will help identify your child's specific problems so that he or she can correct them. I will include suggestions for improving in areas where they need practice in Chapter 11.

Figure 6.1. The Nine Key Elements of Organizational Skills

> • Putting like things together
> • Predicting time
> • Scheduling
> • Remembering
> • Prioritizing
> • Eliminating
> • Reviewing
> • Establishing good habits
> • Maintaining flexibility
>
> Source: Rimm, S. B. (2004). *Sylvia Rimm On Raising Kids Newsletter, 15*(1). Watertown, WI: Apple.

Homework and Study Habits

For students who lack organizational skills, homework and study habits should be structured. The tools for such structuring should be familiar to most parents.

Parent Pointer **Assignment notebooks or some method of remembering assignments is a must. Use large notebooks rather than small ones; small ones get lost. Having a separate folder and notebook for each subject is helpful. A backpack or school bag that is prepared the night before will help children's organization. A place to deposit the school bag and books close to the entryway of your home will help keep books and bags from cluttering the living room, kitchen, bedroom, and family room and will help to make organization a habit without nagging. Insist from the start that studying be done in a quiet place alone at a desk or table—no siblings or parents, and no television, Internet, video games, or stereo until the work is complete.**

If your children are achieving well, quiet music is permissible, but studying in front of a TV is never effective. Reading for school should not be done on the floor or bed. Reclining positions are not conducive to intense concentration, despite your children's arguments that they prefer such comfort. If you insist on organized study, your children will develop organized habits that help them learn. Children who organize their work and are achieving well won't need these guidelines from you, because they probably have developed most of them on their own.

Under no circumstances should your children expect to have you or your partner sitting next to them regularly at homework time. Don't let them convince you that they can't work without you. Your attention should be directed to the completion of their assignments. Certainly, it's reasonable for parents to provide children with occasional help or explanations. However, these should be brief and given only after children have tried understanding the work on their own. If they've studied the material first, parents can quiz them or give them a trial test, but if their performance is poor, the children should return to their desks for independent study. Parents can't be expected to study for their children; however, parents can recommend or teach learning strategies that may be effective in particular situations.

When you introduce these study guidelines for your children, they'll surely debate you. Your directives should be firm. If they achieve well, they may do it their way; if they have not been successful using their own style, they must change to yours until they are clearly achieving for at least a full year.

Grades and Rewards

Grades are important, and **parents should communicate their concern for good grades.** Grades, in one form or another, will always be used to evaluate performance in life, whether they are letter grades for school, verbal comments, written evaluations, or salary increases for job performance. They are a shorthand method of communication and serve their purpose with reasonable effectiveness.

Children will always be able to control their grades to some extent, but never completely. The changeable and dissimilar standards of teachers and evaluators will always influence the outcome. For example, some teachers rarely give A's; others give only A's and B's. You and your children should both keep this variability in mind in interpreting either letter grades or words. Children should be expected to earn the best grades that they are capable of earning, but allowances must be made for teacher and ability differences.

Many parents wonder if they should pay children or give them rewards for good grades, usually A's. They think that paying children for good grades will motivate them to achieve. In my experience, monetary rewards are not especially effective. Children typically will work for A's if they believe that they can achieve them. Underachievers, however, don't really believe that hard work will help them get good grades. If you ask them what grades they would like, many will admit with a smile that they'd like all A's. When you explore further, they typically acknowledge that they don't see A's within their reach and that they really don't see much value in working hard to achieve only B's or C's. Giving added rewards for A's, which they see as unachievable, therefore does not motivate them. The unattainable rewards may, in fact, serve to further confirm their inadequacy. For children who are already achieving A's, monetary rewards are unlikely to do any harm, though they will not provide any major benefits either.

This is not to say that rewards are meaningless. I'll talk about the important places for rewards in later chapters.

The Indulgence Traps

I have already described the ways in which some family patterns result in Underachievement Syndrome. There are some tactics that parents may use to diminish risks in these special situations, starting with avoiding overindulgences. Doing too much for children usually causes problems for them. However, defining what is *too much* is so difficult that parents easily fall into this trap without realizing the harm they've done.

If you are a parent and you recognize that your children are victims of these traps, you can redirect your children despite your former loving errors of too much giving and doing. First, you must convince yourself that under many circumstances, **saying no may be kinder and more loving than saying yes**. This is important because you have so far defined love and kindness as doing things for your children and giving things to them. Depriving them of anything makes you feel guilty, so you try to avoid it if you can. One father stated it this way: "Do you mean that after working so hard to finally earn sufficient money to provide well for my son, I have to say no to him when he asks me for toys that I can now afford and that I would like to give him?"

It was difficult to explain to this warm, generous father that in giving his son so much, he was depriving him of the very quality he valued so much in himself and others—the willingness to work for something. He was stealing from his son the privilege of achieving and earning for himself.

Those parents who want so much to give to their children can measure their appropriate giving by matching efforts. This provides a practical basis for avoiding doing too much. For example, a parent might propose the following to a child: "How about if I work with you to reorganize your room because it's really a mess, but once we organize it together, you'll be able to keep it neat more easily," or, "I used to have some really good strategies for studying spelling (or Spanish or history). I could share those strategies with you, and then you'd find the studying easier on your own."

Other parents match efforts while at the same time rewarding children's initiatives. Parents can use this to guide them in measuring assistance to children with household tasks and schoolwork, as well as with the purchase of material things. If children put forth approximately equal effort or money, they gain an appreciation for their own contributions, as well as their parents' efforts. They earn the confidence that comes from challenge, and parents can feel the pleasure that comes from giving. For example, the parents might suggest that they'll give the child half of the money to buy a desired item if the child will work to earn the other half of the money.

If parents give too much, their gifts are rarely appreciated because the recipient becomes accustomed to expecting lavish material possessions. If parents reverse their earlier generosity and don't give at all, then children are likely to feel angry, resentful, and deprived. The matched-effort compromise permits a phasing in of initiative and provides a parents' vote of confidence for their children's efforts.

Overindulgence traps include giving too much praise and attention, as well as too many material things. **Praise that suggests to children** **that they are the best or smartest is the most damaging.** Though children may recognize that they are, indeed, not the best or smartest, this kind of comparative praise communicates to them that their parents have set competitive goals for them.

Reducing the amount of praise should be done gradually so that the children can move from dependence on outside reinforcement to rewards that come from accomplishing tasks and feeling personal achievement. **Never eliminate your praise entirely.** If you feel that you are lavishing too much praise on your children, begin by tallying the number of times you praise them each day, and set as a goal about half that number. Reducing praise gradually prevents the children from negative acting out to receive attention. You can also reword your praise so that it is positive without being exaggerated. **Emphasize correct learning processes and efforts, and be sure not to praise your children when they have made little effort.** They should earn your compliments, which is not to say that they have to earn your love. Love, of course, should be given unconditionally.

Parent Pointer

It's difficult to measure what is sufficient but not excessive reinforcement. Most adults can recall during childhood being exposed to a gushing adult who praised continually. At first, they were impressed by the continued compliments, but later, they realized that the compliments were meaningless because they were given so freely and were unrelated to efforts or outcomes.

If you are concerned that your children's grandparents are overindulgent, you can use the *Open Letter to Grandparents* which follows. Before giving grandparents the letter, remind them that you are sharing this because you know how much they love their grandchildren.

Dear Grandparents:

Grandparenting is fun! You may enjoy these children of your children with the more relaxed perspective that parents rarely have. You can be patient, loving, and giving, but please remember your own parenting days. You wanted to bring your children up by your own rules. You believed in firm discipline, and you knew that the children were easier to manage if you were consistent and did not always give in to them. When you were rearing your own children, you taught them not to expect an endless stream of material possessions. You expected them to take responsibility, to show effort, and to persevere. The children you parented have grown up responsibly. You must have done many things right.

Now we ask you to permit your children to parent by their own style and standards. Support and encourage your children as parents. It is tempting to play the "good" grandmom or grandpop, but don't do that if it makes your children look like bad parents. If you overrule your children's discipline of their children, your grandchildren will not respect their parents and eventually will not respect you either. Consistent discipline is a key to your grandchildren's growth into fine adults. Give love, give attention, and yes, give gifts—but please don't give so much of any of these that you steal from your grandchildren their initiative, self-discipline, and self-confidence. Moderation—giving less than you would like to give—is a better guide than the generosity you feel. This is a hard message to give you because we know you love your grandchildren so much, but we know you will understand because you were parents, too.

Family Structure Considerations

Family structure has changed, and what we used to think of as typical families—that is, one birth mother, one birth father, and the natural children of these parents—may not be typical in many neighborhoods. Children with a single parent or remarried parents are no longer unique. Nonetheless, the children that I see in the clinic who are no longer in two-parent families usually express the wish to have their original, intact, two-parent families back. They will sometimes add parenthetically, "Without the fighting, of course."

One can hardly ignore the special demands and pressures on these children and their parents in their new family structures. Although many children lead productive lives despite these pressures, many others experience severe emotional trauma. Underachievement is a visible symptom of their stress. The following are some prototypical family arrangements and suggested ways for avoiding typical pitfalls.

After Divorce

Divorce is always traumatic for children, although in many cases, a bad marriage may cause more problems than a divorce. If you are going through a divorce, here are some steps you can take to help your children cope with it:

- Emphasize to the children that the divorce was not their fault.

- Find out how the children view the situation and how they feel about the divorce.

- Look for ways that they may feel caught in the middle between the parents.

- Allow them to express themselves without contradiction about how they wish the situation were the same as it was before the divorce.

- Elicit from them how they think the situation could be improved or what they do not like about it—for example, not liking to visit Dad because he lives at Grandma's and they don't feel comfortable there.

- Be sensitive to whether they are expressing their own feelings or those that they believe will please you.

- Be cautious that your sympathy doesn't foster their manipulation so that they can find "an easy way."

- Give them some strategies for talking to each parent about their feelings. Some parents going through divorce have so much difficulty themselves that they can't seem to avoid trapping their children into impossible conflicts.

- Assure the children that adjustments become easier with time. You may even remind them of some things that have improved already.

- Don't let them use the divorce as an excuse for not being responsible.

- Be sure that they have the opportunity to go for at least brief counseling. They may be fearful of talking with Mom or Dad about issues that they believe might be hurtful to either parent.

Single Parenting

Parenting alone is undoubtedly the most difficult form of child rearing. Parenting alone may come as a result of a divorce or the death of a partner, although some parents choose to parent alone and have never had a partner. Ideal conditions for single parenting exist when the parent has a positive career goal, when there is a second adult who is supportive of the single parent, when regular and reliable childcare providers are available, and when the parent manages to maintain his or her own positive adult social life.

Children of single parents who have the above circumstances are given consistent parenting, view their parent as an achiever, and are treated as children (not adults) with reasonable amounts of attention and independence. Unfortunately, this ideal is rarely achieved, and almost never immediately. More typically, a single parent after divorce is a victim of rejection, feels little confidence about personal achievement, and may be dependent on her (or his) own parents or welfare, or has an overload of work on the job and at home. A single parent after losing a partner due to death may feel lonely and depressed. In either case, children may have multiple caregivers—grandparents, available babysitters, or daycare centers—of varying quality. The parent, in her (or his) loneliness and/or guilt, can easily smother the child with affection and overprotection, seeing the child as the only reason to go on living and thus causing the child to become too dependent.

Alternatively, single parents may take the opposite approach. Because of their loneliness, they may treat the child as an adult, sharing confidences and status and sometimes even an adult bed, thus moving the child into the dominant mode that comes from being given too much power. These single-parent children are frequently surrounded by a variety of adult caretakers and soon develop excellent people sensitivities. However, while they become intuitive about sensing adult moods and emotions, their habits of pushing limits may cause them problems in the classroom.

If you are a single parent, your child may have no problems of underachievement. Even so, you will need to recognize that your job is more difficult. Below are some simple rules to guide you—simple only in that they are few and straightforward. In reality, they are terribly difficult for single parents to negotiate. Pat yourself on the back for each successful day! Here are those rules:

- Find a career direction for your life to give you a sense of purpose and to build your personal self-confidence. Making your children your only purpose gives them too much power and causes them pressure that will be too stressful for them to manage.

- Find some adult social outlets for yourself. Don't feel guilty about enjoying yourself as an adult away from your children.

- Find a reliable babysitter or daycare facility for your children. Consistency in caregivers and surroundings is very important for young children.

- Treat your child as a child, not a toy to be played with or an adult to be depended on. Don't share your bed with your child (except during thunderstorms). That is a place that you should reserve for another adult.

- Don't tell your children that you will love them more than anyone else forever, or your taking a new partner will cause them to believe that you deceived them.

- If your children come home from visitation with their other parent and are unruly, don't blame that poor behavior on the other parent. Instead, tell your children that you're pleased they had a nice time, and if you can manage a nice comment about the other parent, they'll settle down more easily. They need to know that they can love you both.

- Take time (even when you have little) to enjoy your children's achievements, and encourage them to take responsibilities.

Here are some special rules for single mothers who are raising boys:

- Boys should have an older male in their lives to serve as a model. Find effective role models for your boys. Uncles, grandfathers, teachers, Boy Scout leaders, and Big Brothers may all be helpful to your sons in learning to be comfortable with their masculinity.

- If you don't view your children's natural father as an effective role model, absolutely do not tell your boys how much they look like and remind you of their father, especially when you are angry.

- If you do view your children's natural father as an effective role model, do tell your children that they are similar to their father, if that is the case.

- Avoid power struggles with your children's father. If he mistreats you and shows open disrespect, your sons are likely to imitate his behavior.

- Don't complain to your children about their father's lack of financial support. This will cause their father to seem powerful to them. Children unconsciously copy powerful models.

These rules will sound simplistic to some and impossible to others. They may be difficult for you to live by, but they are effective for parenting your children in a single-parent household. Remember: many successful and happy children have been brought up in single-parent families.

The Blended Family

Remarriage brings with it stepparents, stepsiblings and half siblings, new rules, new competitions, and new relationships. Children who have become accustomed to living with one parent are now faced with a multitude of new adjustments and emotions. In what ways can parents and stepparents make these transitions smoother? How can they give consistent messages so that children clearly know that all parent figures expect them to achieve in school? How can parents avoid letting their children manipulate them? How can parents be sensitive to all of their children's feelings?

The blended family, in which the special parent-child camaraderie is disturbed by the parent's adult relationship with a new marriage partner, elicits conflicting emotions in children. They recognize the appropriateness of feeling happy for their parent, but they often feel disappointed at the loss of attention that previously was all theirs. Their feelings toward the stepparent may also be mixed. They certainly may resent this parent's displacing of their own birth parent, but they may also be happy to have both a mother and a father at home. If the single parent previously conferred too much power on the children and has been unable to manage consistent discipline, the children are likely to see the new parent as an intrusion and recognize that their former power will be diminished. These children will certainly not welcome the new adult.

There are guidelines that are helpful in the new family setting. For example, **regular partner discussions of parenting adjustments are a high priority.** These should take place daily, at first, when all children are away or asleep. The children should not be involved in these talks; it becomes too easy for them to manipulate their birth parents, and the main purpose of these daily discussions is to avoid such manipulations. The emphasis in the discussions should be on fairness and consistency. Birth parents should be the main disciplinarians at first. You may benefit from meeting with a counselor to mediate the "my children, your children" problem, if this particular difficulty becomes stressful.

Family meetings that include some or all of the children can also be arranged to provide opportunities for children to help determine study places and times, household responsibilities, and social guidelines. The balance of control between children and parents in these meetings will certainly vary with the ages and responsibility levels of the children, but final decisions should be made by the parents, with consideration to other birth parents or stepparents.

Although there is a temptation to believe that the blended family will be able to participate in all activities together, in actual practice, it seems more effective for birth parents to continue to have some time alone with their own children. It is also important, especially for boys, to have some one-to-one time to develop interests with their fathers, stepfathers, or both. Developing shared interests with their parents outside of school will help children accept messages about school achievement. Stepparents should certainly become involved in children's school-related activities but should avoid setting unreasonable expectations or reinforcing dependent behavior.

The greatest problem in blended families typically comes in the children's wishes to maintain close relationships with their birth parents by ignoring their stepparents. They look for ways to complain about their stepparents, and birth parents are very vulnerable to these manipulations. Problems with schoolwork and discipline are common, and dramatic underachievement becomes a common and powerful tool for manipulation. Daily communication between parents, rather than crisis-oriented overreaction, can prevent this most exasperating problem.

The Visitation Family

The typical arrangement for children after divorce includes living in one parent's home and visiting the other on weekends and for longer periods on holidays and during summers. Because most after-school time is spent at the custodial parent's home, he or she carries the main responsibility for supervising homework and keeping in touch with school. Therefore, this parent is the most important communicator of messages about school.

The parent with visitation rights usually takes on the job of providing fun, games, trips, and gifts. There seems to be little time for school discussions during visitation time. However, **if children are to achieve** **in school, they must have clear messages from their visitation family about the importance of good study habits and school achievement.** Visitation parents must commit time to discussions about grades, projects, and activities at school. They should make an extended effort to support the custodial parents' study expectations. Despite any animosity birth parents may feel toward their former spouse, the two parents should come to a clear agreement on school expectations.

Children whose parents are no longer living together rarely achieve well in school until they are able to address school responsibilities in a way that pleases both parents. Visitation parents should become actively involved in setting achievement expectations for their children and communicating these regularly. These messages can be very effective because the school expectations are paired with brief and happy stays during visitation.

What happens if the expectations of the visitation parents are greater and more realistic than those of the custodial parents? Obviously, the visitation parents will feel much frustration and, without agreement and commitment by the home-based parents, will truly be limited in what they can accomplish. If visitation is weekly or bimonthly, then visitation parents may set weekly goals and responsibilities for their children that they may reinforce with positive activities on the weekend. It will be difficult to monitor progress, but teachers may be cooperative if parents ask for regular feedback.

In difficult cases, clinical help can also be effective in helping underachieving children who receive different achievement messages. Psychologists and counselors can become effective mediators between the two families for clarifying school progress and requirements.

So far, I have emphasized some general patterns of parenting that encourage achievement and should prevent Underachievement Syndrome. If you are already seeing signs of Underachievement Syndrome in your child, you should be concerned, but you shouldn't panic. There are specific steps you can take to reverse underachievement, which will be discussed in later chapters.

Chapter 7
Teaching toward Achievement

Teachers can make a huge difference in preventing and reversing underachievement. Many specific strategies will be recommended in later chapters, but the social-emotional frameworks are introduced in this chapter.

Differentiated Curriculum

Curriculum materials that are too easy or too difficult do not build internal locus of control or self-efficacy in students. They don't contribute to experiences in which children find success by making strong efforts. Figure 7.1 summarizes the appropriate relationship between effort and outcome and also shows the transitional classroom curriculum that causes students to lose their sense of self-efficacy.

Figure 7.1. Relationship between Effort and Outcome

	+ OUTCOME −	
+ **EFFORT** **−**	**Quadrant 1** ++ **Achievers**	**Quadrant 2** + − **Underachievers**
	Quadrant 3 − + **Underachievers**	**Quadrant 4** − − **Underachievers**

Source: Rimm, S. B., Cornale, M., Manos, R., & Behrend, J. (1989). *Guidebook: Underachievement Syndrome causes and cures* (p. 289). Watertown WI: Apple.

Rimm's Law #12 reminds us of the importance of differentiated curriculum for building self-efficacy: Children will continue to achieve if they usually see the relationship between the learning process and its outcomes. Notice the word *usually*. Children are resilient enough to occasionally be expected to complete or attempt schoolwork that is too easy or too difficult. Those experiences could actually be helpful. Experiencing occasional boredom because of repetitiveness is part of life. Also, recognizing some new material as too difficult helps children to be healthily humble about their abilities. It is when inappropriate curriculum predominates that serious harm is done to children's self-efficacy. Because children have different abilities, interests, and learning styles, differentiated curriculum is extremely important for encouraging motivation and achievement.[1]

In reviewing the four quadrants of Figure 7.1, consider that both intrinsic and extrinsic success build self-efficacy. Thus, the love of and interest in learning provide intrinsic rewards, while good grades and teacher and parent praise and pleasure provide extrinsic rewards. Children continue to achieve if they learn that strong effort results in good intrinsic and extrinsic results (Quadrant 1). When children make little effort, they should be disappointed in their learning experiences, grades, and teacher and parent approval (also Quadrant 1). There is a match between effort and outcome, and they learn that making strong effort is meaningful.

Quadrant 4 represents underachievement in which children don't experience a connection between effort and outcome. Even when underachievers describe their study, it's typically unengaged study. For example, they may claim that they have studied when reading something over once lightly and simultaneously watching TV or listening to music. Or they may say, "I was lucky and the teacher gave me an A," or, "Studying just doesn't work for me. I always mess up tests when I study."

Quadrants 2 and 3 represent the inappropriate curriculum environments that, when continuous, lead to underachievement. In Quadrant 2, students initially make good effort, but outcomes are not successful. Learning disabled students, particularly dyslexic students, struggle in this scenario.[2] While they feel intelligent in many ways, in comparing themselves to their classmates, they feel failure related to reading. Because reading is omnipresent in curriculum, it affects these children's abilities to produce successful outcomes in most subjects.

Students who have handwriting or processing speed problems struggle with producing legible work and are slowed down in the completion of workbook pages or speeded math tests. These "pencil anxious" children, mostly boys, who may manipulate screwdrivers and Legos deftly, feel inept and "dumb" because they compare themselves to their classmates invidiously. They often define intelligent students as those who have finished their work first. In one young man's words, when asked how smart he was compared to his classmates, "I'm fifth from the bottom." He explained further that when he completed his work, there were always four other students who hadn't completed theirs. Bright students with disabilities, who had been accustomed to early praise and notice for their intelligence, feel as if something has gone amiss, lose interest, and label their work as "boring."

The too-competitive classroom can also cause students to feel inadequate and is another example of Quadrant 2. Feeling like a loser in most academic endeavors diminishes motivation to work hard. Note that I said "*feeling* like a loser." For some children, feeling third best may feel like being a loser.

Quadrant 3 represents the usual dilemma of gifted students who are unchallenged. In addition to curriculum being repetitive, they find that they can accomplish good grades and significant praise without real effort. Students, parents, and teachers alike remark on how quickly and easily these children learn difficult material. In early grades, outcomes are almost always successful, while effort is minimal. These children don't experience the effort required of students with lesser abilities. Thus, accomplishment with little effort leads to a fixed, rather than a growth, mindset.[3]

If curriculum is appropriately differentiated, gifted children should be challenged. In some cases, they may need to skip subjects or grades in order to learn more. At other times, cluster grouping gifted children within a classroom can provide sufficient new curriculum. Unfortunately, some schools are no longer grouping students according to their achievement levels for fear it will cause children to feel like losers in competition. However, there is probably no better way to make an average or below-average student feel like a loser than to put him or her into competition with a child who does exceptionally well.

Eventually, gifted students will be challenged. For some, curriculum begins to feel difficult by middle school;[4] for others, by high school; while some extremely gifted students may not experience true challenge until college and adulthood. At some point, though, even very gifted children "hit a wall." While some increase their efforts and struggle to meet new challenges, others initiate defensive, avoidance behaviors. They hide their sense of inadequacy for fear that they are no longer intelligent. They avoid difficult work and fall further behind in their skills. Grades decline, and teachers' and parents' disappointment and punishments increase. While for some, parent and teacher consequences are sufficient for immediate reversal of the underachieving pattern, others have lost their sense of self-efficacy and no longer believe that effort can deliver success.

Evaluations of these students' self-efficacy come from comparison to other students, and the increase in complexity of curriculum is typically paired with schools that are larger and more competitive, thus doubling the pressures for these students. It is the lack of early challenge that causes them to assume that bright children should learn quickly and effortlessly. They subconsciously worry that working hard may indicate that they are not intelligent, and this initiates their defensive avoidance patterns that lead to Underachievement Syndrome.

The following story, *The Bicycle Ride*, gives an analogy related to the importance of grouping for curriculum differentiation so that children can develop the relationship between effort and outcome:[5]

> In the interest of enhancing our physical fitness one spring, my husband and I decided that we would do some daily bicycling. Mountain bikes were the appropriate vehicles for our hilly Wisconsin countryside because they provide 21 gears, including a "granny" gear for the steeper climbs. I started our new activity after a fairly rigorous lap-swim regime. I considered myself reasonably physically fit. My husband had not been exercising regularly during the winter, so I had some early stamina advantage.
>
> We rode off in the early morning together, learning the appropriate gear use and appreciating the spring renewal around us. On our first two or three mornings, we were well-matched, and the biking felt like a reasonably social activity. After less than a week, my husband's strength and endurance far exceeded mine. My slow pace no longer provided sufficient physical challenge for him. Because our prime reason for bicycling was fitness, I suggested that he feel free to go ahead at his own speed. The five-mile course provided plenty of challenge for me, but he soon added an extra two miles. We waved as we passed each other going in opposite directions.
>
> Our daughter, Sara, visited from college several weekends. She joined us, and it was very clear that, thanks to her youth and condition, a fitness experience for her demanded more challenge than either my husband or I wanted. Although we could ride together socially for a short time, if we were truly to provide

ourselves with a cardiovascular workout, paces and distances needed be different for each of us.

Reflecting on my feelings of being left behind and my husband's and daughter's needs to bike ahead for fitness, I identified our biking experiences with the controversy that presently surrounds educational grouping in our schools.

First, I imagined that, not three, but 23 of us were biking on that country road. Then, I asked myself many questions about my feelings. These seem to be questions that teachers should ask themselves about grouping in the classroom. Please pretend that you are biking with me and share my questions:

1. Was the main purpose of our biking social or for physical fitness?

2. Would it have been possible for us all to meet our social and physical fitness goals with the same activity?

3. How did I feel being the slowest biker? Would I feel better if there were some other slow bikers near me?

4. How would my husband and daughter have felt if I had asked them to slow their pace for me or spend most of their time teaching me to bike better?

5. How would I feel about myself if the more able bikers were to spend most of their time teaching me or slowing down to wait for me?

6. Would the better bikers enjoy biking with people who have similar skills, strength, and endurance?

7. How could I feel good about my physical fitness activity even though I was slowest?

8. How would I feel if an outsider insisted that I keep up with the faster bikers?

9. How would I feel if others did not see the value of my physical fitness activity for me?

10. How would I feel if my fitness and strength improved but I was forced to continue to ride at my same speed and distance?

If you've wandered through my bicycling questions, please return to the same questions and pretend that you are a student in a classroom. In each of the questions, replace "physical fitness" with "educational fitness." Replace "biking" with "school." Now answer those questions as they relate to classroom grouping. Here are my answers:

1. The primary purpose of school is not social but educational fitness. We cannot and should not ignore the social aspect, but there are many opportunities within the school and community for social life that will not interfere with the pursuit of educational fitness.

2. We can't meet all students' social and educational fitness needs with the same activities. They can be better met by including grouping for some parts of the curriculum, but not for others.

3. No student would like to be considered the slowest in the class. Avoiding small groups of slow readers with only two or three children will prevent that sense of their feeling like losers.

4. Students who need more challenge resent teachers and other students who slow down their learning process. They legitimately feel bored in class and tend to feel superior to other kids if they spend their school time teaching instead of learning.

5. Slower students hesitate to ask questions, volunteer, and discuss if they feel they're slowing other students down, which is not good for their self-concepts.

6. Very capable students do enjoy learning with intellectual peers and often miss the stimulation when peers are not available.

7. Children enjoy the sense of learning if they feel that they are making progress. Setting and reaching personal goals is important for children at all levels.

8. Children feel pressured if they are pushed beyond their capacity.

9. Children who are not viewed as achievers by parents and teachers don't feel good about themselves. All students should feel the sense of accomplishment and the merit of effort.

10. It's important to show children paths for movement between groups, particularly upward mobility through effort.

Based on relatively limited research, the concept of academic grouping has disappeared from many classrooms. As we try to save children from feeling like losers in competition, we are taking from them some important coping skills that they will need in our competitive society.[6]

For very bright children, we are, in a very global way, asking them not to stretch themselves mentally and are actually preventing them from important learning during many of their school years. It is hard to predict the educational outcomes for those students who are being prevented from developing their mental fitness in order to fit in socially with their peers. We may recognize the loss only after an entire generation reaches college.

Other nations that value achievement are demanding much more mental fitness of their students. Their students will not pedal slowly to wait for our country's students to catch up. A bicycle ride provides physical fitness only when all riders are encouraged to exercise to their abilities. Similarly, differentiation of curriculum should provide appropriate effort—not too much or too little—for all students.

Building Task Value

Students are less likely to underachieve if they value either the task or the result of the task.[7] Some tasks may be intrinsically interesting, while others are repetitive and boring. For example, a group science experiment is likely to be viewed as fun, but repetitive foundational elementary skills like practicing multiplication facts or learning to spell words are unlikely to be particularly interesting to most students. It is relatively easy to engage the students in science, but in order to motivate students to participate in the latter tasks, they either have to be convinced that these basic skills are of value to them or they must believe that if they study and do well, their efforts will result in good grades or approval by parents and teachers. However, the grades and approval will motivate them only if they value those results. If they respect or identify with role models who value those results, they are more likely to work to earn them.

Not all students value the same tasks, whether the value comes from the effort or the result. Part of motivating underachievers to reverse their underachievement is encouraging them to either value the task, the outcome, or both. When teachers explicitly point out the reasons for the value of basic curriculum, there is greater likelihood that students will put forth effort. When teachers provide engaging and varied approaches to curriculum, students are more likely to be motivated.

Teaching Healthy Competition

All students should learn to both collaborate and compete in the classroom. Teaching children cooperative and competitive skills is, however, a developmental process. For example, most primary children are not gracious about losing and are discouraged quickly when they do. It may even be difficult for young children to share and take turns. As they mature, they gradually develop an understanding of concepts such as teamwork, good sportsmanship, not being a quitter, and perseverance. They continue to love to win and are motivated and exhilarated by winning, but most learn to cope with defeat and the understanding to continue their efforts. Thus, teaching competition should be done gradually and in developmentally appropriate ways. Ideally, in teaching competition early, teachers need to be nurturing, while later coaches and teachers can set higher standards for coping with competition.[8]

Underachieving students often have highly competitive feelings, but they have not learned the resilience necessary for coping with losing in competition. They can recite the rules of good sportsmanship, but they rarely know how to deal with feelings related to their losing. Because they are poor contenders, they cope with rivalry by denying their competitive feelings. They say they "don't care" or they're "not interested," when they really mean that they don't think they'll do very well. They tend not to like children who are successful because, by comparison, they feel inadequate. They rarely have insight into their feelings about competition and don't reveal the reasons they avoid it. They will typically say that they don't believe in competition and don't enjoy it. Actually, they are so highly competitive that they fear becoming involved and losing. The unfinished work and disinterest in school that causes them to be underachievers is at least partially caused, most often, by their fears of trailing in academic competition.

Some educators believe that any competition that causes a child to feel left behind even temporarily does not belong in schools. The extreme of extinguishing all competition from the classroom seems nonproductive and unrealistic. The classroom should gradually prepare children for both competitive and collaborative experiences. Students cannot learn to function in competition if it is eradicated from schools. Life after graduation will be a shock if students are not prepared during their elementary and secondary school years. If we do not teach competition, the standard of learning in our country will fall further behind Asia and Europe. We need to be competitive.

Individual competition in the classroom should be minimized, even though high achievers thrive on it, because underachievers and even average students become victims in highly competitive environments. Announcing grades to the class is an example of individual competition that can be harmful to children. Instead, small groups or team competition will teach children competitive coping strategies while avoiding the risks that students will feel like losers in competition.

Putting the class in contests against other classes will also assist students in experiencing winning and losing as a group. Team competition helps to foster group solidarity and gives all students reasons to want to contribute. Group competition should be directed carefully by the teacher and structured to include all students. It provides teachers with excellent opportunities to teach good sportsmanship.

Having students compete with their own past performances ("personal best" competition) encourages underachievers by making losses less threatening and demonstrating these students' improvements. Recording their own progress will help them view themselves as competent.

Personal best competition is an excellent strategy and works well even with young children. It can be very effective for helping students build confidence. For example, the timed tests by which students learn their math facts lend themselves well to personal best competition approaches. Each day, the teacher could recognize those children who beat their previous record. This approach leaves fewer children discouraged and enhances the speed of everyone's multiplication or division skills. A special category for those children who manage to maintain their very fast speed, but not exceed it, would eliminate the problem of accidentally penalizing the experts. The teacher could ask for the hands of all children who performed the tests in less than five minutes or who did better than last time. Winning thus becomes possible for all who make effort.

Dominant, conforming underachievers often have special talents and function well in areas where they are winners, but they continue to avoid attempting activities in which they fear losing. Because classrooms are basically competitive, helping children to identify and understand feelings related to competition is a good step toward showing them how to function in other areas where they aren't as strong. Directing them to an activity in which they can share their talents but may not be "first" provides good experience in functioning without an admiring audience. If children become accustomed to this kind of challenging environment, they are not as likely to be devastated when they emerge from their more sheltered high school surroundings. They will be more realistically ready for the real world competition of adulthood.

There are a great many enriched arts, academic, and athletic environments where children who have certain specific talents can meet equally talented students. Even if brief, such experiences can be helpful to the dominant conforming underachievers. During the school year, depending on your location, there may be high-level city youth orchestras, bands, choruses, math competitions, debate meets, and many, many sports opportunities. Specialty teachers usually know about opportunities in their fields, such as clubs and camps for potential writers, photographers, artists, actors and actresses, vocalists, and academically talented children. It's helpful if teachers warn these students of the excellence that they will encounter in these high-powered environments. For some dominant, conforming students, confronting competition for the first time, even in a summer camp, can be a disappointing experience to which it will be difficult to adjust.

Teachers and coaches can also use competition within their own specialty areas to teach young people to manage competition in other areas like academics. Here's an example of a conversation between a counselor and an underachieving student who was captain of his basketball team:

Counselor: Let's talk a little about your team. How do you feel when a talented member of your team comes to practice late, skips practice, or doesn't seem to play his hardest?

Student: It infuriates me because I know he could help us win if he used even half his talent.

Counselor: How do you feel about average guys or really talented players who are positive and practice hard?

Student: I'm really glad to have them on my team. I can count on them, and even if they mess up, I know they did their best.

Counselor: How do you think your feelings compare to your teachers' attitudes about the minimum amount of work you're doing?

Student: (There's a pause as a light comes on) Okay. I get it!

Questioning students about their areas of competitive strengths will help them generalize from their favored activities to the classroom and give them some important insights for improving their attitudes about school.

Dominant nonconforming underachievers are most resistant about entering competition unless they assume that they will win. It is tempting to teach them to compete by engaging them in contests in their areas of strength. Unfortunately, this is hardly ever effective because it is the area in which they most fear failure. It is better to guide them to new areas that they have not yet attempted but where minor victories could provide encouragement. Debate, drama, music, Odyssey of the Mind, and Future Problem Solving are excellent outlets that can introduce them to individual and group competition. If they've withdrawn from music, even though they're talented, you might encourage drama or debate, in which they will feel less pressured. Do not, however, encourage debate by saying something jocular like, "You're always arguing anyway." That will certainly prevent your student from taking the risk.

Any expectations that imply pressure on your students will also deter them. It's better to say to these vulnerable children: "You might be pretty good at debate," instead of, "I'll bet you'd be a super debater." These students are absolutely paralyzed about competition but deny this both to themselves and to others. If they can renew their confidence in a new area, they may even return to compete in their earlier areas of expertise.

Within the classroom, it is ideal for teachers to structure some activities that are described as collaborative—in which students are encouraged to help each other for the good of all—but in order for children to learn to deal with the competitive process, they should have opportunities to experience both wins and losses. Thus, classroom competition should be structured to give all students some of both experiences. Continuous winning or losing is not instructive. It is fun for the winners but disastrous for the persistent losers. If teachers encourage open discussions about winning and losing, this can help children understand and deal with their responses to defeat. An example of a teacher-led discussion about competition can be found in Figure 7.2.

Figure 7.2. Coping with Competition (Classroom Discussion on Competition)

> **Step 1:** Let's begin by making a long list of situations in which children feel competition. Examples: sports; board games; schoolwork; with sisters, brothers, cousins; music; art; dress; popularity.
>
> **Step 2:** Now, let's think of different possible outcomes when we compete in all of those areas. Examples: be first, second, or third; tie for winning; come out in the middle; be in last place; lose; not join in because afraid to lose; quit in the middle of the activity.
>
> **Step 3:** What kinds of feelings might people have if they win, tie, lose, or quit? Examples: excitement, happiness, sadness, depression, anger, smartness, dumbness, rejection, dislike for someone.
>
> **Step 4:** What do kids do when they have these feelings? Examples: shout, clap, jump up and down, throw the bat, curse, lose their temper, blame other people, cry, quit, run away, never play again, say bad things about the winner, start a fight, practice more for next time.

Teaching to the Emotional Needs of Students

While adjusting curriculum to the abilities and learning styles of students is an important task for teachers, it is not the only task. The beginnings of underachievement are too often blamed on teachers by both students and parents, and this blame plays an important psychological role in the initiation of underachievement. Teachers who are blamed by a particular student can be a favorite teacher to other students in the same class. It is a truly talented, insightful teacher that manages to build an alliance with a student who may have lost his or her sense of self-efficacy in the classroom.[9]

In my clinical work, I point out to underachieving students that teachers logically aren't attracted to students who don't turn in assignments, aren't interested in learning, or don't pay attention in class because teachers enjoy teaching those who want to learn. It's often surprising to these students that they actually turn teachers off because of their lack of interest. For excellent teachers, this disinterest should present itself as a challenge because it is within teachers' power to ignite interest in the very students who are disengaged. On the other hand, even excellent teachers can feel worn down by disinterested, discourteous students.

Strategies for how to ally with students to reverse underachievement will be detailed in the steps of the Trifocal Model. Figure 7.3 shows an ALLIANCE acrostic that summarizes the steps as an advance organizer for teachers. The concept of ALLIANCE is critical to student reversal of underachievement. Students should feel that teachers are united with them in their efforts to achieve. Sometimes underachieving students feel that achieving is losing a battle to teachers and that winning is avoiding what teachers want them to do. It's important that students feel like winners, not losers, when they achieve.

Achievers and underachievers alike recall teachers who ignited their interests and initiated their motivation for learning. Teachers who believe in their students provide the spark that initiates their motivation. Psychology has always recognized the importance of positive and firm teaching; punishing students has never motivated them successfully. The strategies that follow in this book are helpful tools, but they are most effective when students recognize that teachers care about them and believe in their abilities to do well. Just as the causes of underachievement are attributed to teachers, the reversal of underachievement is often credited to them as well.

Figure 7.3. ALLIANCE for Reversing Student Underachievement

Ally with the student privately about interests and concerns.

Listen to what the student says.

Learn about what the student is thinking.

Initiate opportunities for recognition of the student's strengths.

Add experimental ideas for engaging curricular and extracurricular activities.

Nurture relationships with appropriate adult and peer role models.

Consequence reasonably but firmly if the student doesn't meet commitments.

Emphasize effort, independence, realistic expectations, and how strengths can be used to cope with problems, and extend possibilities patiently.

Here's a story to remind teachers of how important the "A" for ALLIANCE in the acrostic is:

> My husband and I were dining with an elderly gentleman guest who was a highly esteemed Professor Emeritus of Statistics at Harvard School of Public Health. My husband explained my interest in the childhoods of eminent persons and asked him to share a little about his childhood. I felt a bit embarrassed about my husband's very personal request, but I was actually eager to hear the professor's story.

He began, "Well, I didn't have a very good start in school. They made me repeat kindergarten. My parents didn't get along very well, and I didn't much like my father; I guess my mother didn't either. They eventually divorced. I wasn't doing very well in school, and my mother came in to visit with teachers frequently. She complained to me about the teachers, and I think the teachers weren't very happy with my mother either."

As I listened, I discouragingly ticked off all of the familiar high risks for underachievement, and then the professor continued: "I guess you might say that I was an underachiever until fifth grade. In fifth grade, I fell in love with my teacher."

And with a far-off look in his eyes, he added, "I guess you might say I'm still in love with her. She only taught me for one year and then she left teaching to get married, and I have no idea what happened to her. But I loved her so much that I started working really hard. I enjoyed it, and after that, nothing or no one could stop me."

So you see, while hopefully I am providing you with many tools and clues for the reversal of student underachievement, the most important tool that you have resides within you—the ability to unite in an alliance with students so they believe that you truly care about them and they are tempted to put forth their greatest effort to prove themselves to you. In putting forth that effort, they frequently discover their love of learning.

The two "L's" in the ALLIANCE acrostic remind us to listen and learn from students about what they are thinking. Teachers not only have to listen literally, but also "between the lines" to learn what students are feeling because underachievers use defense mechanisms to protect their fragile self-concepts. Often students are not entirely honest with themselves or others, and many times, they don't have insights into their real problems. You will want to sensitize yourself to what children may mean when they describe school problems. Furthermore, when the pressures of adolescence begin, they may hold back secrets that confound teachers and parents; however, when they share their friends' problems with you, those problems may really represent their own worries.

At Family Achievement Clinic, I often have to listen to what the children are *not* saying so that I can determine what they are feeling and how to guide them. If they listen carefully, teachers can also tune in to what their students' words aren't telling them. Following are some examples from my research and clinical work that will help you understand what children are and are not saying directly but may be feeling.[10]

Competitiveness

Television news anchor Donna Draves remembers telling her mother that she wanted to quit dance lessons because they were becoming boring. However, she revealed to our research interviewer something that she had never before shared with anyone—that her actual reason for quitting was that she was no longer the best dancer in the class.[11] Coping with competition was more at the heart of her quitting than the boredom she gave as her excuse. (*Boring*—doesn't that sound familiar?)

Boyfriend Worries

Sixth grader Ana Maria had recently stopped doing her daily assignments. She told her parents that she couldn't concentrate since her grandfather had died. Her work habits had degenerated at about that time. In counseling, Ana Maria blamed her grandfather's death for missing work, and she had genuine tears in her eyes as she described her feelings. However, she also repeatedly talked about her very first boyfriend and the email that he'd sent to her indicating that he wasn't ready for a girlfriend yet. She insisted that the boyfriend episode no longer bothered her, but the frequency of her insistence that she no longer felt rejected told the true story of her sudden underachievement. Her concern about popularity with boys and feelings of rejection were undoubtedly greater deterrents to her achievement than her genuine sadness about her grandfather.

Power and Peer Issues

Fifth grader Brandon and seventh grader Darius visited Family Achievement Clinic on the same day. Although not related, they had much in common. Both boys were gifted underachievers; both argued incessantly with their teachers; both struggled with peer relationships; both liked their teachers and felt reasonably challenged; both of their parents were divorced but came together to help their sons. Brandon's parents had been told that he was at risk of losing his scholarship to a prestigious independent school, and Darius had been dropped from his public school gifted program contingent on improved behavior.

In my interview, Brandon proclaimed that he didn't know why he couldn't stop himself from arguing and talking, although he realized that his constant debate had earned him the peer label of "pest." Later in our conversation, when I asked Brandon whether he was more like his mother, father, neither, or both, he spontaneously responded, "I'm like my dad; he's against everything, and so am I." Brandon's father had described himself to me as a gifted underachiever, but he needed to make some changes in his oppositional image in order for his son to make a dramatic improvement in his oppositional behavior at school. In Brandon's case, peer pressure for acceptance was helpful.

Darius' story was slightly different. He said that he loved arguing with his teacher and always won the arguments. When the teacher lost her temper at him, he felt the admiration of his peers and believed they thought that he was cool and smart. Darius also said that he didn't know why he couldn't stop arguing, but he hypothesized that it may have started when he was younger and in a school that didn't challenge him. He remembered reporting boredom to his mother, and both he and she would argue with the teacher. The arguing didn't improve his education, but he thought that the experience may have started him enjoying arguing.

Darius hated to lose his time in the gifted resource room and was determined to earn it back. Although I wouldn't have recommended to his teacher that consequence for his bad behavior, it, together with brief therapy, was effective. After a semester, Darius was back in gifted programming. The deliberate argumentativeness had disappeared, and achievement had improved. For both Brandon and Darius, the arguing was a symptom, but underlying were family and peer issues. The anti–arguing alliance for teachers (which can be found in Chapter 13, Figure 13.14) would have been helpful to these teachers.

Finishing the ALLIANCE Acrostic

Students continually compare themselves to other children in their families, schools, and neighborhoods. They also compare their present feelings about achievements to their past experiences. When they feel more or at least equally successful in their comparisons, they're likely to feel good about themselves and achieve. If they fear being less successful, they may or may not report their worries. Instead, they may use defense mechanisms and bend the truth to protect their fragile self-concepts. In order for students to build the resilience required for leading fulfilling adult lives, they have to learn to cope with some less–than–successful experiences in both schoolwork and relationships.

Teachers who listen to what children say, as well as to what they give clues about but deny, are better able to guide and support them as they develop confidence and resilience.

The "I" for "Initiating opportunities for strengths" in the ALLIANCE acrostic reminds teachers about the importance of recognizing strengths and providing opportunities for learning in each student's areas of strength. Every student likes to feel a little special, and those whose strengths are recognized will achieve more in classrooms.

The "A" for "Adding ideas" speaks to the teacher's responsibility to be creative, as well as the underachieving student's need for a change. More of the same approach that has always been used will only foster further underachievement. Recognition of strengths is important, but adding activities that give expression to students' strengths can generalize to overall improvements in self-discipline, work ethic, and self-efficacy.

The "N" for "Nurturing relationships" reminds teachers of their importance as role models to their students who are constantly observing them. There will be more on role models and mentors in Chapter 10.

The "C" for "Consequence" should not be interpreted as punishing students into motivation. It only means that students should clearly understand the reasonable consequences of good or poor work, and educators should follow through on those consequences without being "wishy-washy" or overpunishing.

The final "E" for "Emphasize" incorporates the importance of preventing pressures to achieve and instead encouraging the effort and independence that helps students develop a work ethic. Hopefully, it also reminds educators that reversing underachievement is an effort that requires patience.

Chapter 8
How You Can Reverse Underachievement Syndrome Using the Trifocal Model Step One: Assessment

As the foregoing chapters have suggested, reversing Underachieve-ment Syndrome is not simply a matter of getting a child to clean up his act or pull up her socks. At Family Achievement Clinic, we are able to reverse underachievement in roughly four out of five children by using a three-pronged approach. We call it the Trifocal Model because it focuses on the child, the parents, and the school.

Parents and teachers can prevent and reverse many underachieve-ment problems without a psychologist. Frequently, parents who attend lectures at which I've discussed the Trifocal Model tell me that by fol-lowing my suggestions, they have corrected problems and have improved their children's achievement without requiring further con-sultation. Teachers have also indicated that my workshop presentations of the model have been practical and effective in helping them to reverse underachievement in their students. Although it is possible for teachers or parents to work alone, the strategy is most effective when they coop-erate with each other.

Many schools have also used the Trifocal Model with excellent suc-cess. It has been utilized effectively in regular school programs, programs at Underperforming Schools, special education and gifted programs, and for children in kindergarten through grade 12. It has also been used with college students, although a counselor typically facilitates reversal of underachievement for young adults.

The characteristic behaviors of Underachievement Syndrome were learned; therefore, new behaviors, habits, and attitudes can also be learned. The reversal of underachievement will involve new learning for children and for you as parents and teachers.

The Trifocal Model includes six steps, of which the first five apply to all underachievers. In step six, which is divided into three types of underachieving children, you will select the chapter that most applies to your underachieving child.

Plan to be patient and persevering for success. In the clinic setting, the average reversal time for underachievement is six months. The time varies with the intensity of the problem, the age of the child, and most important, with the consistency and perseverance of parents and teachers. Very young children take only a few months, while high school students usually require at least a full school year. They are often difficult to turn around because of peer pressures and the distractions of alcohol.

Figure 8.1 illustrates the Trifocal Model. Step one, assessment, will be described in this chapter. The second step, communication, will be explained in Chapter 9 and the following three steps in Chapter 10. The final step, modifications at home and school, will be discussed in Chapters 11, 12, and 13.

Figure 8.1. Trifocal Model for Reversing Underachievement Syndrome

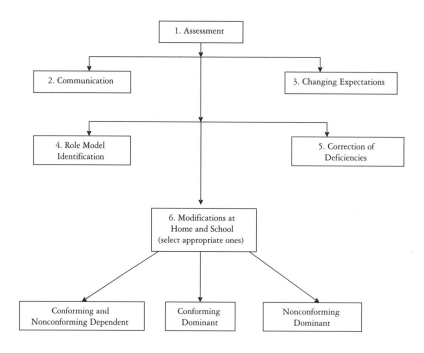

Adapting the Trifocal Model for Disadvantaged Students

While ideally the Trifocal Model should include parent involvement, sometimes parents either refuse to get involved or are experiencing difficult life events that prevent their becoming involved. Students whose parents cannot participate in the model for reversing underachievement are defined as *disadvantaged* for the purpose of reversing their underachievement. They will need an adaptation of the Trifocal Model that a school in Colorado facetiously termed "the bifocal version" of the Trifocal Model. While teachers should continue to communicate with parents about progress for these children, the entire model can be conducted by the school without parent participation. Most steps of the model are similar to the original Trifocal Model, but a person termed a "child advocate" substitutes for the parent reinforcement role and meets with the student weekly to monitor progress. This role can be filled by a counselor, special education teacher, vice principal, or even another classroom teacher. Also, instead of the typical homework routine that parents conduct, an after-school study club can be instituted where students complete all of their homework under teacher supervision. These two modifications make the model very effective for disadvantaged students, despite the lack of active parent involvement.

Assessment

The main purpose of this first step is to determine the extent and direction of a child's underachievement. There are formal and informal methods of assessment. The formal approaches include group or individual intelligence and achievement tests, as well as creativity and underachievement inventories. Informal evaluations involve the questioning and observation of children by their parents and teachers. The formal assessment approaches will be discussed first. Because underachievement is defined as a discrepancy between children's abilities and their school performance, tests can give some important insights into the children's problems.

Many parents are confused about IQ testing. The initials IQ stand for *Intelligence Quotient*. The term comes from tests that were initially created in 1905 by Alfred Binet for the purpose of determining whether children were sufficiently intelligent to benefit from schooling. Binet devised a series of tests for each year of child development to calculate children's mental ages compared to their chronological ages. He multiplied the final score by 100 to arrive at what is called the "intelligence quotient." Children with IQ scores of 100 were considered of average intelligence, those with scores lower than 100 were below average, and those greater than 100 were considered above average. Categories of scores were established and given names, varying from "imbecile" to "genius," and scores were used to make predictions about children's learning abilities.

IQ tests have been changed and revised many times since Binet's first tests, and educators have become much more sophisticated in their use. Although the tests are often referred to as intelligence tests, educators now realize that they measure only some kinds of intelligence and that scores are affected by cultural environments and learning, as well as the individual's inherent intelligence.

Although research has shown that average IQs tend to stay fairly constant throughout peoples lives, my clinical experiences with elementary and secondary students indicate otherwise. Children who underachieve in school for many years often show large declines in IQ scores. New testing can result in scores 10 to 20 points lower than earlier tests. Yet for children who reverse their underachievement, both IQ test and achievement test scores often increase.

Figures 8.2 and 8.3 show examples of group achievement test and IQ test score increases for one student whose underachievement was reversed. This student's individual IQ score increased from 110 to 125 from grade six to eight. Further follow-up of this young man showed that he managed honors classes well in high school and earned a 3.6 grade point average at a highly competitive university where he studied pre-medical education. He attended medical school and is undoubtedly a physician today. If his 110 IQ test score had been accepted as a limit to his ability and he had not reversed his underachievement, his lifetime career would have been very different.

Figure 8.2. Example of Achievement Test Scores for a Student Whose Underachievement Syndrome Was Reversed

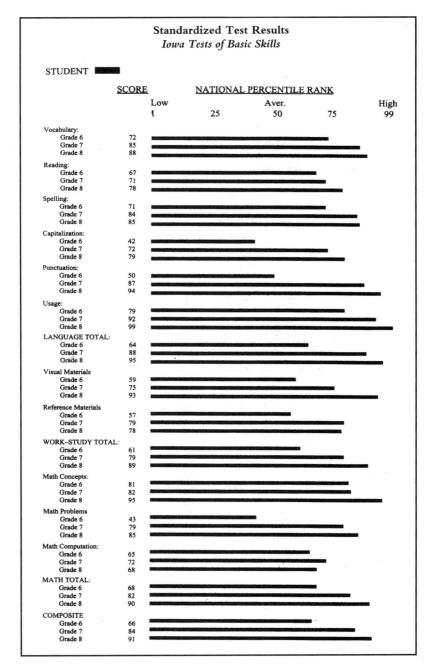

Figure 8.3. Example of IQ Test Scores for a Student Whose Underachievement Syndrome Was Reversed

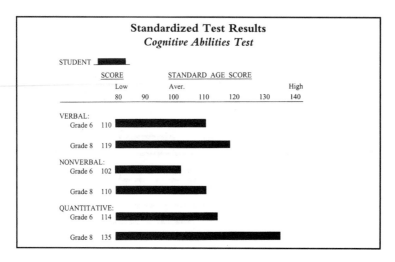

Formal Assessment

Formal measures of underachievement can be divided into two categories: those that measure the extent of the problem, and those that describe the direction of the underachieving behaviors. The extent of underachievement can best be evaluated by reviewing all IQ and achievement scores to date and having a psychologist or teacher administer new test batteries if a recent one is not available.

Once the data is obtained, complete the chart in Figure 8.4 using all test scores and grades available. Ask yourself the following questions to determine the extent of your child's or student's underachievement:

1. Have IQ or achievement test scores, either individual or group, declined more than 10 points during the child's educational career?

2. Is there a difference of two or more categories between IQ and achievement tests?

3. Is there a difference of two or more categories between individual and group intelligence tests, with individual tests being higher?

4. Is there a difference of two or more categories between intelligence tests and school grades?

5. Is there a difference of two or more categories between achievement tests and school grades?

If your answer to any one of these questions is yes, then the child is probably underachieving. If there is more than a 10–point decline in IQ or achievement test scores, or if the differences between variables go beyond two categories, then the degree of underachievement is greater. You may look at underachievement for one subject or for all subjects in this way. The more areas of underachievement that you see or the greater the underachievement in any one area, the greater is the problem that you're confronting.

Figure 8.4. Chart for Analysis of Test and Grade Data to Determine Area and Extent of Underachievement

Chart for Analysis of Test and Grade Data to Determine Area and Extent of Underachievement					
Child's Grade	Individual IQ Test Scores	Individual Achievement Test Scores	Group IQ Test Scores	Group Achievement Test Scores	Grade Point Average
K					
1					
2					
3					
4					
5					
6					
7					
8					
9					
10					
11					
12					

Use the following word categories to describe the test scores and grades:

Word Categories	IQ	Achievement Percentiles	Tests Stanines	Grade Point Averages
Far Below Average	Below 80	0-15	1 or 2	F
Below Average	80-89	16-29	3	D
Low Average	90-94	30-44	4	C-
Average	95-104	45-54	5	C
High Average	105-109	55-69	6	C+
Above Average	110-119	70-70	7	B
Superior	120-129	80-89	8	B+, A-
Very Superior	130+	90-99+	9	A

Other formal assessments that provide help in identifying and describing both the extent and direction of underachievement include parent inventories, teacher observation scales, and child self-report inventories, which can be completed at home or in the classroom. These are helpful in quantifying the underachievement problems and enhancing communication between parents and teachers.

Achievement Identification Measure (AIM)[1]

This is a parent report of typical child behaviors. It serves to standardize, objectify, and simplify information collection. It includes 78 questions that can be answered by using any of the following: "No," "To a Small Extent," "Average," "More than Average," and "Definitely." Parents answer the items, and the inventory is computer scored.

AIM is extremely helpful in communicating to parents the characteristics of their children's achievement motivation. The information that it yields is ideal for parent-teacher conferences because it identifies the extent of Underachievement Syndrome and its main symptoms. There are five dimension scores that closely match the main problems that characterize the syndrome. These are "Competition," "Responsibility," "Control," "Achievement Communication," and "Respect." Children receive a percentile score for each dimension. Descriptions of each dimension and sample questions from AIM are included in Figures 8.5 and 8.6.

Figure 8.5. Dimensions for Achievement Identification Measure (AIM)

Dimension	Explanation
Competition:	High scorers enjoy competition whether they win or lose. They are good sports and handle victories graciously. They don't give up easily. Low scorers get depressed, cry, complain, or lose their temper when they do poorly at something. They tend to brag as winners. They are not skillful in peer relationships because they want to be in charge or prefer not to play.
Responsibility:	High scorers are independent and responsible in their schoolwork. They tend to be well-organized and bring activities to closure. Low scorers depend on adults for help and attention and do not plan or organize their school responsibilities. They may also misbehave in attention-getting ways.

Dimension	Explanation
Control:	High scorers are comfortable in school or home settings without having to dominate or manipulate parents, teachers, or peers. Low scorers tend to be dominant or controlling children who have typically been given too much power as preschoolers by one or both parents. They expect to be the center of attention and to be in control of their peers, their classroom, and their family. They feel angry and out of control even when they are subjected to reasonable discipline.
Achievement Communication:	Children who score high are receiving clear and consistent messages from their parents about the importance of learning and good grades. Their parents have communicated positive feelings about their own school experiences, and there is consistency in messages between Mother and Father. Low scorers have parents who give contradictory or negative messages about achievement in what they do and/or what they say.
Respect:	High scorers are respectful toward their parents and other adults. Low scorers are rebellious or disobedient and ignore their parents' requests and requirements. There is often inconsistency in the discipline philosophy of the parents.

Source: Rimm, S. B. (1986). *Achievement identification measure*. Watertown, WI: Educational Assessment Service.

Figure 8.6. Sample Items from AIM

- I help my child with his/her homework.
- My child had many health problems as a preschooler.
- My child is considered bossy.
- My child does schoolwork at a reasonable speed.
- My child enjoys competitive team sports.
- My child blames others or finds excuses when he/she loses at something.
- My child is anxious to be as similar as possible to friends.
- My child forgets to do homework assignments.
- My child has an older sister who is a high achieving student.
- My child loses his/her temper at school.
- My child usually obeys his/her father.
- My child is very like his/her mother.
- My child is perfectionistic.
- The father in this family liked school.
- My child can get one parent to say "Yes" after the other parent has said "No."
- The father in the family is a more rigid disciplinarian than the mother.

Source: Rimm, S. B. (1986). *Achievement identification measure*. Watertown, WI.: Educational Assessment Service.

Group Achievement Identification Measure (GAIM)[2]

This student self-report is appropriate for preadolescents and teenagers (grades five through 12). It permits students to describe their own behaviors and attitudes. Most schools require parents' permission before administrating it. Like all self-reports, its results are only as valid as the student is honest.

Similar in scope and dimension to AIM, GAIM is an excellent counseling instrument because it quantifies students' self-perceptions and compares them to a national norm of students. If students deny that they have problems, the results will make them look better than parents and teachers observe. This communicates to adults that their children have not even faced up to the issues of achievement. However, sometimes students will share in writing concerns and worries that they have not discussed with anyone. Here's a case example:

> Anne, an eighth grader, scored very low in the "Competition" dimension of GAIM. The scores for her AIM assessment, which was completed by her mother, were very high. Anne's mother assumed that there was something wrong with Anne's test, so she asked her daughter about the differential. Anne broke down into a flood of tears, explaining to her mom how she hated to lose and she hated any competition. She had masked her perfectionism well from both her parents and her teachers.

Although similar, the dimensions of GAIM are slightly different than those of AIM. Dimensions and sample items from GAIM, as well as a description of the relationship between AIM and GAIM dimensions, can be found in *Guidebook—Underachievement Syndrome: Causes and Cures*[3] and at www.sylviarimm.com.

Achievement Identification Measure: Teacher Observation (AIM-TO)[4]

This is a teacher observation instrument. Parents can ask their children's teachers if they would be willing to complete the instrument, or teachers may wish to use the instrument for their own evaluation purposes. AIM-TO is also excellent for measuring children's progress from the beginning to the end of a school year, provided that the same teacher completes the form both times. It is extremely useful when a team of teachers wants to share their observations of a child. Students may respond quite differently in different classes, and AIM-TO scores can document this at a teacher meeting. It is also helpful for communicating to parents or students.

Informal Assessment

The informal approaches to assessing underachievement in your children may be apparent. As parents, if teachers have told you for years that your children are not working up to their abilities, you can safely assume that the problem is real. If teachers see students who rarely pay attention in class, do not do homework or complete assignments, and do little or no studying, they can be certain that the students are underachieving. If these same students complain that teachers don't like them, that much of the work is boring or irrelevant, or that grades aren't important, their statements are probably cover-ups or defenses for their underachievement.

If children are preoccupied with social life, athletics, drama, or music to the exclusion of schoolwork, academic underachievement is usually taking place. If they rarely study or do the homework expected of them, then they are underachieving. Although you can easily determine if your children or students are underachieving, the characteristic patterns or directions of that underachievement may be more difficult to identify. Careful observation at school and at home, or the use of AIM, GAIM, or AIM-TO, will reveal that additional information.

The descriptions in Chapter 1 of underachievers may have already helped you to determine your children's patterns of underachievement. Additionally, Figure 1.2, also located in Chapter 1, will aid you in determining whether their patterns are dependent or dominant. You will want to look back to that figure as you read the following explanation.

Children located in the dependent quadrants of the figure manipulate people in their environments covertly in ways that require more than the typical assistance and encouragement. Their words and body language reach out for more help than they should need.

Children in the dominant quadrants relate to adults in their environments in more overtly aggressive ways. Because they function comfortably only when they are dominating a situation, they feel out of control when they are not mastering their environment. They will argue and debate. They will trap adults into irrationality and then use those adults' behaviors as an excuse for not complying. Furthermore, they'll complain to others and often successfully persuade other adults to side with them against the first adults.

Children who mainly exhibit "poor me" characteristics can be classified as dependent, while those who continuously challenge are usually dominant. However, keep in mind that these categories are not always distinct, but may blend in any one child. By adolescence, most young people exhibit both dependent and dominant characteristics.[5]

Although identifying the difference between conforming and nonconforming underachievers is less important than determining if they're dependent or dominant, this early identification can serve to prevent more extreme problems later. Therefore, it should not be ignored. Conforming underachievers are less visible than nonconforming underachievers. They tend to mask their problems, which are less extreme. Parents and teachers often assume that they will outgrow their troublesome behaviors. It is, however, important to be aware of the characteristics of conforming underachievers because they are at high risk for moving to the nonconforming state. Children who are nonconformers are in a more intense state of Underachievement Syndrome. Their problems are very visible, and they are also more difficult to change.

When you observe children at home and in school, it is most important to note how, and for what behaviors, they gain adult and peer attention. Underachievers are often attention addicts. Knowledge of the ways in which they attract adults to them will help you to discriminate between dependent and dominant underachievers. For example, if they continuously ask for help; act very passive, sad, or shy; work slowly; and don't complete assignments, they are exhibiting dependent behaviors. If they attract attention by bragging, losing their tempers, arguing, or aggressively manipulating, they are more likely to be dominant. The usual pace of dependent children is slow and cautious, while dominant children are more likely to be fast and impulsive.

In order to help you confirm your diagnosis, I'll summarize the characteristics of each quadrant in Figure 1.2 here. Keep in mind, however, that every child is unique, and this information should be used only to focus on main characteristics.

Dependent Conformers

These students are quiet and pleasant and manipulate adults in covert ways. They seek to attract help with their work because it takes more effort than they are accustomed to. They tend to get along well with others, although they are rarely leaders.

Parents and teachers describe these children as especially sensitive. They cry and are frustrated easily. They whine and complain and report headaches, stomachaches, and injuries that are not visible. They exhibit little energy and attract attention at home by their minor illnesses, sadness, and calls for help. At school, they wait for help or ask questions and have trouble following directions. They daydream and stare out the window. They tend not to complete work, although the quality of that work may be very good in elementary school, less so in middle and high school. They definitely prefer easy tasks and will manipulate adults in their environments in order to avoid any pressure or tension.

Dependent conformers may not be noticeable as underachievers in early grades, but their manipulations begin then. Teachers tend to move them to lower reading and math groups to avoid pressuring them. They often don't like to write because it's too hard. They may appear less bright to teachers than they really are. At home, there is usually one parent who is doing too much for them, overprotecting them, and serving as a shelter. If one parent acts as protector and the second as ogre, the dependent pattern is stronger because the children covertly manipulate one parent against the other. This gives these children more dependent power. They usually identify with the sheltering parent.

Dependent Nonconformers

Nonconformers differ from conformers in the greater magnitude of their dependency; thus, they are more readily identifiable. They attract more attention to their problem because they are more visible. Typically, they are noticeably sad and lonely. Their illnesses and psychosomatic complaints are more frequent and cause them to miss more school. Pediatricians often diagnose them as pressured children. They may be teased by other children and use their victimization to attract adult and peer solace.

These children's problems are more difficult because their sadness is real, and their role of victim is less likely to be within their control. As one ninth grader, who exemplified Figure 1.2's Depressed Donna, explained it, "No one is nice to me except when I'm really sad and upset. Then I can usually count on my friends to be helpful and supportive." This girl was mature and introspective enough to understand that although her sadness was effective in attracting friends temporarily at the time of her emergencies, those same friends would not stay around if she continually misused her depressions. However, she also gave assurances that her feelings of sadness were very real.

Dependent Manipulations

Dependent children manipulate covertly and usually are not consciously aware of the manipulations. The targets of their manipulations are caring and sensitive people who find it difficult to deny the children's requests because refusal would make them feel guilty or unkind. Kind parents and solicitous teachers find it extremely difficult not to respond in ways that they intuitively feel are right, even when the manipulations are pointed out to them. It is difficult to convince loving adults that they should allow their children to struggle. Parents and teachers may view higher expectations for these children as being mean and placing too much pressure on them. If this is your concern, let me assure you once more that these children will build self-confidence and competence only through effort and perseverance, and that it is, indeed, a true kindness to permit children to experience some stress.

Rimm's Law #7—Deprivation and excess frequently exhibit the same symptoms—applies here. When dependent children exhibit signs of stress, it is usually assumed that adults have put too much pressure on them, when in fact, the children have so little experience with stress that almost anything causes them to feel pressure. An important warning is that, of course, you should not ignore children's requests for help when they are genuine. All children need help sometimes. It is only when they receive too much help that they begin to act and feel helpless. Following are some common dependent manipulation techniques to watch out for.

Help Me   Children who request help continually, whether it is related to chores at home or schoolwork, are probably getting more assistance than is appropriate. In order to determine if they are truly needy, you can compare them to children of similar age, intelligence, and developmental stage. Child development books can assist you in determining if your children should be dressing and bathing themselves, riding their bicycles, or helping with chores. Individual intelligence and achievement tests will tell you whether your children are capable of reading instructions, completing assignments, and interpreting math problems. Let children do as much as they can do capably.

Children's calls for help at home are directed toward parents, older siblings, or other relatives. In school, they are directed toward teachers, counselors, and peers. Sometimes they are in the form of verbal requests and hand-raising. However, with time, dependent children become experts at "help me" body language. A few tears, facial expressions of stress, nail biting, staring out the window, dropping or playing with pencils, shuffling papers helplessly, or working very slowly become the more subtle requests for assistance. Sensitive parents and teachers are right to pride themselves on recognizing their children's needs, but you must cautiously ask yourself if their needs are real or whether they are signals for your attention in a pattern of helplessness. There is only a fine line between sensitivity and overprotection, but recognizing and respecting that line will help you avoid encouraging the "help me" manipulator.

Nag Me

Dependent children move slowly. If they are not working efficiently, they can count on being reminded by their caring parents and teachers. If you call it *reminding* now, you can count on their calling it *nagging* eventually. They will blame that nagging on the adults in their lives, particularly their mothers or fathers. Spare yourselves; don't fall into their traps. Although initially children don't seem to mind your constant reminders and you truly believe that you are helping them go faster, they will actually slow down. Do you know of anyone who became more efficient through nagging? You don't enjoy nagging, and in the end, it's no kindness to your kids.

Recognize nagging as a reinforcement of dependency. You will prevent your children from learning to organize their own time if you attempt to nurse them through their activities and responsibilities. Parents tend to believe that their children require nagging, or they wouldn't do it; so it's nag to wake them, nag to get them to eat, nag to get them dressed and ready for school, nag to get them to do their homework, and nag to get them to bed. It isn't surprising that these students expect to be nagged to do their work at school as well.

Protect Me

Dependent children use this manipulation to avoid new experiences. Meeting new friends, going to new places, or trying new academic challenges can be avoided by children who tell their parents that they are afraid. Adolescents sometimes label this fear as embarrassment. Whining, clinging, crying, and tantrums underline the proclamations of fear and make them difficult to ignore. When you offer protection, you are again rewarding avoidance behaviors. Sheltering children from irrational fears is another way of telling them that there is good reason to be afraid, or why else would wise adults protect them? Coping with small fear-provoking experiences successfully builds their courage.

Feel Sorry for Me
Children who have genuine problems—for example, difficult financial circumstances, divorce, parent illness, physical or mental abuse, or personal health or handicapping conditions easily move into this dependency pattern. They find out, often by accident, that adults in their environment are willing to center much attention on their problem. It becomes enjoyable for them to receive so much caring.

This pattern is more difficult for adults to deal with than any of the others because these are not totally imagined ills. The children are feeling real pain and have undergone true suffering. It is truly difficult to determine where illnesses end and manipulations begin. Does your child want to stay home from school because of a stomachache, or is she avoiding a confrontation over incomplete homework? Are his asthma attacks real or due to the stress before math tests? Should you insist that children carry through their anxiety-producing responsibilities, or do you ease their burden and excuse them from assignments?

The "feel sorry for me" manipulation is difficult to detect and equally challenging to correct. Physical problems and pain may accidentally serve to provide an escape from dealing with reasonable home and school stresses. Parents, teachers, and pediatricians must work together closely to discern real medical risks, and they should encourage as much independence as is healthfully possible.

Love Me

"Hug me, kiss me, cuddle me, and reassure me of your love." These are manipulations that tear at the heartstrings of affectionate parents and teachers and appear at first to be harmless requests for affection. But they are not at all harmless if tied to children's avoidance of difficult tasks or unpleasant but necessary experiences. When Carlos, a first grader, ran away from his classroom because the teacher insisted he sit at his desk and complete his written assignments, his mother snuggled him and reminded him of her love before she dutifully walked him back to school. On difficult days, Mom also provided special hugs to help him deal with his stress. The snuggles, hugs, and assurances confirmed to him that there was reason for fear. It also served to remove from him any responsibility for changing his behavior. Why change from something easy to something hard, especially when one is given comfort for the easy tasks, but outcomes are uncertain for the more difficult ones?

A question regularly asked by children who have recently misbehaved is "Mom, do you still love me?" Of course, Mom reassures her child that she does. She may try to separate the wrong behavior from the child, but why bother? The child simply manipulates the assurance of love to distract from the irresponsible behavior, and the irresponsibility continues. Mom wonders at the child's insecurity, but what is apparent insecurity is only very convincing manipulation. In some cases, a sincere-sounding note of apology is added to the love me question, and "I'm sorry, forgive me" becomes one more type of manipulation.

There are many opportunities for parents to express love, affection, and forgiveness. However, these should not be in response to a child's regular pattern of avoiding responsibility. The frequency of requests for love and their proximity to avoiding effort will guide you in determining if the requests are genuine or if they are only part of a series of effective manipulations.

If your children tell you that you don't love them or that you love their sibling(s) more than them, you might try a humorous approach, like "You're absolutely right!" accompanied by a wink of the eye. This makes it clear that the "love me" manipulation will no longer be effective.

Adopted children seem to be especially adept at this manipulation. Their quick response to protect them from punishment is: "Mom (or Dad), the reason you don't love me is because I'm adopted." This often causes their parents to assure them of their love and thus prevents the punishment.

Shelter Me The ogre rituals discussed in Chapter 3 cause one parent to take the role of shelterer. Whatever the "ogre" parent requests, the child can find shelter with the protective parent. If Father has commanded that the lawn be mowed before he comes home and Son has not complied, Mother can first remind, then nag, and finally help out to protect her boy from Dad's impatience. If Daughter has not completed her homework after school as mean Mom has insisted, then Dad can spend the evening by her side assisting with that difficult mathematics assignment and protecting her from an angry mother.

These children learn a dependent power pattern to cope with the stresses of meeting even the reasonable requests of one parent. There is no real reason for the child to work if avoiding the work provides a sheltering, loving experience with the other parent. Dependent underachievers are almost always reinforced for their dependency by one sheltering parent.

Dominant Conformers

These students are often not recognized as underachievers, depending on the degree of their problem. They are very overtly competitive in at least one arena and will not make efforts or persevere in domains where they cannot do extremely well. They deprecate all interests and skills except those in which they excel and achieve status. They may indeed be leaders, but that leadership is likely to have a nonacademic orientation. They put down teachers who do not recognize their talents, and they can be powerful influences on their peers.

These children tend to set unreasonably high goals for themselves—they plan to be professional football players, Olympic athletes, concert pianists, Broadway stars, millionaires, and presidents. They demonstrate enormous discipline in the fields of their choice as long as they are winners, but if their status decreases, so do their efforts—they quit.

Because some of these students are very bright, their grades may be average or above without much effort. Thus, their underachievement may not attract attention, although they tend to just get by. If their talent is truly extraordinary, their scholastic underachievement may not cause them future problems. However, because they may have selected highly competitive fields, many will face great disappointment after high school. Their academic underachievement leaves no cushion for them on which to fall back or toward which they can redirect their efforts. Many of these underachievers are not identified until after high school graduation. They are members of the high school extracurricular and social elite who do not achieve the success that their teachers and friends had anticipated.

Dominant Conforming Manipulations

Although dominant conforming manipulations may be learned early in childhood, they are typically unobtrusive at that time. Furthermore, these manipulations actually support the development of intelligence and talent. They are only problematic in degree and not in quality. If children constantly demand praise and notice and if they become accustomed to expecting too much attention, even though it may be positive, it will cause a serious problem.

Determining exactly how much praise to give is difficult but crucial. Dominant conformers have learned to expect too much. They depend on continued exclamations of excellence and admiration. Their admirers are initially few—the adults in their early environment. This expands rapidly to include relatives, peers, parents of peers, and people in the neighborhood, on the street, and in shopping malls. School experiences add teachers and more peers to the growing crowds that these children manipulate positively and unconsciously with their exhibitions of talent and brilliance. The fans vary somewhat, depending on the talent, but there is always an audience.

The main manipulations of dominant conforming children are far fewer and more positive than those of dependent children. Parents and teachers should be alert to them, but only so as not to over-respond.

Ignoring these children's efforts for attention can be harmful, but diminishing the praise somewhat and positively reinforcing more productive alternative behaviors to add balance to their learning experiences will help them.

Because you may feel personally involved and excited about these children's successes, it is more difficult to balance the enthusiastic praise than one would expect. Furthermore, parents, coaches, and teachers can never be sure if these talented children will, indeed, be sufficiently successful to compete at national and world levels. There is nothing wrong with investing your time and energy in a talented child—it may be appropriate and necessary. But you have a responsibility to assist that child in understanding that success beyond high school is not always assured.

Admire Me, Praise Me, Applaud Me Dominant conforming children are constantly on stage. They are tuned in to identifying observers who will admire them and applaud them. They perform best in front of an audience, and their early childhood smiles tell you that they know you are watching. If you're not, they'll attract you quickly. A *pleasant showing off* is probably the best way to label what they actually do, but this seems too harsh a term to describe the way in which a two-year-old charms you by dancing in a circle to family applause or the subtle manner in which a three-year-old selectively enunciates four-syllable words.

The audience gives rave reviews, including "smart," "brilliant," "graceful," "musical," "talented," "like Picasso or Albert Einstein," "genius," "charming," "gorgeous," natural athlete," and a long list of other outstanding qualities. The children continue to improve their performances and internalize the praise as motivators to achieve. Although positive expectations are good, these may be too extreme.

Do Not Criticize Me "I am wonderful, and if you don't tell me that I am wonderful, I will feel hurt, I will cry, I will lose my temper, I will sulk, or I will quit." Because these children are accustomed to accepting only positive praise, even the absence of praise is viewed as negative appraisal. Speaking well of other children's achievements may be seen as painful personal censure, and correction or a suggestion of change or improvement is the worst form of condemnation. And because dominant conforming underachievers equate performance with self, if you should censure their performance, they take it as a personal attack. Anything but praise and admiration produces a defensive response like, "Why do you always criticize me?"

The "do not criticize me" manipulation maintains that there are two groups of audiences, categorized as: "My friends are those who like my performance all of the time; my enemies are those who dare to tell me that I'm performing poorly." Dominant conformers manipulate adults in their environment to avoid any criticism, whether or not it is intended to be constructive. Perhaps surprisingly, then, these children actually do learn to accept the constructive recommendations of a small number of experts in their areas of expertise whom they have learned to respect, admire, and trust. They do not attempt to manipulate this elite group because they recognize the status and expertise of these mentors, do not feel competitive with them, and instead see them as models to emulate. All others beware—the "do not criticize me" manipulation is powerful.

Dominant Nonconformers

These are the most obvious group of underachievers—and the most difficult to reverse. They rarely ask for help and tend to blame their environment—family, the school, and society—for their problems. They actively rebel against adult goals and are determined to live their lives on their own terms with little or no consideration for those who love them.

These children establish their identity by opposition. They push limits and refuse to accept "no." They claim that teachers don't like them, but what they really mean is that they only like teachers who give them special privileges. The more rebellious they become, the fewer teachers they are able to rally to their support. They feel out of control and depressed unless they dominate other people in their environment. They are angry, negative, and sometimes violent. In their adolescent years, they are difficult to help without professional assistance. Therefore, it is helpful to identify these children early to prevent them from extreme acting out. They may rebel for years, but many become effective leaders and achievers after they gain insight into their feelings.

Dominant Nonconforming Manipulations

Dominant nonconforming manipulations are obvious to parents and teachers, although the children will at first deny that they are intentional. By adolescence, they are more likely to acknowledge their tactics to friends and confidants and may even brag about their successes. Despite the fact that adults may be aware of the children's actions, the children are often so persuasive and persevering that parents are simply worn down. Their parents often admit that most of their private discussions center around how to cope with these difficult children.

Dominant manipulators are experts at sensing parent moods, weak moments, and alliances, and their repeated successes encourage them in their machinations. However, their confidence is built precariously on powerful control, and their mood swings—which include tears, tantrums, and depression—help to persuade parents to give them exactly what they want or face the unpleasant consequences. You will need to outmaneuver such children. Here are their manipulations. Be prepared to be creative and patient.

Admire Me, Praise Me, Applaud Me These manipulations are common to both conformers and nonconformers. The major difference between the two groups is that conforming students are more subtle and more successful. Nonconforming youths often find these manipulations unsuccessful, although at some earlier time in their development, they were effective. In other words, the activities that formerly served to make them the center of attention are no longer effective, and their continued search for that earlier sense of security based on adult admiration encourages more extreme manipulations.[6]

The foundation for the pattern is laid by adults providing too much attention. When new circumstances—for example, new siblings in the family, growing up, poor effort, or insufficient talent—place the children in positions in which they don't get the extreme admiration or applause that they are used to, they are disappointed and frustrated. Children who are very verbal and bright may not receive as much attention for their intelligence when a younger sibling begins using impressive vocabulary. The little girl who was the first female child in three generations becomes less noticed when joined by a younger sister. She does not feel as smart, as pretty, or as special as she used to feel, and she thus searches for ways to focus attention on herself. Sometimes these ways are manipulative, sometimes creative, and sometimes only rebellious, negative, and unpleasant. When admired and praised, these children respond well; their rebellion subsides. When ignored, the rebellion increases. They want too much and have learned to struggle too little.

Do Not Criticize Me

This second manipulation is also the same as one of dominant conformers', but again, it is more extreme. The failure of others to respond to such manipulations will be followed not only by sulking, temper, or tears, but also by retaliatory behaviors. If adults criticize, these children look for ways to get even. For the more aggressive adolescents, this may involve fighting or gang warfare. Less physical children will retaliate for being criticized by talking back, talking about, or employing other strategies intended to hurt the critic in return for their own feelings of pain. These children feel mistreated and distrustful when they have been criticized.

Disagree with Me

A major manipulation for these youths is the power struggle. They want to dominate and win and are determined to prove dominance by making losers out of others. They challenge adults to disagree only in areas where they feel confident that they can win, which builds confidence in their personal power. Criticism, to which they are sensitive and overreact, bothers them because they see it as an accusation of weakness. They are practiced debaters and arguers in their territories of strength, but if they feel that they are losing, they fall back to the defenses that other children use when criticized (see above). Parents and teachers are often puzzled by the extremes that these children exhibit—first they act like seasoned battlers, then suddenly they are reduced to flailing tears.

These children have sufficient confidence in their aggressive skills to initiate arguments frequently. Tension pervades the atmosphere around them. Their continuous readiness for argument bewilders parents and teachers alike. They carry the proverbial "chip on the shoulder."

Give Me

"Gimme" is the familiar request of these children—also "I wish," "I want," and "I need more and more." There seems no apparent end to their wished-for material possessions and activities. All must be done instantly; all must be had immediately. "No's" to requests are met with fury or, as the children will explain, justified anger. Sometimes they say "thank you," but more often, there are no words of appreciation or even acknowledgment. It is as though these children take for granted all that is given but never attain a level of contentment. The process of buying, selecting, purchasing, and accumulating never ends and is another avenue for expressing their domination and control. This manipulation is particularly evident in families in which parents have had few material possessions and therefore wish to compensate by giving their children much.

Be Mine

"I want so much to be completely close to someone, to trust them completely, to have them as a very special friend." These seem appropriate expressions of desired relationships for an adolescent or young adult. However, the words understate the feelings. These young people want intense, complete relationships and refuse to share their friends of either the same or the opposite sex with others. They want so much power in their relationships that differences of opinion are viewed as treacherous, differences in activity preference are viewed as disloyalty, other friendships as unfaithfulness, and individuality as opposition. These young people find much reason for distrust because they define trust in an intense and confining way. They invest themselves heavily in others, but their requirements for control are so great that friends resist, reinforcing the sense of disappointment and depression. These are children of extremes, and they literally want to own their friends.

**See My
Difference**

A corollary to the primary manipulation of praise and applause is dominant nonconforming youths' wish to be viewed as different. They want you to see them as belonging to a different group or to no group at all. They ask you to notice their uniqueness, their unusual characteristics, their artiness, and their separateness. They may classify themselves as poets, artists, or musicians as long as the classification includes a sense of being unique.

Because they perceive themselves as different, these children would like that confirmed by exceptions made for them based upon their unique characteristics: "Could you extend the deadline because my story is so creative?" "May I write a longer story since I write so well?" "Can I be exempt from the research paper since I've done my own experiment?" Their requests may not be unreasonable; however, there is a desperate sense of establishing difference by bringing attention to their uniqueness. "See my difference" is not characteristic of all dominant children—only those who view themselves as highly creative.

**How Far
Can I Push?**

This is the most typical manipulation of dominance. For these children, pushing limits establishes both dominance and control. They learned early not to accept "no" without negotiation. For some, it began with a pleasant kind of persuasion that flexible Mom or Dad saw as appropriate under the circumstances. For others, it was more belligerent and angry from the start. In either case, it was effective, and these children have learned the appropriate "people buttons" to push to get most of what they want. A parent's "no" only stirs them to try a different route— sometimes the other parent or a grandparent. A typical comment is, "*Other* parents let *their* kids...." They know how to make parents feel guilty.

The pushing becomes a habit, a way of changing people's minds that helps these children feel in control. It ties their sense of confidence to control. Thus, there is helplessness, depression, and anger when people don't respond to the controllers' demands and insistence. These children continue to push the limits with parents, teachers, and even societal boundaries. For them, there are no "no's"; there are no boundaries— only "How far can I push?"

Figure 8.7. Dependent and Dominant Manipulations

Dependent	Dominant
• Help me.	• Admire me, praise me, applaud me.
• Nag me.	• Do not criticize me.
• Protect me.	• Disagree with me.
• Feel sorry for me.	• Give me.
• Love me.	• Be mine.
• Shelter me.	• See my difference.
	• How far can I push.

Figure 8.7 summarizes the dependent and dominant manipulations. All normal children exhibit these behaviors occasionally, but under-achievers use these manipulations frequently and as defense mechanisms so that they don't have to cope with the risk of finding out that they're not the best or perfect. The manipulations are usually not conscious, mean, or deliberate. They are, however, habitual and dysfunctional and reinforce the underachievement patterns.

Parents and teachers often respond to these defense mechanisms intuitively, helping dependent children too much and arguing with and punishing dominant children too frequently. The Trifocal Model encourages parents and teachers to respond to these students counter-intuitively by gently but firmly insisting on the dependent child's independence and forming an alliance with the dominant under-achiever while setting firm boundaries.

Determining the Next Step

As you review your formal and informal assessments of your children, you need to decide if parent(s) and teacher(s) together can expect to reverse Underachievement Syndrome or if you will require professional help. Underachievement in younger children and less extreme degrees of underachievement are relatively easy to reverse. Also, dependent and conforming underachievement patterns are more man-ageable by parents and teachers than are dominant and nonconforming ones. You may indeed need the assistance of psychologists or counselors to make a reasonable change in children in this latter group.

Peers, alcohol, drugs, and sex can be more powerful motivators than parents and school achievement for these youths. Because many underachievers are concentrated in the less extreme dependent and conforming quadrants, there are many children whose underachievement can be reversed without professional help. Even for those who receive such help, this book can assist you in becoming more effective in confronting the problem.

Chapter 9

Step Two: Communication between Teachers, Parents, and Students

You can reverse Underachievement Syndrome most efficiently when parents, teachers, and students work together. The initiator of the effort may be either a teacher, one or both parents, or the student, but the effectiveness of the result depends on clear communication between them. If parents are initiating the effort to reverse the underachieving pattern, they obviously require the support of teachers. It is also obvious and equally important that teachers who are facilitating a change in children should communicate with parents. Although it is possible for teachers to help their students without parent cooperation, it is much easier to work closely with parents, and the reversal process will take place more quickly.

Teacher-Initiated Communication

If you are a typical teacher, you are already burdened with a full teaching schedule and many additional responsibilities. When you make the decision to reverse student Underachievement Syndrome in your class, be realistic in the number and types of underachievers that you target, especially at first.

Also, your chances for success are greater if your underachievers have parents who are willing to cooperate. Because you will probably be able to reverse underachievement for between two and five children in any one school year, begin with those with whom you are most likely to be successful. Helpful parents increase that likelihood. If you have already communicated with the parents and they have voiced their concern about the problem, that's an especially good beginning.

If you are a teacher who is also a parent, you can empathize with parents' feelings related to their children. They are disappointed in their children's poor achievement. In the process of trying to understand the problem, they feel frustrated and guilty. They feel helpless about changing the school situation and do not know what to do or what to change at home.

If you are a teacher and teaching the same children all day, most children are, in fact, learning. It is difficult to know how to deal with bright children who apparently refuse to learn. Teachers are tempted to attribute causes of the problem to others and simply avoid dealing with such difficult issues. They might blame parents or the children's previous teachers. Sometimes they simply conclude that the children are lazy. **When teachers plan to talk to parents, or vice versa, it is helpful to remember that both environments are reinforcing the underachieving pattern, and both parents and teachers should change their approaches to these children.**

If teachers blame parents, children get caught in the crossfire. They tend to continue to underachieve. If teachers and parents can ally with each other in support of students, then the children can't find any loopholes and are more likely to move forward. The teacher-parent conference sets the stage for that important alliance.

The preparation for a conference should be different for teachers than for parents. Teachers will want to formalize the documentation of the problem in a professional way. One would think that teacher-parent conferences could be approached without trepidation; however, as many teachers and parents know, conferences about problematic children are fraught with tension. **If you are a teacher, speak to a parents as if you were the child's parent—that is, in a caring way that would make you feel comfortable in the school.** Begin with an assurance of concern for the child, as well as the recognition that underachievement is a perplexing and complex problem, and tell the parents that you wish to work with them to foster their child's achievement motivation.

An ALLIANCE acrostic is provided in Figure 9.1 to emphasize the principles that can guide an excellent conference. If you recall the Reversing Student Underachievement ALLIANCE in Chapter 7, you'll understand that the teacher-parent ALLIANCE acrostic is based on the same important psychological principles of allying with and avoiding opposition with parents, listening and learning their thoughts, and then together experimentally altering the program to engage their child in effort.

Figure 9.1. ALLIANCE for Successful Teacher-to-Parent Communication

Ally with the parents privately about their concerns.

Listen to what the parents have observed about their child.

Learn about what the parents think is best for their child.

Initiate a conversation about the student's strengths.

Add experimental ideas for engaging and interesting curricular and extracurricular activities.

Negotiate to find appropriate adult and peer role models.

Consider alternate possibilities if experimental opportunities are not effective.

Extend possibilities patiently.

Figure 9.2. Sample Teacher-Parent Conference Agenda

1. **Strengths and Abilities**
   A thorough description of the student's strengths will encourage your alliance with parents.

2. **Weaknesses and Problems**
   Only priority problems should be presented at this conference. Parents may become overwhelmed by too extensive a list of problems, or they may feel blamed.

3. **Grade Level of Class Performance, Review of Test Scores, and Curriculum Suggestions**
   Go through this slowly and carefully in consideration of parents who are not accustomed to educational jargon. Listen to parent curriculum or extracurricular suggestions. Consider experimental applications.

4. **Peer Relationships**
   These do impact greatly on student achievement, so listen to parent perspectives on peer relationships.

Figure 9.2 provides a potential agenda to discuss with the parents. You may wish to add other issues or information.

Present clearly to the parents the formal assessment discussed in Chapter 8. Explain the student's intelligence and achievement test performance. Parents should understand the limitation of test scores, as well as their benefits. Dimensions of underachievement scores (AIM, GAIM, or AIM-TO) should be described verbally, and interpretation descriptions should be given to parents along with the scores.

You may need to interpret inventory scores further by explaining that they are self-reports, parent reports, or teacher reports, and as such, they represent the way children see themselves or the way parents or teachers see their children compared with a tested group of other children, parents, and teachers. Although these are highly reliable instruments for large groups, they can be inaccurate for any one individual. For example, parents who are extremely optimistic or pessimistic in their descriptions of their children may inflate or deflate scores on the AIM inventory. As you explain the scores to parents, you may be able to determine whether or not they are realistic in their observations.

IQ and achievement test scores are the vehicle for communicating the extent of a child's underachievement. AIM, GAIM, and AIM-TO scores help to succinctly explain the type of underachievement. Because parents have actually been involved in the completion of the AIM inventory, these particular scores are an especially effective means of emphasizing the child's dependency or dominance. It is also good to have ready some specific informal examples of the student's classroom behavior to illustrate how the problems identified in the AIM scores present themselves at school.

After you have described your impression of the problem at school, it is then appropriate to ask the parents what problems they are observing at home. If they are unable to describe concerns (this rarely happens) or if they deny problems (this can happen), you might give them some examples of typical home situations described in this book. As soon as parents acknowledge the dependent or dominant configuration, you have taken your first step toward helping their children.

Next you should describe the changes that you are going to make at school and discuss suggestions for modifications that the parents may be able to make at home. Determine together the behaviors and grade goals that you deem realistic, and emphasize the importance of process and effort rather than immediate outcomes. Grade goals should not be unrealistically high but initially only slightly above where the children are presently performing. Emphasis should be on work completed on time, study, and effort. Once motivated, children will choose higher goals themselves and experience the satisfaction of setting their own goals. Be sure to point out to parents that change is not likely to be immediate and that their children will vacillate before learning to recognize the relationship between their personal efforts and the results.

You can explain that some progress is usually immediate for dependent children; however, that progress is seldom continuous. They tend to have ups and downs while building confidence. Very powerful, dominant children may initially show no immediate progress and only defiance. Caution parents that their children, especially adolescents, may creatively manipulate everyone to avoid any commitment. However, if adults stay firm and positive, the children will begrudgingly begin their work. Once they discover their self-efficacy, resistance will diminish. If parents are prepared for these responses, they are less likely to blame the fluctuations of progress on you, other teachers, or counselors.

Specify the way in which you plan to continue home-school communicating. I suggest daily or weekly reports or emails. (See "Tracking Student Progress" later in this chapter.) Written communication should remain simple. Your own time constraints and the importance of clear messages make brevity necessary. In all communication, it's important to emphasize positive gains. Negative responses will continue for quite a while, but if teachers and parents refuse to see the gains, then the children will become discouraged and the gains will disappear.

Teachers should be cautious about becoming too involved in the personal lives of their students and their families. If it appears that the parents require assistance with problems other than Underachievement Syndrome, recommend the school psychologist or an appropriate community or private counseling service. Psychological counseling is neither an appropriate role for nor the obligation of teachers.

Conclude the conference with a summary of what you and the parents have agreed is taking place and what your mutual goals are for the child. Suggest books or materials that they may use for follow-up support. It is good to express your pleasure at having developed a working relationship with the parents.

Parent-Initiated Communication

Monitoring children's progress and communicating to parents may seem to be the school's responsibility. Obviously, such communication is partially a school's task. However, whether your children are in public or private schools, those schools have a much larger adult-child ratio than you have at home. Therefore, despite good intentions, the risk of the schools not alerting you to underachievement patterns is high. *Falling through the cracks* is a cliché, but it describes what easily happens to those children whose parents do not take an active and orderly approach to communicating with school. I emphasize *orderly* here because sporadic overreaction may seem like communication, but it is not very effective. Parents frequently feel threatened by teachers and vice versa, and so both may tend to wait for an emergency before starting a dialogue. Certainly, emergency communications are sometimes necessary, but steady, persistent efforts of parents to stay in touch with teachers are far more helpful. **Parent-teacher conferences have a purpose, and parents—both parents, if possible—ought to attend them.** However, if you suspect even minor school problems, one or two conferences are not sufficient.

Four to six weeks into the school year is an appropriate time to call a teacher if, for example, your children have a history of not completing assignments or if they exhibit other underachievement symptoms. By this time, the fresh beginning of a new school year is wearing thin, and your children may be resuming some old habits that are unsatisfactory. This timing is also ideal because if there is a problem, the children won't be so far behind that they can't catch up. The early call to the teacher is also appropriate if the children's comments about school cause you to suspect problems. Explain to teachers that you are concerned that your children may not be working up to their abilities, and ask them if they have noticed any problems. If the answer is no but you're still convinced that a problem exists, you might then specify the previous problem areas or the specific difficulties that your children may have mentioned.

If things are going well, you need only to thank the teachers and ask that they notify you if a problem appears. If teachers do indicate concerns, offer to meet at the teacher's convenience. Most teachers will appreciate your interest, and it can be the beginning of a good teacher-parent relationship—one that is important for preventing or curing Underachievement Syndrome.

Your first regular conference should include some specific questions to assure yourself that your children are working at their ability levels. If your children have been underachieving for some time, it may be impossible for the teacher to assess their abilities. Furthermore, if your children tend to be quiet and lacking in confidence, the teacher is less likely to expect as much, and you may actually be a better judge of your children's abilities than their teachers. You've obviously known your children for a much longer time.

Ask the teacher specifically which reading groups your children are in, if there are any. Ask the grade level at which they're reading. Many reading series have multiple levels that are not so clearly tied to grade levels, but the teacher can interpret that information to you very specifically. Similarly, you should ask the grade level at which your children are doing mathematics. Some teachers are more eager to tell you about particular skills mastered. However, it is much harder to assess whether your children are underachieving using those criteria. Also *grade level of performance* is not the same as *grade-equivalent test scores.* The latter may be quite misleading. To judge your children's success in school, you need to know the former, which is the grade level of their textbooks, rather than a test score.

Teachers frequently assume, although mistakenly, that you're putting your children under pressure when you ask for specific achievement information. You can reassure them that this is not the case. Admittedly, such assurances may not be effective, but take courage. Many teachers are also parents, or have been, and most will identify with your reasonable concerns.

When parents initiate a conference, they are in a much less powerful position than are teachers. You, as a parent, are asking teachers to give you personal time and effort beyond that which they allocate to other children. Also, you are not the experts in education that they are, yet it is you who are taking the initiative for recommending a change. Teachers may legitimately feel defensive or uncomfortable about this role reversal. An ALLIANCE acrostic to guide the important principles of a good conference with teachers is shown in Figure 9.3. This acrostic, comparable to the one used for reversing underachievement in students, can be applied to parent-teacher communications following the same psychological principles.

Figure 9.3. ALLIANCE for Successful Parent-to-Teacher Communication

Ally with the teacher privately about your concerns.

Listen to what the teacher has observed about your child.

Learn about what the teacher thinks is best for your child.

Initiate a conversation about your child's strengths and problems.

Ask about experimental ideas for engaging and interesting curricular and extracurricular activities.

Negotiate to find appropriate adult and peer role models.

Consent to alternatives if experimental opportunities are not effective.

Extend possibilities patiently.

You might begin the conversation by expressing your appreciation to the teacher for caring about your child. You could then ask the teacher if she (or he) thinks that your child is working at the level of his or her ability. This question, in a sense, sets up an alliance of caring with the teacher. If she confirms your suspicions that your child may be underachieving—and she probably will—you might examine the difference between the child's test scores and school performance to reach agreement on the extent of the underachievement. If recent IQ or achievement test scores are lower than earlier ones, you might discuss the decline as an indication of underachievement. Together, you can decide what might be reasonable grade expectations for your child and the kind of effort and time commitment typical for achieving those grades.

It is at this point in the conversation that you could share with the teacher the fact that you've been doing some reading about Underachievement Syndrome, and you believe that your child fits a particular category of underachievers. You could explain that, as a result of your reading, you (or you and your child's other parent) are planning certain changes at home, and you would appreciate the teacher's supporting these changes at school. It is likely that the teacher will be happy to cooperate, but it is most important that you suggest some reading materials for her to review. You may want to lend her your copy of this book with your child's appropriate pattern and treatment highlighted. You could also share your child's AIM or GAIM scores, the interpretation manuals of those tests, or information that you have printed off of the Internet from websites listed in the Resources section of this book. Most teachers will be very open to helping you.

However, if your child is a dependent child, be prepared. Very solicitous teachers are likely to believe that you are expecting too much and are therefore putting undue pressure on your child. Refer them to Chapter 11 of this book, which describes how to assess and assist dependent children. If your child is dominant, rigid or weary teachers are unlikely to be supportive of them until the child has indicated a willingness to make an effort. These teachers will resist a change in their own teaching style and will continue to expect the child to comply. Nevertheless, sharing Chapters 12 and 13, which describe dominant children, with these teachers may encourage them. Also, keep in mind that it is difficult for teachers to change their basic teaching approaches because they have found them to be most effective with the majority of their students.

Even if some teachers don't buy into your plan, many will, particularly if you give them information in writing and some time to read about the topic. It isn't reasonable to expect teachers to give you a definite answer until they have read the information that you've given them. Setting up a second appointment at the teacher's convenience would be prudent. At that time, teachers can put together a plan that they can manage during school time. You will then be able to integrate your home plan with their school strategy.

If your child's teacher is not cooperative, don't be discouraged. It's possible to make dramatic and immediate changes in your children if you change patterns at home and make even a few school changes. Parents and teachers often report striking differences that have been brought about in children by merely changing parenting approaches at home. The most typical immediate change in the child is an improvement in self-efficacy. Achievers exhibit an increase in self-confidence when their parents and teachers direct their educational enterprises appropriately. It's important for you to show your confidence to your children and let them know that you have clear ideas about improving their school achievement. They no longer need to flounder by manipulations and limit-pushing; it is an important step in the reversal of their underachievement.

Tracking Student Progress

The central characteristic that distinguishes achievers from underachievers is an internal locus of control, meaning children's sense that they can effectively change their own academic results through effort. One vehicle that helps children to develop this understanding of the relationship between effort and outcome is a student evaluation form that is completed by teachers. Three examples of forms that are used at our clinic and at many schools appear in Figures 9.4, 9.5, and 9.6. These may be modified to deal with specific concerns or behaviors. However, they should remain uncomplicated and general so that teachers will not feel burdened by the time that it takes to complete them. Now that most teachers and many parents have access to the Internet, simple email communications can serve the same purpose.

These forms or teacher emails are shared with and discussed by children and their parents at regular achievement-monitoring conferences. If parents are actively involved, children receive assessments of their progress twice: once from their teachers who distribute the message, and again from their parent(s) who receive the communication. If teachers are undertaking the underachievement reversal process without parent participation (the "bifocal model"), a key teacher or counselor could be the regular receiver of communications about progress. The person with whom the students review their progress can be termed the "child advocate."

Parents or advocates should plan achievement meetings with children on either a daily or weekly basis. For children in primary grades, a brief daily review of accomplishment and reinforcements is appropriate. As the children's achievement and behavior improves, parent and advocate meetings should be set for a regular weekly time. Upper elementary and secondary children should have weekly meetings initially. When they show fairly consistent effort, meetings can move to biweekly or monthly intervals.

Figure 9.4. Daily Evaluation Form

Student Name_____	Teacher Name_____	Date_____

Assignments
Completed: ❏ All ❏ Most ❏ Half ❏ Less than Half

Classroom Effort: ❏ Excellent ❏ Satisfactory
❏ Fair ❏ Unsatisfactory

Behavior: ❏ Excellent ❏ Satisfactory
❏ Fair ❏ Unsatisfactory

Comments and missing assignments:

_____

_____

_____

_____

_____

_____

Thank you very much for your help

Figure 9.5. Weekly Evaluation Form (Sample 1)

Student   Teacher
Name_____Name_____   Date_____

Assignments
Completed: ❏ All   ❏ Most   ❏ Half   ❏ Less than Half

Classroom Effort: ❏ Excellent   ❏ Satisfactory
                            ❏ Fair   ❏ Unsatisfactory

Behavior: ❏ Excellent   ❏ Satisfactory
                            ❏ Fair   ❏ Unsatisfactory

Comments and missing assignments:

_____

_____

_____

_____

_____

_____

Thank you very much for your help

Figure 9.6. Weekly Evaluation Form (Sample 2)

Name_____		Grade____ Date_____			
Week of_____					
Subject	Behavior	Effort	Grade this week (opt.)	Grade to date (opt.)	Teacher Signature
1					
2					
3					
4					
5					
6					
7					
8					
9					

Teacher Comments: Missing Assignments:

_____ _____
_____ _____
_____ _____
_____ _____
_____ _____

Please use the same rating for behavior, effort, and achievement (grades):
A= Excellent B= Above Average C=Average D=Below Average F=Failing

It's important to keep the tone of advocate or parent sessions with students positive and instructive. The sessions provide children with the opportunity to review their gains, to receive encouragement, and to deal with both the positive and negative consequences of their new efforts. They become the means for assessing and reinforcing efforts, setting goals, and clarifying consequences.

Many schools prefer to have children circulate a form from teacher to teacher. Their reasoning is that if students want the information, they should take the responsibility of circulating the forms. However, students do not want negative feedback. Furthermore, underachieving students almost always bend the truth, particularly about school and homework. Thus, the forms may not be as effective if the circulation of them is left to the students. They tend to bring home only the good ones and forget or even alter the ones with bad news. Communication then breaks down. The student blames the teachers, the parents blame the teachers, and of course, the teachers blame both the students and parents.

Therefore, it is critical that there be a foolproof method of tracking progress—one that is not left to the child.

Parents can facilitate this communication by writing the student name, teacher name, and subject on the form and making copies that teachers can fill out more quickly. They can include multiple copies in a file folder with their child's name marked on it. Then the teacher can simply make checkmarks and write brief comments. If there are multiple teachers, the forms can be forwarded to a counselor or team leader mailbox. Parents may want to stop by the school to pick them up, or some students can be trusted to carry sealed envelopes home to their parents to review. The use of regular email serves to ease the process further. If the child advocate is a staff member in the school, the entire communication process is simplified.

Progress reports from a teacher to children and their parents or advocates are an important element in developing children's internal sense of control and self-confidence. These communications build children's sense of accountability, which is a good step toward reversing underachievement.

Chapter 10
The Next Three Steps: Expectations, Role Models, and Deficiencies

The next three steps of the plan to reverse underachievement stem directly from the findings in the children's assessments and the communication between teachers and parents. They take place more or less concurrently. Each of the three steps will be described in this chapter.

Changing Expectations

Underachieving children's habits have led parents, siblings, teachers, and peers to expect continuing low levels of performance, and battles or nagging as well. Even children's expectations of themselves do not match what is potentially possible in their school performance. All parties must change their expectations to match a new level of achievement.

Personal Expectations

In order for children to change their achievement, it is important for those who are close to the child to recognize improvement and then communicate to the child that the different achievement levels are appropriate. This communication is very important because underachieving children have been stuck at a certain level, and it is all too easy for those around them to expect the status quo. Inertia operates to hold underachievers in their place. Therefore, adults will need to let kids know that they expect gradual improvement, not sudden leaps. Those important others in the underachiever's home and school should attempt to recognize even small efforts, although it is better to do so casually. If family members, teachers, and peers don't acknowledge or accept the changes, the children's potential for achievement will seem hopeless to them. After initial attempts, they will give up in despair.

Strangely enough, it is better not to overpraise the improvements. Rimm's Law #4 explains this: Overreactions by parents or teachers to children's successes and failures lead them to feel either intense pressure to succeed or despair and discouragement in dealing with failure. If the children receive exultation or too much excitement for their first A, it has a surprising effect on many of them. They seem to immediately stop working, and the grade drops dramatically. Interviews with children after such experiences provide insights into why this happens. One young man pointed out that his mother's congratulations made him "feel as if she would expect all A's from now on." Another student explained that his teachers' excitement about his good grade made him feel as though they were surprised and didn't really believe he was that capable. Extreme enthusiasm seems to adversely affect kids whose internal locus of control and self-confidence are still precariously balanced.

Underachievers' self-expectations are the first things that need to be changed. These children believe that the whole business of achievement is related to luck or to generous teachers. Many of them have unrealistically high goals; they hope that their luck will suddenly change and that they will become the A+ student they dream of being. They don't believe that their efforts will make a difference, and they are quick to refer to the lucky times they received good grades effortlessly. Depending on the extent and pattern of their underachievement, they either expect a magical solution or they believe that even if they make an effort, nothing will be different. Sometimes they assure the adults in their lives that the intelligence tests used to set expectations for them are too easy and shouldn't be used as an indication that they have the ability to do such difficult work.

Children should be given a clear road map of what is likely to happen if they decide that they would like to become achievers. They should be assisted in establishing reasonable grade goals and timeframes for attaining those goals. Parents and teachers must express their belief that the children can achieve those goals. Students should know that adults in their environment will be patient while they are making new attempts. They should realize that while working, they will sometimes feel stressed, impatient, and disappointed in themselves, but that all of these feelings are signs of motivation and a true index that they are on the correct route.

Sometimes children have so little confidence in themselves that it is appropriate to share with them actual test scores to prove undeniably that they do have the ability to achieve. Although disclosure of children's actual IQ scores is inappropriate, describing their range of abilities is reasonable. Explaining that their test scores show above-average or superior ability should be sufficient to give them confidence. You might also use percentiles. However, a too-high percentile may have the unintended effect of pressuring children. They may assume that, based on such high percentiles, their parents may expect them to accomplish higher grades than they feel capable of. Showing these kids your unwavering belief that they can achieve at higher levels, and pairing that with a constructive insistence on effort, is extraordinarily important to their achievement.

Achieving adults can point out the adults in their own childhood environments who believed in them. They may also be able to name those who did not. However, without the former group of believers, they would not have succeeded. Sometimes those who believed in them were parents, sometimes teachers or friends. Communicating positive expectations to your children is a very high priority for their improved perceptions of themselves.

However, having positive expectations is not the same as having too-high expectations. Parents who have read biographies of eminent people and have discovered the importance of parental belief in children will often try to motivate their children by pointing out their "brilliance." "Your art is as wonderful as Picasso's," "Your poetry will be published when you are discovered," and "You'll make it to Harvard" are examples of unrealistic statements of confidence that are sometimes given by parents to underachieving students. These students are soon paralyzed by their disappointments in themselves. The unrealistic belief that children will suddenly be recognized as extraordinary does little to give them hope and only exaggerates their sense of disappointment about their own poor performance.

Changing student self-expectations can also be accomplished in schools or counseling centers. These expectations can be modified by children's teachers or counselors using the same flexible guidelines recommended for parents. Class groups or small subgroups can also be used for changing self-expectations. Figure 10.1 includes topics used in group therapy at Family Achievement Clinic, as well as in some school classroom groups for changing self-expectations. School counselors may also have the opportunity to modify peer expectations by using these group approaches.

Figure 10.1. Discussion Topics for Students in Small Group Sessions

- Competition: Game Playing—Discussion of Feelings
- Competition: Comparison to Sports
- Peer Relations: Popularity versus Friendship—Reading and Discussion: *It's Dumb to Be Smart*
- Competition and Siblings—Reading and Discussion: *Brothers and Sisters*
- Pressure: How to Cope, and How Much Is Too Much
- Leadership versus "Bossyship": Understanding the Difference
- Understanding Parents
- Responsibility and Organization
- Perfectionism
- Creative Problem Solving

Parent Expectations

How do you determine reasonable expectations for your child? IQ scores remain the most useful guidelines we have, although they are not entirely reliable. There is no excellent way of measuring children's abilities. Below are some factors that you should consider when setting your children's expectations based on IQ scores:

- An IQ score between 100 and 110 indicates average grade-level expectation in an average school district. With reasonable motivation, B and C grades could be expected, and reading and math should be at grade level.

- An IQ score between 110 and 120 (above-average range) predicts B grades in grade-level work, but elementary-grade children in this range who have good study habits can probably achieve A grades as well, depending on the evenness of their specific abilities.

- IQ scores above 120 (superior range) predict A and B grades. IQ becomes less important than study habits in determining grades for children in this range.

- IQ scores in the 130 and above range (very superior) suggest A's and B's in above-grade-level work, but this may also vary with strengths and weaknesses in specific abilities. Some children may have higher verbal than performance scores, while others may have higher performance scores. Thus, reading and social studies may be stronger than math and science or vice versa. It is very important that parents not give intellectually gifted children the message to "be normal," which they may interpret as "get average grades." These children should certainly be encouraged early to use their abilities to learn and to get good grades. They may need acceleration and enrichment beyond the typical curriculum.

- When setting expectations for your children, it is important to modify the expectations based on: (1) the approximate average IQ scores of the general school population, and (2) the academic grading system of the school, as well as of specific teachers. For example, the average IQ scores of a suburban school district may be around 120, and the average grade for a particular teacher may be B. Thus, a child with an IQ of 125 may be achieving well when attaining B grades, considering the school standard and the teacher's grading habits. Most school districts will be happy to tell you the average IQ score for the school. Teachers are less likely to feel comfortable telling you the average grade in their class. You should consider the student and the teacher environment when setting expectations.

These guidelines should be used for underachievers only, although IQ scores should never be considered as ceilings for any children. For children who perform well, their actual performance is a much more important indicator of their potential than their IQ test scores. If children's actual performance is better than their IQ scores predict, don't consider them "overachievers." Consider the inadequacy of IQ scores in prediction. If children are performing well, consider them to be *capable*. In our clinic work, we often find that for high achievers with average IQ test scores, later IQ test scores typically improve.

Before you attach too much credibility to IQ scores, it's important for parents and teachers to understand that although research finds IQ scores to remain constant for groups, IQ scores for individual underachievers often decline over time. Such IQ subtests as Vocabulary, Information, and Arithmetic Reasoning are heavily dependent on school learning and reading. If children are poor readers or do not enjoy reading, or if they are turned off to school, these subtest scores may register their lack of learning.

Adolescents may benefit from hearing that their IQ test scores have decreased. Although exact numbers are probably inappropriate to share, the concept that their lack of effort will cause them to become less capable is somewhat shocking to children and may actually serve as a motivator. In Family Achievement Clinic, we remind them that *if they don't use it, they lose it*; or *the harder they work, the smarter they become. Conversely, the less they work, the dumber they will feel—and may actually become.* These statements are intended to encourage a work ethic and a growth mindset.[1]

It is reasonable to set two expectations for your underachieving children: one short-term, and one long-term. The short-term expectation should be set conservatively, to a point just a little above the children's present grades, but the long-term expectation may be set a bit more optimistically. Goals set too high or too low are equally problematic for underachievers and may also be problematic for underachievers' parents. Parents should be as realistic as possible. If you place emphasis on effort, completing all work on time, and spending a reasonable amount of time studying for tests, students won't feel pressured, and grades will automatically improve.

When parents have set reasonable expectations for their children, they should share them with their children so that the children can incorporate them into their own change in expectations. Parents should provide some rationale for their expectations and should ask children for input to determine whether they consider them fair. Discussion of grade expectations should be arrived at by consensus, based on the parents' knowledge and the children's concerns. Don't be surprised if children set their grade goals higher than you have. Explain to your children that they may consider those grade expectations for long-term goals, but not initially. The too-high goals could provide an excuse for giving up. Finally, consistency between parents is very important in melding parents' new expectations with children's changed perceptions.

Sibling Expectations

When parents and underachieving children reach agreement on expectations, the next step is to inform siblings of the changed expectations. This should be done privately so that each sibling is given support for the expected change in status and a clear message by parents that any putting down of their sibling will be hurtful to all. If this communication is given in private to achieving children, the message is more likely to be taken seriously. Parents should explain that they will understand that their achieving children may have some uncomfortable or jealous feelings, but in the long run, a "whole smart family" will benefit everyone. Emphasis on the cooperation of the family enterprise rather than on competition is the key. Encourage achieving children to be supportive and tell them that you, their parents, will be looking for and admiring them for that support. They should view their sibling's achievements as something in which they can share without feeling that it diminishes their own personal accomplishments.

Teaching siblings to admire each other's performance is a valuable counterbalancing technique in dealing with children's difficult sibling rivalry feelings. If siblings are not included as part of the new expectation plan, you may find a "seesaw" effect taking place. As the underachieving child begins achieving, the balance may shift to cause the achieving child's performance to decline. This will not necessarily happen, but it is a risk if you ignore other siblings in your plan to change expectations of your underachiever. High achievers definitely express feelings of displacement that are important to attend to during the transition.

> Rachel, an eleventh-grade gifted high achiever, seemed to take a real pleasure in helping her ninth-grade underachieving brother get into trouble at home and in school. Although she mainly believed that she was doing this because she loved her brother, it was also clear that she viewed the reversal of his long-standing underachievement problems as threatening to her own standing in the family as being the "good kid."

When children argue that they may never do as well as their "smarter" brother or sister, you will want to reassure the underachieving child that there is no contest in the family and that he or she might still be smarter than the smartest in other families. Assure the underachiever that he or she has the capacity to do well with hard work and that you expect hard work, but it doesn't matter to you at all if the children in the family are first, second, or third because this is a "whole smart family."

Teacher Expectations

Teacher expectations are of critical importance in changing an underachiever's performance. Teachers tend to pay less attention to test scores and are much more attuned to children's past performance—because past performance is usually the best predictor of future effectiveness. However, because parents, teachers, and children are now in a "change" mode, it is particularly important that teachers personally invest in expecting improvement. They may use IQ scores as a guide, but it's important not to use them as a limit to children's performance capabilities. If scores have decreased regularly or are inconsistent, teachers who use these scores might set goals for these children that are too low.

In addition to anticipating better performance by underachievers, teachers should inform the children of their higher expectations. As with parents, when children show success, it's important not to over-react, but rather to display casual pleasure in their achieving what are now reasonable performances. Noticing stronger effort and valuing the child's harder work is of greatest importance. Changing the mindset of students so that they consider the brain as a muscle will help children value the importance of "working out" by learning.[2]

It is equally important not to overreact to occasional setbacks en route to building a consistent achievement pattern because these, too, should be anticipated. A written note of confidence and reassurance of expected future success is often effective. Comments on paper become important communicators of encouragement. Private messages feel much more per-sonal and thoughtful than those given orally in front of the class, and public messages may feel embarrassing, particularly to adolescents.

An important caution: Teachers who insist that children will not make an effort will find exactly what they expect. Negative teacher expectations can be damaging, while positive expectations can turn a child around. Here's a true story:

> It was the first teacher conference of the new year—a time when teachers may not yet know all of the parents of their students. Ms. Dunn, a fourth-grade teacher, had two "Briannas" in her class. One was an excellent student, positive, and well-adjusted; the other had multiple problems and was very negative.

> When the second Brianna's parents came for conference, Ms. Dunn mistook them for the first Brianna's parents. She welcomed them with an enthusiastic description of their daugh-ter's positive attitude, only to be greeted by shocked expressions. She immediately realized her mistake, but rather than embarrass herself and the parents, she continued her discussion about a "few areas" where Brianna needed improvement.

> The parents left the conference feeling more positive about their daughter than ever before and conveyed this excitement to Brianna. The next day, to Ms. Dunn's surprise, Brianna entered school with a big smile and a new, positive attitude. Her self-confidence and her school efforts were completely transformed.

She ended the school year with B's instead of the usual D's that had been typical of earlier report cards. A chance *faux pas* had led to a dramatic change for this girl.[3]

Yes, it really is a true story!

Peer Expectations

The effect of peer expectations on achievement is very different in elementary school than it is in middle and high school. However, at all levels, peers have a definite impact on the reversal of Underachievement Syndrome.

At the elementary level, the "dummy" or "troublemaker" of the class is in an unpopular position. Teachers become the interpreter to the class of who the "dummies" and "troublemakers" are. Much of this can be avoided if teachers can manage to keep most negative comments private yet make some positive comments public. Obviously, teachers can't be expected to manage that kind of control at all times. However, they will generally set the peer expectations of student achievement by their comments about each child. Because they are in a powerful position to influence negative peer expectations, they are in an equally strong position to affect positive change in peer expectations.

Teachers should be careful to make positive statements gradually and not as if a miracle of transformation is taking place. As mentioned previously, an overreaction to an underachiever's early success may cause that child to give up if he or she isn't consistently successful. Peers will accept a new image of success if underachievers are gradually given increased recognition for achievement and decreased negative feedback. Positive peer acceptance will follow easily.

When a teacher wants to help a student with a behavior problem, it is often tempting to suggest, in the name of cultivating kindness, that the class cooperate to help the student with the problem. Unfortunately, the exact opposite will result. The more teacher-class referential talk there is about the child's problem, the less the child feels he or she can do about it. Many stubborn problems have been eradicated by the elimination of teacher-class referential discussion. Here's a classic example:

Alisha was an elective mute. She had not spoken even once in her classroom or on the playground from kindergarten through the end of first grade. Many behavior modification strategies had been tried without success. At home, Alisha talked comfortably and didn't seem shy at all.

Alisha's parents were asked to discontinue all referential discussion about the school problem. Her teacher was asked to discontinue class participation in the project of helping Alisha talk and to not even take notice if the girl spoke accidentally. These behavior modification strategies were kept private, and Alisha was informed that no one much cared if she talked or not. It was entirely her choice as to whether or not she wished to speak in school.

Approximately six weeks later, after expectations were subdued, Alisha began talking normally. The problem disappeared, and the teacher found herself facetiously admonishing Alisha to stop the flood of words. The elimination of home and class referential talk had changed Alisha's expectations for herself.

There are some key words that teachers can use to change descriptions of children in the class and reduce negative expectations. Examples are included in Figure 10.2.

Figure 10.2. Reducing Negative Expectations in the Classroom

Negative	Positive
• Scott has strange ideas.	• Scott has creative insights.
• Sherice, don't be so bossy.	• Sherice, you're a good leader. Here's a suggestion to guide you.
• Quinton, the slowpoke, is finally done.	• Quinton, you're doing quality work. I'm glad you don't speed through it.
• The class is waiting for Colin to organize his materials again.	• Almost everyone is organized. I'll set my stopwatch for 15 seconds so that everyone can be ready.

Changing peer expectations in middle and high school is a very different matter. Here, teachers are much less effective in influencing peers, although well-liked teachers can continue to make positive differences in peer acceptance. If underachievers are part of a peer group with pro-school attitudes, their improved achievement may be viewed by their friends as what might be expected of them, and thus they find encouragement from their friends. However, if underachievers are part of an anti-school peer group, improved grades may make them unacceptable to friends. Parents may want to talk to their children about actually changing friendship groups. However, it might seem impossible to move children into a different peer group in light of their reputation and school performance.

When parents ask their children to change peer groups, the children may not agree. Emphasizing that even adults are affected by peer pressures may help these children understand that adults are not "talking down" to them in this request. Of course, the children enjoy their present peers and feel included by them, so parents can't expect ready acceptance. Encouraging children to join more than one group may help. Children often like to consider themselves able to bridge different crowds.

In some cases, when peers are extremely negative, changing schools is a reasonable alternative. A change should not be made hastily, though, because many children may simply gravitate toward negative peers in the new school. However, a move from public to private school or the reverse, coupled with new achievement efforts, may facilitate a child's being accepted by a new set of peers.

Research indicates that peer groups have a mediating impact on adolescent achievement. One study found that achievement of adolescents who were parented well decreased if their peers were not achievers—and that the reverse was also true. Even when adolescents came from families in which parenting was inadequate, participation in positive peer groups improved their achievement.[4]

There may also be cultural and gender peer pressure on adolescents who carry too many books or appear too studious. In a study of 8,000 high school students, it was found that only 10% of high achievers would acknowledge association with the "brain" crowd. The percentage was slightly lower for females and somewhat higher for Asian-American students. Among African-Americans, none of the students wished to be associated with the "brains."[5] High achieving African-Americans may be called "acting white" by their peers, and studious American Indians may be chastised as "apples" (red on the outside and white on the inside). In addition, girls take the risk of being considered too smart by some boys who find their intelligence threatening. To ignore adolescent peer pressure is to miss an important issue in the discussion of underachievement. Here's an example:

> Andre, an African-American sixth grader, was asked what he
> had learned from the reversal of his underachievement that he

could share with other kids. He had two suggestions: they should start their year off on the right foot, and they should stay friends with kids who wanted to get good grades.

Placing a student in special education classes should always be done with great care. Children who are labeled "emotionally disturbed," "mentally retarded," or "behaviorally disabled" often have great difficulty dealing with peer expectations. Adults must weigh the value of the educational or emotional support that the children receive in the special classroom against negative expectations that peers will probably establish. It's always a difficult decision for parents and educators to make. In most school districts, all children are entitled to an attempt at inclusion in regular classes. Whenever it's possible, inclusion is best for children because negative labels cause them to lose confidence and to be excluded from peer groups.

This is why special education can have the unintended effect of reinforcing an underachievement pattern. For example, dependent underachievers are frequently and mistakenly placed in classes for the learning disabled or educable mentally retarded because their behavior resembles that of slow learners or learning-disabled children. Learning disability classes often provide the one-to-one and small group help that reinforces these children's and their teachers' perceptions that they can learn only on a one-to-one basis. Dominant underachievers are more frequently placed in classes for the emotionally or behaviorally disturbed. The students' determination to control the classroom causes them to be viewed as having behavioral problems that are not easily solvable in a regular classroom without outside psychological help.

Special placements reinforce these children's sense of being different. Peers who are not receiving special help label these children as "unusual" or worse. At the secondary level, special education students are often expected to find friends only among others in similar classes. Thus, many of the educational efforts intended by parents and educators to be helpful have very negative and not easily measured side effects. Negative peer expectations adversely affect personal self-confidence for many years and may impede the reversal of underachievement patterns.

Whether children with diagnosed disabilities should be labeled as such is controversial. The misdiagnosing of underachieving children as learning disabled, mentally handicapped, or emotionally disturbed is a much more serious problem because the label limits expectations by teachers, family, and peers. This inappropriate categorization literally stops the effective reversal of Underachievement Syndrome. Schools have become very aware of this problem; however, diagnosis is still difficult. Figure 11.15 in Chapter 11 lists differences between learning-disabled children and dependent underachievers. Some schools have effectively used the Trifocal Model for children who appeared to have special educational needs and have prevented dependent underachievers from being placed in special classes.[6]

Role Model Identification

Children learn appropriate behaviors more easily when they have effective models to imitate—Rimm's Law #2. As you may recall from Chapter 3, the process by which children select and unconsciously copy family models is called *identification*. When underachievers spontaneously reverse patterns of underachievement, they frequently cite important persons who were pivotal in their change of direction. These adults were the models with whom they identified and from whom they adopted adjustment patterns, work habits, studying practices, and general life philosophies and career goals. Several people may serve as models for any one person. However, the adults in an individual's immediate environment are especially important. Children and adolescents frequently refer to some adults around them as people they would like to grow up to be like.

Because imitation of models is so important to the reversal of underachievement, we should focus on the sources of models, as well as the processes by which we can encourage identification with appropriate models. Sometimes the models chosen may not be appropriate for achievement motivation.[7] Children may choose rock stars, sports heroes, and multi-millionaires about whom legends of miraculous and magical success are woven. They imitate these unrealistic models in their dress, speech, and musical styles. "Real people" models seem inadequate by comparison because they're not as prestigious as the stage and sports idols.

Underachievers tend to select these idols as models to be copied without any thought about the process by which these persons have arrived at such a lofty height and without any conception of the many thousands who have fallen by the wayside in competition. They would rather fantasize in rapturous expectation about the miraculous discovery of their own hidden talent than invest in the more mundane efforts that would build their skills toward a realistic goal. Hero fantasy is not harmful in itself, but when it becomes a substitute for effort and for the emulation of more realistic models, it can prevent the necessary learning of skills that would lead to achievement. Fantasy becomes an excuse for avoiding responsibility.

Sources of Models

For many children, family members are the best source of identification models. Fathers and mothers, if they are positive and achievement-oriented, are ideal. It's important, however, that their achievement orientation be visible to their children because children can only copy what they see. Thus, if parents' positive-thinking "work selves" are reserved for the workplace, and only their grouchy, negative selves are displayed at home, there is little opportunity for beneficial emulation.

Although this seems obvious enough when you think about it, many parents are not sensitive to the selves that they present to their children. The achievement orientation that they would like their children to imitate is frequently invisible. Since it is not possible for most children to see their parents in the workplace, mothers and fathers should interpret and describe their jobs to their children. This interpretation should include enthusiasm, challenge, effort, and satisfaction if it is to convey a suitable work message.

It is certainly realistic and honest to mention discouragement, frustration, and failure experiences to your kids, but if you always describe your work negatively, then there will be no reason for them to be inspired toward effort. They will see only a negative achievement model and will use it as a rationale for either rejecting their parents as models or adopting their parents' negative attitudes. They become anti-work kids. They will convince themselves that they don't want to work hard because they prefer a value system that is much better than that of their parents—a "fun" ethic that avoids drudgery and is based on a happy-go-lucky lifestyle.

Selecting parents as appropriate role models is the most practical way of teaching achievement motivation. To do this successfully, parents must convey what is reasonably interesting and fulfilling about their work.

Many parents in our society are not happy with their work but see no alternative opportunities for earning a livelihood. They may, indeed, feel as though they are in "dead-end" jobs but do accept the responsibility of making a living despite their desire for more interesting work. They cannot honestly share good news about satisfaction derived from accomplishment. However, they can tell their children about products or services that they contribute to, or they can at least discuss with them the pride that they take in being responsible. If they get themselves to work on time and are committed to performing well on the job without constant complaint, they, too, are good models for responsibility. In talking with their children, these parents may also wish to add that if they had continued their education, they might have had more choices of careers. They can hope that this message will encourage their children to study hard in school in order to broaden their own opportunities.

The increase in one-, three-, and four-parent families makes it challenging to help underachieving children view a parent's work favorably. Certainly, stepparents can be appropriate models. However, this becomes difficult if the children's birth parent criticizes and belittles the stepparent. Children can look to both parents and stepparents as role models if the adults involved respect each other.

Certainly, other relatives, including grandparents, uncles, aunts, and cousins, may also be good models for emulation. These models need not be frequently available because descriptions of their activities can partly substitute for their actual presence. Oddly enough, parents or grandparents who are deceased can also be good role models for children. Stories about a grandparent's achievement, perseverance, or risk taking can be tailored to children's special needs, and of course, the real grandparent is not there to show any contradictions.

Older siblings can also be important as role models. Younger children typically admire their older siblings, and it takes only a small step beyond admiration to build that important identification. However, when parents make comparisons deliberately, they will quickly be told, "Don't always compare me to my sister or brother." In addition, if older siblings have not yet managed to focus their own lives, identification with them can bring problems. Parents have good reason to worry that a younger sibling will follow in the footsteps of a rebellious adolescent. That older sibling appears very powerful to younger sisters or brothers.

Teachers are especially valuable as models. Children often report the special admiration that they feel for a particular teacher. They may spontaneously choose one as a model, and particular teachers may have dozens of students who aspire to be like them. However, it takes very special teachers to win the admiration of students, and only exceptional teachers are willing to invest the time and effort to guide the youths who see them as identification figures. Teachers can make positive differences to literally hundreds of underachieving students during their careers, although their day-to-day routines and responsibilities may prevent them from sensing the impact that they are making. Kids hardly ever thank their teachers for the differences they make because it may be years before they understand the teachers' impact on their lives.

For children without appropriate role models, teachers fill an important vacuum. In a society where the structure of marriage is so precarious, positive and caring teacher models become even more critical to children. Here's a letter from a student about his teacher:

> After I finished sixth grade, I started seventh grade at middle school. Middle school was very different from elementary school. I got a lot more homework than I did at elementary school, but I also got a lot more privileges.
>
> Eighth grade, so far, has been pretty good. Although my grades have dropped since I have been at middle school, I have also learned a lot since I have been here. The things I am talking about are not physical, but mental. I have learned a lot about myself and others from a very important person. Believe it or not, this person is a teacher. His name is Mr. Talbert. He is not a regular teacher; he is more like a father or something.
>
> There are about 24 of us in his class, and I feel that he has touched each and every one of us in a way I do not think anyone else on this earth could do. I know that he is my favorite teacher ever, and I am pretty sure he has some other great admirers. One of the reasons I enjoy him so much is because I think we are alike in many ways. In his class, we learn about the values of life and friendship. He has taught me more than social studies. He has taught me what life is all about.

In my research into the childhoods of successful women, women repeatedly thanked their teachers for inspiring them to success. ABC's *20/20* reporter Deborah Roberts thanked her eighth-grade English teacher who held her to high expectations, Jane Pauley thanked her debate coach for inspiring her toward her media career, and astronaut Cady Coleman credited her teachers in the gifted program for inspiring her toward science.[8] The list of those who appreciated their teacher's or counselor's inspiration could continue *ad infinitum*. Successful men and women typically attribute part of their success to the teachers who encouraged them.

In general, society should place a greater value on the role of educators so that children can view them as persons worthy of emulation. It is equally important that teachers value their roles as educators. There are some unfortunate cases of disgruntled teachers who use their classroom power to grieve to children about unfair administrative or school board practices. Others bemoan their choice of career to their students, thus unwittingly sharing powerlessness and preaching an anti-education message. The teaching profession is often not sufficiently honored or rewarded. Nevertheless, students are not the appropriate audience for teachers' complaints. Disenchanted teachers are poor role models for children in their classrooms and can have major negative impacts on underachieving oppositional youngsters.

Community leaders can also be models. Adults who invest their time in scouts, 4-H, religious youth groups, and athletic coaching can make that time commitment more valuable to children if they understand the importance of identification. As adults take special interest in young people, they can also become effective models. Although communities frequently find a scarcity of volunteers to lead youth, those who accept these volunteer responsibilities can make major contributions for many adolescents searching for adults to admire. If you serve in the significant role of youth leader, it is important for you to communicate to children the value of academic achievement.

Schools that implement the Trifocal Model may wish to include a community component, in which volunteers are invited to share with classes their stories of their achievements. Small group sessions can encourage questions and discussions. Mentorships, in which students are actually given opportunities to work with adults in the community, provide excellent opportunities for adopting role models. Local industries may encourage executives and supervisors to share their stories, and successful workers at every level can talk about achievement and accomplishment. Video-recorded sessions can provide opportunities for future students to share in especially interesting stories by appropriate role models. Kids value photographs and autographs of their heroes as well, and adults are often happy to oblige.

Peer models spontaneously influence youths who have not selected adult models. Peer imitation may be very problematic when the peer group is anti-school and anti-parents. Ironically, members of negative peer groups such as gangs can occasionally provide a good role model for some young people. Here's a case example:

Reverend Frost was a leader in the African-American community and was certainly an appropriate role model for the kids he was trying to help. He was an authority on gangs and had been a gang member as a child. As he discussed his own childhood role models, he explained that he watched one of his friends, with whom he had always felt competitive, leave the gang and go on to college. When he realized that his former friend had completed his first year of college successfully, he was encouraged to try college himself. Thus, this initially negative peer was the first model who inspired him to leave the gang and choose a very different lifestyle and educational opportunity. Later he acknowledged that there were many other important role models along his educational route.

Of course, positive peer groups provide a pro-academic message and encourage enthusiasm for study and learning. Peers may also serve as models for appropriate social behaviors, although it is difficult to point out another young person for imitation to an adolescent without engendering competition and resentment. However, younger children may be successfully guided toward selecting good models to improve awareness of staying on task in school, appropriate and enthusiastic hand raising, eye contact, pleasant or friendly body language, good manners, and general social skills.

When parents and teachers suggest that children copy others, it is important to remind them that the imitation should only be of specific skills that will be helpful to them. Asking children to actually copy another child's general actions is implicitly a comparison and is likely to decrease their self-confidence. However, calling attention to two or three behaviors for imitation is not likely to cause harm and makes the positive social learning process easier. Pointing out good behaviors is even more effective if the children that you suggest as models are already liked or admired by the children to whom you're making the recommendation. If they don't like or respect the child you're suggesting that they emulate, it won't work.

Fiction, history, films, and biography are rich with descriptive material to inspire youths toward perseverance, education, and heroism and can provide effective models for many children. Identifying similarities between their own lives and those of their heroes, and emphasizing how these achievers met failures and overcame them, can introduce young people to the pairing of struggle with success.

For underachievers, seeing the extensive time that their heroes invested in work and practice will help them understand the amount of effort required to accomplish serious goals. Identifying with such heroes should help young people realistically assess their own efforts and talents and can provide positive models for success. Unfortunately, society has many heroes on stage and in sports who provide negative messages in their lifestyles. Children are easily inspired to follow these models because of their attractiveness, power, and wealth. In guiding youth in adopting heroes as models for achievement, parents should provide the criteria for quality that their children will hopefully choose to follow.

Process for Encouraging Identification

"When I was your age, I remember having some of those very same feelings" may be the sincere statement of fact that ties a child to an adult in an identification relationship. For a child, this makes the grown-up very human and approachable. It also encourages the child to see similarities between him- or herself and that adult.

A precaution to follow in establishing your similarity to a child is that you don't want to become a model for underachievement. For example, if you say, "I was an underachiever and outgrew the problem," then your child may assume that he, too, will automatically outgrow his problem. You may recall that two of the three variables that lead to unconscious copying of an adult model are nurturance and similarities between the two. In a statement that couples personal concern and similarity, the adult may be taking a big step in influencing a child to find personal direction. The third variable to enhance identification is power, but all three variables need not be present for imitative learning to take place. In deliberately selecting models for role model identification, similarities between adult and child are helpful; however, it is certainly wiser to look for positive similarities.

Unfortunately, when children are underachieving and have poor self-concepts or are oppositional, they are likely to be attracted to inappropriate models who share the same talents, experiences, and underachieving attitudes. Thus, young adults who may not have established their own identities, or who may be confused about their own direction, may be readily available negative models for underachieving teenagers. Because they are older and appear more experienced, powerful, and exciting, youths who see their own frustrations as similar to those of flashy young adults are ready prey. The young adults may think that they can help these youths, with whom they may counteridentify, and the helping process gives them a sense of personal self-importance. However, because neither truly has a sense of realistic direction, they may flail—and fail—together. Young adults who attract high school youths to rock performance groups, traveling drama troupes, an arts community, or a religious cult provide models and inspiration to these youths. They offer temporary security, shelter, and support for the youths' opposition to their parents. These rarely are permanent or positive, and in the process, educational opportunity doors may be closed. Sometimes these adolescents drop out of school or give up college scholarships. Sometimes they alienate their families irreparably.

How can you avoid these negative identifications? Protect your children from the vacuum that evolves when potentially appropriate models no longer see anything positive in your adolescents. When parents and teachers continually criticize children, the children cannot select these critics as models. Avoid this negative cycle so often generated by rebellious adolescents. Search for the positive in children, and they will be more likely to follow your guidance in selecting environments in which they will be surrounded by appropriate role models.

Music, art, language, science, computer and drama summer camps, youth travel, camping groups, and special schools may be effective in channeling adolescents' choices of models. Visiting an out-of-town family member and taking a career-oriented job can allow your children to encounter positive models. Changing the physical setting can have the effect of preventing the children from following the "path of least resistance" and inspiring them by exposure to people who are positively involved in growth experiences. An environment in which adolescents are surrounded by other motivated young people who share their interests and by dedicated teachers who inspire them can be pivotal in giving purpose to underachieving children. Increasing numbers of such opportunities are being made available by camps, universities, and private schools during the summer months. An inspirational summer can make a difference, particularly if participants maintain communication during the school year.

A one-to-one parent-child adventure is an excellent way to encourage identification with a parent model. A negative father-son relationship or stepfather situation can change into a pairing of admirers after the two have shared a week-long camping or boating experience. A one-to-one car travel adventure, in which two family members are not distracted by parent or sibling rivalry or pressures of the job or school, can provide the bonding that causes two formerly oppositional individuals to admire and respect each other. Children may see, for the first time, reasons to admire and copy qualities of their parents. One spectacular week can provide a strong foundation for positive identification and emulation. It can melt the opposition and provide a solid basis for parents to influence and guide their children. Although the parent who stays home may feel left out of the experience, a loving, kind, well-meaning mother or father can unconsciously interfere with the one-to-one bonding that had been lacking earlier. Father-son, mother-daughter, mother-son, and father-daughter trips can be extremely effective for healing wounds and building new close relationships.

Correcting Deficiencies

The next step of underachievement reversal is the least difficult, but it cannot be neglected or the entire plan may fail. Underachievers who are faring poorly in school may not have learned basic educational skills that will be necessary for their further success. For very gifted children, skills gaps may be minimal, but for most children, depending on the length of time of their problem and on their abilities, there may be major deficits in their skills. The subject areas fall into four basic categories: reading, writing, math, and language.

A tutorial system is most expedient for efficiently eliminating skills gaps. However, there are a great many risks in one-to-one instruction. Therefore, Figure 10.3 includes some suggestions that tutors should follow to avoid reinforcing Underachievement Syndrome.

Figure 10.3. Tips for Tutors

- Avoid fostering dependence. Explain concepts, and then have children demonstrate their understanding. Insist on independent problem solving and carry-through of assignments. Children should absolutely *not* have someone sitting by their side as they complete all of their assignments. Encourage them to push their own limits.
- Provide a goal-oriented framework for the students, including timelines and the charting of accomplishment. Tutoring should feel purposeful. Will they be able to test out to a higher reading or math group? Can they learn to write for a school newspaper? When they achieve their goal, will they be able to choose to discontinue tutoring?
- Move children through material as quickly as they can handle the skills. These are bright children receiving individualized instruction. The sense of rapid progress will encourage their confidence in their achievement and will generalize to their classroom.
- Poor tutoring can reinforce the underachieving pattern. Good tutoring can provide a springboard to better achievement in school. Underachieving children can easily trap tutors into their manipulations. Tutors, therefore, should understand children's patterns to avoid the trap and help them correct the deficiencies as quickly as possible.

Source: Rimm, S. B. (2005). *How to Raise a Happy, Achieving Child, 15*(3). Watertown, WI: Educational Assessment Service.

Anxieties and Special Skill Deficits

Although some recommendations will be included in the following chapters, special tips for reading, writing, math, and listening anxieties are described in Figures 10.4, 10.5, 10.6, and 10.7.

Figure 10.4. Tips for Reducing Reading Anxiety

Reading is a first-priority subject for comfortable learning in the classroom. For children who don't care for reading or who struggle with learning to read, the educational process will be considerably more difficult. Special recommendations for children with reading problems will help parents and teachers guide children toward self-confidence and independence, despite their reading problems.

- Children should not be forced to read aloud to their parents at home because the parents' anxieties about their children's reading may be conveyed to the children. Most parents feel tense when poor readers read aloud to them. Children may, of course, read aloud if they choose to do so. Also, as adult readers, they will rarely find oral reading important.

- Parents should read aloud to their children as long as the children enjoy it (eighth grade is not too old).

- Children should be permitted to stay up half an hour later at night if they're in their beds reading to themselves (children don't usually like to sleep; it's adults who do).

- Encourage children to read whatever they like during that pre-bedtime half-hour. Don't insist that they read grade-level material. Comics, cartoons, sports magazines, easy material, and books read multiple times are all good for reading enjoyment. If they love reading, they will expand their interests as their reading improves.

- Encourage children to read stories while listening to recordings of the stories. Don't hover over them to be sure they're actually reading; they will eventually.

- Model reading by keeping a book around that your children see you enjoying. Newspapers and magazines also serve well.

- Encourage children to read to their younger siblings, provided that those siblings aren't better readers than they are. They shouldn't do this in their parents' presence, but alone with their sisters or brothers.

- Visit and browse through bookstores and libraries in your travels or on shopping trips.

Source: Rimm, S. B. (2001). *Sylvia Rimm On Raising Kids Newsletter, 12*(2). Watertown, WI: Educational Assessment Service.

Figure 10.5. Tips for Reducing "Pencil Anxiety" (Processing Speed)

If your children write slowly and therefore hate writing, they can overcome this problem. Many elementary school-age children have uneven development; the small muscle coordination needed for printing and writing seems to develop more slowly than other thinking and learning abilities. This seems to be a more frequent problem for boys than for girls. (Surprisingly, it has no effect on their use of screwdrivers, Legos, or computer games.) Some children with writing speed difficulties may simply solve problems more slowly than others, and parents and teachers may wish to obtain formal testing of these children's mental Processing Speed to determine if this is a factor.

Whether or not assignments are timed, these children often develop an anxiety related to written work because they may lag behind their classmates in completing assignments. They equate fast with "smart," and they search for ways to avoid feeling "dumb." They may not finish their work or do fast and careless work and make excuses about written work being boring. These easily become bad habits that may cause children to learn to dislike writing and to develop anxieties about written assignments.

Here are some general suggestions that may help children who have "pencil anxiety":

- Occupational therapy is often helpful, especially for young children.

- Encourage your children's use of the computer for all drafts when writing stories or reports.

- Ask your children to talk their story into a microphone before actually writing it. This will allow them to get their ideas out.

- Permit your children to use fine-line markers or number 2 pencils for assignments—whichever seem to work better.

- Have your children practice this "speeding" exercise. It's a personal self-competition model. They will need a stopwatch and multiple sheets of the same written material to copy. They first copy the material and set a baseline time to record on a calendar. The next day, they write the same material and mark the time. The goal is to beat their own time. Writing the same material every day may get boring, but they'll soon find that they can write much faster. They'll become much more relaxed about timed tests if timing becomes a daily habit and they can see their improvement. The selections they choose for writing can be short or long depending on their age and can be varied every week or two. This same approach can also be used for speeding math fact knowledge.

- Children who write slowly may not score up to their ability on timed tests. Time limits may have to be extended.

- Change expectations by making specific comments that emphasize that intelligence and speed are not the same. Some examples of things you can say follow:

  Although some intelligent children finish work quickly, other very intelligent children are slow workers.

  Quality is more important than quantity.

  Authors always write many drafts before they feel satisfied.

  Although some assignments require fast writing, others are best completed slowly.

Source: Rimm, S. B. (2008). *Sylvia Rimm On Raising Kids Newsletter, 18*(3). Watertown, WI: Educational Assessment Service.

Figure 10.6. Tips for Helping Children with Math or Spatial Disabilities

Teachers often describe their feelings about tutoring students who have inordinate difficulty learning mathematics in this way:

When I explain the mathematics concept to the students, they seem to catch on to the explanation. However, two hours later, they no longer seem to understand it—almost as if I had never taught it.

One can't predict whether these students will continue to have problems in math or whether the problem is related only to memory. The serious concern related to an inability to learn basic math facts is that children lose confidence in their capacity to do all math. That's the advantage of identifying the real root of the problem. If memory is the issue, an emphasis on concrete counting techniques such as using tokens or calculators and computers can permit them to function well in math class. If mathematical concepts are difficult for children to understand, real-life shopping or work problems will help them to concretize abstract concepts.

Sometimes children's early math problems are related to spatial disabilities. Difficulty doing puzzles; telling time; counting money; understanding maps, geography, and directions; solving math story problems; comprehending geometry; and working with computers are symptomatic of spatial problems. A school psychologist can test the student for spatial disabilities.

Regardless of the cause of the math problems, many games are excellent for developing number concepts and spatial skills that contribute to better math competence, especially board games involving money. Games that can help build these basic skills include Monopoly, Chinese checkers, dominoes, card games like War and Go Fish, checkers, chess, puzzles, video games, tangrams, Concentration, Legos, and blocks.

Your children may require tutoring for many years if they continue to struggle with math. This disability may cause them to lose some self-confidence. Because the problem seems to be at least partially genetic, you can't expect to completely change it, but only to improve it somewhat with practice or by making creative adjustments when required. Although a lack of math skills will reduce career choices, there remain many opportunities available for verbal young people.

Source: Rimm, S. B. (2001). *Sylvia Rimm On Raising Kids Newsletter, 12*(2). Watertown, WI: Educational Assessment Service.

Figure 10.7. Tips for Improving Listening Skills

Our media-driven society has provided children with opportunities to access information and entertainment from television, movie, and computer screens almost since birth. Perhaps because visual stimuli are omnipresent, many children have poor auditory processing skills. Our clinical experience has found that practice with using only auditory stimuli can enhance listening skills.

Here are some listening suggestions that may help your children process auditory verbal stimuli better:

- Books on tape
- Stories on radio
- Sports casting on radio
- Personal storytelling
- Poetry readings
- Participation in two-way conversations
- Establishing eye contact when giving instructions

Scotopic Sensitivity

Some children have a reading disability known as scotopic sensitivity, which can be corrected by colored lenses. For some of these children, reading can be improved using various colored plastic overlays. Typically, children who have scotopic sensitivity have inherited the problem from a family member who has also had reading problems. The recommendations to diminish reading anxiety (Figure 10.4) are also applicable for these children, and they can show dramatic reading comprehension improvement.[9]

The Last Step

The final step of the Underachievement Syndrome treatment plan, correction, is divided into three sections, discussed in Chapters 11, 12, and 13. I recommend that you read all three chapters regardless of your child's or student's diagnosis. Then select the modifications to be made at home and at school that are most appropriate for your child or student.

Chapter 11

What You Can Do for Dependent Children

The recommended environmental changes for dependent children are the same for both conformers and nonconformers. You may be tempted to assume that the first group will outgrow their minor problems. This outgrowth is unlikely unless responses change at home and school. Parents and teachers who are willing to interpret the problems and react to these children in new, counterintuitive ways will alter the habits that have maintained their Underachievement Syndrome.

Suggestions for parents will be given first, followed by ideas for teachers. It will be helpful to parents and teachers to read both groups of suggestions because they sometimes overlap. Although you should expect much more effort from these children, you can also continue to communicate with them in a kind, sensitive manner while they gradually gain courage and confidence.

What You Can Do as Parents

Understanding the causes and characteristics of your children's underachievement patterns is the first important component of change. However, as kind and sympathetic parents, you may have difficulty finding the courage to replace many of the reinforcements that you have accidentally and intuitively provided to your children. As responses are modified, you may fear that you're not being sufficiently sympathetic or supportive. You might feel guilty about the ways in which you are parenting and may even think of yourself as unkind or inadequate. You may worry that these differences will cause your children to suffer further or fail. You might sense so much internal pressure about your fear of their failure that you experience anxiety, as if these fears were for your own personal failures. Because any or all of this is likely to happen to you, read the following words of encouragement several times before you begin making modifications:

- If you don't permit your children to work independently now, they will surely fail later and blame you for that failure.

- If you overprotect and do too much for your children, they will resent you for stealing away their independence.

- Your children can't learn independently when you don't believe that they are capable of independence.

- Your children's dependence causes you to unintentionally diminish their self-confidence.

- If your children use tears, whining, complaints, physical ailments, or non-eating as manipulations, you are being unkind if you respond to them as though they were truly suffering.

These precautions should help you through the difficult days ahead. If you have the courage to weather these changes, be assured that you will feel more confident as a parent, and after your children's initial struggles are accomplished, you will enjoy with delight their rapid growth in competence and confidence.

Vote of Confidence

Don't do for your children those things that they are capable of doing and should do for themselves. Any child development book will indicate what typical children of your children's ages and stages should be doing. Dressing, washing, doing chores, and most important, doing homework should require little, if any, help from you. If your children are accustomed to reminders, nagging, sympathy, and assistance, they have learned to get you to focus your attention on their dependence.

You need to learn to refocus that valued attention to the completed task. Remove yourself physically from the scene of attention-getting dependence, but be available and quietly complimentary when the job is complete. To give you an example of how you can do this, compare the two examples in Figure 11.1 for dependent and independent morning routines. If your children are dependent, they probably fit the first example. Try the instructions in the second example to strengthen their morning independence without nagging. Add a timer to make a game of it.

Figure 11.1. Morning Routines

Morning Routine #1 (Dependent)

Mom: Michael, are you up?
Michael: (No answer)
Mom: Michael, it's time to get up!
Michael: Um...awfully tired...a few more minutes.
Mom: Michael, you'd better get up. You'll miss the bus! (Repeated with increasing volume three to 10 times)

This is only the beginning. Admonitions to wash face; brush teeth; eat breakfast; hurry; wear different clothes; remember lunch money, schoolbooks, notes; and finally, warnings about the soon-to-arrive school bus or carpool add to the din. Arguments between siblings on bathroom use, clothes exchange, and breakfast choices punctuate the distressing beginning of the day. If two parents are awake, interparent debate about the degree of nagging reinforces the hassled start to each new morning.

Morning Routine #2 (Independent)

Step 1: Announce to your children one at a time the guidelines for the new beginning. From this day forth, they will be responsible for getting themselves ready for school. Your job will be to await them at the breakfast table for a pleasant morning chat.

Step 2: Night-before preparations include the laying out of their clothes and getting their books ready in their book bags. An evening checklist will let them prepare without your help. They should set the alarm early enough to allow plenty of morning time. They will feel just as tired at 7 A.M. as they will at 6:30, but the earlier start will prevent their usual rush.

Step 3: Children wake themselves up (absolutely no calls from others), wash, dress, and pick up their room. A morning checklist can help them to remember each task. Breakfast comes only when they are ready for school. Absolutely *no* nagging!

Step 4: A parent (or parents) *waits* at the breakfast table and is not anywhere around them prior to their meal together. Then, enjoy a pleasant family breakfast and conversation about the day ahead.

Step 5: (Optional) If the children are ready early and enjoy a morning television program, they can watch until it's time to leave.

Morning Routine #2 (Independent) Q & A

Question: What happens if the kids don't dress in time for breakfast?
Answer: No breakfast. (This will only happen two or three times!)
Question: What happens if my children don't like to eat breakfast?
Answer: Offering 15 minutes of TV after breakfast, when they're ready for school, will probably be effective.

Question: What happens if they don't get up?

Answer: They miss school and stay in their room all day (this will happen no more than once), or you drive them to school and they pay you for taxi fare out of their allowance, or they ride their bikes or walk. They deal with the school consequence of being late. Don't write them notes to excuse them.

Question: What happens if they don't have enough time?

Answer: They go to bed 30 minutes earlier and set the alarm 30 minutes earlier until they find the right amount of time necessary for independent mornings.

Question: Does this routine really work?

Answer: Absolutely, with elementary-aged children; they hate to miss school. Sometimes, with high school students.

Source: Rimm, S. B. (1996). *Learning leads Q-Cards: Parent pointers.* Watertown, WI: Apple.

The ingredients of a parent's vote of confidence include: (1) encouraging and insisting on children's independence, (2) withdrawing your nagging attention from dependence, and (3) relocating that positive attention and reinforcement to the completion of the independent task. Make sure that there is a negative consequence that takes place if your children don't complete the task—for example, a child's not waking up and getting out of bed at the sound of the alarm could result in their having a shortened breakfast. The negative consequence should rarely be used but absolutely enforced if necessary. The positive should be emphasized. Try to voice confidence in your children, even if you don't feel it initially.

The steps below can be applied in reversing any dependent pattern. They fit well with bedtime routines, chores, trying new experiences, mealtimes, and of course, homework, which will be given special attention later.

- Explain the task to your children briefly, and include them in the plan of how they will complete it independently.

- Move your attention from an incomplete task to the completed task.

- Reward the children's completing the task with a pleasant consequence.

- Emphasize positive accomplishment, not potential negative consequences.

The Place of Shelter

Protection is certainly appropriate for children who are being physically or sexually abused by a parent. Sometimes shelter from verbal abuse is also necessary. However, if parents shelter their children from any harsh voice or reasonable demands for responsibility, they aren't helping them.

Mothers especially have a tendency to recoil from a husband's occasional scolding of their children and seem to fear that it will cause the children permanent damage. They may even consider it to be verbal abuse. Typically, these same mothers may scold and lose their own tempers without a similar concern for any negative impact of *their* scolding on the children. Evidently, these mothers hear their own voices as being quieter and gentler than their husbands'.

Children are resilient enough to deal with a loving parent's angry voice and need no cushion from the other parent. However, if parents lose their tempers frequently, this is an indication that they lack control of their children. Their children are not listening, respecting, or complying. The parent who provides a shelter or protection for the child being scolded is thereby encouraging the child to further disobey and giving the child permission to be disrespectful. If the scolding parent is demanding reasonable effort and discipline, the sheltering parent is reinforcing reduction of effort and avoidance of responsibility. Yet mothers and fathers often do this to each other. By undermining each other's requests and demands, they steal children's self-confidence. The sheltering parent teaches avoidance manipulations instead of helping children to develop competence and confidence. The protected children learn that when tasks are difficult or uncomfortable or involve high risk, it is appropriate to escape and search for protection rather than cope with the stressful challenge. These children are also learning to challenge a loving authority figure to whom they should be looking for leadership.

If you and your spouse have differing perspectives on child rearing and discipline, make some compromises. There is no single correct way to discipline except the one on which the two parents agree. It is better to be too strict or too lenient than to teach children to manipulate their parents to avoid responsibilities. The sheltering parent may feel like a good parent and more loved at the time that he or she provides shelter; however, as children grow more discerning, they are likely to label that parent as weak. The parent who views the sheltering as kindness will have difficulty interpreting the children's later lack of respect and will feel as if it is unearned rejection and punishment. Furthermore, both parents may get disgusted with their children as they watch the children's expertise in avoiding, making excuses, giving up, and complaining.

Of course, there is a place for shelter. If a parent is abusive, the other parent must assertively take a stand to protect the child, report the abuse, and receive shelter for self and children. This is a different form of protection and is unrelated to the dependency issue.

Encouraging Same-Gender Identification for Boys

The importance of modeling was discussed previously, but it must be reemphasized, particularly for boys. It is very important for boys' self-confidence and achievement to have a male identification figure. Mother-dependent and mother-identifying boys frequently have underachievement problems. There are two main reasons for this: first, they tend to achieve only when they receive more than the typical amount of attention and assistance because they are accustomed to too much attention in a too-close, one-to-one relationship with Mother; second, they tend to have social problems based on society's continued hostility toward boys who do not appear to fit the male gender stereotype.

For the mother who has a close one-to-one relationship with her verbally bright, delightful son—whom she adores and in whom she has tremendously invested herself—this request for a male role model may seem to be an impossible and unfair demand. Furthermore, because it isn't necessary to make a similar demand of fathers, this suggestion may be viewed by women's equity groups as a "call to arms." The only way that I can redeem myself is to remind you that even though the close one-to-one relationship of mother and child undoubtedly provided the child with his enhanced verbal ability and improved intelligence, this child must grow from dependence to independence. For a boy in our society, at least at this time, that growth seems much more difficult without identification with a male role model.

This is *not* a recommendation to mothers to sever relationships with their sons. The mother-son relationship is an important basis for the son's relationship to other women and ultimately to his wife, if he chooses to marry a woman. However, Mother must loosen the ties to permit growth and freedom.

The easiest way to encourage male identification with a father or stepfather is to permit the father or stepfather and the son some time together, including work and play activities that both enjoy. Hiking, fishing a quiet stream, cooking a meal together, or visiting an art show or sports event are relationship builders that seem effortless. Fathers, don't let your son bring his friends with him. The friend interferes with the father-son bonding.

Time constraints may be a major problem. Father may not have long vacation times and may either put a priority on spending time with the whole family or on being in the company of other men. Wives may not wish to be alone with the remainder of the family or give up valued time with their husbands. The special one-to-one father-son time may involve sacrifices and may be short. Nevertheless, the potential for quality relationship-building is so good that reasonable sacrifices should be made to make it possible. It can provide the basis for close identification that can serve as an inspiration for independence in young men.

Mothers should not be involved in orchestrating these male bonding experiences. The relationships should be established based on comfortable male communication terms. Too many boys know their fathers only through their mother's interpretations and don't ever build relationships with them. This causes a great void for many young men.

If you happen to be a fortunate woman who loves and respects her husband and you make that known to your son, you will be able to stand back and give them space for closeness. The necessary identification will follow spontaneously, and you will enjoy your son's confidence that comes with the change.

For homes without fathers or for situations in which fathers may not be appropriate models, there are substitute activities. Wilderness trips, work experiences, Big Brothers, Boy Scouts, and other situations that bring boys together in an intense living/working alliance encourage boys to deal with the challenge of independence and the discovery of appropriate male role models and behaviors.

Although there are many successful and happy young men who have been brought up without fathers in their households, there is a much greater risk of underachievement among boys brought up in single-parent homes led by females. Successful boys and young men can usually specify one or multiple male role models who influenced them. Coaches, band directors, bosses, teachers, ministers, college professors, and family physicians are often among their models.

Expressing Feelings

Everyone would agree that it is good for children to be in touch with their feelings and to understand and communicate their sadness, anger, or frustration. Certainly, it is not good for them to harbor thoughts without expressing them because then the feelings often become exaggerated. After feelings build up, one can become irrationally angry and can no longer identify the reason for the anger. It is better to teach children to talk things out productively.

However, Poor Pollys, Perfectionist Pearls, Taunted Terris', and Depressed Donnas may find, unconsciously, that talking about sad feelings can be a passive, dependent way to control an adult. Hypersensitivity and feeling sorry for oneself, and talking about it, can become ways of avoiding more productive problem-solving techniques. The kind parents' attention may unintentionally serve to teach children to overreact to criticism or peer teasing and to feel sorry for themselves. Expressions of self-pity may also be used to maneuver one parent against the other—as in ogre rituals, in which children tell one parent how terrible the other parent is making them feel.

How do caring parents determine if talks with children are productive or if they are mainly manipulative sympathy sessions? The fine line that divides appropriate empathizing from a "feel sorry for me" ritual is not always clear, and changing a manipulation pattern is usually temporarily painful for parents and children. It engenders guilt in the parents and frustration for the children, so be prepared for both. Some helpful guidelines are included in Figure 11.2.

Figure 11.2. How Much Sympathy Is Too Much

- Frequency of sympathy sessions is an important clue to manipulation. Children who need to continuously express their sadness are overreacting or overexpressing. Shorten the sessions and direct children to more productive activities. If the sessions appear to be your children's way of cornering your attention, be sure to focus your attention on more positive and independent activities.

- Examine the facts. If children use sympathy sessions as a way to dramatize their nonacceptance by peers, check out that information with teachers, coaches, or even scout leaders. These children may already be well-accepted but would prefer greater popularity or power. Perhaps they have only discovered your oversensitivity.

- Encourage better problem-solving techniques. Children may have to settle for your advice to not evaluate themselves based on whether other people like them or not. It may be that your encouragement of independence will help them through adolescence, a time in which popularity is too revered.

- Attending to children's expressions of feelings makes sense, but dwelling on their sadness only encourages it in a nonproductive way. Keep sympathy sessions brief and helpful to your children.

- Stay alert for "villains." If the focus of your children's constant complaint is your spouse or a sibling or a teacher, then they are learning a style of becoming close to you based on having a common enemy. This is especially problematic in an oppositional marriage or a pre-divorce situation. Too many children trap their parents into unwarranted sympathy when a spouse makes reasonable requests for responsible behavior. The kind of sympathy that shelters your child and alienates your spouse is bad for the marriage but even worse for the child. It teaches children a style of controlling the people that they love by "putting down" the competition for that love. An example of subtle sibling rivalry is, "Isn't it too bad that my younger brother isn't nice to my friends?" In saying this, the child is making his brother look bad. If dependent children are using manipulative sympathy sessions, each session will be directed toward blaming others for their own problems. Your tip-off will be that the sessions are always person-centered, with your child gaining your sympathy based on an alliance with you against another person.

The underlying consideration of parents of dependent children should be that they provide an opportunity for the children to talk to them about concerns, but these talks should lead to constructive action rather than reinforce avoidance of challenge. Children's successes should also be encouraged with loving talk sessions so that they learn that growth, not just failure, fosters intimacy.

Organizational Skills

Dependent underachievers often lack organization skills. To clarify the specific organizational skills that they are deficient in, it's best to examine the elements of organization, identify those that apply to your child, and attempt to help the child correct them. Descriptions of some elements and suggestions for correction follow.[1] (These elements were listed in Figure 6.1 in Chapter 6.)

Putting Like Things Together

This concept is basic to organization. Whether children learn to pair socks, put their library books together in a special place on a shelf, organize incomplete homework separate from complete homework, or arrange their favorite CDs, they're learning an essential first of organization that will help them find necessary items. This skill is so basic that even preschool children can begin learning to put like things together.

Predicting Time

Sensitize children to how long it takes them to bathe, dress, brush their teeth, or walk to the bus stop, and it will help them to be ready on time for school or activities. Noticing how much time it takes to study for a test or complete a math assignment will help them plan. Making them time-conscious will permit them to allocate enough preparation time and prevent the daily frenzy that some parents and children experience when they're always late. Timers and stopwatches are essential measurement tools, and time can be charted. Once children are more realistic about their needed time for preparation, they'll learn how much time to allow and are more likely to be ready for everything.

Scheduling

After children calculate the time it takes for daily activities and study, they can prepare a weekly schedule to visually understand and communicate their activities for the week. Children can keep their own schedules and add their personal activities to a family schedule that can be posted on a refrigerator or bulletin board. In this way, parents and children can better manage carpools, taxiing, and duplication of activities. It may take a fair amount of juggling on the parents' part to cope with gymnastics, soccer, and music lessons of several children. A realistic schedule helps.

Remembering

Assignment notebooks for children and electronic organizers for teens are great for remembering assignments, as long as children don't forget to use them. Children like to believe that they'll remember their homework or activities without writing them down, but this often is only an excuse for forgetting to do something or be somewhere. They have amazing facility at remembering what's important to them but falter when their responsibilities are not first priority. Parents who make lists for their own remembering are good role models for kids who must also learn to keep track of responsibilities. Children can invent their own special system for remembering, but they need to prove that it's effective if they plan to continue to use it.

Prioritizing

As children's lives get busier, it's important to join them in prioritizing their most important responsibilities. Discussing priorities helps kids learn to evaluate their activities and determine which ones they absolutely must do and those they can accomplish only if time allows. Prioritizing helps families to balance work and play. Doing homework before watching television or chatting online with their friends may not be a choice that children prefer, but they'll find it more effective.

Eliminating

In the process of prioritizing, parents and children together may decide that children simply have to drop a sport or activity. By discussing what should be eliminated, children clarify their own values while also understanding their parents' perspectives on activities. Sometimes you may have to insist that children drop an activity, but it's better to make this a joint decision and ask for their thoughts on which activity they'd like to drop. There may be times when you'll disagree. Listen to your children's perspectives, but don't hesitate to speak up if you consider their choices harmful.

Reviewing

The process of reviewing helps children to realize that their decisions aren't permanent and can be revised at a later date. Prioritizing and eliminating will need repetition every few months if schedules become too hectic again. Children can add activities that they've dropped or drop some that they've added as they learn to evaluate their daily lives and interests regularly. Reviewing homework or tests after they're complete can also organize, correct, and help children become more careful and thoughtful.

Establishing Good Habits

Study, chores, and organization become much more automatic and less frustrating if children develop good habits. Doing schoolwork and chores before play is a good habit that prevents procrastination. Rechecking assignments is a good practice for curbing carelessness. It's also important to avoid bad habits because they, too, can become automatic. Bad habits like skipping breakfast, arguing daily, staying up late, or ignoring homework cause great problems for children.

Maintaining Flexibility

The quotation I enjoy sharing is: "Habits are the best of servants and the worst of masters." It's true that good habits can foster efficiency, but it's just as true that children who are mastered by inflexible habits lose opportunities for creativity, spontaneity, and fun. Intentionally teaching children to make exceptions to their schedules can prepare them to adjust to change and can enhance their lives without destroying their organization and efficiency.

Teaching Competition

Dependent children avoid competition. They don't like sports because they don't want to lose. They don't necessarily get angry or throw the bat; instead, they avoid the entire process. They will say that they don't like the activity or don't feel like participating. This expression of their wish to not participate then attracts parent attention and persuasion.

Family game playing is a good exercise in learning to compete. Humor also helps children to deal with losing. Don't give a lot of attention to poor losers. Label it *poor sportsmanship,* ignore the loser, and go on with the fun of the game. Let kids hear your laughter as you play. If it sounds to them as if they're missing fun by withdrawing, they'll soon rejoin you. Permit them to do this without a lot of attention or explanation, and they'll soon forget their sadness. Absolutely *do not* make an issue of persuading them—that just makes it difficult for children to rejoin without losing face.

Game playing should always be designed as fair competition. This may mean that you need to give children a handicap, but don't just let them win every game. Doing so takes away their sense of control and teaches them to depend on winning for fun. Learning the balance between winning and losing is the key factor. Any time winning is fixed before the game is played, it invalidates the objective of teaching competition.

Having dependent children compete against themselves encourages them to learn to enjoy the process. Keeping track of their personal records for basketball throws, speed or accuracy of reciting math facts, or number of books read will set in motion ideas about the fun of personal competition. The *Guinness Book of Records* may be used to initiate and inspire these concepts at home or school.[2]

Group or team competitions such as Future Problem Solving,[3] Odyssey of the Mind, debates, or group music or drama meets are all approaches to encourage participation in competition with support. When children are ready for individual competition, 4-H, debate, and individual music contests, in addition to school sports teams like track and swim team, are all ways to teach the underlying concept that both winning and losing are normal and healthy.

Too much competition appears to cause problems for children at home, especially when the roles of "winner" and "loser" are fixed within the family. Siblings experience pressure if the winner feels forced to keep first place and the loser sees no chance of changing that outcome.

Structuring games in which the outcome is not assured helps children to express sibling rivalry in acceptable and fun ways and aids in dissipating their negative feelings about competition. The hilarity and laughter that accompany game playing relaxes tension, encourages all to do their best to win, and gives dependent children the opening to take the risk of playing. However, if the game playing gets too serious, it only encourages the existing competitive pressure and will deter the child who feels sure of losing.

Because dependent children have learned to avoid competition due to fear of failure, you can encourage their risk taking and help them build self-confidence by providing a safe environment in which they can compete with family members by self-competition, encouraging team competition, and gradually introducing low-key forms of individual competition. Behaviors to absolutely avoid with dependent children are listed in Figure 11.3.

Figure 11.3. Don'ts for Dependent Children Who Avoid Competition

---

- Don't just let them win.
- Don't feel sorry for them or overreact when they lose.
- Don't pay a lot of attention to their being afraid to try.
- Don't let their avoidance of competition keep the rest of the family from having fun.

Teaching Social Skills

Teaching effective social skills is helpful to achievement. Dependent little girls rarely have problems with social skills; there are many other little girls who are happy to dominate them. Although they may be teased occasionally, unless they object to the control by others, these dependent young children frequently boast many friends. However, as they approach preadolescence and adolescence, they may feel much less comfortable with their dependent role and may voice their complaints to mothers or teachers. Teaching girls reasonable assertiveness will protect them from feeling like their more dominant friends' pawns. It's better for them to learn to tell their friends that they'd rather not go somewhere than for them to learn that you will offer them excuses that they can use.[4] The first is more difficult initially, but your excuses for them only train them to lie and avoid.

If your dependent daughters or sons find it difficult to say "I'd rather stay home and not go to the party," or "I'd rather go with my family," give them some role-playing experiences before they try their assertiveness on their friends.

Sports talk is very important for social skills among boys. If you listen, you will notice that most adult male conversations begin with the score of the last game. Boys who never listen to sports on the radio or watch them on TV experience some real gaps in their social interchanges. Of course, you can continue to encourage your sons to ignore what you and they may believe is unimportant. However, it would only be a small adjustment to your schedule for you and your son to spend a few minutes watching the TV sports news or perusing the sports section of the newspaper or Internet together, and this minor modification in your routine may lead to major differences in your son's ability to participate in casual conversations with others. It takes only a few key observations to provide the jargon that bridges the social gaps for boys. They don't need to become steeped in sports news. They don't even have to play. Just knowing some sports language increases male social confidence.

If your children have few friends, it's better not to agonize about their loneliness. Encouraging their interests quickly gives them something to talk about with other kids who share similar interests. Computers, chess, reading, pets, horseback riding, music, and collecting model cars, coins, or stamps are interest areas that provide for social sharing without causing children to feel pressured about friendships.

Encouraging Activities with Intrinsic Interest

Modeling intrinsically interesting activities helps dependent children's motivation. Because they often fear competition, these children have learned to escape to noncompetitive, passive activities such as reading, watching television, surfing the Internet, or playing computer games. Don't hesitate to limit escapist activity, particularly television, the Internet, and video games. Although children may learn a great deal through them, these types of activities don't encourage personal investment of self. Instead, share or develop interests or hobbies that are satisfying and active. Whether it is hiking, biking, art, or building, these activities build confidence. Although there is no competitive goal, modeling active pursuits may provide the first steps in improving children's self-concepts and independence.

Obviously, intrinsic interests that provide personal satisfaction without competition are appropriate throughout life, but for dependent children, they play a special role. There is little risk. Potential gains include increased activity, planning, and goal direction, as well as opportunities for sharing interests with peers and adults. For a child who's a "loner," it provides the basis for developing friendships. For Sick Sam, there is the possibility of focusing attention on productive activity instead of his illnesses. Perfectionist Pearl will have the opportunity to work without the pressure of excellence, and Passive Paul and Depressed Donna will find that such activities initiate self-confidence and personal control. Plants, animals, science, stamps, dolls, and coin collections are only a few of a long list of activities that are noncompetitive but will broaden children's interests.

You might initiate your child's interest with a small gift, and absorption in one activity may attract children to two or three others. With added confidence, children may rapidly expand their curiosity and involve themselves in more than you expected. If you have problems getting children started, include them in your own activities, and model the excitement and enthusiasm that can grow from noncompetitive involvement.

Getting children interested in something doesn't mean that they must be passionate about it. Parents' concern that their children become passionate about activities often causes these children to quit the activity unless they perform best. Explain that engagement toward passion takes time and typically emerges as children become more skilled and knowledgeable about the activity. Sometimes it doesn't happen until they're adults and are immersed in their work. At the beginning, some creativity and enjoyment should be enough to encourage participation.

Easing Perfectionism

Striving for perfection in an area of expertise can represent a healthy development of talent or healthy excellence. However, when perfectionism becomes pervasive and compulsive, it goes beyond excellence. It leaves no room for error. It provides little satisfaction and much self-criticism because the results never feel good enough to the doer. Perfection is impossible for children who apply unrealizably high standards to too many activities too frequently.[5]

Perfectionistic children don't feel good enough about themselves unless they are "the best" and avoid taking risks when they fear that the results will not be perfect. They may procrastinate or feel anxious and fearful when they believe that they cannot meet their high standards. They may experience stomachaches, headaches, and depression when they worry that they will make mistakes or perform worse than their perfect expectations. Sometimes, they avoid accomplishing the most basic work and make excuses and blame others for their problems. They may even become defiant and rebellious to hide their feelings of failure.

Some children may only be specifically or partially perfectionistic. For example, some are perfectionistic about their grades and intellectual abilities, others may be perfectionistic about their clothes and appearance, some about their athletic prowess or their musical or artistic talent, and others about their room organization and cleanliness. Some children are perfectionistic in two or three areas, although there are some areas that apparently don't pressure or bother them at all. Those children whose perfectionism is directed toward grades and schoolwork have the greatest risk of becoming underachievers in school.

The pressures that children feel to be perfect may originate from extreme praise that they hear from the adults in their environment. The pressures may also come from watching their parents model perfectionistic characteristics, or they may simply stem from their own continuously successful experiences, which they then feel they must live up to. Easy curriculum for gifted students is often to blame for not providing opportunity for error or effort, thus perpetuating perfectionism.[6]

In the *See Jane Win* study of the childhoods of more than 1,000 successful women,[7] the authors found that 30% of the women viewed themselves as perfectionistic in high school. For the most part, they considered their perfectionism positive, but there were some exceptions. For example, television news anchor Donna Draves quit many childhood activities shortly after starting them. She would tell her parents that the activity was boring, which may sound familiar to educators. Donna admitted that she would drop out if she was not the best in the activity. She would never attempt activities like sports and math because she considered her brother to be the best at those. Fortunately, she was the best at speech, and she carried excellence in speech to her career.

Donna's perfectionism even affected her eating habits. Although she was a size three, she continuously compared herself to two other girls in her class who were skinnier than she. She felt unattractive unless she was the thinnest. Donna is successful today, but the near pitfalls of perfectionism could have easily derailed her and prevented her from making the mark that she so wished to make.

Perfectionism can be difficult to detect because children with apparently healthy perfectionistic tendencies are at risk of regressing to unhealthy perfectionism when curriculum becomes more challenging or when faced with greater competition. Read Rebecca's story:

Rebecca's school history showed her to be a perfect A student throughout elementary school. In middle school, she earned a few B's but ended her freshman year in high school with a 3.7 average. During her sophomore year, she studied less and occasionally missed assignments. Her grade point average decreased dramatically. By the second semester of her junior year, her grade point average had plummeted to a 0.3. Rebecca's peer group had changed from students who all planned to attend college to those who might never attend.

Rebecca's perfectionism at home had caused problems for many years. A first child, first grandchild, and first niece, she was initially the designated "queen." Rebecca was not happy about the eventual addition of three brothers, whom she bossed mercilessly. Temper tantrums were common when plans didn't work as Rebecca wanted them to, and these outbursts effectively gave her control of the household. She manipulated her father against her mother and competed with her mother. Her father blamed her mother for being too controlling, while her mother felt totally powerless.

Rebecca was angry and oppositional at her visit to Family Achievement Clinic. She admitted quitting on schoolwork when she couldn't get A's in her sophomore year. She told the therapist that her only goal was to be a good person. She was angry at her parents, her brothers, and her teachers as well. When asked what she might wish for if her therapist were a fairy godmother and could grant her three wishes, her first wish was *to be able to control all people,* her second for a million dollars, and her third for *a guaranteed successful career.*

While Rebecca's struggle with perfectionism was clear from her interview, she was motivated to raise her grades for college admission. Returning to the former, more positive peer group helped, and uniting her parents also made a difference. No teacher could have predicted Rebecca's perfectionism problem when she was in elementary school. Rebecca is in college now. Only time will tell if she can manage to cope with her perfectionism.

Here are some suggestions for ways in which parents and teachers can help perfectionists:

- Help children to understand that they can feel satisfied when they've done *their best*—not necessarily *the best*. Statements of praise that are more moderate convey values that children can achieve—for example, "excellent" is better than "perfect," and "You're a good thinker" is better than "You're brilliant." Also, avoid comparative praise; "You're the best" makes children think that they must *be* the best.

- Explain to children that they may not be learning if all of their schoolwork is perfect. Help them understand that mistakes are part of challenge.

- Teach appropriate self-evaluation, and encourage children to learn to accept criticism from adults and other students so that they can learn from others.

- Read biographies together that demonstrate how successful people experienced and learned from failures. Emphasize their failure and rejection experiences, as well as their successes. Help children to identify with the feelings of those eminent persons as they must have felt when they experienced their rejections. Stories from *How Jane Won*[8] are helpful to discuss.

- Share the lessons you've learned from your mistakes.

- Humor and gentle teasing help perfectionists. Don't overprotect them. Help children to laugh at their mistakes.

- Teach children empathy and how bragging affects others. Help them to put themselves in the position of others. Say, "Suppose you messed up at your piano recital and the winner told you that she had her best performance ever. How would you feel?"

- Show children how to congratulate others on their successes. They will feel that they are coping better as they congratulate others.

- Teach children routines, habits, and organization, but help them to understand that their habits should not be so rigid that they can't change them. Purposefully break routines so that your children are not enslaved by them. For example, if they make their beds daily, permit them to skip this chore on a day when you're in a hurry. If you read to them at night and it's late, insist that they go to sleep without reading.

- Explain to children that there is more than one correct way to do most everything.

- If your children are underachievers and avoid effort because they fear not achieving perfection, help them to gradually increase their efforts, and show them how this relates to their progress. Emphasize that effort counts.

- If your children are high achievers but over-study for fear of not receiving an A+, help them to gradually study a little less to show them that it has only a little effect on their grade. Help them to feel satisfied with their excellent grades with reasonable study so that they can balance work with fun.

- Be a role model of healthy excellence. Take pride in the quality of your work, but don't hide your mistakes or criticize yourself constantly. Congratulate yourself when you've done a good job, and let your children know that your own accomplishments give you satisfaction. Don't overwork. You, too, need to have some fun and relaxation.

- If your children's perfectionism is preventing accomplishment, or if your children show symptoms of anxiety related to perfection-ism, like stomachaches, headaches, or eating disorders, get profes-sional psychological help for your children and your family.

The dilemma for parents and teachers is to balance helping children be successful and good without also causing them to be burdened by the negative side effects of too much pressure to be the best. We want children to grow up to work hard and take pride in their work, but they also need to feel the satisfaction that they have earned.

Teaching Deferred Judgment

Dependent children are often afraid to contribute creative ideas. They are highly critical of themselves. They fear that they must produce perfect or correct ideas, and they evaluate so frequently that they may be unable to think of almost anything at all. It is difficult to encourage some dependent children to volunteer any but shallow or brief answers, while others may contribute very rarely, although the quality of their contri-butions is extremely creative. Their production of ideas is disrupted by their continued negative self-evaluation. Teaching children to defer or postpone judging their ideas thus enhances their creative problem-solving skills, their risk taking, and their self-confidence.

There are many specific strategies for developing creative thinking.[9] Underlying all of these strategies is the basic concept of postponing the evaluation of ideas until the individual or group has an opportunity to stretch the imagination and accumulate an extensive list of thoughts. Highly creative people are fluent and express many ideas, although only a small fraction of their ideas may be original or practical. Removing the pressure for high quality will enable children to produce more ideas. Providing enough time for idea production and letting them know that creative thinking may be either fast or slow also lessen tension. They must be given a safe environment in which "bad" or "dumb" ideas are also accepted. The concept of deferred judgment means that during a period of time allocated for idea production, no one, not even the children themselves, will be permitted to criticize—either positively or negatively—the ideas that are produced.

This strategy for idea production can be conducted on an individual or group basis. *Brainstorming* is the term given to the popular group process for creative idea production. Figure 11.4 includes four simple rules to govern this process.

Figure 11.4. Ground Rules for Brainstorming

1. Criticism is ruled out. This is deferred judgment, which contributes to the creative atmosphere so essential for uninhibited imaginations.

2. Freewheeling is welcomed. The wilder the idea, the better. Seemingly preposterous ideas sometimes lead to imaginative yet workable solutions.

3. Quantity is wanted. This principle reflects the purpose of the session: to produce a long list of ideas, thus increasing the likelihood of finding good problem solutions.

4. Combination and improvement are sought. This lengthens the idea list. Actually, during the session, students will spontaneously "hitchhike" on each other's ideas, with one idea inspiring the next.

Source: Adapted from Osborn, A. F. (1993). *Applied imagination.* Buffalo, NY: CEF Press.

Brainstorming is an extremely effective method for encouraging groups of children to originate ideas that are not likely to be thought of under evaluative pressures. Children can be taught to individually find ideas for problems using a similar model. For example, suppose your child needs to come up with an idea for a science fair project. Dependent children often come to their parents for suggestions because they have little confidence in their own abilities to initiate good projects. Parents typically respond first by suggesting that the children think of their own idea. However, after a few minutes (or days or weeks) of dependent manipulations, parents who don't recognize the dependency trap will sit with their children and make suggestions for possible projects. Together they may review books or former winning ideas until the parent finally recommends something that appeals to the child. The child may resist trying anything and thus causes the parent to spend even more time assuring the child of the parent's willingness to assist.

Although the child and parent feel that cooperation between them is good, the entire project has reinforced the child's dependency and provided the "vote of no confidence" from parent to child that maintains the child's fear of risk taking and the paucity of idea production. The deferred judgment approach should be used instead. It will encourage idea production and independence. Figure 11.5 provides the script to encourage idea production. You need to practice your part as parent only a few times to feel comfortable and encourage your child's independence.

Figure 11.5. Script for Idea Finding for a Science Project

Mom:	Aemilio, your teacher sent a note home, and it says that the science fair project ideas are due by next Friday. That's only a few days away. Do you have your project planned yet?
Aemilio:	Naw, Mom. I don't think I'll enter this year. I just can't think of any good ideas—unless, Mom, you have any suggestions?
Mom:	Aemilio, I learned a good way of thinking of ideas, and after I show you how, I just know you'll be able to develop your own project plan.
Aemilio:	I don't think so. I'm not good at science ideas.
Mom:	You don't have to be good at this plan; anyone can do it. (Sits down with Aemilio, and together they write out steps for the plan.) 1. Gather up your science book from school and science books around the house. Take them up to your room to your desk. 2. Get pencils and paper. 3. Leaf through the books, and daydream a bit about ideas that you see. 4. Write down any possible project ideas. They can be silly; they can be hard; they can be impossible; they can seem dumb. 5. Don't criticize any of your ideas; just keep writing. 6. You can put some ideas together. 7. You can borrow ideas from books or pictures or other kids. 8. Remember, don't criticize any ideas.

9. If you run out of ideas from books, look around the room; you may see some more. Look out the window to find more ideas. Anything can be on your list.
10. Try to write down at least 30 ideas before you stop.
11. Now go back and look over your list.
12. Cross out the ones that don't interest you or seem truly impossible.
13. Leave four or five ideas on your list that look pretty good. You may combine ideas.
14. Think through your plans for those four or five ideas.
15. Bring your plans to Dad and me, and we can all have a little meeting. We can hear all about your plans and help you if you should need a little bit of help. I know you'll be able to find ideas this way because I've tried it, and it really works.

Children who are taught techniques for idea production begin to incorporate these approaches into their general thinking and develop the confidence that dissipates passivity and perfectionism. Encourage these techniques by teaching them and personally modeling them by incorporating them into your own problem-solving approaches.

Independent Homework

Dependent children typically establish ways to avoid doing homework alone. Sometimes they manipulate parents to sit with them at the kitchen or dining room table; sometimes having a parent in the same room to nag them or answer their questions suffices. Some children ask only for occasional help, others expect parents to take turns answering questions ("You do this one; I'll do the next"), and some very dependent children manage to persuade their parents to do most of the work ("If you don't help me get it done tonight, I'm afraid I'll fail"). Parents frequently comment that their children will not work unless they, the parents, are sitting at their side.

This "help me" pattern frequently begins with the recommendation of a teacher because the child seems to require more than the typical amount of assistance in school. Threats and worries about failure keep children in the habit and prevent them from building the self-confidence that comes from working independently. Because these are attention-addicted children, moving the focus of your attention from your children's dependency while doing homework to the successful completion of that homework is critical.

Parents who want to change this pattern (and you must, if you hope to transform your child into an achiever) should plan to prepare for an initial struggle. Children who are accustomed to getting help with homework will creatively uncover dozens of reasons why they cannot work without you, or they will suffer aloud so that you can hear their moans and complaints. Sometimes they will daydream and produce nothing to prove their point and to establish to you that doing their assignments alone is an impossible feat.

A new desk or the clearing of a thoroughly buried work surface sets the stage for the new independence. The desk or table should be in a separate room away from the family traffic. No parents or siblings should interrupt the homework flow, and radios, stereos, and TVs are definitely taboo in the initial stage of establishing independence. For teenagers who insist that they cannot work without music, you can point out that they have already established that they are not very effective working *with* music. You may also wish to remind them that teachers will not play music in their classes to enhance their test performances, nor will college professors ever play music during exam time. You can assure them that when teachers communicate to you that homework and study have improved, they can certainly add quiet music to their study time on an experimental basis. Be firm but positive. They really are more likely to concentrate better in silence initially, although children who are established good studiers may have some choice of study environments; they have earned it. Dependent children have not yet proven themselves.

In order to encourage independence, you must be absolutely firm. To make it fun and to focus attention from help to completing the task alone, reinforcement by your attention will be necessary initially. Usually the best reward for all dependent children is personal, one-to-one attention. Try a game of chess or checkers or some time working together on airplane models afterward. Sharing a special snack—a banana split, ice cream soda, or popcorn—is also excellent. (For families that are worried about weight control, this should be modified to something less caloric.)

You should set up a specific timeframe for study, initially, although exceptions may be made for scout meetings, sports, or music lessons on some days. Creating regular study times and places provides the basis for good study habits and moves the responsibility from parents to children.

A general guideline for daily study time follows:

Grades 1 to 2........... 15 minutes
Grades 3 to 4........... 30 minutes
Grades 5 to 6........... 45 minutes
Grades 7 to 8........... 1 to 1½ hours
Grades 9 to 12......... 1½ to 3 hours

These are minimum times, and you can adjust them for your children. They will vary somewhat with the requirements of the school and the ability of the child. You should increase the time if assignments are not being completed, and it may be decreased if the children's achievement is very good. Once Underachievement Syndrome is reversed, children may set their own time requirements. Explain to them that you look forward to giving them that independence.

Scheduling homework time for before the evening meal works well with many families and leaves the evening free for family fun or television viewing. However, for many families, this time can't be monitored because the parents are at work. In that case, scheduling homework time directly after the meal is reasonable.

Avoid scheduling study for just before bedtime, if possible. Children rarely like to go to sleep, so they will use long periods of inattentive homework as a means to push bedtime limits. Giving them something to look forward to after finishing their homework is very helpful. To direct children away from dependence on nagging, try awarding extra bonuses for initiating study and setting an oven timer to give a signal to begin studying. Of course, parents will have to use maximum self-discipline to refrain from their typical reminders. You can establish the initiative on the child's part right at the beginning by making a contract. I'll explain contracts later in this section.

What do you do if you are concerned about the quality of your children's work? You may need to look over homework for each subject at first. When you check your children's work each night after it is completed, a brief perusal should indicate whether your children have made reasonable effort. If the work is carelessly done, send the children back to their desk to redo the assignment carefully. Don't go through it and correct each example, and don't lose your temper and scold. A few direct sentences and an insistence on quality should be sufficient to inform your children that you expect good quality. A sample statement is: "This work is not as good as you are capable of. Our family takes pride in our work. Go back to your room and do it over. As soon as you're finished, I'll be waiting to work on your model with you."

What happens if your children say that they don't understand the work, and you're not sure whether it is honest lack of comprehension or manipulation? Tell your children to try to understand the work on their own at least three times before coming for help. If they can't do the lesson after that, they may come to you for an explanation. Describe the concept slowly, and permit them to try one or two examples or questions in front of you. Then insist that they go back to their study area to finish the rest. A word of praise about your children's new independence to your spouse within your children's hearing range (referential speaking) will serve to send them off feeling pride in their independence.

Who should be the prime monitor of homework? For girls, it may be mothers or fathers, but for boys, if at all possible, it should be fathers. Mothers and female teachers are frequently the main communicators of educational tasks. From a boy's perspective, learning may appear to be "women's work." Conscientious mothers are often hesitant about passing to their spouses the responsibility of giving their children important messages about learning, particularly if fathers or stepfathers do not appear to show interest. However, I repeat: *Interested, persistent, and positive fathers are extremely effective in communicating serious schoolwork messages to dependent boys.* Although fathers are often less picky about the quality of the actual schoolwork, boys seem more willing to accept the responsibility and challenge of handling the homework independently if the homework message comes from a male. In homes where there are no fathers at home each night, mothers will have to supervise. They have the disadvantage of not being a same-gender model, but they, too, can be effective if they follow the guidelines in this chapter.

A study plan is most important in changing your children's study habits. Figure 11.6 includes a conversation you might have with your child to initiate a study plan.

Figure 11.6. Study Plan to Encourage Independent Homework

Dad:	Vincent, I've talked to your teacher, and he assures me that you have very good ability. Now that I know that, I want you to get into the habit of doing your schoolwork on your own.
Vincent:	Dad, I need Mom's help. Can't she just help me a little bit? (A few tears) I just can't do it without her.
Dad:	No, neither Mom nor I can help you because we really want you to prove to yourself that you can do it, but we have some good ideas that will make it fun.
Vincent:	(With sad face, but listening)
Dad:	We'll start by moving Grandpa's old desk up to your room so that you can have your own study space.
Vincent:	(Faint smile of interest)

Dad:	Then we'll set up a study time. Your teacher suggested that one hour a day for a sixth grader would be about right; so we'll start with that. Of course, that's only for five days. You get two days free of homework. They could be either Friday and Saturday or Saturday and Sunday. If your work seems to be very good and you don't need that much time, we can cut it down. Of course, if you don't finish your work in an hour, you will have to work longer than that. That study time will take place in your room, at your new desk, before watching TV or playing video games and with no radio or stereo on.
Vincent:	Dad, that definitely won't work. I have to watch cartoons when I get home to relax and unwind after school.
Dad:	Son, that cartoon watching will have to wait. I like to watch TV to relax, too, but when I sit down in front of the television, it's really hard to get back up to do any work. So I wait to watch TV until I've finished my work. You'll have to do the same thing. I don't mind if you have a snack or sit around or go outside for a while, but by 4:15, I expect you in your room working, and absolutely no TV until you're done and I've checked your work.* That way, you'll be all done with your study time before dinner, and we can shoot some baskets after dinner and watch TV when it gets dark.
Vincent:	I know this just won't work. I think I should watch TV for half an hour before homework.
Dad:	Vincent, part of this new homework plan is that you are going to earn some fun things for doing your homework on your own. It's not that your mom and I paying you for doing your homework, but we thought that we might help you to make a game of it. Now you'll need to think of something you might want to save for.
Vincent:	(Full smile) Dad, that sounds great. What kinds of things can I save for, and how do I get the prize?

* For information on plug locks and to purchase them online, visit www.familysafemedia.com/powerstop_power_plug_lock.html.

When parents and children have decided together on their study plan and reinforcement schedule, it's best that they write an agreement or contract agreed to by all. Children and parents, and even the teacher, should sign the contract, and it should be taped in an appropriately visible location to remind children and parents of their commitments. Keep a second copy in a separate place should the first disappear. An example of such a contract is shown in Figure 11.7.

Figure 11.7. Sample Study Plan Contract

Vincent, his mom, his dad, and Mrs. Norbert agree that Vincent will spend at least one hour each day, five days a week, studying and doing his homework independently at his desk in his room. He will do this before he watches TV, and there will be no radio, stereo, or TV on in his room during study time. After his work is complete, his father will review his materials. At the end of the week, if all work is complete in class and homework has been handed in on time, Vincent will receive 10 points, which may be saved toward a mountain bike. Each point is worth one dollar toward the price of the bike. Vincent may also receive extra credit points for doing special projects. Vincent's mother and father will not remind him to study, and he will take the initiative independently. If Vincent has not completed his homework, he will bring all of his books home on Friday, and he will not be allowed any weekend activities until he completes all missing work.

Vincent
Dad
Mom
Mrs. Norbert

What kind of rewards should you offer for completed homework? Young children do well with daily or weekend activities or small prizes as reinforcers. Adolescents typically prefer money or larger gifts. A sample activity chart, which can be copied or modified for use in your reward system, is found in Figure 11.8. The reason that these children require rewards is that they don't yet have the confidence or good habits to get consistent good grades. If they did, the grades would be their rewards.

Figure 11.8. Sample Activity Chart

Activity	Day							Weekly
	S	M	T	W	TH	F	S	Total
Math homework	4	2	4	4	2			16
Science homework	2	4			4			10
Social Studies (reading)	5		6					11
Spelling (study)		2			2			4
Reading (extra credit)			5	10			10	25
Extra creative writing					8			8
Feed the dog	1	1	1	1	1	1	1	7
Make the bed	1	1	1	1	1	1	1	7
						TOTAL		88

Figure 11.9. Point System for Younger Children (15-30 Minutes of Study for Children in Grades 1-4)

Homework Completed	Number of Points
Reading a story	1
Reading a workbook page	1
Practicing flashcards (10 cards three times)	1
One math or writing page	1
All schoolwork completed in school	3
Set 3-point minimum for daily sticker or baseball card; extra sticker or card for each 3 points; extra points may be added to the next day's total.	

Figure 11.10. Point System for Typical Homework Schedule (One Hour of Study for Children in Grades 5-12)

Homework Completed	Number of Points
Each page of reading	1
Each page of writing (includes workbooks, social studies, science questions, or copied writing)	2
Each math page	5
Each page of creative writing	5
Each page studied (read and outlined)	5
Weekly bonus for all homework in on time	25

Figure 11.11. Suggested Rewards for Point Systems

Daily Minimum Points

Days with a minimum of 20 points earned can be counted up. Children who reach 30 to 50 days of successfully completing the minimum requirements could earn a family excursion, a night baseball game with Dad, a fishing trip, or a pizza party. A special game or toy is also effective. For younger children, this may seem too long-term, and weekly goals should be established—for example, five days per week with 20 points each could earn bowling with Mom, a special meal out, or having a friend overnight. Daily minimum schedules work especially well with slow workers.

Cumulative Points

Points can be accumulated toward short-term or long-term goals. Very long-term goals are rarely effective at first, but as the children accumulate points, they often gain momentum. Cumulative points work better with children above fourth grade level and can be saved toward toys, cameras, movie rentals, bicycles, and computer games. Points are equated to money (10 to 20 cents per point may be effective). A record of earnings is charted and maintained until enough has accrued to redeem the earnings for the reward. Some adolescents enjoy using the point system to earn spending money, and if parents have no objection to "paying" children for homework, it is effective, particularly if the children have no other source for earning money. Cumulative systems work well for motivating children to do extra work.

In selecting a menu for rewards, you'll want to consider your own budget and the quantity of material possessions and privileges to which your child is accustomed. Don't give away too much or there will be little left with which to motivate your child. For the child who already has too many material possessions and experiences, it is sometimes difficult to find a reinforcer. A guiding rule is to use as little rewarding as possible, but just enough to be effective. Children must see the reward as worth working for, and you must view it as a reasonable commitment that is consistent with both your budget and your value system. Don't offer or suggest anything that you do not want your children to have. Sample reward systems are described in Figures 11.9, 11.10, and 11.11.

Incomplete Schoolwork or Homework

The first signs of underachievement are usually incomplete work at school or required assignments not handed in on time. Dependent children frequently do not finish their work in school because it may seem simpler for them to bring their work home, where they know that they will receive help and attention from their parents. An appropriate report to parents from teachers (see Chapter 9, Figure 9.4) will help encourage elementary children to complete their work in school, especially if this is reinforced at home by a daily reward activity. You may want to provide special attention or treats on days that work is completed.

Daily reports are not appropriate for most children beyond fifth or sixth grade. By this grade level, the incomplete work has shifted from classwork to homework, and the problem is students not handing in assigned homework. Weekly forms (see Figures 9.5 and 9.6 in Chapter 9) are appropriate for communication where there are many subjects and teachers. Children should not be required to circulate the forms. The forms can be sent to the guidance counselor or child advocate for communication to the parent. Adolescents usually hate to carry forms and experience considerable peer pressure and internal pressure to not collect them. If teachers are cooperative and supportive, it encourages the students to be responsible about their homework. The weekly forms document incomplete work and help students catch up before they are so far behind in their work that they give up. Email messages to parents are even more effective than the forms.

Because incomplete homework and inadequate study are the main causes of poor grades for underachievers, regular school-home communication is a most important key to reversing underachievement. It requires perseverance and effort on the part of teachers to cooperate in the enterprise, and parents who ask teachers to help should certainly let them know how much this extra effort is appreciated.

Middle and high school children can benefit by noting on an achievement schedule (Figure 11.12) the amount of time and the time of day that they have completed their homework. Sometimes these students create their own achievement schedules on computers. Parents can help children compare their weekly report from teachers to their time invested in study and homework. The relationship between effort and outcome will thus become very apparent.

Figure 11.12. Achievement Schedule

	Mon	Tues	Weds	Thurs	Fri	Sat	Sun
8-9							
9-10							
10-11	M: 25 min E: 10 min		M: 20 min E: 20 min		M: 30 min		
11-12							
12-1							
1-2							
2-3							
3-4							
4-5							
5-6	SS: 45 min.	M: 30 min. Sp: 20 min	M: 10 min. SS: 15 min.	M: 40 min.			
6-7				Sc: 50 min.			M: 10 min. SS: 30 min.
7-8							
8-9							
9-10							
M=Math, SS=Social Studies, Sc=Science, E=English, Sp=Spanish							

The school–home communications should continue until students are working consistently and have learned by experience that one failure will not be terminal; they can recover and continue to make efforts to maintain good grades. Before the daily or weekly communications are discontinued, be sure that students are able to realistically and honestly evaluate their own progress. When you feel confident that your children's own self-report matches what the teacher would be telling you, you can move from dependence on written communications to the students' personal reports. Do this cautiously because it is common for dependent children to return to a pattern of defensive lying and regress to old habits if they have not yet confidently established new ones. However, if they fall back into old patterns, you can quickly return to report forms. Some students tire of these, but only their own motivation can signal the discontinuation of them. On the other hand, some dependent students are fearful about discontinuing these reports. For these children, gradual weaning from the use of forms is important.

There are some pitfalls of which parents should be aware. First, some teachers simply will not agree to daily or weekly reports. Fortunately, they are in the minority, but if your children happen to be in their classes, they will soon sabotage your efforts. Instead, ask them for their preferred form of communication. They may have an alternative suggestion worth trying; email is often most effective and not labor intensive.

Second, elementary-age children are likely to avoid carrying notes home. They may start, but they usually won't follow through. You may need to attach both a reward for bringing home the report and a penalty for not bringing it home. The consequences should not be great. They can vary with the children's value system and their cooperation. The most effective reward for good behavior, including delivery of the form and completing work, is 15 minutes of parent-child time alone each night. Negative consequences should be used only if children don't bring the report home. Loss of TV privileges or outdoor playtime for one day will likely keep the communications coming.

Most critical to the communication system is teacher and parent consistency. This means that no matter how busy they are after school, parents must review the teachers' reports faithfully and must positively encourage progress. If students bring their reports home on Fridays, their weekend social life can be delayed until they finish their homework. Don't use other penalties for dependent children because punishments may easily move them toward depression. Be absolutely firm, hopeful, and consistent if you expect your children to take the responsibility seriously.

Figure 11.13 describes a reward system for grades that can be used with weekly reports. For most children, it is better to start with the process reward system described earlier, in which actual completed schoolwork is rewarded rather than grades. However, for some older children or for students who have shown good initial progress with the first system, moving to this weekly reward system for grades will encourage a sense of change and growth. It's important to reward effort in the same way that you reward actual grades, and for some children, you may want to reward effort more than grades. You want children to learn that if they make the effort and have reasonable ability, then acceptable outcomes will follow with time. Remember: Children will continue to achieve if they usually see the relationship between the learning process and its outcomes—Rimm's Law #12.

Figure 11.13. Sample Suggested Reward System for Grades

Rewards for report card grades are not effective motivators for dependent children because they are too long-term. Children will typically begin the quarter enthusiastically but will give up with the first poor grade. Monetary reward systems, geared to saving up for something special, can be very effective if based on weekly grade reports. Both effort and weekly grades, but not the cumulative grades, should be counted. An example of such a system follows but should vary based on reasonable grade goals for your child and on the number of weekly grades:

A = $1.00 per week
B = 50 cents per week
C = 25 cents per week
D = minus 50 cents
F = minus $1.00

Bonuses for improvements, exams, and report cards may be offered as the end of the semester approaches, but they are only effective if outcomes seem clearly within reach.

Monitor reward systems regularly, and pay children or record amounts as agreed to. Don't take away earnings or alter agreed-upon arrangements as punishment for unrelated activities.

Once you have set up positive and negative consequences, avoid overreaction (Rimm's Law #4)—that is, don't tell your children that they are doing superb work when their efforts have improved only slightly. Most important, don't give up, get angry, or lose control when failures come after initial successes. You are helping your children cope constructively with failure. They should view failures as learning experiences to determine the extent of effort necessary to reach their goals. If you overreact, you confirm their suspicions that they cannot really be as successful as their tests indicate. If your dependent children are already in high school and only a few years remain in which to prevent their closing doors on a college education, your own feelings of tension may be so extreme that you may feel as if you will explode each time they fail. Calmly remind yourself that if you persevere with both positive and negative consequences, you are demonstrating the most important characteristic that your children must learn—patience and persistence in a difficult task.

Teaching Concentration

Dependent children are sometimes diagnosed as having inattentive-type attention deficit disorders. They don't exhibit hyperactivity or impulsivity but daydream and appear to simply have difficulty concentrating when the teacher is talking or when they are doing assignments in class. For such children, review the suggestions in this book for reducing dependency before you consider medication. These suggestions may also be helpful if children are already receiving medication.

Figure 11.14 explains how to encourage children's eye contact with the teacher.

Figure 11.14. Encouraging Children's Eye Contact in the Classroom

- Explain to your children that teachers enjoy teaching students who like to learn, and if they can look at the teacher's eyes when the teacher is talking (eye contact), then the teacher will assume that they like to learn. Whether the children are concentrating or not, the teacher will think that they are. (Actually, children will probably concentrate better if they are looking at the teacher.)
- Indicate to your children that you will ask them daily how their eye contact is progressing.
- Dad's making these suggestions to a son may be even more effective than Mom's doing so.
- The children will consider this a fun trick to play on the teacher. Everybody wins.

If your dependent children are not participating in class, explain that you would like them to speak up or volunteer at least once a day. Ask them each night before bedtime what they contributed in school that day. Simply targeting one behavior at a time builds courage. Once they start, they'll soon feel much more comfortable about speaking up. For very young children, you may wish to put a star on the calendar on days when they've contributed orally.

Dependent children may have trouble with concentration during homework. A hovering parent only maintains their inability to focus attention. Suggest that your children get up and show you or your spouse their work after completing each subject. Eventually, they will be able to wait until the end of homework time to have you review their work.

A stopwatch can also help children focus their attention. After each 10- or 15-minute period, they may write down or record orally into an audio recorder the essence of what they've learned. As their attention to the task increases, the stopwatch can be set for longer intervals. The writing or recording serves as review, and their stopwatches help keep them on task and make a game out of the homework activity.

Extra-Credit Work

Depending on your children's skill deficiency, extra-credit reading, writing, or math should be added to their study time. This additional work should be encouraged so that children can take pride in the quantity of reading that they have accomplished or the pages of math practice that they've completed. Keeping the extra-credit work goal-directed or determining ways in which children can earn extra credit in school will help them gain a sense of success and confidence in their academic performance. You can encourage extra reading during study time only if the child is not already a strong reader. Children who love to read may use reading as an escape from homework.

Many dependent children write slowly. It is impossible to determine the chicken-egg relationship in these cases—whether slow writing encourages parental attention to dependency or dependent children write more slowly because they are less confident. Nevertheless, increasing writing speed is a goal worth pursuing. Encourage children to practice the timed exercise described in Figure 10.5 in Chapter 10.

As your children get in the habit of doing more than expected and you take pride in the additional work that the children learn to do, their habit of doing only enough to get by will change to one of always accomplishing a little bit more than is expected. Doing extra work is characteristic of achieving persons, and giving recognition to the extra efforts that your children make will help them to change their negative self-image. It will be helpful if teachers also reinforce their students' new images of doing more instead of less than expected. However, if teachers prefer not to give credit for extra work, parents can develop a bonus system for creative stories, extra reading, book reports, science experiments, social studies projects, or foreign language practice, depending on your children's own needs. They will enjoy the bonuses, and their accomplishments will build confidence.

Goal-Directed Tutoring

Dependent children sometimes fall behind and aren't placed in academic groups appropriate to their abilities. Temporary tutoring to bring them up to speed and help them make the gains that they need to move up in placement encourages them. Tutors and students can devise a plan of accomplishments to reach the students' goals. Keeping visual records of progress helps to give the students feelings of self-efficacy and encourages progress. Tutors need to be sure to nurture students' independence while they are accomplishing the goal.

Keeping Children in the Mainstream

School staff meetings about dependent children often conclude that these children work well on a one-to-one basis but not within the larger class. This assumption should never be used as a reason for labeling the child as having a learning disability. Dependent underachievers often exhibit many of the characteristics of the learning disabled, but dependency is not reason enough to separate these children from the mainstream.

Parents often believe that their children will be getting something extra by being placed in a learning-disabled (LD) class. Unless your children have true disabilities, it would be better not to label them and give them and their teachers an escape from dealing with the real tasks at hand. Children misuse the LD label as a convenient excuse for not taking full responsibility for assignments and for getting more help from teachers and adults than is truly necessary. School placement into LD or other special education classes is an institutionalized way of convincing children, teachers, and parents that the children lack abilities, when their poor skills may actually come primarily from a dependent achievement pattern. The funding allocated for learning-disabled children should be reserved for those with very real needs. Figure 11.15 will help you discern the difference between disability and dependency in your children.

Figure 11.15. Ways to Discriminate between Dependence and Disability

Dependence	Disability
1. Child asks for explanations regularly, despite differences in subject matter.	Child asks for explanations in particular subjects that are difficult.
2. Child asks for explanations of instructions regardless of style used, either auditory or visual.	Child asks for explanations of instructions only when given in one instruction style, either auditory or visual, but not both.
3. Child's questions are not specific to material but appear to be mainly to gain adult attention.	Child's questions are specific to material, and once process is explained, child works efficiently.
4. Child is disorganized or slow in assignments but becomes much more efficient when a meaningful reward is presented as motivation.	Child's disorganization or slow pace continues despite motivating rewards.
5. Child works only when an adult is nearby at school and/or at home.	Child works independently once process is clearly explained.

Dependence	Disability
6. Individually administered measures of ability indicate that the child is capable of learning the material. Individual tests improve with tester encouragement and support. Group measures may not indicate good abilities or skills.	Both individual and group measures indicate lack of specific abilities or skills. Tester encouragement has no significant effect on scores.
7. Child exhibits "poor me" body language (tears, helplessness, pouting, copying) regularly when new work is presented. Teacher or adult attention eases the symptoms.	Child exhibits "poor me" body language only with instructions or assignments in specific disability areas and accepts chalenges in areas of strength.
8. Parents report whining, complaining, attention getting, temper tantrums, and poor sportsmanship at home.	Although parents may find similar symptoms at home, they tend to be more sporadic than regular, particularly the whining and complaining.
9. Child's "poor me" behavior appears only with one parent and not with the other, only with some teachers and not with others. With some teachers or with the other parent, the child functions fairly well independently.	Although the child's "poor me" behaviours may appear only with one parent or with solicitous teachers, performance is not adequate even when behavior is acceptable.
10. Child learns only when given one-to-one instruction but will not learn in groups, even when instructional mode is varied.	Although child may learn more quickly in a one-to-one setting, he/she will also learn efficiently in a group setting, provided that the child's disability is taken into consideration when instructions are given.

Some children who are truly disabled also become dependent. The key to distinguishing between disability and dependence is the children's responses to adult support. If the children perform only with adult support when new material is presented, they are too dependent, whether or not there is also a disability.

Source: Rimm, S. B. (2001). *Sylvia Rimm On Raising Kids Newsletter, 12*(2). Watertown, WI: Educational Assessment Service.

Retention

Holding children back for a year before kindergarten entrance and considering children for retention in a grade are common approaches for coping with dependent children because they seem to require so much help. However, research indicates that, by and large, neither is effective.[10] The negative impact of retention on children's self-concept seems to cancel the advantage of attaining better skills. Nevertheless, under some special circumstances, retention can be considered.

For some underachieving children whose skills have fallen so far behind, tutoring will be insufficient for catching up in the classroom, even with substantial effort. If a child is young in the class and small in size, adjustment to retention is easier. First grade is a recommended grade for retention because mastery of those initial basic skills is critical to further progress. Kindergarten is not a recommended grade for retention unless the child is moved from a half-day kindergarten the first year to an all-day highly academic program.

As children get older, retention is a higher risk psychologically and less useful for basic skill remediation. A move to a new city or a new school makes retention easier for older children to handle because their peers will not be aware of the repeated grade.

Retention is not enough treatment for an underachiever. If counseling for the problem is not provided, retention alone will not cure the problem. A second bad year after retention increases the child's risk of school failure. Never retain a child without a plan to identify the causes of the problem and for helping the student change his or her underachieving pattern.

What You Can Do as a Teacher

If you're a teacher, many of the changes you can make for underachievers at school are similar to the changes parents should make at home because the children may interact with adults in similar styles in both environments. Be sure to read the parent recommendations in this book to see the applications of the same processes. The changes at school directly complement home changes. If parents won't participate, it is nevertheless possible for you to reverse underachievement in school, although it probably will be more difficult. In order to apply some of the home strategies to the school environment, enlist the help of a counselor, school psychologist, special education teacher, or one of the child's classroom teachers. Thus, the alliance between parent and teacher will become an alliance of counselor and teacher, with the counselor providing brief one-to-one attention, reinforcement, and support for the child's independent accomplishments in the classroom.

Vote of Confidence

Most children and parents like a kind, solicitous teacher, a sensitive person who genuinely cares about children. Yet an effective teacher must be able to avoid inappropriate sympathy. Children who show signs of pressure—for example, nail biting, frequent tears, sad body language, or shyness—may be telling you that parents are expecting too much from them, but they may just as likely be letting you know that they are overprotected, are unaccustomed to hard work, and that parents are not expecting enough of them.

If children's intelligence and other diagnostic tests indicate above-average or superior abilities and you, as their teacher, are expecting them to produce only grade-level performance, those indications of pressure are much more likely to mean that parents are not expecting enough of their children. Teachers often worry that they may be placing too much pressure on these students. If you communicate to parents your concern about too much pressure, they compound the problem further. It is at this point that you must tell yourself to be kind, strong, and firm. Your message to the pressured children should be that they are hard workers and therefore can complete the required tasks. Assure them that hard workers don't give up and that once they are good at hard work, it becomes easier. If you pretend not to see those little tears and gently comment on the children's perseverance and problem-solving skills, the tears will gradually disappear to be replaced by confidence.

Sensitivity is a good quality to develop in children. Hypersensitivity, however, can destroy self-confidence and should not be encouraged. Ignoring it is the best way to extinguish the symptoms of helplessness that seem to accompany the slightest effort for these children. If ignoring children's tears makes you feel guilty, tell yourself each time that you are truly being kind to them by not noticing their signs of helplessness and that you are enabling them to develop a better self-concept. Although these recommendations may cause you a great deal of stress, you will soon see the favorable outcomes in these children, and your own personal anxiety will subside. You may wish to review Rimm's Law #6, which states that children build self-confidence through struggle. If you take away the children's struggle, you also steal their self-confidence. Small experiences with anxiety in secure environments prepare children to cope with greater stresses in the future.

Multiple Methods for Giving Instructions

Children exhibit such variations in learning styles and abilities that it's safest if you give assignment instructions and homework reminders in several forms. Homework assignments should be given orally and then written on the board or given out as a handout. Instructions for assignments can be given orally to the class and recorded on an audio-recording device simultaneously. Dependent children or children who don't remember the instructions can listen to the recorded instructions and pass them to other children who require a repeat of them.

Schools can also post homework assignments on Internet sites so that students can be sure to have the correct assignments. This will help them become less dependent on you personally, and parents will also be able to confirm the homework assignments that are due for their children.

Sometimes students do not have the ability to understand concepts in instructions. They may truly need your help. In this case, you should take the extra time to explain and help, and you should not assume that the children are only dependent. Figure 11.16 will help you teach to all of your students' senses.

Figure 11.16. Teaching to All of Their Senses

We know that students show variations in the ways in which they learn best. Some students learn more efficiently visually. Others are more effective listeners and prefer auditory learning, and still others learn best by tactile senses or through hands-on activities. Stories that involve feelings or emotions enhance learning for most children.

Using all four styles can reach many children and encourage them to utilize their strengths in the learning process. If children are visual learners, writing, copying, and drawing or collecting pictures will reinforce their memory for information. If they are auditory learners, listening to recordings, talking into audio-recording devices, and oral repetition will assist them in improving their memory. If they are kinesthetic learners, they will learn better by manipulating counters, markers, or flash cards. Making up stories, rhymes, or mnemonic devices will assist them in involving their feelings or emotions in improving their memory. Using as many sensory approaches as possible when teaching any concept—such as writing on the board, passing pictures or models around, and then telling a story or joke—if used all together, will reach most of the students in the class.

Source: Rimm, S. B. (2002). *Sylvia Rimm On Raising Kids Newsletter, 13*(1). Watertown, WI: Educational Assessment Service.

Completing Classwork and Homework

As stated in the recommendations for parents, most dependent children don't complete classwork in school or don't finish their homework. It is even more frustrating to find that some will do the assignments and not hand them in to you. The communication and home reinforcement described earlier in this chapter for parents work ideally to eliminate these bad habits. If you, the teacher, can encourage effective parent cooperation, it is likely that you will be successful in changing students' patterns. The length of time expected for change will vary with the strength of the pattern, the age of the child, and the follow-through of the parent-teacher pair. If you can persuade the child's same-gender parent to cooperate, it will enhance your chances of success.

The communication forms provided in Chapter 9 are effective, but you may want to design your own to direct parents toward special problems that the child exhibits. It's important not to incorporate too many behaviors into the form. Concentrate on one or two areas at a time. You may add others after the first have been improved. Brief emails are also effective.

There are many underachieving children whose parents are not willing or able to cooperate effectively. This does not prevent you, as classroom teacher, from reversing the pattern. However, it will take a bit longer, and it will involve more of your personal time and commitment. You can provide the daily or weekly feedback directly to students because attention is the most potent reinforcer of good behaviors. Your personal time spent with a child can make a tremendous difference. Time is a scarce commodity, but there are other school resource people to assist you. Guidance counselors, school psychologists, speech therapists, learning disabilities teachers, gifted class teachers, and subject teachers may be happy to help. At one elementary school, a classroom teacher and a learning disabilities teacher made a most successful team for encouraging work completion, independence, and positive behavior in a very dependent third grader. They effectively reversed the underachievement pattern in school even before changes were made at home.

Other potential reinforcements that you can use are time with a friend, computer time, game time with an adult, a few extra minutes at recess, or an extra library privilege. Stickers, stars, and smiley faces work well for young children.

For children whose parents can't follow through, after-school study clubs are effective. These differ from detention in that they are voluntary. Children can be encouraged to stay for study club because they can combine a social break and a snack with study and homework help. Community organizations or industries are sometimes willing to fund snacks for study clubs. Additionally, if children complete their homework in study club, they are, of course, relieved of carrying any books home.

The underlying counterintuitive principle that will help you design your approach to changing these children's achievement patterns is that you must redirect your attention from dependency and inadequacy to effort and accomplishment. Your personal interest in the child and the communication of your confidence, along with a feedback system that emphasizes effort and patience, will provide the critical change.

Teaching a Growth Mindset[11]

In my clinical work, I explain to children that their brains are growing rapidly, and if they make great efforts, they are likely to change the hard wiring of their brains. This is especially effective for middle and high school boys since it also fits with my encouraging them to exercise to build their muscular potential. As preadolescents or adolescents, it makes sense to them because they understand physical growth spurts. If they can have physical growth spurts, they can imagine having mental growth spurts and can relate to working out both physically and mentally. I summarize the explanation with: "The harder you work, the smarter you'll get, and the smarter you are, the harder you'll work." My goal is for them to believe that intelligence is not necessarily fast and easy but requires exercising challenge. A growth mindset encourages dependent children to persevere.

Building Resilience through Biography

Studying the biographies of successful people will help students recognize how these people had to cope with repeated frustration and failure before they were successful.[12] This will help children to better understand that their own failures are not symptoms of their inadequacies, but only indicators that they have accepted opportunities for challenge. In our study of successful women's childhoods, we found that many of the women were inspired to success by reading biographies of successful people,[13] and another study found that reading biographies about perseverance encouraged students' perseverance.[14]

Focusing Attention

Dependent children are daydreamers and are, thus, frequently diagnosed with inattentive-type attention deficit disorders. Their apparent inability to focus attention and concentrate cause them to absorb information poorly in the classroom and to have poor study skills. Their staring out the window, looking off into space, and restlessly moving hands and feet are annoyances to both parents and teachers. However, if they are engrossed in an activity, they do show complete concentration, and although this may happen infrequently, it does provide indisputable evidence that they're capable of paying attention.

As their motivation and goal direction improve, these children's attention spans are likely to increase. Involvement in intrinsically rewarding activities also enhances their concentration. However, teachers and parents may want to devise some special signals for assisting children in attention control.

As suggested earlier in this chapter, explaining the importance of eye contact for communicating is one effective means of encouraging children's concentration on your verbal presentations and instructions (see Figure 11.14). You may also want to arrange a secret signal to assist children in looking directly at you while you're speaking. For example, you might touch your own eye or eyeglasses or tap the desk with a ruler as a signal to the willing child who is attempting to improve concentration. This is only effective if the signal is considered a secret between the teacher and child; otherwise, it will cause children to feel as if the teacher is constantly observing them.

Adolescents who are attempting to teach themselves to concentrate at school and at home should monitor their own focused attention by setting a stopwatch for 15-minute intervals to estimate the percentage of that time period in which they were actively tuned in to their task. By charting their on-task thinking on squares of graph paper, they can gradually learn to improve those percentages and can gain a sense of control over their productive study. You should discuss their progress and give them feedback and encouragement. This exercise requires willing learners; initial motivation must precede this attention-monitoring exercise.

Other devices that assist children in concentrating at home include actively reciting or writing material, summarizing material learned orally or in writing, using special mnemonic techniques, and forcing meaning into rote memorization tasks. Adolescents may create their own inventions for helping themselves to attend to teachers' presentations. Encourage them to do so.

When children don't pay attention in school, it's helpful to know what they are thinking about. Most children I have talked to say that their wandering thoughts are mundane—for example, yesterday's baseball game or what one student said to another. A few may be creatively engrossed, and some may be troubled by school or home worries. For this latter group, setting aside some time for discussion of their concerns is appropriate. For the imaginative students, some appropriate outlets for their creative thinking may be very helpful. These creative thinkers may wish to jot down ideas on notepads. However, for most children who are spaced out in your classroom, lack of interest, incomprehension, or ordinary daydreaming are the time wasters that prevent them from learning.

Teaching Goal Setting

Dependent children rarely set realistic goals for themselves. In their day-to-day school world, they usually set no goals at all. Their distant future goals are either nonexistent, romanticized, or illogical. Living self-sufficiently and independently in the mountains of Colorado or becoming a great baseball announcer or player are typical future plans of these children, but even more frequently, such children will answer "I don't know" when asked what their future plans are. They will require a teacher's assistance in setting short-term realistic goals so that they can experience some sense of internal locus of control and some confidence that they can accomplish something.

Often, when you suggest goals, these children show no interest initially. This disinterest is mostly because they have had so few success experiences that they fear another failure, or else they don't see the goals as sufficiently lofty to reward them with the recognition that they would like to have. You will have to persuade these children that they are capable of achieving these goals and that, once they have attained them, they will feel good about that success. They will require a step-by-step description of the process that they will need to follow to attain the goal, the strategy that they must use, and markers by which they can measure their success. Any conversation with children about goal setting should be a private and individual one. You may include parents after the initial meeting with the child.

Appropriate goals for bright underachieving children are movement into higher reading or math groups, inclusion in enrichment or gifted programs, inclusion in special classes or performing groups, participation in specific enrichment experiences, participation in sports programs, removal from special education classes, or for a few very gifted underachievers, it could mean skipping a whole subject or grade. Being promoted to a higher reading or math group is typically an appropriate goal for many elementary children, and a special enrichment honors class or a class at a nearby college or technical school is an attractive opportunity for a middle or high school student.

Dependent children are so lacking in confidence that they may fear not being successful in higher groups. Explanations that assure them that they will get assistance during the transition will be helpful. Figures 11.17 and 11.18 present two sample goal-setting conversations between a teacher and student and are intended to guide teachers in the persuasion process.

Figure 11.17. Helping an Elementary Student Move to a Higher Reading Group

Mr. Reed:	You know, Marcus, since the school psychologist tested you and since you've been completing more of your reading workbook pages, I've realized that you have the ability to move up to the high reading group. You really are a very good reader, and I would like to see you challenged.
Marcus:	(Smiling) Mr. Reed, I think I could read with the "Blue Birds," but they have too much work to do, and I don't think I could finish it all.
Mr. Reed:	Well, the tests tell me that you could with a little practice and a little catching up. You know, you're quite a bit smarter than you think, and you can really do hard work well. All of the reading you do at home has been a big help.
Marcus:	(Still smiling) You mean I could just read with the other group right away?
Mr. Reed:	No, not exactly, but let me show you what you would have to do. (Demonstrates with textbook and workbook.) Here's where your group is. There are 20 stories that I would want you to read. There are 40 workbook pages that come between where you are and the next group, but I've picked out 20 of the most important ones. I've written each story name and each workbook page number that you need to do on this chart. If you come see me for a few minutes after school every day, I can teach you some new words and make sure that you understand the instructions for the workbook page. Then all you would do is read one story a day and do one workbook page a day at home. You can tell your mom and dad about the story, bring the workbook page in to me, and mark what you've done on the chart. If you read a story a day and do a workbook page, too, in 20 days, you'd be ready to take your reading test. I feel almost certain that you could pass it, and then I know you'd be ready for the challenge of that high group.
Marcus:	(Hesitatingly) Do you really think I could do all that?
Mr. Reed:	Absolutely. It won't seem so hard because you'd do just a little at a time.
Marcus:	I guess I'll try. I'd really like to be up there with my friend Alan.
Mr. Reed:	Well, that's where you belong, so let's write a little agreement. I'll bet that your mom and dad will be proud of you, too.

Source: Rimm, S. B. (2006). *Sylvia Rimm On Raising Kids Newsletter, 17*(2). Watertown, WI: Educational Assessment Service.

Figure 11.18. Helping a High School Student Establish Eligibility for an Honors Biology Course

Mrs. Lopez:	Scott, do you have any idea of the career direction you'll be taking? I mean, now that you're taking initiative, you can see that you have some real talents
Scott:	Mrs. Lopez, teachers have been telling me since I was a little kid that I'm smart and not working up to my ability. I think they're wrong. The tests that the psychologists give are just easy, but the schoolwork is really hard for me. Even now that I've been doing my homework, I'm just getting B's and C's. So what's so smart about that? It doesn't even seem worth the effort.
Mrs. Lopez:	Scott, the tests really aren't wrong, and they only seem easy to you because you really are so capable. Actually, your scores are in the top 1% of students your age, and that really does mean that you're capable. I know you're doing your home-work now, but you've really just started doing that, and it'll take a little while to bring your grades up to A's and B's, where they belong.
Scott:	It's hard for me to stay motivated. The work seems so routine and boring. Even in science, my favorite subject, the work just seems dull.
Mrs. Lopez:	Scott, what if we try an experiment? You know, you really have the ability to be in the honors science class, and you would probably find that more stimulating. You have just one more quarter of the school year left—not enough to bring up your whole year grade average, but it is enough to demon-strate that you really can accept a challenge in science. If you could do just three things for me, I believe that you could prove to yourself and to the science teacher that you could handle the accelerated program.
Scott:	But I'm not sure I want to be with all of those smart kids. All they do is study.
Mrs. Lopez:	Well, what about just trying my experiment, and if you don't want to move up, you won't have to. It's just a way to let you see what you really can accomplish with just a little more effort. I think you'll like the feeling.
Scott:	Maybe. What do you want me to do?

Mrs. Lopez:	First, Scott, I'd like you to add 15 minutes a day to your science study after you've done your homework. I'll meet with you a couple of times to show you how to use that 15 minutes. Second, I'd like you to read two or three autobiographies of famous scientists so that you can understand the excitement and challenge they feel. And last, I'd like you to work on an independent science project of your choice between now and the end of the year. I'll be glad to help you plan it. If you do all that—and only if you want to—I'm sure that you'll be ready for the honors science class. Scott, I really know you have the ability, and our country needs good scientists. It takes a lot of work to reach a career in science, but it can be really satisfying. You ought to at least find out what you can accomplish.
Scott:	I don't think it'll work out, but I do like science, so I guess I'll try it. How do I start?
Mrs. Lopez:	Well, let's write down our agreement first. Then we'll set up a weekly meeting during your study hall so that I can help you with the details. I know that this is a big decision for you, Scott, but I have a lot of confidence in you, and I know you won't disappoint me.

Source: Rimm, S. B. (1990). *Learning leads Q-cards: Teacher tips.* Watertown, WI: Apple.

Be sure when selecting an upwardly mobile goal for underachieving children that it is likely to be achievable and, furthermore, that school policy will permit upward movement for them if they show appropriate progress. It is important that school policymakers set reasonably flexible guidelines for vertical movement by children into higher skill groups. Finally, it's critical that the children make a personal commitment to striving for higher status, which is difficult for dependent children because they are so lacking in confidence.

When students succeed in reaching their initial goals, it adds a great deal to their self-confidence and makes a perceptible change in their motivation. They feel a sense of control and accomplishment, which may extend to much of their other schoolwork. However, in setting their second set of goals, they may easily fall back into a pattern of setting goals too high, thus increasing the risk of failure. You will need to remind them to be patient. A's may certainly be within the students' abilities, but B's or perhaps C's are more reasonable for them at first if they have just moved into an honors group. More modest goals will help to build the confidence that will eventually lead them to the excitement of excellent achievement. However, they are often very disappointed in themselves when they are not immediately more successful. They can give up easily if you don't give them special permission for realistic expectations.

Help these children take satisfaction in becoming one of the smart students, rather than "the smartest student." As they accomplish more and more of their achievement goals, they should be reminded that they are opening doors to personal growth opportunities. During their underachievement period, they were continually closing those doors and limiting their futures. Remind them to not always expect to succeed at everything; no one does.

As their balance of success and failure shifts, help these children identify their positive accomplishments. Plan a weekly 15-minute meeting with them to review their successes and to encourage their personal goal setting. The 15 minutes may be reduced to five as they become more successful, but don't lose the weekly opportunity to reinforce their progress. Prior to changing their reinforcements, you were spending much more time attending to their inadequacies and dependencies. Now they've learned to attract your attention more positively, but their performance and confidence may not be secure for a long time, so your investment in positive attention may remain critical to them for quite a while.

As a teacher, you'll want to reward yourself frequently, too. Remind yourself that you are truly important to these underachieving students. If you become the pivotal person in their lives—the one who changes their achievement direction—they'll remember you throughout their adult lives as the person who made the difference. Changing that underachiever may take major effort and a good deal of persistence, so don't hesitate to give yourself credit for your quality teaching. You deserve it.

Teaching Organizational Strategies

Dependent students are sometimes very organized, such as Perfectionist Pearl, and sometimes completely disorganized, as with Passive Paul. They tend to choose one extreme or the other, and their organizational failings may relate to time, materials, and/or information. It is easier to discourage rigid organization than to deal with poor organization. Children who depend on rigid structure should respond favorably to creative problem-solving exercises to learn to increase their divergent thinking.

Teaching organizational strategies can best be facilitated by modeling good organization and by allowing time in the school day for children to gather materials, file papers, clean desks and lockers, and write assignments in assignment notebooks (see Figure 11.19). Demonstrating personal organization approaches and encouraging students to share exemplary and creative organization strategies with their classmates will help them to value order in their school lives. Figure 11.20 includes a student example.

Figure 11.19. Assignment Notebooks

Underachieving children usually lose regular assignment notebooks. Sometimes achieving children do also. Here are some effective assignment reminder alternatives. Give children a chance to choose their favorite approach when possible.

- Assignment notebooks can be full-size spiral notebooks. Each day's assignments should be written on a fresh page. The page is torn out when all assignments are complete. The advantages are that: (1) the notebooks are less likely to be lost because of size, (2) children derive satisfaction from tearing out completed pages and showing them to parents or teachers, and (3) the new assignments are always on the top page. One disadvantage is that it is somewhat wasteful of paper, although you can encourage your children to recycle.

- Children can have an assignment notebook for each subject. All subject notebooks should be carried home each day.

- Teachers can prepare a special assignment form for children to be placed in a loose-leaf notebook. Time at the end of day can be allotted so that children can copy assignments into the appropriate notebooks and gather necessary books.

- Teachers can pass out weekly assignment sheets for children to place in a binder. The children can check off assignments as they accomplish them.

- Schools can provide homework assignments on a website available for parents and students.

- Children can be permitted to create their own assignment reminder strategies. Some children are very inventive, and once they invest in their own devices, they remain committed.

Source: Rimm, S. B. (2002). *Sylvia Rimm On Raising Kids Newsletter, 13*(1). Watertown, WI: Educational Assessment Service.

Figure 11.20. One Student's Technique for Remembering Assignments

To remember my assignments, in the morning, I put all of my books in order on the top shelf of my locker. As the day goes by, I put the books that I don't have homework in on the bottom shelf and the ones that I do have homework in on the top shelf. At the end of the day, I leave the books on the bottom shelf in my locker and take the ones on the top shelf home. That way, I don't forget my homework books.

Source: Rimm, S. B. (1990). *How to Stop Underachievement, 1*(2). Watertown, WI: Educational Assessment Service.

There is a fallacy that equates creativity with chaos. Although it is true that many creative people appear to live in disordered environments, this is an illusion. Creative individuals do not depend on rigidity and do tolerate ambiguity well, but they have a real skill for organizing chaos, and they frequently are very detail-oriented. Their workspace may appear to be a mess, but they can typically find exactly what they want when they want it. You may wish to explain this concept to your students. Dependent underachievers take no responsibility for ordering their time and materials. Modeling organizational strategies and allowing specific time for organizational tasks will be helpful.

Organizing information for study is such a critical skill that achievers and underachievers alike should practice these organizational skills. Too many young people arrive at post-high school education without an understanding of the study process. Study skills appropriate to content areas should be taught and exercised in every classroom. Of course, many teachers do teach children to study for their particular subject, but many would prefer to delegate learning of study skills to a special course. So many children hesitantly admit that they don't know how to study that many teachers must assume that someone else will surely teach them.

Just in case your underachievers have not learned effective study techniques, teach them, and permit them to rehearse those content-appropriate study skills for the specific subjects that you teach. Repetition in learning content-oriented study skills can help all children. You may also be able to share some creative study ideas that they've never tried, and kids may share their own suggestions with other kids.

Long-Term Assignments

Even when dependent underachievers competently complete daily assignments, they often feel overwhelmed by long-term assignments. They postpone and procrastinate. They begin their work when most students are completing theirs. They may work all night just before the assignment is due and thus build in an excuse for less-than-perfect products.

You can help these students by meeting with them the first day after you've announced a long-term assignment to provide them with planning techniques for the completion of the assignment in a timely manner. Or you may wish to review with the entire class a plan for organizing long-term assignments, as shown in Figure 11.21.

Figure 11.21. How to Plan a Long-Term Assignment and Fight Procrastination

- Determine how many study days remain between today and the due date for the assignment—for example, 15 days.

- Divide the assignment into parts for the number of days available—in this instance, 15 parts. Students may need help in dividing the assignment, but here's an example of how to allot the 15 days for writing a paper:

  five days: library research and notecards
  one day: organizing notecards
  two days: forming an outline, three sections to outline
  three days: writing one section each day
  two days: revisions and changes
  one day: preparing final draft
  one day: extra day in case needed

- Students should then describe each part of the assignment in their assignment notebook for each day it is to be accomplished.

- One or two extra days should be left over should any part of the assignment take more time than expected.

Source: Rimm, S. B. (2004). *Sylvia Rimm On Raising Kids Newsletter, 15*(1). Watertown, WI: Educational Assessment Service.

Test Anxiety

Dependent children who consistently perform worse on tests than they expect often develop test anxiety. This anxiety may further interfere with their performance, thus causing a self-perpetuating cycle. Study feels increasingly hopeless to these children, so they decrease time spent studying.

Anxiety can actually interfere with memory. Children will feel that they know the material well until the test is in front of them. After the test is over and they leave the room, they remember again the information that they studied for the test but forgot during the test.

Highly creative students who tend to interpret questions in unusual ways may also develop test anxiety. Their continual misinterpretation causes them to lose confidence in their test-taking skills and often in their intelligence as well.

You'll find that students actually become less anxious if they can both make up and take their own practice tests, either for themselves or for other students. The practice of designing tests and answering questions in a variety of ways takes much of the mystery away and dissipates anxiety.

Social Rewards

Social acceptance by peers is important to students of any age. For some, acceptance feels more consequential than for others, and it takes on its greatest urgency during middle school.[15] Dependent children are frequently well-liked by adults, and some are accepted by peers as well. However, if their dependency receives a considerable amount of negative attention from teachers, they may become known to peers as "dummies," "stupids," or one of the many other hurtful labels that exclude them from their classmates. Sometimes dependent boys are teased as being gay, and this teasing can be very confusing to preadolescent boys.

In changing dependent children's self-images and peer perceptions, it is important to heighten their awareness of how dependent behaviors have caused them to become alienated from friendship groups. Don't give these children the impression that being popular is a first priority, but let them know that earning the respect of some peers is a worthwhile goal. Of course, in schools where peer groups condone non-achievement, helping kids earn peer respect is not an effective technique for reducing their underachievement. However, children who attract attention to their helplessness and to their irresponsibility are usually not accepted by any peer groups. It will be helpful for teachers to point out that reasonable class performance will actually help them be accepted by appropriate other students. Your underachievers will not be easily convinced, but if you can point out some student examples, it will help. Don't suggest peer respect as a primary goal, but as school performance improves, underachievers do tend to gain respect among classmates and are less likely to be victims of teasing and jokes. As they develop confidence, they also become less vulnerable. It is worthwhile for teachers to tell a child privately that changes are visible, because they may evolve gradually without the child's awareness.

As a teacher, you may also facilitate social acceptance for dependent children. For example, you can appoint partnerships for projects. Pairing dependent children with other students who are accepted by the class will foster peer support, provided that the partner is not so dominant that the dependent child becomes overwhelmed. Because the dependent partner may easily fail to accept responsibility, team members should each be required to list their individual tasks as part of the total project. Task groups of three are not nearly as effective as pairings of two in assuring the inclusion of dependent children. Larger groups of four to eight children will be helpful only if the division of responsibility can be clearly designated and monitored. However, if each child can be made to feel like an integral part of a project, then grouping will be effective in encouraging dependent children's cooperation, confidence, and group acceptance.

Creating a competition between the total group and another class or school group encourages cohesion and inclusion of the dependent children. Dependent underachievers may benefit by some hints on how to be effective group members. Their self-esteem will grow as members of the peer group voice their support and as they, too, learn to encourage the efforts of their peers. It's usually worth discussing in class how to become a good team member. Also, crediting a few students with exemplary teamwork, particularly if you can include dependent underachievers with socially accepted high achievers, is an effective strategy for changing their peer image. Teachers who are well-liked by most students can be amazingly effective in influencing peer acceptance.

Teaching Other Children

Many teachers ask children to tutor or help others. Dependent underachievers are hardly ever selected for this opportunity because they show so little leadership. However, it is exactly their lack of leadership skill that makes them more in need of the confidence-building experience of teaching others. They may teach other children in their own class, but they will gain in confidence most if they are given opportunities to tutor, read to, or in some way mentor younger children. This teaching of other children can take place in their areas of either strength or weakness, although if it is an area of weakness, they may require some guidance.

All teachers recognize how much knowledge and confidence kids can gain when they are required to teach in a new and challenging area. Difficult curriculum material becomes crystal clear as they explain it to a younger child. Dependent children rise to independence when guiding others.

Punishment

Teachers should reexamine some common punishments before using them with dependent children. Keeping children in from recess to complete school assignments is usually not effective for these children. They may prefer the time alone with their teacher to the company of their peer group at recess, which they may actually find quite uncomfortable. Thus, the threat of a lost recess may either serve no appropriate purpose or may even reinforce their failure to complete assignments.

Writing names on the board for unfinished work is equally inappropriate. It highlights dependent children's inadequacies to the class and serves only to confirm the children's suspicions that they don't measure up to typical student performance. For most children, whose names may appear only occasionally, it does no harm and may serve as a reminder to stay on task. Dependent underachieving children will see their names on the board daily. How can they ever hope to escape their dilemma?

Withdrawing privileges based on incomplete work is something to do sparingly. Doing it frequently will only prevent dependent children from participating in important and rewarding activities. These children give up so easily that you will soon find that they miss most of the privileges that you hope to use for motivating them—for example, taking away a team sport activity is counterproductive for dependent underachievers.

As a classroom teacher, you will find yourself in dilemmas similar to those that the parents of these dependent children experience. Punishments aren't very effective in motivating them. The children lose confidence, become depressed, and very soon, there is little left to take away from them. Your use of punishment typically has no effect on improving their performance. You will soon conclude, as their parents will, that punishment is not a helpful motivator for dependent children.

Why do so many teachers use punishment for dependent children even though it is usually ineffective? Teachers also need to feel an internal locus of control. It is important for you, the teacher, to feel that you are accomplishing something with your students. When typical teaching methods are not effective, it seems logical that taking away privileges may be an alternative approach. However, although it seems rational and logical, this is only effective if children personally feel that they can do something to change the consequences. Unfortunately, dependent children easily begin to feel doomed to failure, depressed, and helpless. You wish that you could shake them out of their lethargy, but no matter how you scold, lecture, reason, explain, threaten, or punish, they show no signs of the energetic application of which you know they are capable.

Save yourself the frustration. Only personal attention, inspiration, individual interest, persuasion, creativity, and short-term activity reinforcements will be effective. Teachers, you'll need great patience. These children will depend on your support and encouragement, but they will be weaned only gradually from dependence as they learn to be motivated by intrinsic interest, achievement, good grades, and positive attention.

Creative Problem Solving

Deferred judgment and brainstorming were discussed in the parent section of this chapter. Creative problem-solving approaches should be built into the curriculum of every classroom for all children. They are as basic to school learning as the "three R's." Although they are essential for all children, there are some specific ways in which creative thinking serves the special needs of dependent children. These passive children, who tend to think that they are not very good at originating ideas, will discover that they can depend on some specific strategies for making creative classroom contributions.

For the perfectionists who prefer the structure of right and wrong answers, creative processes may feel uncomfortable and will not be their preferred style of learning. But with practice and encouragement, they will be much more willing to risk the indefiniteness inherent in novel ideas, and they will expand their educational risk taking. Their initial discomfort will change to the enjoyment of producing ideas as the satisfaction of being right expands to the fulfillment that comes with the creative process. Some non-graded assignments may help these children.

Learning creative-thinking strategies needs to be a high priority for the Passive Pauls and Perfectionist Pearls. These strategies will help these dependent children in deciding on projects or stories and reports, in addition to helping them deal with peer relationships and other personal dilemmas. A few strategies that adapt easily to the classroom are described in Figure 11.22. Others can be found in the book *Education of the Gifted and Talented.*[16]

Figure 11.22. Creativity Exercise: Attribute Listing

Students list the main characteristics or attributes of a problem and then write down the various ways in which each can be changed or modified. An example of using attribute listing for designing a science project would include the following basic attributes:

Statement of the problem
Materials and equipment
Methodology
Conclusions
Applications

Modifying each step of the experiment forces the students to creatively examine the impact on the next step. You could also use attribute listing in creative writing for children who have difficulty finding ideas for a story. The children can begin with another story but modify some or all of the listed attributes:

Title
Characters
Setting Beginning
Climax Ending

The children will not only learn a great deal about the structure of stories, but will find that their modifications have resulted in an entirely new and creative story, which they previously thought themselves incapable of writing.

Source: Davis, G. A., & Rimm, S. B. (2004). *Education of the gifted and talented* (5th ed.). Boston: Pearson Education; Crawford, R. P. (1978). The techniques of creative thinking. In G. A. Davis & J. A. Scott (Eds.), *Training creative thinking* (pp. 52-57). Huntington, NY: Krieger.

One fifth-grade teacher planned a daily creative thinking time of just five to 10 minutes each morning for a fun activity that encouraged children to expand their thinking and defer judgment. She fostered a truly creative atmosphere that extended to all school learning. The activity was appropriate to achievers, underachievers, gifted, average, and below-average children. Creative thinking is a basic skill, and teaching children to postpone their evaluations frees them to build confidence in personal idea production. The quality of their ideas will improve as quantity increases. Encouraging quantity reduces pressure on the students who believe that they must always produce high-quality creative ideas. Humor and a fun atmosphere are hospitable to encouraging creative thinking.

Chapter 12
What You Can Do for Dominant Conforming Underachievers

Dominant conforming underachievers are difficult to identify because the extent of their underachievement tends to be much less extreme. They rarely fail courses, doing just enough to get by. Their underachieving patterns are often not recognized at all by their families. During their grade school years, they may not be viewed as having school problems. As a matter of fact, these children usually function precisely in the style preferred by their parents. They act more like achievers than other underachieving children, and it may not be until after high school graduation that their earlier underachievement becomes apparent.

Dominant conforming children will move into nonconforming patterns, either dominant or dependent, if the competition in their areas of expertise becomes too intense and they no longer dominate in their fields. This is less likely to happen in high school, but when it does occur, these children may become manipulative, rebellious, anorexic, or depressed. It is more likely to present itself in college or in their careers when they are confronted with a profusion of talent and must make the adjustment to comparatively lower levels of success.

Dominant conforming children are frequently multitalented. Their good intellectual capability, paired with such additional qualities as social leadership, dramatic or musical talent, excellent physical coordination, and attractive appearance, provides them well with the raw materials for success. Their home environments foster success in positive, motivating ways. These children receive much attention for their superior skills in their areas of expertise. They excel from the start and are able to maintain their excellence, despite competition in sports, music, drama, schoolwork, or social life. They appear to be good competitors because they work hard and exhibit excellent perseverance in their chosen areas of dominance. However, they manage to avoid learning to cope with failure by not getting involved or just getting by in areas where they are not first or extraordinary.

Parents may observe this in their children, but because the children seem happy and successful, they decide it best not to overreact to the B's that should be A's, the C's that should be B's, or the sudden loss of interest in basketball in favor of the swim team. When the son who was a former class president announces that he's no longer interested in school government, or when a daughter decides to drop out of the school play because she got only a small part, parents assume that these symptoms are a normal part of growing up or of adolescent decision making. Those parents may be correct. Adolescents should certainly have the right to change interests and decide for themselves where they want to invest their time and energies. However, a pattern in which children choose activities only when they can be recognized for excellence portends more serious problems later.

These children manipulate home and school environments to avoid competition. This may eventually cause dramatic underachievement and often some related emotional problems. Parents and teachers can prevent the problems if they are alert to them. However, parents often have so strongly counteridentified with their children's successes that they are blinded to the potential problems. The needed changes in school and at home are not complex, but it is difficult to convince parents and teachers to make them. This will become clear as the necessary changes are described.

The root of dominant conforming patterns in children comes from receiving too much attention for excellence. Although the attention has enhanced their talents, the children have internalized a pressure for continued attention. They become addicted to this attention and are willing to maintain high performance only in areas that elicit the attention. They will not function well if they are not assured of an audience and of success.

What You Can Do as Parents

Changing your method of parenting when you don't see a problem but are only told that there is potential for one someday may seem like an unreasonable action. Why should you do anything different if your children seem content and successful? Of course, you don't need to make changes unless you see some of the symptoms of Underachievement Syndrome. If those signs appear, however, they are the tip of the iceberg, and it makes sense to deal with the problems that lie beneath the surface. The changes will seem logical and not at all drastic once you become comfortable with them. Making small changes can be a genuine long-range kindness to your children.

Monitoring Counteridentification

One or both parents of gifted underachievers frequently share a similar interest or talent with them. Research certainly supports the crucial role of parent interest, enthusiasm, and shared abilities in enhancing achievers' accomplishments.[1] However, that same intense interest can cause problems. If you are a competitive, achievement-oriented adult, you may feel extreme excitement when your children are successful and intense disappointment when they fail. It is as though your children's experiences are your own personal wins or losses. Your children seem like extensions of yourself. The more similar their expertise or experiences are to those of your own childhood, the more intense and personal their victories and defeats feel to you.

It is difficult to separate yourself from your children, in whom you've invested so much of yourself. If you are an artist, your children's art talent may represent the fulfillment of your own dreams. You are sure that the artistic achievement that excited and rewarded you should provide similar excitement to them, and you personally share the thrill of the praise that they receive from their teachers. Socially, if you were well-liked and popular—or if, in contrast, you felt unaccepted—you can identify with the awe of your daughter's first date or your son's early phone calls from girls. If you were an athlete and received the glories of senior high trophies and peer adulation, or if you didn't quite qualify for awards, you can imagine how your son will feel as the crowds cheer and marvel at his football successes. Here's an academic case study example:

> Juan, a freshman in college, had failed or withdrawn from all of his second-semester classes. In an effort to help Juan set reasonable goals, a counselor reviewed his aptitude test scores and explained that college would be more difficult than high school, and although his abilities were excellent, it would take hard work for him to accomplish a B+ average. His mother, who was part of the conference, took the counselor aside afterward in frustration and asked why the counselor wasn't reassuring Juan of his high intelligence and telling him that college should be easy for him. She said that it should not be difficult for him because college hadn't been hard for her. She counteridentified with Juan so intensely that she couldn't imagine his having lesser skills, abilities, or motivation than she.

Why is it important to separate yourself from your children and to be enthusiastic without being overwhelming or disappointed without being depressed? It is because the intensity of your feelings conveys to your children such strong emotional messages that there develops an urgency to their victories and a distress to their defeats that go far beyond the impact of the actual events. Of course, your children should enjoy the thrill of winning and should learn to deal with the disappointment of losing, but when parents overreact, winning becomes so important that kids dare not participate in activities in which there is a risk of losing.

It is irrational to expect your children to be continually victorious, and you don't truly expect that, but your emotional intensity conveys this impossible message to them. You should ask yourself whether it really is important to your children to be the most popular person, best athlete, star in the play, or valedictorian, or whether these are *your* emotional pressures that you are unintentionally attributing to them. Certainly, you want your children to compete and to make their best efforts, but the pressures that you feel send a different message. Celebrate your children's excellent performances and empathize with their struggles, but permit them to feel their own experiences without burdening them with your personal pressures.

Dr. Robert Sapolsky, professor of biology and neurology at Stanford University and author of the book *Why Zebras Don't Get Ulcers*,[2] discussed how difficult experiences serve to "inoculate" people from feeling like failures while increasing their resilience. Thus, small stresses that children learn to cope with will "vaccinate" them to cope better with the larger stresses that life is likely to deliver. If parents counteridentify with their children too greatly and thus overprotect them from experiencing failures, they may be withholding the vaccination that can lead those children to the resilience that they will require in adult life.

Competition

You will find that competition is discussed in all of these chapters describing modifications for underachieving children. It is basic to the underachievement problem, regardless of the underachievement style. I won't repeat the recommendations for teaching competition at home from Chapter 11. You may refer to them if you've skipped that chapter. There are, however, some additional competition issues that need to be addressed with dominant children.

Dominant children usually live in highly competitive families. Dominant conforming youngsters have found areas of activity in which they can be winners. They need only to put winning in perspective.

They can value excellence as long as they don't feel valued only for their excellence. If you have been sending the messages that you like children who win, who are the smartest, and who excel, then change them to: "We want children to try, to be responsible, and to make positive and sincere effort." If children feel that they have to perform best to earn their parents' love and attention, they will select only areas of participation in which they are convinced that they can excel.

As parents, you should get involved in some activities where you don't always win. You will want to voice respect for the talent and skill of your competitors so that your children can hear that admiration. However, the admiration shouldn't mean that you hope or expect your children to attain those great heights. For example, if you and your son play tennis and you're watching the Wimbledon tennis championships, explain to him how to observe the players and learn from their skills, but please don't suggest, as so many parents do, that if he practices regularly, he may be playing tennis at Wimbledon someday. You are building unlikely dreams and unreasonable competitiveness. There will be time enough later for such lofty goals if he displays extraordinary talent. At this early date, competition with his friends is a reasonable standard to set for both fun and glory.

Parents frequently tell their children that they can do anything if they're willing to work hard enough. Although it's true that practice enhances skill, your children, despite all of their efforts, may not make it to Olympic sports, the Metropolitan Opera, Harvard Medical School, the Broadway stage, the National Ballet, the Cleveland Indians, or the Green Bay Packers.

Although these expectations are usually delivered in jest, children often take them seriously. Dominant conforming children may begin their efforts immediately and may assume that if they're stars of the sixth-grade basketball team, they're on the way to professional basketball. They practice basketball earnestly but don't want to make a similar commitment to schoolwork. Learning to work in arenas where they are not stars is an essential component of learning to function effectively in a competitive society.

Intrinsic Motivation

In addition to learning to function in competitive environments, competitive children should develop interests that are intrinsically enjoyable and participate in activities that are neither competitive nor rewarded by outsiders. They don't often do this because they invest so heavily in their areas of expertise. The urgency to win is so strong that they can hardly imagine spending time on activities that are noncompetitive. Gifted adolescents have often told me of their sudden realization that they have developed very few interests other than those in their specialty areas. There seems to be no purpose to participation if there is no contest and no recognition for their success. This narrows experiences for young persons who should be exploring their world.

Involving children in activities that are intrinsically rewarding, as has already been mentioned, is an important way to expand their interests—that is, sharing noncompetitive activities with your children will broaden their enthusiasm and encourage participation. Membership in peer groups that are interest-centered or participation in specialized summer camp experiences will encourage children to broaden their involvement. There are, for example, camps for science, language, computer, drama, music, basketball, and art, to mention a few. If the children's special talent is drama and they are already stars, a drama camp would only increase their experiences in competition, while a language camp would introduce them to a new area of interest. If sports is their field, then drama camp might lure them to the excitement and fun of the stage. Specialty programs present varying values for children. They can be used to teach and encourage competition and challenge, but they can also open up new experiences outside of children's typical talent areas.

Learning to enjoy noncompetitive interests is important for all children, but it seems especially important for dominant conformers who focus only on winning.

Parent Messages

Communications from parents in the form of verbal statements and actions are amazingly effective in guiding dominant conforming children. Messages to elementary-age children are much more important than those given in the teenage years, when these highly competitive children have already discovered their strengths and internalized their competitive pressures.

The most important message about school achievement is that academic learning is central, while all other school-related activities are of lesser importance. Activities like band, chorus, sports, and drama are important because they provide a full and enriched life for children and adults alike. Certainly, developing interests and participation in competitive activities in these areas is appropriate and should be encouraged, but schoolwork and study should take first priority. If you state this message clearly when children are younger, they will know by high school that geometry homework is to be completed even though play rehearsals last until 9:30, and a heavy basketball schedule is not an excuse for skipping a class just because they didn't finish the homework. But there are many parents who inadvertently give the opposite message. For example, one parent told her daughter, who was quite bright, that the most important part of school was her extracurricular activities. This woman gave a clear message to her child of the secondary importance of school learning.

If you take your children out of school for shopping trips and sports events, you are sending a message that schoolwork is unimportant. When children are excused from school, there should be a definite educational or medical reason for that excuse. Field trips or family trips that provide unique learning experiences obviously qualify. If other family events should make it necessary to take children out of school, then you should require your children to collect and complete all school assignments. This will provide reasonable flexibility for the family while making clear that you value academic responsibility.

This central-versus-peripheral message is especially important to dominant conforming children because their fields of expertise or showmanship are so much more enticing than the more mundane activities of the classroom. If children demonstrate unusual competence in a talent area, parents and schools should certainly make allowances for their special training and practice needs. It may be that such talented children should have a lightened number of academic requirements. However, they should be cautioned to maintain the minimum number to permit them to have alternative career options, should they not qualify in their highly competitive talent areas. They should also be expected to meet quality standards in subjects that may be important to those alternative careers. For example, the aspiring dramatic actress may eventually need to compromise and teach drama and English. Although this may seem an unlikely outcome to the star of the high school production of *Carousel* or *Fiddler on the Roof,* she certainly will have to learn math and science to attain that college degree.

Many youths from first grade through college declare to their parents and peers their rationalizations for not studying or doing homework in subjects that they are certain are irrelevant to their future. Sometimes, I feel convinced that parents are telling these children that educators don't know anything about education. There truly is a basic core of skills that educated citizens should master by adulthood. You should communicate to your children that they are expected to learn to read, write, and do math, even if they hate any or all of those subjects.

I don't mean that in emphasizing academics you should suggest that you do not support music, art, drama, or athletics. To the contrary, all of these forms of creative enrichment are extremely important. But for most children, they should be viewed as supplementary to the core of good academic learning and thinking. Time and experience will permit the extraordinarily talented to make more definite decisions later.

Sensitivity

Dominant conforming children, except for the specifically academic type, are usually well-liked by their peers. Their elementary and secondary school days are typically productive and active. They view themselves as winners by virtue of the fact that they have selected only activities in which they are successful.

Because they are usually happy, peer-oriented youngsters, these children rarely take the time or have the wish to develop sensitivity to the feelings of others who may be less successful. A line from Daddy Warbucks from the musical Annie—"You don't have to be nice to the people you meet on the way up if you're not coming back down again"—summarizes succinctly the confident air of success that surrounds the popular high school sports, drama, and music stars. These youngsters are often ill-prepared for the reality that frequently follows their peak teenage years. They may indeed come back down again, and the effect of seeing less successful peers surpassing them as they descend is cause for depression in these youths who are so accustomed to thinking of themselves as being at center stage and superior.

These once-confident kids are likely to face their initial defeats and failure experiences as young adults in college or in the working world, sometimes far from supportive family members. How can you as parents best prepare your children for the real world with all its potential disappointments? Children who often brag enthusiastically about their accomplishments and boast with bravado of their victories should be sensitized early to the feelings of the majority of people who meet failure frequently. If you can teach them empathy and support for others, they may vicariously learn coping strategies that will help them adjust to the balance of failures and successes which is part of all adult lives.

You can encourage empathy by asking questions and making comments that direct their attention to the feelings of others. However, because your children will be counting on your applause for their performance, your suggestions of sensitivity to losers must be made in a way that does not take credit from your children's own successes. If they feel that you are giving more attention to the losers than to those who are victorious, they may reasonably complain about your lack of support. Some appropriate sample statements and questions that may be helpful to you are presented in Figure 12.1.

Figure 12.1. Sample Statements to Encourage Empathy

> • "Josh, that was a really great game! You truly were a sports hero, and your dad and I were impressed. But I think your friend Troy had a really bad game. I never saw him play so poorly. Do you think he could use some of your encouragement?"
>
> • "Trayvon, your brother is really in a bad mood. He did terribly at the track meet. You've always handled losses well. Do you have any ideas on how you could make him feel better about trying again in the future?"
>
> • During a party, Mom calls Madeline into the kitchen and privately has this conversation with her: "Your friend LaKeisha keeps coming in to talk to me. I don't mind her coming in here, but I think she feels left out. You're so popular; do you have any ideas on how you could help her to feel included?"
>
> • "Two standing ovations! I don't think I ever saw such an enthusiastic audience. You are really a star. Wouldn't it be neat if on the last night, the cast could figure out a way to get the backstage people to come out and take a bow so they could share that applause?"

Notice that in each statement, the parent comments to the children on the success of their performances before suggesting consideration of how others could use their support. If parents don't do this, it becomes so much of a "root for the underdog" message that the winning children feel deflated by the unappreciation of their own efforts. Children will not always follow through on suggestions like these, but bringing the suggestions to their attention even at the time of such victory will help them form a habit of empathy. As they share with their friends those experiences of defeat that must sometimes come to all, they can vicariously learn strategies for coping with defeat themselves.

As mentioned earlier, teaching admiration is another means of developing sensitivity that can assist the high school star in the real world beyond high school. Even while your children are winning, they can learn to notice, admire, and communicate their admiration to other performers. Because they are in the habit of competing, they tend to feel inadequate each time someone performs better than they do. When there is real competition, even when it is from the other team, the gracious good sport should develop skill at showing respect for, rather than deprecating, the talent of a rival. Although this is truly a difficult skill for highly competitive children to develop, it gives them a mentally healthy way to deal with being second best, which they tend never to consider. For dominant conforming children who are accustomed to winning, congratulating more skilled players is an act of courage that will prepare them for the realistic appraisal of their own skills in later adult competition.

Teaching winners to be sensitive to the feelings of others without dampening their own enthusiasm is more difficult than it may appear. They feel more comfortable savoring victory than appreciating the skill or effort of competitors. Try having these children teach and coach others in their fields of expertise. This allows them to see how others cope with victory and defeat. They may find it easier to console younger children than their own peers and may well become the first to teach younger children how to win graciously.

Academically talented children must also develop coping skills for the world beyond high school, where they are going to face greater intellectual competition. They, too, must be reminded to avoid boastfulness. They may not realize that their enthusiastic exaltation in success can have the effect of discouraging others who are losers by comparison. Learning to be sensitive, to admire other scholars, and to recognize the future will help them be healthily competitive and prepare them for the more challenging intellectual environments that they will meet in college and in their careers.

Acceptance of Criticism

Dominant children prefer to do things their own way. They feel good about themselves only when they are fully in control of their activities. Criticism of their performance causes them to feel out of control. Their defensive reaction to criticism is a symptom of their problem. Obviously, it is irrational for them to believe that they are perfect at a given skill, yet they invest considerable effort to avoid performances in which they might not be praised. For example, musically talented children may manipulate you into persuading them to perform, on the pretense that they are shy. They are thus avoiding any risk of criticism because they know that your response to their reticent performance can only be applause. You would withhold any negative comments because you assume that it might injure the child's already precarious self-confidence. Don't bother persuading them; ignore their manipulation. They love to perform and will soon volunteer if you don't turn it into a power struggle.

As another example, your children may prepare a class report or a story that they feel certain is excellent and are positive that their teacher will admire. However, they don't want to show it to you until it is graded. After all, you may recommend that they make a few minor changes that would undoubtedly improve the grammar or the story, and any such criticism would be intolerable because then the story would not be completely theirs. They don't want to change a sentence—that would take their control away. After they've received their A, they'll be happy to show it to you, but any criticism will be met with "Well, I got an A, so I guess it's fine." Anything that produces less than an A may not make it into your hands for review unless you request it.

If children are to truly develop their potential talents and not become underachievers, they must learn to cope with criticism. Don't permit them to manipulate you into backing off. Teach them to be analytical, especially in their talent areas. If they become accustomed to constructive criticism, both positive and negative, they will take it in stride. Children who receive only praise do not tolerate negative criticism well.

Evaluate briefly in writing. It helps children to accept the criticism without becoming defensive. Your notes to them may seem too harsh at first, but when they look at them a second time, they'll feel more ready to think about your suggestions. Make it an analysis of strengths and weaknesses, and permit them to decide whether or not to act on your suggestions. In this way, they become accustomed to evaluation and will not feel that they are in a power struggle that they must win or lose. Eventually, they may even thank you for your suggestions, although this is unlikely to happen immediately.

If your children are already defensive about criticism, begin the process in a new area of learning first. They will not need to be so protective of their reputation in an area in which they do not perceive themselves as experts. A few tears should be ignored in initial assessment stages. They indicate hypersensitivity that is not conducive to accepting challenge. You will want to tread carefully at first, but persevere. Also, analyzing other people's performances together in a positive way will help dominant conforming children to recognize it as a constructive and invaluable activity. Teaching your children to deal with criticism constructively will be helpful to them throughout their lives.

There are times to postpone evaluation or avoid it altogether. The emotional times that accompany victory or defeat are not good times to evaluate. Children can't be objective at such moments and are certainly likely to overreact, especially in the case of the defeated. Time-pressured situations also do not invite criticism. Children will not welcome appraisals when they are completing the typing of their composition in the morning just before catching the bus. Of course, they may have deliberately arranged this time-pressured situation to avoid evaluation. Nevertheless, it is better to say nothing than to precipitate a crisis that will certainly not accomplish your purpose.

Times of initial idea production are also not good for evaluation. Deferring judgment until children have had plenty of time to play with ideas encourages creativity. You should consciously state the rules for deferring judgment as a reminder that you will definitely not evaluate at an early stage. Finally, don't get into the habit of criticizing or evaluating everything. Children should have areas of freedom in which they can count on minimal or no evaluation. If parents literally criticize everything, children have justifiable complaints.

What You Can Do as a Teacher

Modifications at school will again match the changes recommended for parents at home. However, some teachers are in dramatically powerful positions to make impacts on dominant conforming children. Coaches, music teachers, drama advisers, and specialists in the youths' talent areas are viewed as models. They may be much more influential than parents, particularly in adolescence. You can show these children how to put their talent areas in competitive perspective for future planning. Tell them that they should participate in their fields of excellence, but they must also pursue an appropriate education to avoid closing the doors to careers and lifestyles that may be more realistic after all.

Keeping Academics Central

Basketball coaches or music or drama teachers may be very enthusiastic about the most talented children with whom they work. They may counteridentify with these students much as parents do. They might see within them the talents, ambitions, wishes, and disappointments that they felt as adolescents. Influenced by their own unfulfilled wishes, they may inadvertently direct these youths toward concentrating too heavily on their own specialty field. Their enthusiasm for and commitment to the field, mixed with the belief that they have discovered unusual talent, can cause them to emphasize the talent area at the expense of other learning. Because these youths tend to have excellent rapport with their coaches and mentors, they may accept every communication as gospel truth.

Coaches are in a superb position to alert talented children about real-life competition and about the central importance of broad academic preparation. Specialty teachers are probably not as excited about math as drama, nor as good at writing compositions as playing tennis. Nonetheless, they should familiarize themselves with the total child that they are educating in order to avoid influencing these youths to invest so much time and energy in their specialty that they neglect less glamorous endeavors.

Other faculty members who observe these children's lack of interest or underachievement should ask the specialty coaches or teachers to make appropriate compromises that allow children to participate and develop their special talents but permit them to maintain achievement in all of their courses. Certainly both are possible, and the drama or football coaches are in excellent positions to give messages to children about central and peripheral activities. Strong academic preparation is central but obviously not sufficient for these children. Keeping extracurricular activities extra will permit them to enjoy the special challenge of their talents while continuing to participate in areas where they do not excel—that is, other course work.

Acceleration or Grade Skipping

Some highly gifted children will not experience challenge with their age mates even when their curriculum is adjusted because their intellectual abilities and skills are so advanced. There is considerable research on all forms of acceleration, including early entrance to kindergarten, compacting curriculum, grade skipping, advanced placement courses, and early entrance to college.[3] It is appropriate to consider subject and/or grade acceleration if students' IQ and achievement test scores suggest that they are not being challenged.

Emotional maturity and good peer relationships will probably predict a healthy adjustment to a higher grade level but are not the main factors to consider. There are actually several factors that contribute to positive and negative outcomes when grade skipping a child. An excellent resource to use when determining the appropriateness of a whole grade skip is the *Iowa Acceleration Scale*,[4] which allows teachers, administrators, and parents to use objective measures to rate a particular child on whether or not a grade skip is advisable.

In general, skipping only one grade at a time seems to facilitate better adjustment. However, exceptions should be made for students with extreme talent or skills. Studies of even extreme acceleration indicate excellent success from both academic and social perspectives.[5]

Continuous monitoring is important to ascertain whether further curriculum modifications are necessary.

The attitude of the receiving teacher is an issue to be considered when deciding upon acceleration because grade-skipped children may feel considerable pressure if their teachers do not believe that acceleration is appropriate. Despite the conclusive research indicating the success of grade skipping, many administrators and teachers tend to be set against the concept. The opposition to acceleration likely comes from two main sources:

- Extremely gifted children tend to have more social problems during adolescence than other gifted children or average children, whether or not they are grade skipped.

- Adolescents tend to have some social problems, whether or not they are grade skipped.

When students are grade skipped, typical problems of adolescence and of the highly gifted are blamed on the grade skipping. However, when they have not been grade skipped, the problems are attributed to their adolescence or their giftedness.

If the child is a perfectionist and earning all As, some kind of acceleration is probably appropriate. You should take a proactive position toward acceleration. Don't wait until the child is manifesting behavioral problems, underachieving, or complaining about boredom to make a decision to accelerate in a subject or skip a grade. Once the acceleration takes place, make sure that the child has sufficient counseling to make the move successful, both academically and emotionally. Appropriate grade skipping is most frequently viewed as successful from the students', parents', and teachers' points of view.

Acceptance of Criticism

Underachieving students will be more willing to accept criticism from favorite coaches and teachers in their specialty areas than from other classroom teachers or their parents. If English or math teachers criticize the basketball stars or rock singers, their response will typically be: "The teacher just doesn't like me," or "I can't do math." Remember, dominant children are "show-people," and they see lack of praise as criticism. It is difficult for adults to give them enough assurance, but here are some suggestions.

Don't criticize these children in front of their peers. They lose face easily, and you may become a permanent enemy if you embarrass them.

Sarcasm and humor are also likely to be viewed as unfair, unreasonable, and insulting. They don't laugh at themselves easily. Reserve humor and light sarcasm until after they've accepted you as a friend. Then, handling humorous sarcasm will be a good exercise for them.

At first, you will want to begin almost every criticism with a compliment—for example, "I really think you're getting the idea, but your paragraph includes a few too many subjects." This approach may sound a bit awkward and indirect, but teachers should pair honest observations of effort with the criticisms, at least some of the time. The key is to make these children see you as an ally. They tend to dichotomize people into either friends or enemies. It takes a special effort for teachers to evaluate in a supportive way, but it will facilitate these youths' acceptance of criticism. When they have identified you as a supportive person, you'll find that you can be a bit more direct. However, don't be manipulated into backing away from the evaluation process entirely. Students become less defensive and more comfortable with criticism when they become accustomed to recognizing the constructive part that it plays in their learning.

Dominant children often compete with teachers in power struggles and may choose unpredictable class times for establishing their superior power. The intellectually and socially dominant are particularly adept at attempting to show their peers how smart and powerful they are by proving their teachers wrong. Furthermore, the dominant conformers, who tend not to be troublemaking students, will frequently find allies in peers and parents, and you may discover that what you thought was a simple deserved criticism of a child's work or behavior becomes a major social battle with formidable opponents. These children are seasoned battlers, and they like to win. If you take them on in contests, don't expect them to be fair. You are likely to hear things about yourself with which you can't even remotely identify that they've told to other students, teachers, or their parents. They will manipulate to win, and because they have a strong reputation based on their excellence, their audiences believe them.

Remember Rimm's Law #10: Adults should avoid confrontations with children unless they are reasonably sure that they can control the outcomes. If you remain these children's ally, you can help and even criticize them. If they cast you as their enemy, you will feel frustrated and helpless and will not be able to assist them in change. Sometimes you may find yourself in confrontations with these children even though you cannot recall the origin of the problem.

When you sense that this has happened, your best chance of success will be to have a private conference with them. In discussing the situation with them, your position should be one of strength and fairness—neither too rigid nor too weak. The conference should focus on the problem, with no winner or loser. If you are punitive, the confrontation will go on. If you appear ineffective, these children may apologize but continue to badmouth you and try to dominate you in the presence of peers. You should maintain respect by your own power and by recognizing the children's strength. Dominant children can be equally unkind to those whom they view as weak or whom they have cast as rivals.

Intrinsic Motivation

Engaging in activities without an audience seems boring to dominant children. They expect continuous praise, feedback, and admiration. They tend not to get involved in intrinsically motivating activities because it is not the process but the outcome that interests them.

Teachers can use this dependence on feedback as a bridge to introduce these children to new interest areas that are noncompetitive and have no external rewards. Students should develop interests and activities for which personal growth and satisfaction are motivators. Some examples of classroom assignments that stimulate children to work for intrinsic satisfactions appear in Figure 12.2. These can be interspersed among the more typical graded lessons for variety and to teach children to do work without external reward.

Figure 12.2. Class Assignments to Encourage Intrinsic Interests

- Projects graded by pass/fail
- Self-graded assignments
- Individually selected projects
- Special-interest trips and speakers
- Discussion sessions on personal interests and hobbies
- Small group projects
- Total class cooperative projects—for example, murals or plays (these have audiences but are cooperative ventures without class stars)
- Community member interviews
- Surveys and questionnaire analysis
- Scientific experiments
- Extra-credit projects

Source: Rimm, S. B. (1990). *Learning leads Q-cards: Teacher tips.* Watertown, WI: Apple.

The last item on the list, extra-credit projects, may appear to be an extrinsically motivated assignment. Certainly, it is the actual awarding of credit that motivates the child to begin the independent effort. However, once involved in an activity for which they are more or less assured of credit, children will develop the personal sense of accomplishment that we call *intrinsic reinforcement*. Extra-credit projects are an excellent way to tempt dominant children into the world of self-directed exploration of interests.

Many teachers withdraw the opportunity for earning extra credit from those who are doing poorly on regular assignments, telling them to invest their time in studying instead. Dominant underachievers, who don't expect to get good grades when they conform to teachers' rules and who prefer directing their own study, will be much more willing to do productive work if you encourage them with extra credit to engage in some personally selected learning experiences. You should, of course, guide them to truly challenging and worthwhile activities in order to assure that they are learning relevant material in their individual projects.

Biographical Study

Reading biographies can be inspiring to all students. However, dominant conforming students have already experienced a great deal of success and have developed self-confidence directly related to continued successes. They often consider themselves to be extremely talented in their areas of expertise. They'll require preparation for competition beyond high school, whether that be a college or in their careers. Biographies can teach the concept that successful people fail multiple times and either persevere toward success or change direction creatively to find other outlets for their talents.

In one study, elementary students were encouraged toward greater effort when they were exposed to biographies of how successful people develop their skills. On the other hand, when children were exposed to biographies that primarily emphasized the natural talent of eminent persons, it discouraged student learning.[6]

Reading biographies was a frequent childhood activity of successful people. Many have described the motivational effect of their biography reading. For example, African-American neurosurgeon Alexa Canady recalls reading 10 or 12 little blue biographies a week, and Senator Kay Bailey Hutchison remembered having read all of the biographies in her school library.[7]

Biographies are suitable for reading aloud to classes to be followed up by discussion, and they are also suitable for individual reading for book reports. In order to emphasize effort, questions that direct students' attention toward perseverance and coping with failure experiences are likely to enhance their own persistence and resilience.

Preparation for College

Dominant conformers are probably the underachievers most in need of preparation for college. For the most part, they graduate from high school ranking reasonably high in their class; they are self-confident, skilled, and ready to take on the world. They've worked hard in their areas of expertise and coped with competition in those areas well. Colleges have not only accepted them but welcomed them with sports, music, drama, and academic scholarships. Their "just getting by" in academics was acceptable to their parents or teachers, who assumed that college would encourage their maturity. Almost no one was really worried.

In college, these students can meet a tall wall. An injury prevents Joe from playing football. Khana's first major exam is graded with a C. The drama department expects Emma to work behind the scenes. Alex doesn't qualify for the highest band or orchestra. Inside, these students continue to feel capable, but they can't seem to impress others with that capability. They have their IQs retested. They determine that engineering or music is the wrong major. They decide to stay as far away from the stage as possible.

Many of these students mature, adjust, and regroup. They may choose different careers. They may learn to function in competition. They may come to terms with the recognition that they won't dominate their field. A very few actually do go on to dominate their talent areas and become Olympic athletes, professional sports stars, accomplished artists or musicians, cancer research scientists, and business magnates. Of course, even they must learn to cope with setbacks in competition.

Many others view the wall as an impossible barrier. They become depressed or anxious. Their grades drop; they drop out. They give up lifelong goals and feel like failures for years. Here is a case study of a talented violinist:

> Lacey was determined to be a violinist. Her talent led her to victory at all contest levels. She also did quite well academically. She entered an excellent university that had a fine music department. But by her sophomore year, Lacey had given up on

music and had failed most of her courses. Depressed, she dropped out of school. She could not even listen to music for years afterward without being flooded by terrible disappointment.

Lacey emerged and regrouped later, determined to build a new career. She will surely be successful eventually. However, this highly intelligent and talented young woman cannot erase her record and must explain the problem at every attempt to reenter college or meet a challenge. Her confidence is now very precarious, and many more years will need to be invested before she can arrive at her career goals.

Following are excerpts from two letters that I received after speaking about underachieving gifted students on the *Today* show:

Dear Dr. Rimm,

I am 27 years old. As a young child, I was labeled *gifted* and sent to a special school for two days a week. I always received a lot of attention from teachers and felt a lot of pressure to do well in school. Nobody in my family had ever gone to college. In fact, my mother dropped out of school in the tenth grade, and my father had a sixth-grade education.

I dreamed of leaving my hometown and going to a prestigious college. I was a nearly straight-A student throughout high school and scored very well on the SATs. Consequently, I left home to attend Smith College on an academic scholarship. I was ill-prepared for the stress of living far from home and the pressures of being thrown into a competitive academic environment with some of the best students in the country. By my sophomore year, I was suffering from acute anxiety attacks, and it was all I could do to sit through a class without leaving the room. I graduated from college on time, and while my grades were far from abysmal, they certainly did not reflect my true academic ability.

I had dreamed of being a doctor since I was a little girl, yet I had defeated myself to a large degree. Four years later, I decided that it was time to pursue the dream again. Today, I have been rejected from medical school two years running and feel that it may be a long time before I can look as good on paper as I once did. Medical schools don't care about my high IQ or my high school record. They look at my college performance, without regard for any of the reasons that I failed to live up to expectations during that period in my life. So you see, I am a good example of a gifted child gone awry—so much potential, so little guidance at the right time.

Dear Dr. Rimm,

My lack of academic success in college has led to unrelenting disappointment in myself, frustration, depression, severe migraine headaches, and insomnia. My dream has always been, since I was a little girl, to become an attorney. I see this dream slipping away.

I am an only child who graduated in the top 10% of my high school class with a 3.5 GPA. I took all advanced and college preparatory classes throughout junior high and high school.

Feeling confident about my academic abilities, I entered the University of North Carolina at Chapel Hill, where I graduated with a 2.2 GPA. I was so overwhelmed by this that I cried myself to sleep almost every night for two months.

The GPA with which I graduated is not in any way reflective of my true abilities. However, law schools look at two things—the GPA and the LSAT.

Figure 12.3. Guidelines to Success for New College Students

- Never miss a class, no matter how boring or irrelevant you believe it to be. You've paid for this education, so you might as well get your money's worth. The lecture or explanation you miss may become the exam question that you don't quite remember learning,

- Plan to study at least two hours for each hour of class time. Colleges recommend this guideline; take their advice literally.

- Structure your study time on a schedule or calendar for at least one week ahead of time. Visualizing the time allocated for study will lessen the pressure you feel.

- If you're struggling with course content, find help before you fail. Writing labs, tutors, study groups, and counseling abound on college campuses. No one is going to take you by your hand to help you; you will have to initiate the search, but there is plenty of willing and free help available. Even A students get help.

Figure 12.3 includes some suggestions from which these students might have benefited and that you may wish to share with students who will be entering college. These are most important for young people whose parents have not attended college and for dominant conformers who are convinced that they will be able to climb any mountain.

Chapter 13

What You Can Do for Dominant Nonconforming Children

Reversing underachievement in dominant nonconforming children is a difficult challenge. These children are the most resistant to change. Their behaviors make them unpleasant to live with. They are often belligerent, rebellious, cocky, and even hostile. Yet beneath their protective shield, these are typically bright, sensitive children who are easily hurt. They feel confident only when they are in control. Unlike dominant conforming children, they feel that they do not have acceptable areas of expertise in which they perform well and receive attention. They are dethroned youths who remember their earlier childhood as a more satisfying time—when they were adored, when they were "perfect," when they earned all A's, or when they were Daddy's little girls.[1] These are young people whose position of being center stage has been removed, and their manipulative and rebellious behaviors are efforts to return to the glorious period of their lives when they were so admired. They are often negative, angry, and even violent. Alcohol and drug abuse become approaches that temporarily restore power. When the effects wear off, their feelings of powerlessness return until they use further alcohol or drugs to restore the sense of power again.

These children struggle and resist acknowledging their problems as their own. You'd like to put them in their place, shake them, spank them, and somehow convince them that you're the adult. They make you feel powerless, trapped. You lose your cool with them again and again. You wonder why you lose control and what initiates the brouhahas. They push you continually, yet pushing back doesn't work. Your intuitive responses are almost always ineffective. Nowhere is Rimm's Law #10 so applicable: Adults should avoid confrontations with children unless they are reasonably sure that they can control the outcomes.

Consider the pattern that dominant nonconformers habitually follow. When they don't feel in control, they argue. You as parent or teacher feel pushed and undoubtedly say no to almost every request they make. This doesn't stop them. They debate further. You feel obligated to counter with reasoning. But they're planning to win. They pursue the argument relentlessly until you find yourself completely irrational. You're out of control. Now they can use your irrationality as the basis for refusing your requests and being angry at you. Furthermore, they can usually find someone to take their side against you because you've been so irrational. This cycle and their power continue until they argue with almost everyone. They then claim that no one understands them, and they are actually correct—no one does, least of all themselves.

There is a more effective response to these students, though it will seem counterintuitive. The first step is a positive and firm alliance with these children based on understanding the strong pressures that they feel—for example, to be smart, creative, artistic, or popular. Before ever responding to their requests, give them plenty of time to talk. While they're talking, they feel smart and in an alliance with you. You should try to be confident and authoritative and to really show them that you're listening. After they've completed their discourse, take time to think about your response so that you can avoid overreacting or being trapped. When you give your answer, it should be absolutely firm and irreversible. It should also include a few reasons so that you model the reasoning process. If your children or students try to continue pushing, you simply need to stop, walk away, or time them or yourself out.

Never reopen negotiations. Instead, remain positive but absolutely firm. They may not like your reasons. They may not be happy. But with time, they will respect you. Wishy-washy adults get trampled by dominant nonconforming kids. Dominant kids view wishy-washy adults as weak, dumb, and as having been born a thousand years ago. If you're still smiling and in control, if they continue to feel that you're in an alliance with them, if they can respect your fairness, then they're more likely to respect the limits you set.

Some dominant nonconforming children will require psychological help. As young children, they may have been diagnosed as having Attention Deficit Hyperactivity Disorder (with hyperactivity and impulsivity), and later, depending on their acting-out behavior, they may be diagnosed as oppositional defiant or depressed. As children, their goals were set impossibly high; they wanted to do something spectacular or reach stardom. As adolescents and young adults, they feel like failures as they perceive their peers surpassing them in accomplishments. They flip-flop from the highs of dominance to the lows of depression with little of the patience and perseverance needed to direct their high energy toward productiveness.

You will have a challenging task in effecting change in these kids. If your children are of preschool age, the job is relatively easy. For children in elementary grades and junior high school, it is a bit more difficult. The senior high years are the hardest. However, after high school, if they are on their own, they may be motivated toward change and may actually be more likely to reverse their underachievement than they would have earlier. Be prepared for patience, and expect many failures. However, if you can persevere in attacking these children's problems, you can expect them to become successful adults. Achievement orientation, competitiveness, and motivation are all within them, though they have masked it well.

What You Can Do as Parents

You probably have no doubt that changes should be made for your dominant nonconforming children. You probably also feel helpless and out of control—not sure when or how to intervene in their lives. If you ask the advice of any two people, you get two different responses. You feel confused, disappointed, guilty, disgusted with parenting, and not at all sure where to turn. Despite the fact that it seems that your children control you, it is important to realize that they don't feel secure at all. To the contrary, as long as their lives are a struggle for power over others, you can be sure that they are suffering and feeling unsure of their own personal direction.

In changing these children's reinforcements at home, it is important to see the world from their perspective, but not necessarily to act toward them in ways that will gratify their immediate wants. As parents, you must take the long-range view; as children, they can't. It's your role to direct them according to their needs, but not necessarily according to their present wishes. If your children are difficult to live with and also unhappy, you surely know that something more must be done, even if you are convinced that you've tried your best. The recommendations that follow have been proven effective but are not easy. They are the practices that we use with children who come to our clinic. If you feel that you can't make a difference, keep in mind that these children are in the most extreme quadrant of underachievers. You may need professional help, and positive results may not be immediate.

Reversing Early Childhood Dominance

Some children seem to seek dominance from birth, almost as if it is an integral part of their personalities. It seems that by instinct, they sense that their parents won't manage to control them, and although they are fed, cared for, and loved, they are not content. Some parents tell me that by the time their children are at age three, the children are controlling them, and they find themselves yelling, screaming, and acting in irrational ways that they never imagined for parenthood. Parents say such things as, "I ask him to sit in the corner, and he won't," "I put her in her room, and she comes out," and, "I tell him that he must eat his vegetables; he eats them and throws them up right at the table." These parents can hardly believe that they've given birth to such misbehaving monsters. Their children have somehow discovered that they are in charge of their caretakers. They have developed an early and very severe case of nonconforming dominance. However, there is great hope when this situation is discovered early. You can redirect their power. You can take charge—*and you must.*

With preschool-age children, there's an almost magic wand solution to regaining control that is nearly always effective. It is also effective with many children up to age eight. Beyond that age, it works with some, but not with others. It is not intended for adolescents. The method is the "time-out," and it is described in Figure 13.1. Many parents use time-outs, but often, they don't do so effectively.

Figure 13.1. Recipe for Successful Time-Outs (Follow *Exactly*)

- One adult should tell the child briefly that the consequence for naughty behaviors will be to stay in his or her room for 10 minutes of quiet (as determined by a timer) with the door closed. The naughty behaviors should be specified. Don't select all—just the worst (for example, hitting, temper tantrums).

- If the child is likely to open the door when it's closed, arrange it so that the door can be locked from the outside (some parents loop the end of a rope around the doorknob of the child's room and loop the other end around the knob of the door of an adjacent room). For very strong children, some kind of lock is initially required. Of course, parents should always be nearby for safety.

- Every time the child misbehaves in the stated way, the child should be escorted to the room without the parent's losing his or her temper and with only a sentence of explanation.

- If the child slams the door, loses his or her temper, bangs on walls, throws toys, screams, shouts, or talks, there should be absolutely no response from anyone. Expect the first few times to be terrible. Set the timer only when the child is quiet.

- After 10 minutes, open the door to permit the child to leave. There should be no further explanation, apology, warning, or discussion of love. Act as if nothing unusual has happened. DON'T HUG! Repeat as necessary.

- After one week, only a warning of the closed door should be necessary to prevent the undesirable behavior. Give only one warning. ALWAYS follow through.

Source: Rimm, S. B. (1996). *Learning leads Q-cards: Parent pointers.* Watertown, WI: Apple.

This method will work if you follow it exactly. Your children will become much calmer and will actually obey your requests most of the time. You will be in control of your children, and you will be a much more confident parent. As long as you maintain that control and don't regress to the powerless tactics of screaming and impossible threats, your children will not return to the routine of continually pushing limits. The change is usually dramatic.

As you read this, I know that you won't believe me about the effectiveness of this procedure. Parents who come to my office don't believe me either. However, they come to their next visit smiling, convinced, and ready for the next guidelines. When you use time-outs, the dramatic reversal will take place because you have changed your role from follower to leader. Prior to the time-outs, your children were in command and didn't know how to cope with the excessive power. You are giving your children positive direction, and they will feel so much more secure. You are bigger and in charge, and they will be content to follow your secure lead. Although initially they may be furious at losing their power, they're young enough to feel a new confidence in their own childhood.

Some of you may feel that the time-out procedure is cruel and unusual punishment that you would not inflict on your children. You may be inclined to modify it by explaining to your children afterward how much you love them. However, if you do, you will cancel the effect of the time-out by giving them double messages. The time-out is effective because it completely withdraws attention. If it is punctuated by words of love, your children will continue to control you. If you're reading this book, your children know that you love them. It certainly is appropriate to remind them of your love, but not at times when they've behaved poorly, and certainly not immediately following a time-out.

Dominant children are "show-people." They like to function with an audience. Withdrawing their audience tells them that their act is ineffective and that they should select more appropriate showmanship. As long as you deal consistently with your children's unacceptable actions by completely removing their audience, they will search for more praiseworthy behaviors. However, this is a strong habit that you are changing, so expect them to make every effort to upstage you in their last scenes.

The locked door time-out procedure is not intended for all children, but only for those who are too powerful and would not otherwise remain in the time-out room. After you've used the locked door just a few times, even dominant children will be willing to stay in their room without your needing to lock the door.

There are some occasions when children don't respond to the time-out treatment. Figure 13.2 lists some mistakes that are easy to make in timing out very powerful children. Remember, your goal is to avoid accelerating the power struggle. If you take children's possessions out of their rooms, give all of their toys away, or use too tough an approach, you only exacerbate the struggle. Your kids will dig in their heels, and you will lose your alliance with them. They will try to defy you and tell you by words or actions that time-outs won't work with them. If they're telling you this, you know that they hate it. Don't add further punishments.

Figure 13.2. Mistakes in Using Time-Outs

- When children time themselves out, they often slam the door. Parents respond by telling them not to slam the door. The children thus realize that they have power over their parents, and they continue to slam the door.

- Sometimes, when the children call out and ask how much time they have left, parents will make the mistake of talking to or actually arguing with them. This conversation cancels the effect of withdrawn attention.

- Some parents are hesitant about locking the door and will hold it closed or not even close it at all. If the parent holds the door, children know that the parent is holding it, and thus, the power struggle continues. If it is not closed at all, children just walk in and out, proving that the parent is not in control.

- Sometimes after children have thrown things around their rooms, parents insist that they go back in to pick up what they have thrown around. Another power struggle ensues, in which case children take charge of the parent by argument again.

- Sometimes parents use a time-out only after they've yelled and screamed and lost their temper. That's too late. It has to be executed reasonably calmly, showing that parents are in charge.

Source: Rimm, S. B. (1996). *Learning leads Q-cards: Parent pointers.* Watertown, WI: Apple.

Explain to these children at a time when they're calm that you're helping them cope with their own anger and that they're welcome to punch a pillow or yell or scream as a way of venting their anger. They can also play, color, or read to calm themselves. However, only when they feel calm will their door be opened. Remind them that they and you will feel better afterward. Even with time-outs, you're after positive alliance and firmness, not punishment.

Children should be given opportunities to make choices and participate in decision making, even in early childhood. However, you should always define the choices for them. Let them choose from an established range of activities, behaviors, and material possessions. As they get older, you may broaden the range available to them, but throughout childhood and adolescence, *you* should set those limits. If you progressively extend their freedom as they make responsible choices, they will feel independent, trusted, and in reasonable control of their lives.

Ironically, if children are given too much freedom too early, they feel out of control and search for a sense of control. They take freedom from adults and trample adults' rights by requiring continuous surveillance. By providing them structure and then flexibility within that structure, children and adults can live together comfortably.

Wish, Want, Work, Wait

Parents who struggled through their own childhoods and are now successful are anxious to reward their children with the material possessions and enjoyable experiences of which they were deprived. Parents who as children had unlimited material possessions may also be tempted to shower costly toys, clothes, and activities upon their children. Children who find that all of their requests, and later their demands, are responded to immediately grow accustomed to it and expect it to continue. At the same time, parents who give so much so easily are taking away from their children the sense of efficacy and confidence that comes when "wishes and wants" are followed by "work and waiting." The sense of instantaneous delivery by someone else gives children the power and audacity to ask continuously for material possessions, gifts, and activities.

When children learn to expect instant gratification, they find themselves unprepared for education and schooling. They have learned only to wish and want, not to work or wait. They want to be instantly smart, immediately successful, and to easily complete their responsibilities. They want to wave a magic wand and be declared bright, talented, and creative, and they expect intelligence to provide immediate results. They assume that other good students learn instantly and get good grades with quick study, so they deny themselves the satisfaction that comes with effort.

Teach your children to work and wait. Whatever material possessions and experiences they have, they should be learning a process of effort and patience. They can learn the process from planning, working, and saving with you for events that will be meaningful. Savings accounts or charts that plan their savings for material possessions show them visually that saving up works. You can also help them to apply these concepts to education, where planning, effort, and patience will reward them with deserved success. No matter how much you wanted all of those possessions and experiences that you were denied, don't give them to your children without their effort. Don't steal their work or their wait!

Attention Deficit Hyperactivity Disorder

Attention Deficit Hyperactivity Disorder (ADHD) can be caused biologically, environmentally, or both ways. There is not yet a biological test for diagnosing this disorder, although scientists are trying to develop one. Rating scales, which are based on the descriptions given in the *Diagnostic and Statistical Manual of Mental Disorders* (4th edition),[2] are the basis for all diagnoses. Figure 13.3 includes some of the main characteristics of ADHD. Six of these characteristics, which must have originated before the age of seven, are required to qualify children for each diagnosis. These characteristics should be present in at least two settings—for example, home and school.

Figure 13.3. Characteristics of Attention Deficit Hyperactivity Disorder

---

314.00 Attention Deficit Hyperactivity Disorder, Predominantly Inattentive Type*

A. Often fails to give close attention to details or makes careless mistakes in schoolwork, work, or other activities.

B. Often has difficulty sustaining attention in tasks or play activities.

C. Often does not seem to listen when spoken to directly.

D. Often does not follow through on instructions and fails to finish schoolwork, chores, or duties in the workplace (not due to oppositional behavior or failure to understand instructions).

E. Often has difficulty organizing tasks and activities.

F. Often avoids, dislikes, or is reluctant to engage in tasks that require sustained mental effort (such as schoolwork or homework).

G. Often loses things necessary for tasks or activities (e.g., toys, school assignments, pencils, books, or tools).

H. Is often easily distracted by extraneous stimuli.

I. Is often forgetful in daily activities.

314.01 Attention Deficit Hyperactivity Disorder, Predominantly Hyperactive-Impulse Type*

Hyperactivity

A. Often fidgets with hands or feet or squirms in seat.

B. Often leaves seat in classroom or in other situations in which remaining seated is expected.

C. Often runs about or climbs excessively in situations in which it is inappropriate (in adolescents or adults, may be limited to subjective feelings of restlessness).

D. Is often "on the go" or often acts as if "driven by a motor."

E. Often talks excessively.

Impulsivity

F. Often blurts out answers before questions have been completed.

G. Often has difficulty awaiting turn.

H. Often interrupts or intrudes on others (e.g., butts into conversations or games).

*Must show at least six characteristics that have begun before age seven

Source: American Psychiatric Association. (2000). *Diagnostic and statistical manual of mental disorders* (4th ed., text revision). Washington, DC: Author.

Although parenting problems always happen with ADHD, this does not mean that ADHD is caused by poor parenting. However, high-energy children are especially difficult ones to raise.

Biological interventions for ADHD include stimulant medications such as Ritalin and Adderall. Both medications are available in long-acting form so that children won't have to take pills during the school day. There are also non-stimulant medications available, but your family physician or a child psychiatrist is the best source of information on medications. At this time, ADHD is over-diagnosed, and medication is being over-prescribed. Don't hurry to your physician to ask for medication. Try behavioral changes first. Medication often has side effects and should be used only with the careful supervision of a physician.

Figure 13.4 lists some of the side effects of Ritalin. Although these side effects take place in fewer than 50% of the children using it—and for some children, there are no side effects—Ritalin or other medications should not be taken without careful consideration. However, for some children, these medications are very helpful for both calming them and heightening their ability to pay attention.

Figure 13.4. Side Effects of Ritalin

More Common Side Effects	
• Loss of appetite • Abdominal pain • Weight loss during long-term therapy • Inability to fall or stay asleep • Abnormally fast heartbeat	
Less Common Side Effects	
• Abnormal heartbeat • Abnormal muscular movements • Blood pressure changes • Chest pain • Dizziness • Drowsiness • Fever • Headache • Hives • Jerking • Joint pain	• Nausea • Palpitations • Pulse changes • Rapid heartbeat • Red or purple skin spots • Skin inflammation • Skin rash • Tourette's Syndrome (severe and multiple twitching) • Writhing movements

Only a small percentage of children with symptoms of ADHD actually require medication. Many children can be helped behaviorally. Blind controlled tests are best for determining if children require medication. "Blind" doesn't mean that parents or teachers should be blind—only that they should not know if the children are on medication or on a placebo (an inert pill that looks like the real medication) when reviewing the children's behavior. For those who believe that medication provides a cure-all, there is absolutely no long-term research that indicates that medication improves children's grades in school. And for those who think that medication only causes more problems, there is also no indication that medication increases the likelihood that children will use illicit drugs. On the other hand, whether or not ADHD children are medicated, they are more than twice as likely to be involved in substance abuse than children without ADHD (17.4% vs. 7.8%).[3] Unfortunately, there have been problems related to teenagers selling their prescription medication for misuse by others. In summary, medication can be helpful to children who are correctly diagnosed as having ADHD, but its use requires parent precautions.

Behavioral approaches that help these children include all of the suggestions given in this chapter. In addition, look at the attentional and organizational suggestions in Chapter 11 on dependent children. Time-outs, united parenting, and firm consistency are important. Redirecting children's energy toward constructive activities is a high priority. However, over-scheduling can cause them problems. They require structure and consistent expectations. Too hurried a pace will cause stress for them and their parents and will lead to overreaction and impulsiveness.

ADHD children thrive on some one-to-one time doing physical work and chores with a parent. Keep television watching to a minimum, and there should be none within an hour of bedtime. Keep them away from violent television programming, including violence in cartoons. Avoid activities that foster wrestling and physical contact with parents or siblings, although for most other children, these are not harmful. ADHD children extend this physically active show of affection to peers and easily get themselves into trouble, especially at school. Direct their energy toward sports or work projects.

Parents with ADHD children need support. They often benefit by joining parent support groups and going for regular counseling help. Some adolescents and adults continue to have ADHD symptoms. Others seem to outgrow the problems. Home and school environments make important differences for children with ADHD.

Be sure not to call your children your "ADHD kids," either directly or referentially. It will cause them to feel as though they have no responsibility for appropriate behavior and that their behaviors are, indeed, completely out of their control. Parent referential talk that these children are impossible to handle also adversely affects them. Moderate direct praise and positive referential talk are encouraging to all dominant nonconforming children, but especially to ADHD children.

Avoiding Confrontations

Dominant nonconforming children have built their confidence based on winning power struggles. Because this is a tenuous basis of self-esteem, they must continually manipulate people in their environments to reinforce the sense of power that comes only from winning and being right. In order for them to feel good about themselves, others must feel bad. They continuously compete against almost everyone, especially their parents. When comparison and competition are not part of a relationship, they invent methods of making comparisons. Of course, one method is to brag or put down others. They talk to adults as if the adults were children and they themselves were the adults. An equally common habit is to instigate an argument or confrontation that they expect to win.

This custom of arguing about everything with everyone can make home and school life quite unpleasant. Bright children will insist that they are being reasonable and will cleverly chastise their parents about being dictatorial rather than rational. They obviously enjoy the process of debate; however, if you observe carefully, you will notice that they rarely settle for reasonable solutions. They continue in the arguments until they win or until they have pushed their parents beyond self-control. When parents or teachers have lost their tempers, children automatically consider themselves right or winners because they view their adversaries' loss of self-control as weakness or failure.

Dominant children enjoy the sense of victory over their parents or peers because it makes them feel successful and powerful, and it gives them fuel for further debate because their opposition is perceived as an inadequacy. They search for ways in which to prove their power by initiating struggles in which they are assured of success. This habit begins when parents feel that they should explain reasons for all that they require of their children. Next, the parents are persuaded by their children's counter-reasoning to ease these requirements. As the children find themselves more frequently victorious, their ritual arguing is reinforced. This habitual struggle for power actually has little to do with reason or logic but is based on competition for control. Some children capture authority from their parents very early. By adolescence, children who are accustomed to the power struggle rituals feel depressed and angry unless they are victorious. They consider adults entirely unfair and dictatorial.

As parents, you should recast your interactions with your children to avoid this style of interchange. Be sure in children's discussions and debates that they are rationally evaluating ideas and are not just arguing for the sake of winning power. Once again, Rimm's Law #10 can guide your relationship with your children: Adults should avoid confrontation with children unless they are reasonably sure that they can control the outcomes. In other, more familiar words, pick your battles.

Your role is to continually guide your children without becoming dictatorial. Certainly, with increasing age and maturity, your children should earn increasing freedom and decision-making opportunities. However, you are their guide and leader, and if you relinquish your power before they are mature enough to find their own direction, they wander aimlessly searching for someone's guidance. There is a vacuum where there should be parental direction, and influential peers and various adults will move in to fill the void before the children have developed a value system by which to judge them wisely.

In order to win confrontations with your children, you must have the power to follow through and ensure that they will comply with your requests. Thus, sending young children to their rooms for time-outs is effective. It asserts your power and is enforceable. Sending rebellious teenagers to their rooms is usually ineffective. They will delight in proving you powerless by climbing out a window or cleverly engineering some other way to escape or flout you. Don't try it. It only reassures them that they can outmaneuver you.

It is a great challenge for parents and teachers of nonconforming, powerful children to outperform and outthink them. As children get older, there are fewer controls that a parent can utilize. By high school, there is money (sometimes), a driver's license, or access to the car, a cell phone, a computer, or perhaps some other special material possession that you can regulate. Sometimes even these are ineffectual. It is better to try to maintain an alliance with your children than for them to use all of their energies to oppose you.

Again, *if you can't control the outcome, don't confront.* Persuade, inspire, excite, influence, model by example, but don't argue. Every power struggle you lose reinforces your children's habits of domination and puts you into a weaker and weaker position. The louder you shout to motivate your children, the less they will respect you. The increased volume represents decreased control. As you lose power, they become further addicted to owning all control.

Families are not intended to be adversarial relationships. You will build respect with quiet control. Take your time. Don't rise immediately to your kids' bait. Tell them that you need time to think about requests or punishments. They may worry, but they will learn patience. Responding too quickly is what traps you into battle. Envision yourself as a wise, patient parent. Choose confrontations carefully so that you don't develop an atmosphere of combat. If 90% of family time is spent disputing differences of opinion or arguing for control, there is little remaining time in which to develop an atmosphere of positive growth.

If you initially invited your children to discuss issues and express their opinions in order to encourage democratic involvement of family members, you will see that you have overshot your mark. Families are not meant to be democracies. Children don't have the experience to have equal power. Now you must show authority where you still have power to control, and replace all other power struggles with less confrontational approaches—for example, inspiration, persuasion, suggestion, demonstration, and fun activities. These latter approaches give children choices within limits that you can regulate, yet they still keep the home atmosphere sufficiently positive so that children will want to please you instead of spite you. Strive to be authoritative but not authoritarian.

Use caution. Dominant nonconforming children are habitual fighters. They automatically manipulate for confrontation and victory. Adjusting to a less confrontational atmosphere will seem counterintuitive, but alliances leave more time and space for mutual growth and trust.

Following are anti-arguing instructions that can help you keep an alliance with dominant nonconformers.[4] An ALLIANCE acrostic following in Figure 13.5 summarizes these instructions.

1. When arguers come at you (they always choose an inconvenient time because they instinctively know that you're vulnerable), remind yourself not to say yes or no immediately. Instead, after they've made their request, ask them for their reasons. If you've asked for their reasons, they can never accuse you of not listening. Also, you'll feel better by not cutting off their expressions of feelings, and they'll feel better because they've had plenty of time to talk (talking makes them feel smart).

2. After you've heard their reasons, say, "Let me think about it. I'll get back to you in a few minutes" (minutes for a small request; more time for a larger one). There are three marvelous benefits to the second step of this arguing process. First, it permits you to continue to be rational (that's what you wanted to be when you accidentally trained your arguers). Second, it teaches children to be patient. Third, since arguers are often bright, manipulative children and because you haven't yet responded with either a yes or a no, they know that their good behavior increases the likelihood of your saying yes. Therefore, while you're taking time to be rational and while they're learning patience, these lovely, dominant children will be on their best behavior. How nice!

3. Think about their request and their reasons. Don't be negatively biased by their pushiness. If your answer is yes, smile and be positive and enthusiastic. Arguers rarely see adults smile.

4. If your answer is no—and you do have the right and obligation to say no sometimes—then say no firmly. Include a few reasons as part of your refusal. *Absolutely never* change your decision, and don't

engage in further discussion. Don't let them make you feel guilty. It is healthy for children to learn to accept no's in an environment where they are loved.

5. If they begin to argue again, review with them calmly that you've heard their request, you've listened to their reasons, you've taken time to think about them, you've given them your answer and your reasons, and the discussion is now over. Don't get trapped back into discussion of the initial request.

6. If they continue arguing and they're below age 10 and not too big, escort them to their room for a time-out. If they're too big for you to time them out, go calmly and assertively to your own room and close and lock your door. If they beat on your door, ignore them. Relax with a good book. Finally, they'll learn that parents have earned the privilege of saying no. They'll also have learned that they may continue to have the opportunity to remain children. They may not appreciate the latter at the time. However, your home will become a more pleasant and positive place in which to live, and your children will find that you are positive, fair, and rational, but not a wimp, and they'll respect you.

Figure 13.5. Parent Anti-Arguing ALLIANCE

Ally with a positive statement of interest.

Listen to what the child says.

Learn about what the child is thinking.

Inquire to determine if there are other issues missed.

Answer wisely only after taking time to think about the request.

Name two or three reasons for your response.

Consequence if the child reinitiates arguing.

End. Absolutely do not re-engage in the argument.

Emotional Ups and Downs

Victory in competition, control of others, and a sense of power provide emotional highs for dominant nonconforming children. As they approach victory and feel confident of winning, they also become enthusiastic. However, an absence of goals or losses of power cause these children to feel lethargic and depressed. Of course, it should not be surprising to parents to find their children disappointed or depressed in response to an obvious loss because they can recognize the cause of the problem. If a child performs poorly in a tennis match or breaks up with a boyfriend, there's good reason for sadness. However, it is often much more difficult to uncover other reasons for depression. Extreme mood swings are very common and worry parents. It is important to identify the cause(s) of their depression so that you can guide your children toward a more effective problem-solving pattern.

Dominant nonconforming children become depressed when adults say no to something that they want very much. If you, as parents, have refused permission for your children to see a girlfriend, participate in an activity, or buy a new outfit that they have selected, then they will use depression to manipulate you into changing your decision. These children may cease communication with the family, close themselves up in their rooms, not come to meals, and ignore your questions that indicate that you are worried about their mood. Depending on how determined they are—and how successful they've been before—they will eventually lure you into granting their original request or doing some alternative favor for them that will make them feel that they have won the power contest. Their depression will then completely dissipate, and they will swing into a high mood again; you will be left wondering at the amazing change in their temperament. If you've given in to their wishes, despite the fact that you resolved not to, you will feel helpless, out of control, and not sure of how you arrived at this point. How you need to handle this problem will depend largely on how extreme the problem has become.

If you have small children who show sadness, tears, or depression when events don't go their way, begin early to ignore the sadness and tears or respond to them simply. For example, you might say to your daughter, "I know you're disappointed that you can't go to your friend's party, but you must go to Grandma's house for her birthday dinner. There just isn't any sense in crying about it." Give her a pat on the head or a hug to comfort her, but don't overreact to the sadness, and certainly don't permit her to convince you that this week's friend is more important than her grandmother. If she continues to pout at Grandma's, ask other family members to ignore the sad face, take her aside, and privately voice your disappointment in her behavior; then go on with the party. If she is not an extreme case, she will rejoin the family fun within half an hour. If she is already an expert mood manipulator, she may act despondent all weekend. Because you know the cause of her depression and because you don't want to allow further manipulation, persevere in your unresponsiveness. You may not feel as if you're accomplishing anything, but you are actively breaking a very difficult behavioral habit that can get very much out of control in later years.

The most important skill that you must teach these small children is the habit of accepting "no" graciously. Permit them to suffer a bit. Don't feel so sorry for them in those minor disappointments that each sadness is met with a too-comforting release from their sorrow or a compensating favor or material possession. Permit them to work through minor disappointments to prepare them for tolerating larger difficulties ahead.

If you have adolescent children who habitually manipulate you with depression and you have clearly identified the "no's" that you give as the reasons for their depression, then they are already in a dangerously powerful position. The most critical change that you should make is to think carefully about your responses to their requests before giving them. Avoid saying no unless you are absolutely sure that you can and will be able to defend and maintain that position. An alternative to saying no that helps them to break the habit of always expecting to get what they want is the "wish, want, work, and wait" position described earlier. This moves responsibility from you to them and focuses their attention from manipulating you to their own personal effort. Here's an example:

> Thirteen-year-old Sierra is determined to get contact lenses instead of glasses, which she sees as no longer fashionable. You are tempted to say no because her glasses are only one year old. Contact lenses aren't expensive, but you're not sure that Sierra will handle them responsibly. If you say no, be prepared for depression and manipulation until she makes you change your mind. Don't confront unless you can win—but you can't win this one because her manipulative depressions are already extensive. Instead, the conversation should sound like this:

> "Sierra, I can understand why you'd like contact lenses, and I think it's a good idea to get them as long as you understand the additional risks and responsibilities that go with them. I think it's fair for you to pay for them, because we did buy glasses recently. If you save your babysitting money for the cost of the contacts, we'll let you try them and show us that you can be responsible."

This response avoids a power struggle and allies you on your daughter's side. It permits her to work and wait for her request instead of expecting it immediately. Furthermore, it permits her a graceful way out of a power struggle. Should she decide that the contact lenses aren't worth saving her money for, she can simply forget the whole issue or let you know that she has decided to direct her funds toward something else she wants. This is far better than the more typical "No, we can't afford it," or "No, you can't have everything you want," which would probably be followed by days or weeks of depressive manipulations and the final decision by parents to purchase the contacts.

Obviously, not all requests can be met with so easy an alternative response. However, if your dominant nonconforming children are accustomed to manipulating you with depression, you should make every effort to change the habit by not rewarding it. There are two main ways to prevent this manipulation:

1. Don't give children what they want only in response to their irrational sadness and depression.

2. Direct their requests toward opportunities in which they can earn privileges and thus earn the confidence that comes with personal control based on effort rather than manipulations.

Threats of suicide are the most powerful manipulation that dominant nonconforming adolescents may use. **Threats of suicide, even if you feel sure that they are manipulations, should always be taken seriously.** Young people who threaten to kill themselves should receive professional help, whether or not they think they need it. Suicide attempts are even more potent as manipulations than are threats, and professionals can usually help to prevent children's actual attempts. Obviously, the act of suicide is final. It typically results from feelings of powerlessness. When children who have become accustomed to a great amount of control find themselves unable to control multiple factors in their lives, they feel powerless. Of course, adolescent suicides do not all stem from a history of reinforcing depressive frustration. Some severe depressions may be biochemical in nature.

The moping and depression of dominant children, either conforming or nonconforming, is not always a tool for manipulation. There is a less serious form of the problem that appears frequently and causes parents to worry unnecessarily. It is depression from boredom. This kind of depression causes parents to probe adolescents with questions that these young people probably don't know how to answer. It takes parent observation to determine the cause of the problem and, usually, patience to permit adolescents to resolve it themselves.

Dominant children are usually very active socially. Because they gain their confidence from involving themselves with friends, any lull in activity that many adults would see as relaxation is boring to them. It is a feeling of lack of direction, a malaise—or as they would say, "nothing to do." It is especially acute immediately after an intense or very successful, goal-directed activity. The contrast between a highly social summer, a championship tennis season, or a successful musical and an inactive period with no immediate goals or social life feels dull by comparison. Dominant children experience an emptiness and listlessness that they don't quite understand.

If the adolescents are dominant conforming types, the contrasting letdown that comes after an exciting football season will dissipate in some new social or extracurricular activity, and parents need do nothing but observe and understand the transition. However, in the case of dominant nonconforming children, the boredom and sadness are more likely to erupt into an unforeseeable display of power or a deep depression. It is almost as if the lack of other goals causes them to invent a battle and a power struggle. Here's an example:

> Dell's parents had sent him to a private military school against his wishes in response to his underachievement and general irresponsibility at home and with peers. Dell, a dominant nonconforming child, was determined to win the power struggle, directed mainly toward his father. He failed his classes in the military school in defiance of all of the school's efforts at control. He contrived stories about the school and his parents and finally wrote letters home that included vague threats of suicide. Dell's parents were heavily involved in a confrontation that they couldn't win and decided to permit Dell to return home and continue school in the local community.
>
> With the glorious power of victory over his parents, Dell returned to spend a quiet summer home before the school year began. His parents felt safe and confident about the summer. They lived in a country home on a lake. Neither Dell nor his friends drove yet, but with fishing, swimming, and boating activities to keep the boy busy, his parents felt that although summer might be tense, it would at least be uncomplicated.
>
> The early part of the summer found Dell sad and uncommunicative. When given the opportunity to invite friends to the lake

323

or to visit selected peers, he was uninterested. Family activity was not sufficiently appealing either. Dell fished or watched television and had little positive conversation with family or friends. There were occasional small arguments with his father, as if Dell were attempting to let the family know that his dad remained the enemy.

About six weeks after Dell's return, he got drunk at home alone when his parents were out for the evening. He then drove the family car into town in his inebriated condition, stopped briefly to talk to a few friends, and went for a further drive, during which he managed to drive the vehicle into a ditch. He survived the accident with no injuries to himself or others, although the car repair bill approached $1,000.

When asked for his reasons for the sudden alcoholic binge and the illegal and irresponsible driving, Dell could only say that he was bored and didn't really know why he had taken the apparently impulsive action. He claimed that he'd had no prior plan. However, he had been storing one beer at a time from the refrigerator for several days in order to accumulate the eight beers that he consumed during his night of boredom.

If there is no apparent cause for frustration, the quiet depression of a dominant nonconformer may signify a sense of lack of purpose. These are energetic youths who rarely enjoy inactivity or relaxation. For them, life is boring if it is not busy. Before their pent-up energy turns into depression, find a creative outlet for it, or it will result in senseless destructive actions whose only purpose is to provide excitement and conflict. Although Dell could verbalize that he was bored and angry at his parents for having sent him to military school, the reason for his anger no longer existed—he had won that battle and felt the excitement and power of that victory. Afterward, with nothing to direct his energies toward, the drinking and driving allowed him to assert his power in a new father-son duel.

It is better to prevent dominant nonconformers' behavior than to punish afterward, so look for the symptoms and creatively distract the opposition to a cooperative adventure. A "wish, want, work, and wait" regimen might have served some diversion for Dell. Of course, finding the right combination is not always easy. However, within one week of Dell's arrival at home, his parents could have initiated a regular work project, in which he could earn money toward something that he wanted. A job, by itself, would not have been sufficient because there should be an important goal direction for the child's work—for example, saving up for a guitar or a bicycle during the summer. Planning an adventure trip with his father for later in the summer would have helped heal the wounds and cement a more positive relationship. Redecorating his bedroom or remodeling the boathouse into a clubhouse for parties would have given integration to his returning home and his social life. It might have also provided him with the courage to again initiate peer relationships.

For dominant nonconforming children, you will have to subtly inspire them toward a positive cause or support their creative projects in order to avoid their being distracted to negative, nonconforming activities that only maintain family combat. However, keep in mind that their drive is toward nonconformity, so the activities that will appeal to them will need to be unusual and different—such as a trip with a parent to a new place, remodeling the barn into a social hall, sewing a different wardrobe for fall, writing a drama to be produced by peers, or preparing for an art exhibit or other special contest. These children are often driven by an inner pressure to be different, so try to help them make their difference positive and productive.

It is difficult to respond to these children's depressions without reinforcing them. Reacting to their successes is much easier and more fun—and more important than it may seem. When your children do something positive, celebrate with them and praise (don't overpraise) their efforts. Emphasize their perseverance and their victories. Of course, you must also sensitize them to the feelings of the vanquished, but not so much that you take away from the pleasure in their accomplishment that you enjoy together.

Some parents feel that because these children exhibit mood swings, they should try to calm them down in victory. However, don't deflate their celebration by suggesting that they're enjoying it too much or by criticizing their performance. This will only make them feel that you wish they hadn't done so well and that you begrudge them their success. It will also encourage oppositional feelings that are just below the surface. Sharing their joy enthusiastically, spontaneously, and without overreaction will feel good to them and assure them of your support. Later, when the emotional high is over, you may make comments about bragging or the need to be sensitive, if necessary.

However, even if such reminders are appropriate, be sure to begin the conversation with your delight at their success. These are oppositional children who, if not reminded of your support for them, will feel as if they are being criticized. Prevent a defensive reaction by providing them the psychological safety of your alliance.

Encouraging Time Alone

Giving very young children some time alone during which they learn to invent ways to keep themselves busy can pay off in adolescence. If children have learned early to initiate their own activities and to derive satisfaction from non-oppositional involvement, they are not likely to suffer from depression caused by boredom. Therefore, if your children are of elementary school age or below, it's wise to respond to "I don't know what to do" by sending them off to do their own activities by themselves, instead of feeling that you must provide a continuous flow of activities for them.

Paradoxically, the way to prevent boredom depression for young children is to insist that they use their own time to discover their potential for inventing activities. Early childhood individual play teaches children intrinsic motivation that isn't tied to the winning in competition and attracting attention that dominant children seem to search for. For dominant nonconforming adolescents, it is typically too late for this approach. They've not learned inner control, only manipulation and opposition. You may have to take the first steps to inspire them toward constructive activities in which they can become intrinsically interested. Unfortunately, inspiring without attracting opposition from these children is difficult.

Maintaining the Positive

How can you remain positive when dominant nonconforming children are determined to push parents and teachers toward negativity? How do you manage to avoid overreaction in the form of severe punishments, which, after you think them through, you decide are too extreme and should be modified? Dominant nonconforming children have developed antennae that tune into your every mood. They know your weak moments and the appropriate buttons to push. They are practiced at manipulation and well-rehearsed in advocacy. They are established, persevering persuaders, and the brighter they are, the more expert they are at convincing you of their points of view. If they have established power as children, they will not give it away. If you talked to them as adults at age six, don't plan to treat them as children at age 12. Such treatment feels like a put-down, and it angers them because it seems so irrational. If you wrench your children's freedom away once it is given, you can expect them to feel controlled, punished, and resentful. They will become defiant, and you will find yourself in a continual power struggle that you and your children will feel helpless to avoid.

In order to elude the endless negative cycle of punishments and put-downs, you will have to negotiate with these children. Your first step is to create a negotiation inventory. Include four components in your stock-taking: strengths, weaknesses, controls, and rewards. The first, *strengths*, includes talent areas and positive qualities that your children have managed to retain. The second, *weaknesses*, includes all of those personality qualities that your children exhibit that you dislike. The third, *controls*, includes those areas of adult power that you have not given away. The last, *rewards*, includes those tangible and intangible incentives that will continue to motivate your children. For a sample inventory of one adolescent girl, see Figure 13.6. Tack your inventory in an unobtrusive spot so that you and your spouse may review it or add to it each night, out of view of your youngsters. The list provides you with your negotiating options.

Figure 13.6. Sample Negotiation Inventory for an Adolescent Girl

Strengths	Weaknesses	Controls	Rewards
• Creativity • Sensitivity to others • Kindness • Intelligence • Attractiveness • Creative writer • Cooking ability • Good taste in clothing • Musical talent	• Disrespect for parents and teachers • Argumentativeness • Overeating • Procrastination with schoolwork • Poor study habits	• Spending allowance • Clothing allowance • Driver's license • Specific social events • General weekend social activity • Concerts, ballet, or drama productions	• Additional monies for clothes, gas, or special events • Use of car • Special trips • Invitations to friends to join family events • Tickets for concerts, ballet, and drama productions

Make an effort to notice and mention one of your child's strengths at least once a day, and try to extinguish as many weaknesses as possible by not responding to them. Obviously, there will be some problem areas for which you must take a much firmer position. Pick the one or two problems that are highest in priority to you, and select your negotiating tools from your controls and potential rewards. Select the least potent control and the smallest reward that you believe will be effective in controlling your most pressing issue. Present this alternative to your child in a positive and persuasive manner. See Figure 13.7 for an example.

Figure 13.7. Sample Negotiation Conversation with an Adolescent Using the Negotiation Inventory

Parent:	Jane, we would really like to help you get out of your school procrastination habit. You're intelligent and creative, but your grades reflect neither because you put off doing your homework and studying. It would be good if teachers could appreciate what you can do when you make the effort.
Jane:	The schoolwork is not creative and not challenging, and I just don't see why I should do it. The teachers give more and more busywork.
Parent:	I'm sure that's true for some assignments, but I can't believe that all of the work is busywork, and I know that all of the assignments are part of a plan for your learning. What about if you agree to an experiment with doing your work on time?
Jane:	(With rolled-back eyes) Yeah, right!
Parent:	Your dad and I have agreed that you do have to, but we're hoping that you'll do it willingly and positively, and we're willing to pay you for your efforts as part of the experiment.
Jane:	Pay? Money? Now that sounds interesting. I've spent all of my allowance, and I was hoping to get some new clothes for school.
Parent:	Well, that would be great to save toward. Here's our plan. We've arranged with your counselor to give us a weekly report from your teachers every Friday. Here's the report form [see form in Chapter 9]. There is a space for missing assignments. For every week that there are no missing assignments, you will receive $5.00. For every grade of B or above, you will get an extra dollar. That would mean $10.00 a week for just doing your work.
Jane:	Not bad. It wouldn't take too long to get those jeans I want.
Parent:	Now here's the part you won't like. If there are any missing assignments on Friday, then you have to bring your books home and complete the assignment before you go out on Friday nights.
Jane:	Ha! Then I won't do it. I just won't bring my report back. Then how will you know?
Parent:	I guess we'll just have to assume that you haven't done your assignments, so you'll miss the Friday nights at the football games. But Jane, we wish you wouldn't do that. We really don't want to punish you at all, and if you just keep up with your homework and not get behind, we won't have to punish you and you can make some extra money. And Jane, the real bonus is that you'll accidentally find out that you can be a pretty good student. Will you give it a try?
Jane:	I guess I don't have much choice. Okay, I'll try it.

Maintain this technique as long as it is effective. If it is ineffective, you may wish to select a more potent control or a more powerful reinforcer, but be absolutely certain not to use up your controls or rewards prematurely; the long list of negative behaviors to be changed will remind you that you should hold on to all of the power that you have.

Be very sure not to use punishments that are not on your list, because you have not thought them through and you may not be able to follow through on them. You may be able to modify some behaviors without rewards if you can stay in an alliance with your children. Be absolutely certain that you don't unintentionally follow a negative behavior with a reward, despite your children's efforts to coerce you to do this. Finally, make every effort to notice and mention your children's strengths privately to them, as well as referentially to your spouse or relatives. Don't hesitate to follow positive behavior sometimes—but not always—with one of the sample rewards. Intermittent or occasional rewards are more powerful than continuous ones.

Teach yourself to be flexible in your rules but rigid in delivering the consequences. For example, children may select the time of day to work on a long-term assignment and may choose their style of work. You can even move deadlines slightly if they show intense effort. However, if they do not complete their long-term assignment and are not even close to finishing, then as agreed, they miss the weekend party, regardless of all their persuading. They will try to convince you that they'll take their punishment next week, that this is the party of their very best friend, but you must be absolutely rigid and unbending if you expect them to take your threats seriously. In your initial negotiations, leave them room for choices and control, but don't change the consequences once they have been definitely set. Again, provide the framework of flexibility and alliance at first, with calm and absolute firmness after the decision has been made.

Don't overreact and double the punishment or expand the negative consequences, because your children will then simply try to get even. They do care, even if they say they don't. Don't add to their resentment by irrational threats and punishments that you can't truly control. Using your inventory as a guide will help you plan carefully and fairly and will prevent one incident from escalating into the series of negative actions and reactions that are typical for dominant nonconformers. Notice in the conversation in Figure 13.7 how many opportunities the parents used to remind Jane of her strengths and their alliance with her. At the same time, her parents were firm without overreacting. The withdrawal of social privileges is effective only if parents are confident, definite, and continue to emphasize the positive.

United Parenting

Team parenting of dominant nonconforming children is the greatest challenge. You feel all extremes of emotion, from despair at their frequent stubborn opposition to the exhilaration and pride that go with their successes. It is difficult to parent in unison as you watch your children struggle and as they manipulate one of you against the other or both of you against the school. You repeatedly resolve not to become engulfed in their manipulations, then suddenly find that somehow you are misunderstood or misquoted and right in the center of a confusing muddle of miscommunication. Children like this are very powerful at manipulating parents against stepparents as well. More than once, you will try to remove yourself from the entire morass of parenting these children only to find that your guilt and your love have not permitted you to escape, and you will resolve to make one last effort.

You and your spouse will find that these children are the continuing center of your conversations and your attention, despite all of your efforts to back away from their overwhelming problems. However, these talks are not merely discussions, but constant debate, disagreement, and argument about the best way to deal with these difficult kids. It's not surprising that united parenting is so difficult. It may even be the most difficult test of your marriage. Remember that any time you feel like a better parent than your partner when dealing with oppositional adolescents, you've probably sabotaged the other parent—and unfortunately, you will both suffer the consequences.

Figure 13.8 includes precautions to help you parent as a team without isolating these children, whose self-concepts are dependent on their succeeding against opposition. Rimm's Law #9—Children become oppositional if one adult allies with them against a parent or a teacher, making them more powerful than an adult—summarizes these precautions.

Figure 13.8. Precautions to Prevent Opposition

- **Be certain not to say anything negative about your spouse in one-to-one conversations with your child, even if you disagree with your spouse's behavior.** Dominant nonconforming children manipulate parents against each other because they feel secure and mature in an alliance with one adult against another. It is not unlike an alliance between nations that have a common enemy. These children search and even compete for such powerful relationships, and they will manipulate and misquote you when they change positions and attempt to build a partnership with your spouse. If you disagree with your spouse's approach, then you should talk it through privately and make your compromises. This may be difficult—and almost impossible if you're divorced—but it is the only way to avoid the manipulations.

- **If your child is misquoting you to your spouse or others, use one of several alternatives.** Write down your agreements and sign them. Include both parents in your discussions with your children, and be sure that the children explain to you in your presence their understanding of any agreements.

- **Use conversations with your children to point out the excellent qualities of your spouse (even if you're divorced).** They will respect that parent only if you give them a clear message of high regard. If you teach children to oppose one parent, they are also learning to oppose other adults, including yourself. They should build their feelings of confidence based on accomplishment, not opposition.

- **Reassure your oppositional children frequently of their parents' mutual support for them.** However, be positively firm in not permitting them to manipulate either of you. Because they are in a habit of seeing relationships between others as a betrayal of commitments to them, you should assure them frequently that spouses can respect each other while both still love their children. This is a difficult reality for these youths to cope with, and they may feel emotionally isolated unless they are reassured frequently.

One of the parents (the "good" one) will be placed in the position of mediator by these children in order to persuade the other, unless the parent absolutely refuses to play that role. Although it may be tempting to one parent to use that mediator position in the hope of being better able to support the child, in reality, this mediator role does not succeed. It is an effort by the child to maintain an alliance with one adult in order to feel more powerful than the rival parent. If you take the child's position against the other parent, you may feel like the "good" parent. However, you are relegating your spouse to the position of "bad" or "dumb" parent, which leaves no alternative for your child but rebellion and/or underachievement. Stay together and reassure the child that you are both supportive. Because you are taking power away from the child, he or she will need continued assurance of your mutual support, coupled with very firm limits.

If your children are dominant nonconformers, you already know how difficult parenting can be. You have often found yourselves trapped in their manipulations and have wondered just how all of those miscommunications could have taken place. If you attempt the changes described here, you'll initially be greeted by further anger, rebellion, and depression. However, if you parent together and continue to cultivate the positive in these children, they will eventually feel more secure in a family where both parents clearly love them but also discipline them appropriately.

Communicating about Achievement

Internally pressured children who fit in the dominant nonconforming quadrant typically blame the pressure that they feel on others, usually their parents or their teachers. Although you may never have even suggested that you expect them to get straight A's, unless they are excellent achievers, they will say that you are pushing them toward impossible goals. They will also communicate this message to others— for example, their counselors, their teachers, their mediator parent, and sometimes a convenient grandparent, aunt, or uncle.

These other adults may easily be fooled into believing that the children's difficult behavior is caused by the pressure that you are placing on them to achieve, instead of realizing that this is a defensive manipulation. It puts you, as a parent, in a most difficult position. If you expect less of your children, their manipulations will have been successful, and they can avoid responsibly achieving and blame you. If you set realistic expectations of achievement that are beyond their present performance and require that they put forth reasonable effort, you will soon hear from aunts, grandparents, and teachers about how much you are pressuring your kids. Because your children are already having problems, these well-meaning adults will reinforce your guilt, and you will be tempted to lower your expectations. It will indeed feel like a no-win situation.

There are some appropriate yet safe messages to give to these children. You can say that you expect them to put forth effort, and you can quantify that effort in terms of reasonable time spent studying. You should probably confirm the amount of time that is considered reasonable with their teachers. You can also set logical grade goals for underachieving students that fit with their abilities and reflect their strong and weak subjects. Slight improvements are always reasonable goals. One step above the level at which they're presently achieving can't be too much pressure for children who have been making little effort.

Don't worry about not setting goals high enough for them. If they are complaining to you or others about the pressure that you're placing on them, then you can assume that they really would like to achieve those grade goals that they've attributed to you. They already feel pressure; by setting your expectations above their present level but below where they'd like to be, there's a reasonable chance for success.

If you notice an improved effort and continue to encourage their work, your chidren's grades will gradually improve. However, each time you overreact in disgust when they receive poor grades, they build evidence for your pressuring them. Instead, be patient in awaiting the improvement, and comment on how much better they're studying. They probably have little study experience and poor study skills. It will take time for them to learn the process. Gradually raise your expectations for their efforts. Eventually, when the positive results are fairly consistent, you'll be able to move into the background except for occasional encouragement for their successes. They want to achieve, and once they've discovered that they can, the defenses that they were accustomed to using will no longer be necessary.

To reverse underachievement patterns for dominant nonconformers, you should plan to meet with your elementary-age children daily. For students in grades five through 12, specific weekly meetings are usually enough. The meetings should include a review of the children's daily or weekly progress in each subject, discussion of behavior problems and improvements, and any rewards or punishments that you have built into your contractual agreement (see Chapter 11 for information on contracts). The meetings should be set at specific times and should vary for emergencies only. Ideally, the weekly appointment should be with the same-gender parent or both parents. In either case, it must be very clear that neither parent will let children escape from their commitment to making a strong effort.

The daily or weekly meetings should be kept as positive in tone as possible. If oppositional children try to use them for a power struggle, be firm and don't let them engage you in debate. Be sure that contractual agreements are in writing so that rule bending can be avoided by referring to the contract. Don't be rigid when your children make reasonable requests; however, be careful. Their cry of rigidity may only be a ploy to escape their responsibilities.

Communicating with Schools

You can be sure that school administrators, teachers, and others will take the initiative to communicate with you if your children are dominant nonconforming underachievers. These children cause teachers sufficient stress—to which you may already be accustomed and which is making you fearful of teacher conference day. Teachers may blame you, just as you find yourself blaming them for your children's problems. Neither of you will benefit by that process, but all of you are undoubtedly feeling helpless. Remember, an alliance between teacher and parents in support of these children is the goal.

Disagreements between parents and teachers can often be one cause of these children's oppositional patterns. If parents take their children's side against the teacher, they provide children with reinforcement for their oppositional behavior, and the children will not respect the teacher's authority. Remember Rimm's Law #9: Children become oppositional if one adult allies with them against a parent or a teacher, making them more powerful than an adult.

Certainly, not all teachers and schools are right in their approach to teaching children, but neither are all parents. Because many children will exploit these oppositional positions by underachieving or misbehaving, it is best that communications between teachers and parents are kept private. Sometimes, even when parents try not to involve their children in arguments with school staff, they make the mistake of telling their spouses or telephoning a friend about the conflict within the hearing of their children. This referential speaking allies these children with their parents against their teachers, and although they delight in the support of their own parents, they are now engaged in a battle with their teachers that they feel they must win. Knowing about their parents' disputes with teachers supports their "do it my way" position, whether or not their way is a wise one. Even when parents explain to me that they have not shared their nonsupport of teachers with their children, children almost always report to me that their parents agree with them that the teacher is bad.

Of course, it is vital that parents become advocates for appropriate education. This advocacy may involve differences in opinions with teachers and recommendations for changes in the system. You should make every effort to keep your role as positive and respectful as possible and to avoid confrontations with the school about issues in which you as parents are powerless to win. What follows is one case of a parent-school conflict that was successfully resolved.

Evan, a third-grade gifted achiever with an IQ score exceeding 145, was an applicant for a specialty school for gifted children. Although his ability and achievement ranked him at the very top of eligible applicants, the school had opted to use a random selection system based on a pool of eligible applicants. Evan was not selected, despite his undisputed high priority need. Because the criteria for eligibility into the selection pool were fairly low, many students who were selected had considerably less need for a differentiated curriculum than did Evan.

Initially, Evan's parents visited with school administration. This was followed by an official appeal process. Neither attempt was successful. Evan's parents turned to the legal process. They consulted with a psychologist in order to get expert support for their position. The psychologist agreed with their legal position but did not consider their efforts to be in Evan's best educational interests. In the six months since the beginning of their battle with the schools, Evan began to underachieve dramatically. If Evan's parents continued with the lawsuit, the time involved would not permit him to enter the gifted school during that school year—and perhaps not even in the following school year. Furthermore, if the case were decided in their favor, it was not clear that it would affect the future selection procedure because there was a strong possibility of modification of that system.

The psychologist recommended that the parents consider enrolling Evan in a nearby private school, perhaps not as excellent as the gifted school, but of a quality that would prove challenging to him and that would take him out of the oppositional position in which he was presently involved. They could then separate him from the court case and perhaps pursue the case on its legal merits. The fear was that a year or two of opposing the system with the support of his parents would be sufficient to propel Evan into a downward cycle of underachievement that later would be difficult to reverse.

If there had been a reasonable likelihood of Evan's rapid inclusion in the gifted school, or if the court decision could have had the effect of ensuring appropriate educational opportunities for other gifted children, there would have been value to the oppositional position. However, the chances of a positive impact on

Evan were small, and the adverse effect on his attitude toward education and on his efforts was dramatic. He was not a dominant nonconforming child initially, but in his new position as advocate for a different school, he was focusing a great deal of energy on directing his teacher regarding how he should learn and refusing to conform to that teacher's assigned requirements.

It seemed more important to be a child advocate than an issue advocate. The risk was too high. Evan transferred to a private school with a much more positive attitude and renewed effort.

Any communication between parents and school contains a high risk of being reinterpreted or misinterpreted by dominant nonconformers because they feel more secure in oppositional situations with a declared ally and enemy. They also may choose to change sides and confuse parents and teachers alike, so it is very important that you do not conclude prematurely that teachers have wronged your children. Make efforts to clarify communications whenever in doubt.

In setting up a reporting system with the teacher, it is very important that you also arrange for feedback to the teacher—that is, if teachers are writing reports to keep you aware of your children's daily or weekly progress and those forms do not reach you, the teachers should be told about the problem.

Actually, because working with dominant nonconforming children is difficult and trying for all involved, you and the teacher will want all the support you can give each other. You will wonder how children can render intelligent adults so powerless.

Changing Peer Environments

Peers begin to play a crucial part in children's educational environments by the time they are in the upper elementary grades. If peer relationships have been poor for dominant nonconforming children, becoming popular becomes an extremely important goal for them by junior and senior high school. Because they view popularity as a dominant role, they want more than ever to take a leadership position among their friends. In order to lead, they must conform to adolescent peer values, such as expressing opposition to adults. This is not difficult for them. It actually fits well with their developmental history of choosing allies who share similar enemies—the allies being their peers, the enemies being all parents and teachers. The rebellious adolescent model fits well with their manipulative skill. Their self-confidence and peer popularity grow if they can display the greatest anger at the adult world. Gangs are a perfect fit for them.

This fit, of course, will depend on their finding a rebellious adolescent peer group. Gangs exist in many secondary schools. They establish their group identity in opposition to schools, parents, and achievement. Dominant nonconforming students gravitate toward such groups and feel most accepted among rebellious friends. These groups also reinforce the underachieving pattern that feels right. Underachievement is a ticket to acceptance and popularity. High school peer groups that oppose school achievement and carry a "do the least you can" banner reinforce the adolescent underachievement pattern and make it extremely difficult to reverse. Members of these peer groups are often called "losers" by parents; unfortunately, it is the parents who feel like the losers.

If you are parents of younger children, hold on to your right to place limits on your children's friendships. They certainly need to select their own friends, but it is not wrong or controlling to impose standards on your children's friendships. The standards may be different for each family, but you should make them clear to your children. You can control friendships while the children are in elementary school, although you probably won't be able to by the time they enter high school. Both parents should agree on the same standards, or the children will fight them. Furthermore, if one parent wants to set standards and the other parent thinks that children should make all of the choices, the first parent is rendered powerless by the second parent. Stay united for the sake of your children. If children internalize your values early, they will probably automatically consider them in selecting friends later. Be sure to stress effort to achieve as one of those values if you want your children to achieve.

There are many situations in which you can't control friendships for adolescents, even though you realize that these friends are having adverse effects on your children. Changing peer groups is usually an expensive and not-too-popular alternative. Moving children to a private school is an effective approach if you are confident that the private school has a more positive peer population. Sometimes the reverse— moving from a private to a public school—is an equally good choice. Moving to another community can be effective, but I would not recommend moving only to change a peer group. Besides, your child may find an oppositional peer group in the next school district, in which case you've inconvenienced your family for naught. Special summer programs for highly motivated students who share your children's interests are excellent for promoting a pro-learning attitude and can help children think anew about their anti-achievement attitude. Summer travel or wilderness experiences are also excellent for encouraging personal self-discipline, confidence, and achievement orientation.

If peers can get together, so can parents. Don't hesitate to contact some of the parents of your children's friends. If they share your concerns, you can support each other in providing guidelines and positive peer social experiences. In one large suburban high school, those parents who promised to provide drug- and alcohol-free parties published a list of their names. For many students, this modified a destructive social norm, although it certainly didn't erase the problem.

The impact of peers on dominant nonconformers is both dramatic and extremely difficult to change. When you find that your children are with a positive peer group, be sure to be hospitable. The test of whether those peers are actually positive will be the effect that they have on your child. Sometimes seemingly desirable peers have an influence that you will later regret.

Getting Professional Help

Of all groups, dominant nonconforming students are most likely to need and least willing to want professional help. Finding appropriate professionals can be problematic. It is important to seek therapists who will not use an adult therapy model for children. Adolescents can easily be further empowered by therapists who don't stay in close communication with parents. Family therapy can be counterproductive if teenagers are given power equal to their parents.

A therapy model that provides a separate time for children or adolescents and parents is best. Because teenagers may worry about confidentiality, it may work better if a team of therapists work together—one therapist with the parents and another with the teenager. Weekly sessions with the teenager and separate monthly sessions with parents may work out. For elementary and middle school youngsters, sessions can be divided with some time for parents, some time for children, and a concluding time together.

Children and adolescents should not expect complete confidentiality. Of course, confidentiality is limited by law for any patient. Expectation of harm to self or others is always a legal reason to break confidentiality. Some states may have other exceptions. Parents do at least require a framework within which to understand their children, and although therapists need not repeat details of therapy sessions with children, parents should not be made to feel like outsiders in the therapy process.

Dominant nonconformers almost always resist therapy. They extend their usual manipulations to therapists by assuring their parents that therapy is a waste of time and money. They are also quick to say that they don't like a therapist if the therapist expects them to do something that they'd rather not do. Therapy is very precarious for these oppositional defiant youngsters because staying in an alliance with them and moving them forward in confidence and responsibility are difficult to combine. Nevertheless, in extreme cases, parents need to be strong supporters of the therapist as an assistant in helping their children or adolescents reverse their underachievement and improve relationships.

What You Can Do as a Teacher

As they are for parents, dominant nonconforming children are the most difficult group for teachers to change. If the children have begun their nonconformity early, they tend to have behavior problems in school. By middle and high school, their nonconformity and opposition have extended far beyond underachievement and classroom misbehavior. For some, the problems may be extreme and may extend to their social environment. Some students may also have problems with the law and may be beyond teacher control. In these cases, the greatest assistance that teachers can give is to refer these children for outside help and to be supportive of those professional efforts.

The following recommendations for modifications in the classroom will usually work for younger children and for the many less extreme cases in middle and high school. For these children, there is much that teachers can do to help avoid problems and provide good school experiences.

Forming a Teacher-Student Alliance

The first step in helping these children is forming an alliance with them. You'll want to review the ALLIANCE acrostic in Chapter 7, Figure 7.3, for reducing student underachievement. Oppositional children will form alliances with those whom they perceive as strong enough to respect, provided that these persons can get through the children's defenses and communicate that they value something within the children. Because these children were brought up in an early environment of extensive praise and admiration, and because they no longer earn that praise easily, if you are perceptive enough to see their good inner qualities, they will value their relationship with you. However, what you tell them must be accurate and sincere. For some of these youths, their confidence in you will depend on your perception of their intelligence, creativity, attractiveness, kindness, openness, or street wisdom. If you honestly identify their valued strengths, you accomplish the first step of your alliance.

The second step involves your power. Dominant nonconformers are accustomed to pushing limits. However, once they have overpowered people, they no longer respect them. If you are perceived as being within their control, they won't respect you. They will take advantage of your weaknesses by not doing their work and not taking responsibilities seriously. If they are within your control, they may either respect or resent you. If your control is coupled with the perception that you truly like them, they will respect you and perform at their best for you. If your control lacks that special positive relationship, you will be viewed as an enemy. They will manipulate confrontations and do all within their power (and their power is extensive) to avoid meeting their responsibilities and your expectations. You have very few controls to use with these children. Failing grades, detentions, reprimands, and punishments tend to be completely ineffective in motivating them toward effort. It is much safer to keep things as positive as possible. You will be much more effective using inspiration, persuasion, and rewards rather than anger and hostility.

Brief personal and confidential meetings are the most effective way to convince children that you care. Working with them to set short-term, attainable goals and clearly agreeing on positive and negative consequences combines closeness with respect. Be sure to write down any mutual or contractual agreements to ensure that both of you understand the obligations and consequences. Always keep a copy of the agreement, because they will probably lose theirs. The contract will avoid misunderstandings and "memories of convenience." Figure 13.9 will help you determine how and when to write a contract. An example of a contract can be found in Chapter 11 (Figure 11.7).

Figure 13.9. How and When to Write a Contract

- Use a contract for all dominant children and for older dependent children. It's optional for younger dependent children.

- Use a contract for behavior problems, work completion problems, or special projects or arrangements. Use a short time framework—for example, two or three months.

- Arrange for the teacher, child, parent, and/or child advocate to sign it. More signatures are better.

- Review the contract for clarification before it is signed. Be sure that the child understands responsibilities, rewards, and possible negative consequences.

- Make copies of the contract for everyone.

- Renegotiate only if *absolutely* necessary.

- Stay with and hold the child to the contract. Don't add further rewards or punishments.

How can you take the time to give such individual attention? It is certainly more than is required by your job. You can't do it for all children, but two or three amazing turnarounds a year definitely would be an exciting accomplishment, and it is possible. Those close, positive, and respectful relationships with these children will encourage them to perform in your classroom, and you will be delightfully surprised by the evidence of hidden talent.

Behavior Problems and Attention Deficit Hyperactivity Disorder

Refer to the earlier section in this chapter on ADHD for a better understanding of Attention Deficit Hyperactivity Disorder. Children who have this disorder will always be problematic in school. However, teachers should be sure not to quickly refer these children for medication. There are effective behavioral approaches to try in the classroom before children should be considered for medication. If you suspect ADHD, complete a behavioral rating scale, which can be obtained from the school psychologist, before you begin behavioral interventions. After several months, complete the checklist again. If the behavior is improving, avoid referral. If it's continuing or worsening, your school psychologist may be able to help you, or you may wish to request that the parents seek further help.

Children who begin their dominant nonconformity early are often serious behavior problems in elementary classrooms. They demand attention. They insist on pushing limits and disobeying rules. Boys may be physically belligerent; girls are more likely to be verbally aggressive. They frustrate the most tolerant teachers, and you are likely to find yourself scolding them often and inventing punishments to keep their misbehavior in control. They will probably cause you to lose your temper, although you repeatedly resolve that you won't.

The principle underlying goal of these children seems to be class domination. They want to be noticed by teachers and students. They want to be in charge on the playground, they want to do only the assignments that they enjoy, and they want all of these things—and more—instantly. They are impulsive and impatient. They have not learned the "wait and work" of effective learning and quality performance. Your scolding, writing their name on the chalkboard, or showing your impatience rewards them with class attention, and they earn a reputation as the class "troublemaker." They fulfill this reputation almost as if they have no choice, and indeed, they often feel that they have no alternative. Their mischief-maker stereotype moves ahead of them in schools, and teachers and peers alike anticipate the annoyance. Parents tell their children not to play with them—and as a matter of fact, children avoid them because they fear that they will be similarly labeled. Friendless or paired with other children who have behavior problems, they aggressively search for ways to make friends. They don't see the relationship between their naughtiness and their peer problems.

You will not be effective with these children by using attention-getting reprimands of any kind. Neither scolding nor placing these children's names on the board will improve their behavior. Seating them near the teacher's desk, in the corner, against the wall, in the back of the classroom, or in the hall will not serve to take away their negative attention and will further label them as troublemakers. Quiet reprimands, personal signals, and brief time-outs (see Figure 13.10) are more effective in modifying behavior. Small, daily rewards or privileges may also be effective.

Figure 13.10. Time-Out in the Classroom

An appropriate place:
• A separate room with a window for the teacher to check in but too high for children to see out. It should at least have a table and chair. A book storage room may often do. Children will not disrupt or destroy books, although you may feel worried about this.
• An unused office. A counselor's or principal's office is fine if it is not in use at the time. Secretaries or the principal should not converse with children during time-outs.

An appropriate place:
• A bulletin board enclosure or folding screen within the classroom with a desk or table behind it. It can be called the "creativity or concentration corner" and can have alternative uses. Children should not be able to see out or be seen.
An appropriate time:
• Time-outs should always be brief. Ten minutes may work, or the children may choose to return to class quietly when they feel ready.
An appropriate signal:
• In an alliance with the child, the teacher should use a covert signal (for example, a hand on the shoulder) to let the child know that he or she needs a little time away from the class. Time-outs should be explained to children as a way to control themselves without embarrassment or scolding or even the knowledge by the class that they are having a problem.

Withdrawal of privileges serves as an effective negative consequence. However, for elementary children, both positive and negative outcomes must be short-term so that each day, children have a new chance to establish that they can be good. Power and attention, unfortunately, are the most effective rewards for these children. Consequently, withdrawal of attention is the most effective negative consequence. Figure 13.11 suggests a token system that has been used effectively for encouraging concentration on tasks, and Figure 13.12 is a specific example of a behavior change plan made for elementary school-age youngsters.

Figures 13.11. Token System for Serious Behavior Problems of Young, Dominant, Nonconforming Children

> • Select only one major behavior problem to work on initially. For example, aggressive hitting is typically the first behavior chosen, to be followed by in-seat behavior, on-task activity, and finally, good attention to the teacher.
>
> • Plan private meetings with the child. The agenda for the first meeting should include the following:
>
> Behavior to be changed.
>
> Menus of activities that the child would like to earn—for example, computer time, a game with friends, special time with teacher or parents.
>
> Positive consequences: one token for every hour during which no inappropriate behaviors have been shown.
>
> Negative consequences: time-out at the signal in an enclosed attention-free area for 10 minutes of quiet time or voluntary return when the child feels ready.
>
> Determination of price in tokens for menu items.

- All contingencies should be decided together at a private meeting. The teacher should indicate that he or she is trying to help the child improve behavior and be accepted by classmates. All tokens and signals should be prearranged and private.

- Daily meetings should be held with the child to note improvement, show support, and encourage continued improvement.

- If parents are cooperating, daily or weekly communications should be sent home.

Source: Rimm, S. B. (1990). *Learning leads Q-cards: Teacher tips.* Watertown, WI: Apple.

Figure 13.12. Sample Behavior Change Plan: The Four-Star Day for In-Seat Behavior

1. The teacher has a private conference with the child and parents to explain how important sitting at the desk is. The example of pretending to put glue on a child's bottom makes the instruction graphic. Teacher definition of sitting should be anything in approximation to contact with the chair—for example, one leg on the chair should be considered sitting.

2. The teacher divides the day into four parts: morning to recess, recess to lunch, lunch to recess, and recess until the end of the day. The teacher explains to the child that each part of the day that the child is in-seat earns a star on a card. The goal is four stars. Three stars can be a temporary goal for the first week. Emphasize that stars are earned only for sitting.

3. The child brings the card home to the parents (or child advocate in school) at the end of each day. If the child receives four stars, he or she earns a home prize, game, attention, or points toward a gift or weekend activity.

4. Parents are cautioned privately to be encouraged and not too easily disappointed. The first four-star day may take time to accomplish, but much else will fall into place while the child concentrates on sitting.

Source: Rimm, S. B. (2007). *Sylvia Rimm On Raising Kids Newsletter,* 17(4). Watertown, WI: Educational Assessment Service.

Daily notes describing behavior to be reinforced at home are effective in improving behavior if teachers and parents cooperate. A form similar to the one in Figure 9.4 (Chapter 9) can be used for behavior problems. Good days can be rewarded with special individual play or model airplane time with Mom or Dad. Food treats (ice cream or candy) are effective primary reinforcers but shouldn't be used if there are weight problems in the child's family. For children who are slightly older, good days can be counted up for a weekly activity with parents—for example, bowling, a movie, or a pizza treat.

Unfortunately, rewards alone may not be sufficiently effective. Unsatisfactory days should be followed with consistently negative consequences—for example, no television, video games, or bicycle use; early bedtime; or time-outs in the children's rooms. Parent-teacher consistency is the key. For children who are a continuous behavior problem, there is little room for flexibility. Consistent positive and negative consequences for appropriate and inappropriate behaviors, respectively, will make it very clear that only appropriate behavior will be accepted. Five cardinal rules for behavior management of these children are:

1. Focus attention mainly on positive behaviors; completely remove attention for negative behaviors.

2. Be consistent, firm, and don't overreact.

3. Use short-term consequences, or you will use up the few controls available to you.

4. Keep noticing the positive qualities that these children show, but don't overreact to those qualities either.

5. Focus these children's high energy constructively by finding engaging activities for them.

These are often difficult and intense children. However, your patience and perseverance will be rewarded when you are able to divert their intensity to learning.

Anti-Arguing Instructions

The routine described in Figure 13.13 provides effective instructions for avoiding continual arguments in class. Dominant nonconformers will want to do math their different way, tell you how to run the class, and complain that you treat the girls better than the boys. As they wave their hands at you trying to attract attention and peer power, consider that they are calling out to you, "Look at me, look at me, I'm smart, notice me." You will not be able to help them by your intuitive response to put them in their place. They will feel put down, and they will wish to get even.

Figure 13.13. Anti–Arguing Instructions for Teachers

1. Dominant students who pride themselves on their debating skills know that you are more vulnerable if they argue in front of the class. If they lose in front of their peers, they inspire peer sympathy; if they win, peer admiration. If you lose in front of the class, you also lose respect from the other students. If you win, they side with the "poor student." Therefore, when the arguer raises his or her hand to say, "I've got a better way to do this math," immediately remove the debate from the classroom arena by a positive response that sets up an alliance: "I'd be very interested in hearing about your idea. Let's meet right after class."

2. After class, don't say yes or no to the student. Instead, say, "Please describe your idea," or "Could you tell me what you have in mind?"

3. If you're not sure of how you want to respond, say, "Let me think about it; I'll get back to you."

4. If the idea sounds good but may not work for more advanced work, say, "I like your idea. Let's have an experiment. You do part my way and part your way experimentally. If your way continues to work, you may continue to do it half and half. If not, you must promise me that you'll do all the work the way I've suggested it. [Student smiles] Let's write this down now so I don't forget the special privileges I've promised you." (Always keep a copy of your agreement.)

5. If the student is obviously trying to avoid work and can't explain the process, you will have to say no. Explain to the student that you've thought about it; however, he or she can't use the idea at this time. Add that you like his or her excellent thinking and that you will be interested in any other ideas.

6. If the student continues to argue, remind him or her that you have listened attentively to the idea, taken time to think about it, and given a carefully thought-out "no," along with a reason for your "no." The discussion is now over. If the student continues arguing, excuse yourself and briefly visit the teachers' room for shelter.

7. Treat each arguing attempt in the same manner. Students will value your encouragement of their creative thinking, and they will recognize that you are not a "wimpy" teacher. Your classroom leadership will not be threatened.

Source: Rimm, S. B. (2006). *Sylvia Rimm On Raising Kids Newsletter, 17*(1). Watertown, WI: Educational Assessment Service.

In the counterintuitive approach, you provide these children privacy and an alliance. After you negotiate with them, write down your agreements; keep a copy and hold them absolutely firmly to their word. Remind them of how much you like and trust them, and smile at them a lot. They are much less likely to rush to get even with their favorite teacher (and maybe the only one left who they like at all) than they are with a teacher who is angry at them. An ALLIANCE acrostic that sum-marizes the anti-arguing instructions is shown in Figure 13.14.

Figure 13.14. Teacher Anti-Arguing ALLIANCE

Ally with a positive interest in talking to the student privately.

Listen to what the student says.

Learn about what the student is thinking.

Initiate an experimental compromise, if possible.

Add a written agreement with two copies.

Nurture your relationship as a role model.

Consequence reasonably if the child doesn't follow through according to the written agreement.

End discussion by positively encouraging the student to initiate new ideas in the future.

Giving Them Power and an Audience

Dominant nonconforming adolescents who have some insight into their own behavior may admit to you that they often view their own actions as if they were on stage. They plan their behaviors with attention to how other people will react. It is truly as if they automatically and spon-taneously manipulate people around them, almost without awareness. Some who are especially sensitive and bright realize that they are manip-ulating others and even feel uncomfortable about the habit, but they don't know how to change. They were trained in showmanship as chil-dren and measure their self-worth by their impact on others.

Channeling their energies into an interest that gives them an intrin-sic sense of accomplishment is the most effective way to help these children build inner confidence and get them off the manipulation track. Their dependence on an audience can be used positively in select-ing areas of strength from which they can build weak areas. It is a two-step process. Step one includes finding an activity in which they are proficient and that provides an audience. Step two expands the activity, with the same audience, to develop a weaker area for the student. In step one, they are focusing energy positively. This step provides the vehicle that moves them to the second step, where they can challenge them-selves with an experience that intrinsically rewards them for their involvement. Figure 12.2 (Chapter 12) suggests some additional class assignments to encourage intrinsic interests. Figure 13.15 includes suggestions for some audience–activating projects.

Figure 13.15. Projects that Help Students Use Strengths to Improve Weak Areas

Strength	Weak Area	Step 1 Strength Activity	Step 2 Weakness Activity
Reading	Writing	Reading to children in lower grades	Writing stories for these same children
Verbal ability, computers	Writing	Talking into a recording device	Writing a story using a computer
Musical talent	Lack of perseverance, depression	Prepare for the school musical	Take challenging vocal lessons
Creative writing	Organization of time	Independent study course in creative writing	Part-time job contingent on successful organization of school time and assignments
Creative art design	Oppositional behavior at home	Redecorate barn next to home or basement rec room for peer social activities	Organizing a party with friends contingent upon respectful behavior toward parents
Computers	Math facts	Use video game that teaches math facts	Participation in math facts game individually or, later, in peer-chosen competition
General academic excellence	Behavior problems or lack of confidence	Partial acceleration in area of strength	Total acceleration based on behavioral improvement or improved skills in areas of weaknesses

This method allows dominant nonconformers to use their dependence on an audience to develop a level of confidence that they have rarely experienced. They will feel good about their accomplishment and realize that it is not an empty reward that comes from manipulation. As they build this new sense of confidence in one area, their performance in other school subjects and other behaviors should improve. Feelings of pressure and tension will disappear as they finally realize that they are capable and that their ability is not merely a facade. It is as though they are lifting a mask to find a real self underneath that is more effective and more satisfying than the face that they wore for show.

This approach of using an audience and a strength to remediate a weakness and build confidence is most effective for reversing underachievement with children who are manipulative, rebellious, and creative. It is not as effective for the more aggressive and delinquent youngsters, who typically require more help than you, the classroom teacher, can provide.

Avoiding Student Manipulation

Dominant nonconforming children find that alliances with one person against another are so comfortable that they easily trap kind teachers and counselors against parents and other teachers. If you seem to listen without disagreeing, they assume that you agree. You will have to become a creative reframer of their arguments, or you will soon be quoted as saying something negative about their parents or teachers. Their parents will come rushing in to blame you for something that you know little about.

Figure 13.16 provides some insight into what students may really mean when they bring you complaints. If you think that there may be real problems, you may surely listen and investigate their complaints further. Figure 13.17 provides some reframing examples that correspond to the student complaints listed in Figure 13.16.

Figure 13.16. What Do Children Really Mean?

Young children's cognitive development affects their moral development. Kohlberg tells us that in early childhood, children define right by what is rewarded or punished.* Later, right becomes what pleases or displeases the important "others" in their lives. They repeat what they've heard and learned. They combine and reorganize adult ideas and restate them. When we hear the words that we or someone else has taught them, we respond to them as if the ideas were theirs in the first place.

Examine the information that you have about your students before you respond to their expressions of feelings. There are many possibilities for the true meanings of what they say. Listen to their words, and interpret them with your adult wisdom. When children communicate to you about their home lives, here are some possible interpretations of what they may mean.

What Children Say	What Children May Mean
1. My parents love my sister/brother more than they love me.	• It may be true, or... • The child may have been accustomed to total attention and now feels deprived. • The child may have been punished recently.

What Children Say	What Children May Mean
2. My parents make me work all the time.	• The child may have too many chores, or... • The child may be required to do one chore a day and argues about that. • The child may never have had chores before and is being required to do something for the first time.
3. My parents don't ever buy me things.	• The parents may be economically disadvantaged and may not be able to provide for the child's basic needs, or... • The parents may buy the child many things but have recently said no to something. • The parents may be concerned about buying their children too many material things and may be intentionally educating them not to be so materialistic.
4. My parents are getting divorced.	• The parents may be getting a divorce, or... • The child may have overheard his or her parents argue for the first time. • The child's friend's parents are getting a divorce, and he or she may think that all parents get divorced.
5. My parents never help me with my homework.	• The parents may not help, even when the child has an appropriate need, or... • The parents may have helped regularly and are now trying to encourage independence. • The parents may have been out and couldn't help last night.

*Kohlberg, L. (1976). Moral states and moralization: The cognitive developmental approach. In T. Lockona (Ed.), *Moral development and behavior*. New York: Holt, Rinehart, & Winston.
Source: Rimm, S. B. (1990). *Learning leads Q-cards: Teacher tips*. Watertown, WI: Apple.

Figure 13.17. How to Reframe Students' Complaints

1. I know that your parents love you. You're a nice person, and I'm sure that this reflects how much they care. I also remember a few times when your sister/brother was in trouble with them.

2. That's excellent. They're teaching you real responsibility. I'll bet that you're a good worker.

3. I know that your parents are having financial difficulties. They always manage to provide you with food and clothes. I remember when I always wished I could have more, too.

4. Even when it seems that parents don't get along sometimes, they usually resolve their problems. One thing is sure: they both love you.

5. Good. That means you're growing in independence. Always try things at least three or four times before you ask for help. I'll always be happy to help you if you've really tried.

Changing Academic Grouping

Because dominant nonconforming children search for sources of attention within their classrooms and families, acceleration in reading or math groups is a potent way to direct their urges toward positive accomplishment. Underachieving children are typically placed in achievement groups below their actual abilities and skills. Nevertheless, it is unfair to other children to move these underachievers to higher groups unless they have proven themselves able to learn the skills and to pass the proficiency tests that will permit them to move forward. Be sure to caution them that they may remain in the higher groups only if they can maintain a reasonable quality of performance. Refer to Figures 11.17 and 11.18 in Chapter 11 for samples of conversations about moving students to higher levels in certain subjects.

Moving to a higher group is a very visible indication of these children's improved competence and helps to channel their wish for dominance much more constructively. Even skipping a grade can be appropriate for some highly gifted children, despite their behavior problems. If monitored carefully, it may provide the positive attention toward which the children's earlier behavior problems were targeted.

Research on grade and subject skipping has consistently found both options to be very effective for building children's achievement motivation.[5] Even when many other changes take place within their personal lives, acceleration provides children with a leap of confidence. One eighth grader wrote to me years after I worked with him, saying that he believed that his taking algebra in high school was the cause of his entire behavioral change.

Providing a Sanctuary

Some dominant nonconforming children will benefit if you can provide them a learning sanctuary within their learning environments. This special, safe place can be within their existing school, outside of the school but within the community, or within a different school. Those who will benefit from a haven include children who wish to dominate based on their intellectual, creative, artistic, or political nonconformity. If their environment is labeled as *special* because it is intellectually challenging, creative or artistic, or politically stimulating, it reduces the pressure that they feel to dominate. Placement in such groups provides recognition of their status so that they no longer feel that they must prove themselves superior. Within the group, they find peer support for their personal nonconformity, while the pressure to be different and superior is reduced. For example, Creative Chris, within a group of children identified as highly creative, can feel secure in the uniqueness of the group and can experience personal creative expression without the stress of having to be the most creative. Academic Alice can reduce her personal pressure by telling herself that within the group, all children are very bright, and she doesn't have to prove her brilliance.

In order for a sanctuary group to be effective, it must emphasize non-competitiveness and solidarity within the group, it must be self-labeled or recognized as different from typical peer groups, and it must support achievement of all its members. Gifted classes in schools, special-purpose religious groups, private schools, community art or drama groups, and political youth groups can provide avenues for positive nonconformity in creative, intellectual, and political areas. The only risk of being involved in such groups is if the leadership redirects the participants' nonconformity to nonproductive ends. It is extremely important that the group leadership maintains a positive direction that helps the participants learn and mature.

Sanctuaries that support uniqueness are a good way to use children's strengths to improve their weaknesses. Their strength lies in their creativity or their intellectual or artistic difference. Their weakness is their inability to conform long enough to learn skills that are important for productivity in society. If they are not included in a sanctuary group that provides positive direction, they are likely to be attracted to unproductive shelter or peer groups and gangs. If you hope to educate these children, you can guide them better if they recognize and legitimize their nonconformity. You can ignite their enthusiasm toward productiveness. They will respond at their best within a sanctuary that values their nonconformity. Figure 13.18 summarizes how you can help these creative underachievers.

Figure 13.18. How to Help Creative Underachievers

- Encourage creative children to be productive in at least one area of creative expression at all times, and help them to find an audience for their performance. Whether their choice of creative expression is art, drama, music, or poetry, a creative outlet frees them of some of their internalized pressure to be nonconformists in other areas and permits them to feel good about themselves.
- Be sure not to permit them to use their creative outlet as a means of evading academic assignments. Demanding music practice or impending art show deadlines are reasons for flexibility in academic requirements but not excuses for avoidance of responsibility.
- Find appropriate models or mentors in areas of students' creativity. The word appropriate should be emphasized. These students, particularly in adolescence, easily discover inappropriate models who are also creative underachievers. They are attracted to them because they see the similarities between themselves and these models. Appropriate models should share their creative talent area but must also give the message of self-discipline and reasonable conformity. An appropriate model should be an achieving, creative person.
- Provide a peer environment that combines creativity and achievement so that these children may feel comfortably accepted by other achieving and creative young people. Gifted resource and pull-out programs frequently provide a haven for creative underachievers, and they often achieve in this safe environment.
- Encourage children to become involved in summer opportunities for drama, music, art, photography, computers, science, math, or foreign languages where there are creative outlets and supportive peer groups and where they don't feel labeled as an underachiever.
- Encourage intrinsic motivation while also teaching competition. Children should learn to enjoy the creative process for the joy and satisfaction of their personal involvement. They shouldn't feel that all of their work must be judged in competition. However, they shouldn't be permitted to entirely avoid the competitive arena, either. They may fear failure to the extent that they refuse to perform in competition. Although winning builds confidence, taking the risk of losing provides their entrée toward real accomplishment.
- Use creative strengths to build up weaknesses. Children don't have to be equally strong in all areas, but they do have to accomplish at least minimally in school-required subjects so that they don't close educational doors for themselves. Artists who don't like math or creative writers who don't like memory work can use their creative strengths as a means of adjusting to their weaknesses. For the creative writer, unique mnemonic devices will often make dull memory tasks more interesting. Artistic folders or assignment notebooks may help the non-mathematician remember to do assignments, particularly if he or she is encouraged to share these artistic creations with peers.

• Help creative adolescents plan a creative future. Students should understand that most creative careers are open to achievers only. If they are not willing to compromise and conform to reasonable requirements, they are likely to close doors to future creative opportunities. On the other hand, if they are willing to recognize that preparation for a creative career demands a combination of conformity, self-discipline, and creativity, they will have taken the most important step toward creative achievement.

Helping Students Find Balance

Dominant, nonconforming students are almost always intense. They love people or hate them; they feel amazingly happy or incredibly sad; they have too many wonderful friends or feel isolated and lonely; they earn A's or F's. The list of opposite intensities is long.

These children's intensity makes them exciting and interesting but difficult young people to work with. Introducing the concept of balance to them entices them into examining their own extremes. I like to explain that people aren't totally balanced, but searching for reasonable equilibrium is a logical goal. I typically discuss with them the need to balance achievement and affiliation (relationship) goals, explaining that concentrating only on achievement (which they rarely do if they're underachievers) makes as little sense as concentrating only on social relationships. On the other hand, I point out that concentrating on relationships only (which they are often doing) is not good for future opportunities in life. Young people who concentrate only on friendship groups soon find themselves bored and gradually leave their tight friendships to search for the challenge of accomplishment. This seems to inspire them to step out cautiously to achieving.

Appealing to Altruism

Although establishing one's identity is an important task of adolescence and young adulthood, underachieving young people are often caught up in what they oppose. Many feel as though they are different, and in middle and high school, they direct anger or disdain at "preppies," "jocks," and even "nerds," none with whom they claim to want to be associated. This attitude unites them only with anti-school kids in the name of either their idealism or their uniqueness.

In college, young-adult underachievers who feel out of the mainstream often avoid achievement in the name of being anti-establishment and wishing to be more humane toward poor minority groups and/or by indicating that they are too creative to go along with the structure of college courses. These anti-mainstream students are typically extremely idealistic and nourish their affiliation needs with friendship groups that fight social norms in the name of improving society. They find time for protests, marches, and angry music. Typically, drugs that they believe should be legalized cement their intense relations with other idealistic, rebellious young people. Together, they are so immersed in oppositional activities that they find little time to study or complete course work.

Establishing an alliance with such young people, in agreement with their sensitive concerns and their first oppositional steps in the search for their identity, and issuing a challenge to use their strengths to identify and contribute to what they believe in usually attracts their attention. I point out that opposing what is unfair is only a first step toward making the world a better place. Educating themselves for a career in which they can contribute most effectively to improving our society is the great challenge. Appealing to their altruism is typically most effective in helping them recognize that looking forward to "smoking the best weed" does little to improve the problems in our world.

Specific activities that help others who are in need now and setting goals for careers that can improve the world in the future can help these underachievers who are caught up in a rut of overindulgence in virtue. They are stuck in the role of considering it virtuous to spend their energies in alliances with friends who bemoan the terrible world but do little to improve it. When issued a challenge that asks them to "get off their butt and make things better," they can become very excited about changing to a positive direction.

At every age—elementary, middle school, high school, or college—students become engaged when they help others. Whether they read to or tutor younger children, clean up after a hurricane, collect food for the homeless, or consult about computers at a senior citizen center, underachieving dominant students learn both humility and self-efficacy through altruistic contributions.

Alcohol and Drug Abuse

Dominant nonconformers, in their quest for power, are the group most likely to drink and do drugs. Here's a case study:

Fourteen-year-old Jerod discussed with his counselor his reasons for drinking to drunkenness on weekends. He explained that he felt worried and frustrated all week, but at parties, he could drink, smoke, and do drugs, and he would feel wonderful again. Nothing bothered him, and he would drink himself into unconsciousness. Although he admitted that he had terrible hangovers, the great high feelings were well worth it.

Whether or not teenagers use alcohol and drugs during the week or on weekends, sudden worsening of their behavior and motivations may be more noticeable to you as teacher than to their parents, who are more likely to deny the problem. If you have an alcohol and drug assessment program in the school, notify the counselor in charge. A successful treatment program can bring these children back to school more ready to work on their underachievement problems and help them to be much more communicative.

Maintaining Open Doors

A major concern of parents and teachers of dominant non-conforming adolescents is helping these youths avoid closing doors on future education and career opportunities because of their present rebellion. The careers in which they will eventually be happiest will involve challenge, creativity, leadership, and typically, preparation beyond high school. Each time they push school and societal limits, they risk shutting off potentially bright futures. If you, as teachers, can assist them in jumping the necessary hurdles that will keep those potential directions open, you can make a real difference in their lives.

Unfortunately, there will be many times when adolescents return to you too late to finally acknowledge that they now understand your former message and wish that they had heeded it. They realize that their preferred career opportunities are no longer available. Their creativity and intelligence may go unutilized for years because life or family circumstances now force them to work in an area far below their abilities. Their path has narrowed to one of lifetime underachievement, although they recognize how different it could have been if they had been able to get control of their need for dominance. In order for capable students to train themselves for careers that will eventually offer challenge and creative outlets, they must often forgo the immediate expressions of their independence. If you can help them see this bigger picture, your influence will be felt throughout their lives.

Chapter 14
Overview

The Why

Underachievement Syndrome is epidemic. The increasing numbers of children displaying symptoms of Underachievement Syndrome have been documented by statistics. Teachers can also substantiate this conclusion based on their own classroom observations. There is certainly no simple explanation for the tens of thousands of children with good abilities who are not learning within the same classrooms where teachers successfully teach other youngsters. However, by examining both the main psychological causes for children's underachievement and current environments, one readily recognizes that the interaction of the two is responsible for the increasing number of underachieving children. A parent or teacher alone is likely to have little effect on overall conditions in society, but together or separately, they can adjust the home and school environments to compensate for social problems and can thus foster achievement in their children.

Essential Elements of Underachievement Syndrome

The characteristics of Underachievement Syndrome and five essential causes of it have been described in this book. Although some of the factors of underachievement may also be found in achieving children, they are less severe. The more factors that are present, and the more severe they are, the greater the underachievement problem will be.

Initiating Situation

Most, although not all, underachievement risks develop in the first years of life. Some of these very same behaviors can lead to high achievement, depending on later environments. Attention addiction caused by children being overwelcomed, gifted, handicapped, or ill may begin the problem. Parents who are determined to do or give everything to their children or who see their children as the centers of their universe and their only purpose for being will unintentionally foster the dilemma. Inadequate, inconsistent caretakers or particularly competitive sibling combinations also provide high risks for initiating the syndrome. Although these early home situations are typically the first culprits, actual underachieving patterns may not show themselves until late elementary grades, middle or high school, or even later.

In some circumstances, the conditions that actually initiate the patterns arise later in childhood. A poor teacher relationship can begin an underachieving pattern, and two consecutive bad school years present a high likelihood of the start of underachievement problems for children. Life circumstances such as the death of a parent, divorce, or a dramatic change in environment can also initiate underachieving patterns in a formerly achieving child. There is usually an identifiable point at which the telltale symptoms of the syndrome begin, although the obvious underachievement characteristics may not show themselves until later.

Excessive Power

Excessive power in childhood is characteristic of all underachievers. Although these children have too much power, they typically feel as if they have too little. Their power is directed toward manipulating others in order to avoid responsibility rather than toward actual accomplishment. Of course, they don't intentionally control others to cause themselves, their parents, or their teachers grief; they simply have learned a comfortable—although nonproductive—style of human engineering. Their maneuvering feels immediately gratifying, and they do not understand that other kinds of interaction might benefit them more in the long run.

These children typically relate unconsciously to people around them in either dependent or dominant modes. The former involves covert manipulation, including verbal and body language that requests excessive sympathy and assistance. The latter is more overtly manipulative; the children pressure parents, teachers, and peers to conform to their wishes and preferences. Parents and teachers do not guide these children; they are powerless, allowing the children to take their own paths, regardless of their lack of wisdom or experience. Struggles for power are frequent, and children continuously trap their parents and teachers into arguments and debates. Children conclude these debates by either dominance, anger, or rebellion, and adults lose their tempers and feel angry and frustrated. Both dependent and dominant children refuse to live within guidelines set by their parents and their teachers but instead push adult limits continually in either passive-aggressive or overtly aggressive styles.

Appropriate power for children comes when they are encouraged to be independent within limits set by adults. Their range of independent activities should grow with maturity and their demonstration of responsible choices.

Inconsistency and Opposition

Caretakers and parents are typically inconsistent and/or oppositional in the lives of underachievers. Whether these caretakers are birth parents, grandparents, stepparents, foster parents, daycare teachers, or babysitters, when adults have conflicting sets of requirements, the stage is set early for underachievement. The inconsistency may take place within one adult or among many adults. For example, the parent who is living through a difficult period in her own life is likely to be inconsistent in disciplining and coping with her children. If there are numerous adults in the child's immediate environment (grandparents, aunts, uncles, and childcare providers—all of whom have very different ideas about child rearing), not only is there a lack of consistency, there is also probably opposition.

Opposition takes place in the intact, traditional, two-parent family; in the single-parent family; and even more frequently, in the divorced family. The characteristic dispute between parents and/or other caregivers involves how firm or how lenient to be with the children, with the adults unconsciously competing to be viewed as the "better" parent. The contraposition of a mean or strict parent with a kind or sheltering parent will foster underachievement. The children compete and become antagonistic with the more demanding parent. That parent feels frustration, anger, and lack of control and becomes even more oppressive. The sheltering parent feels pressure to protect the children from the ogre parent. Although sheltering parents wish that the children would apply more effort, they empathize with the children's feelings of inadequacy, poor self-concepts, and their concerns with never being able to meet the difficult standards imposed by the ogre parent. Thus, the children's escape behavior is actually unintentionally fostered by the loving, protecting parent. Although neither adult is entirely at fault, if they both give contradictory messages to their children, they will create a pattern of avoidance and poor self-concept.

Oppositional caretakers can also be responsible for the children's dominance or dependency. There is little reward for these children in achievement because success does not create the close, sheltering relationship caused by failure. Opposition robs the children of an achievement-oriented model with whom they could identify and provides instead an opponent with whom they can compete.

Inappropriate Classroom Environments

Schools and teachers are very important. They do make a difference. Classroom teachers who don't recognize the telltale symptoms of underachievement are likely to unintentionally feed the dependent or dominant manipulations of these children. Particularly in elementary grades, these symptoms are easily misidentified as immaturity, parent pressure, learning disabilities, attention deficit disorders, or emotional disturbances. Intuitively, teachers are likely to respond to dependent children in ways that reinforce their passivity and to dominant youngsters in ways that maintain their combative stance. The typical teaching approaches that are effective with achieving children may not work for underachievers. Achievers are much more receptive than underachievers to a wide variety of effective teaching methods. Even the best teachers may fall into the unintentional traps set by children with Underachievement Syndrome.

For gifted children, insufficient challenge in the classroom can pose special school problems. Unstimulating environments may actually initiate and maintain underachievement, even when a child has no particular parenting problems. Parent-school antagonism may have equally detrimental effects. Children in these situations may accidentally receive the message from their parents that because school is not meeting their educational needs, they are not expected to complete boring assignments. Furthermore, teachers may inform the children that their high abilities are imaginary because their school performance is so poor. These children easily fall victim to Underachievement Syndrome.

For children from culturally deprived and academically disadvantaged backgrounds, teachers may not provide sufficient challenge because of preconceived notions about these children's abilities and may unintentionally teach them dullness. All children need to learn to stretch themselves to achieve.

Although all children need to extend what they can learn, there are clearly individual differences. When the same curriculum and speed of learning are used for all children, some children will not be challenged, while other children will give up in despair because the curriculum is beyond their comprehension. Neither of these groups will experience the relationship between effort and outcome.

Finally, although the majority of teachers in our classrooms are effective, some children fall prey to that minority of ineffective instructors. A few bad school years due to bad teaching, high teacher absenteeism, or a teacher-student match with outright antagonism between a teacher and a child can be a factor in Underachievement Syndrome for some children. It is unlikely to be the sole cause of the problem, but it certainly may have an exacerbating effect.

The most important quality of classrooms in which children maintain an achieving mode is the presence of an appropriate relationship between the learning process and its outcomes. If assignments are either consistently too easy or too difficult, the conditions that cultivate Underachievement Syndrome are present, and the syndrome will worsen.

Competition

An environment that does not teach children to cope with competition fosters underachievement. Life is always competitive, but if there is a competitive climate in which children find themselves consistently in the position of being either losers or winners, they are unlikely to learn a healthy attitude toward competition. Students who always lose see no reason to make an effort because there appears to be no possibility of success. They withdraw from competition entirely. Winners who have never had to cope with failure are disabled when they are not continuously victorious. They lose confidence when they are not at the top, and they stop putting forth an effort. The winner role is less likely to result in permanent underachievement because these children have developed a better history of accomplishment. They are more likely to be resilient enough to adjust their goals based on their foundation of past achievements. The continuous loser is less easily motivated toward effort because previous sporadic attempts have resulted in failure. Such children are more likely to daydream about a magical deliverance than risk investing energy in tasks that they perceive as impossible.

Classrooms and families are inherently competitive because children automatically compare themselves with peers, teachers, siblings, cousins, and parents. When they perceive that they are falling short, either because of their own inadequacies or the superior achievements of their competitors, they may not understand their loss of motivation. They may set more realistic goals and continue to achieve, or they may decide that their inadequacies leave them little reason to exert effort. The latter decision results in Underachievement Syndrome. The source and degree of competition certainly feed into the syndrome, but children's appraisal of and response to that competition is much more important.

Social Changes

Social changes in our country have had a dramatic impact on the psychological elements that cause Underachievement Syndrome. Although this book is not intended as a treatise on social or ethical directions in the United States or the world, there are some obvious underpinnings to the problem. Although this description is not all-inclusive, the main social changes that lead to Underachievement Syndrome are readily apparent.

Family

The structure and fabric of American family life have changed so dramatically that our great-grandparents would be stunned. The mix includes mothers with full-time careers, daycare centers, babysitters, relatives who take over child rearing, lack of clarity of roles for men and women, extramarital relationships, increasing divorce, living together without marriage arrangements, single parenting, and disorienting visitation privileges and custody disputes. Young parents who look back to their own families and wish to use them as a framework for guiding their children are likely to find themselves without a model. The old-fashioned nuclear family with one set of loyal parents who are primarily responsible for child rearing still exists, but the actual number of children brought up in such secure, structured environments diminishes continuously.

Education

The size of schools and the tasks of educators expand regularly. Beyond the basics and the familiar three B's—"beans, buses, and basketball"—are three more B's—"breakfast, babysitting, and bargaining." Educators who used to feel that too much school personnel time was being devoted to discussing hot-lunch programs, transportation, and sports programs are now being asked to provide morning meals, social services, and after-school care for children of working parents. However, these represent only a fraction of additional roles tagged on to teaching. The responsibilities of administrators and teachers have multiplied exponentially. Certainly, there are many teachers who continue enthusiastically to excite children toward learning, but the ways in which their time and energy must be divided into so many tasks and so many children detracts from their holistic pedagogic zeal. Many teachers feel discouraged.

Moral Standards

Some readers will lament disintegrating moral standards, others may say that nothing has changed, and still others may agree that there has been change but prefer these new standards of conduct. This book's task is not to provide commentary on changing moral standards, but only to note that an environment that supports extensive alcohol consumption, drug abuse, gang violence, and permissive sexual behavior provides considerable temptation for adolescents. Adolescents announce that, among other things, they have a right to an adult sex life and that adults may not steal this from them. The ready availability of such distractions from the educational scene increases the difficulty of exciting adolescents toward learning. By comparison, school may indeed appear boring.

Competitive Pressure

An increasing population, career requirements for more extensive education, fragmentation in job responsibilities, narrowing career options, the complexity of business and government, and diminishing moral directives are only a few of the changes that dramatically add to the competitive pressures in our society. Children are affected by adult competitive pressure because, as their parents struggle in the dog-eat-dog world, these adults model to their children survival techniques, as well as escape routes. Their children may copy any of these that they see or hear. Parents communicate their own anxieties to their kids without ever intending to put pressure on them.

Adults, reflecting on their own career pressures, feel a legitimate and anxious concern for their nonachieving bright children. How will they make it in society if they can't even succeed in the small arena of school? Out of their tension over their children's poor performance, they overreact to the children's victories and defeats, communicating a pressure far different from the problem-solving approaches that the children should be learning.

Media

Television, computers, movies, and video and computer games display the lifestyles and financial rewards of the most successful—and they do so right in our living rooms. Commercials incite an unquenchable thirst for material possessions. Sports and music heroes are more reputed for the fantastic salaries that they command than for their hard work or talent. Furthermore, the stories of their successes sound like magical fairytales, with little struggle and much luck. Heroes' value systems appear free of ethical structure. Alcohol, drugs, sex, violence, and illegal activities are associated with fame and success. The traditional "rags to riches" image that modeled for American children of previous generations the path by which hardworking, intelligent, and creative people climbed the ladder from poverty to wealth has been replaced by the media's magical system, which any child would like to follow. Brilliant talent is miraculously discovered. A powerful fairy godmother transforms a poor, unrecognized teenager to instant stardom, or the child could even win the lottery—more magic without work.

Interaction between Underachievement Factors and Social Changes

Figure 14.1 illustrates the ramifications of social changes for the key factors that cause Underachievement Syndrome. Each of the social changes described has a separate impact on each of the key factors that cause the syndrome, and taken together, their force is so great that it is unreasonable to expect schools alone to halt the epidemic. There is no immediate method of funneling taxpayers' money for school reform, no specific message to give to your congressperson, and no particular bill or law that will lead to prevention or cure. The problem is too complex to remedy in so simplistic a fashion.

Figure 14.1. Ramifications of Social Change on Underachievement Syndrome

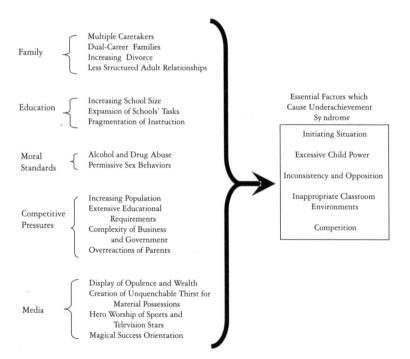

The social changes that have dramatic impact on underachieving children can be mitigated in your own homes and schools. Although you may feel helpless in terms of making major changes in our culture, you can shape and temper how that culture acts on the children or students in your own care. For example, individual parents can do much to maintain a reasonably secure family structure. We can lend support to our schools and teachers and help decrease the unreasonable demands that communities place on educators. Individual teachers can inspire underachieving students toward development of talent. We can teach our own children and students reasonable moral and ethical principles, and we can model these. We can show them how to cope with competition, and we can demonstrate valid temporary ways of relieving too much pressure. Finally, we can limit their exposure to damaging mass media and interpret the "rags-to-riches" story without glorifying the magically produced heroes. In these ways, we can lessen the risk that our children will fall victim to the underachievement epidemic.

Recognition of the essential elements that cause Underachievement Syndrome will assist in preventing the problem in your own families and classrooms. You may or may not be able to prevent the initiating situation, but awareness will assist you in diminishing the harmful effects on your children. Those of you who are parents can have the greatest impact by changing the power, inconsistency, and opposition variables in your family. Those of you who are teachers can be instrumental in improving the school environment for many underachievers, although there may be many classroom issues beyond your control. As parents and teachers, instruction and modeling of competition can make a major contribution in your families and classrooms. You cannot entirely prevent underachievement, but understanding the causes of the syndrome can assist you in reversing it.

The What

The reversal of underachievement is possible for the children in your homes and the students in your classrooms. It isn't easy, nor is it likely that you can change every child who underachieves. Although most of this book has focused on methods that have been implemented effectively by parents and teachers through Family Achievement Clinic and through many schools, there are countless other alternatives for you to select or invent to use with your own children. I have provided the Trifocal Model because I know that it works. Within that framework, there is space for your own innovation and adaptation.

Rimm's Laws of Achievement

As you create your own innovative approaches to helping children toward achievement, Rimm's Laws of Achievement should assist you in predicting the likelihood of their effectiveness. You have already seen these laws earlier in this book, but I repeat them here because they summarize the main principles that have been presented in these pages.

Rimm's Law #1

Children are more likely to be achievers if their parents join together to give the same clear and positive message about school effort and expectations. Meeting the expectations of parents is developmentally normal and a high priority for most children, provided that the parents' goals are clear, consistent, and within reach by reasonable effort. When one parent expects more of the children than the other parent, or when the second parent feels compelled to shelter the children from the first parent, underachievement and rebellion will surely follow. Compromise by all parents involved and a clear, unified message of reasonable goals should underlie all parent and teacher initiatives for dealing with underachieving children. When adults who raise and teach children are respectful of each other, children are more likely to respect the adults who guide them.

Rimm's Law #2

Children learn appropriate behaviors more easily if they have effective models to imitate. Parents are the models most frequently available to children. As such, they should be aware of both the potential effectiveness and the problems of modeling attitudes and behaviors that children can copy. Parents should also describe their partners to their children in a manner that will encourage their role model identification. Nurturance, power, and similarities are the three qualities that foster identification. If parents are not available or are inappropriate as models, then school, community, or other family relationships can be used to inspire children toward appropriate imitation. It is especially important for males to find same-gender models; for females, same-gender models are not as critical but do help the necessary alliances take place more easily.

Rimm's Law #3

What adults say to each other about children within their hearing (referential speaking) dramatically affects children's behaviors and self-perceptions. Parents and teachers should be sensitive to what they say to other adults within their children's hearing. If you talk about positive accomplishments, you will encourage children to take pride in their achievements, but continually expressing frustration with children's inadequate behaviors may damage their self-confidence. If you discuss your inability to control children's behavior, you will foster disrespect and belligerence. Referential speaking between adults sets a self-fulfilling expectation for children.

Rimm's Law #4

Overreactions by parents or teachers to children's successes and failures lead them to feel either intense pressure to succeed or despair and discouragement in dealing with failure. A moderate problem-solving approach to their failures helps your children cope with losing and see failure as a normal component of learning. It helps them learn to accept criticism and to patiently persevere. Similarly, your pleasure, not your ecstasy, is an appropriate response to their success. Not only does the latter not seem genuine, but it encumbers them with the pressure to perform continuously, which may not be possible. As they become more confident in their successes, you may increase your level of delight without fearing that they will be overwhelmed by pressure.

Rimm's Law #5

Children feel more tension when they are worrying about their work than when they are doing that work. Children who exhibit symptoms of tension usually do not need to have their workload reduced or simplified. For the most part, they only need your assurance that they can accomplish their lessons and a clearly structured plan for producing their completed assignments. Organizing their tasks and providing visual reinforcement of accomplishments will help them successfully complete their work. Their tension will diminish as they work harder and build confidence in their accomplishment. Children can be "vaccinated" for some of their anxiety by gradually learning to cope with small amounts of tension.

Rimm's Law #6

Children develop self-confidence and resilience through struggle. It is difficult for parents and teachers to calmly witness children's suffering. However, to deny them the opportunity to push their own limits is to deny them the efficacy and growth that comes from accomplishment. Obviously, children who make sincere efforts without ever attaining success will not be encouraged to achieve. However, when persistence results in reasonably frequent successes, children build the confidence and the character to cope with challenge and disappointment.

Rimm's Law #7

Deprivation and excess frequently exhibit the same symptoms. Our Freudian heritage leads us to evaluate children's psychological symptoms in some misleading ways. For example, we assume that attention-seeking children have not received enough affection, that angry youths have not been given enough power or freedom by their parents, and that children who exhibit tension have been pressured too much by adults. All of these may be true, but children exhibit identical symptoms if they are accustomed to receiving too much affection, if they have had too much power over their parents, or if adults have done so much for them that they have not learned to cope with any pressure. Too much and too little are equally problematic, but one needs to determine which is the culprit before providing appropriate assistance.

Rimm's Law #8

Children develop confidence and an internal sense of control if they are given power in gradually increasing increments as they show maturity and responsibility. If children are not given enough independence, they do not develop a good self-concept. However, if power is given too early and then must be reduced as they reach adolescence, they feel controlled and angry, even though their limits are no different than those of their peers. Adults can better identify with this experience if they imagine how they would feel if their freedom to make choices was restricted by some outside force. The angry feelings of these adolescents are genuine, but they are not caused so much by imposing too much structure as by having failed to impose reasonable limitations earlier. Relative to their earlier power, they feel powerless.

Rimm's Law #9

Children become oppositional if one adult allies with them against a parent or a teacher, making them more powerful than an adult. The feeling of control that children receive from dominating other powerful persons makes them feel both excitingly powerful and frighteningly insecure. It creates an impulse within them to maintain dominance over others as a measure of their self-confidence. When that feeling of control over others disappears, they return to their frightening sense of inadequacy. The opposition that provides power without wisdom thrusts them into mood swings that vary with their control; these children are very difficult to cope with during adolescence and young adulthood. Appropriate independence and internal locus of control can be fostered without oppositional alliances, but these alliances are reinforcing to adults as well as children, so beware.

Children need not go through a rebellious and angry adolescence if parents follow Rimm's Laws #8 and #9.

Rimm's Law #10

Adults should avoid confrontations with children unless they are reasonably sure that they can control the outcomes. Entering a confrontation without true control of the result only provokes further active or passive opposition. For many children, it's less effective for adults to command or demand than to persuade, inspire, model, share efforts, cooperate, encourage, and create a positive alliance. Make a realistic appraisal of what will be effective with a child before plunging ahead with what feels right to you at the moment. There are multiple ALLIANCE acrostics throughout this book to assist parents and teachers in reversing opposition with children and with each other.

Rimm's Law #11

Children will become achievers only if they learn to function in competition. Children should learn early that winning and losing are temporary. They should understand how to function when they fail or lose. They thrive when they have experiences of both failure and success and can learn to use failure constructively to build success. Home, school, and society are all competitive. It is not possible to continually withdraw from competition and still remain confident. Parents and teachers can gradually teach children to learn to function both collaboratively and competitively. Some environments should be encouraged to decrease competition, while others should increase collaborative opportunities.

Rimm's Law #12

Children will continue to achieve if they usually see the relationship between the learning process and its outcomes. Children acquire an internal sense of control by investing themselves in an enterprise and finding that they have performed well. This same sense of efficacy is reinforced by discovering that lack of effort leads to a less successful outcome. Children are usually aware that there are differences in abilities, in teachers' perceptions, and in levels of difficulty of assignments and tests that can also affect scholastic outcomes. However, when children make little effort and highly successful outcomes follow, or when they make a serious commitment to study with no success, or when the relationship between their work and their grades seems random, they lose that sense of internal locus of control. They begin to attribute their grades to luck—or lack thereof. They blame teachers for their failures, or they claim that they are really not very smart. Frequently, they may say that they should study harder, but they rarely follow through because they don't truly believe that studying will have an impact on their grades or their learning.

To establish self-efficacy, a clear study time and structure combined with feedback that explains the performance grades, as well as the basis for earning them, are important. Although children are resilient enough to adjust to reasonable differences in criteria and teachers, they cannot establish that inner sense of control with unclear or random grades or academic material that is too easy or too difficult.

Reversal of an Epidemic?

This book holds no wonder cure. It will not cause Under-achievement Syndrome to disappear from society. However, it is not mere theory. It is based on many real-life experiences in homes and classrooms. Whether you are a parent or a teacher, if you take time to understand your underachievers, follow the steps of the Trifocal Model patiently, and apply Rimm's Laws of Achievement, you will make a positive impact on your children's school performance. Their symptoms of the syndrome will decrease, and their achievement motivation will improve. It happens daily for the underachieving children in clinics and schools that use the Trifocal Model.

Resources

Academy for Educational Development
National Literacy and Learning Disabilities
www.novel.nifl.gov

C.H.A.D.D.
(Children with Attention Deficit Disorder)
www.chad.org

Council for Exceptional Children
(Also provides information about learning disabilities)
www.cec.sped.org

The Davidson Institute for Talent Development
www.ditd.org

Educational Assessment Service, Inc.
www.sylviarimm.com

ERIC Digests (Former ERIC Clearinghouse System)
www.ericdigests.org

Family Achievement Clinic
www.familyachievement.com
www.sylviarimm.com

Gifted Child Society, Inc.
www.gifted.org

Hoagies Gifted Education Page
www.hoagiesgifted.org

Irlen Institute (information on scotopic sensitivity syndrome)
www.irlen.org

National Adult Literacy and Learning Disabilities Academy for Educational Development
www.nifl.gov/nalldtop.htm

National Association for Gifted Children (NAGC)
www.nagc.org

The National Research Center on the Gifted and Talented
www.nrcgt.org

Recording for the Blind & Dyslexic® (RFB&D®)
www.rfbd.org

Supporting Emotional Needs of Gifted (SENG)
www.sengifted.org

Sylvia Rimm
www.sylviarimm.com
www.seejanewin.com

Twice-Exceptional Newsletter
www.2enewsletter.com

References

American Psychiatric Association. (2000). *Diagnostic and statistical manual of mental disorders* (4th ed.). Washington, DC: Author.

Assouline, S., Colangelo, N., Lupkowski-Shoplik, A., Lipscomb, J., & Forstadt, L. (2003). *Iowa acceleration scale* (2nd ed.). Scottsdale, AZ: Great Potential Press.

Baum, S. (2004). The promise of talent development for two exceptional youngsters. *Gifted Education Communicator, 34*(4), 13.

Baker, J. A. (1996). Everyday stressors of academically gifted adolescents. *Journal of Secondary Gifted Education, 7*, 356-368.

Benbow, C. P., & Stanley, J. C. (1983). Sex differences in mathematical reasoning ability: More facts. *Science, 222*, 1029-1031.

Berg, A. (1993). *The application of the Trifocal model in the special education program.* Paper presented at Rimm Underachievement Institute, Milwaukee, WI.

Bloom, B. S. (Ed.). (1985). *Developing talent in young people.* New York: Ballantine.

Bloom, B. S., & Sosniak, L. A. (1981). Talent development vs. schooling. *Educational Leadership, 39*, 86-94.

Brody, L. E., & Benbow, C. P. (1987). Accelerative strategies: How effective are they for the gifted? *Gifted Child Quarterly, 31*, 105-110.

Brown, B., & Steinberg, L. (1990). Academic achievement and social acceptance: Skirting the "brain-nerd" connection. *Education Digest, 55*(7), 55-60.

Clasen, D. R., & Clasen, R. E. (1995). Underachievement of highly able students and the peer society. *Gifted and Talented International, 10*(2), 67-76.

Cornale, M. (1988). *Dependence and dominance in preadolescent academic underachievers.* Unpublished research paper, University of Wisconsin-Madison.

Covington, M. V., & Beery, R. G. (1976). *Self-worth and school learning.* New York: Holt.

Davis, G. A. (1992). *Creativity is forever* (3rd ed.). Dubuque, IA: Kendall/Hunt.

Davis, G. A. (2006). *Gifted children and gifted education.* Scottsdale, AZ: Great Potential Press.

Davis, G. A., & Rimm, S. B. (2004). *Education of the gifted and talented* (5th ed.). Boston: Pearson Education.

Dweck, C. S. (1999).*Self-theories: Their role in motivation, personality, and development.* Philadelphia: Psychology Press.

Dweck, C. S. (2006). *Mindset: The new psychology of success.* New York: Random House.

Emerick, L. (1992). Academic underachievement among the gifted: Students' perceptions of factors that reverse the pattern. *Gifted Child Quarterly, 36*, 140-146.

Feldhusen, J. (1993). *Creative thinking and problem solving in gifted education.* Dubuque, IA: Kendall/Hunt.

Glenday, C. (Ed.). (2008). *Guinness world book of records 2008*. New York: Bantam Books.

Goertzel, V., Goertzel, M. G., Goertzel, T. G., & Hansen, A. M. W. (2004). *Cradles of eminence: Childhoods of more than 700 famous men and women* (2nd ed.). Scottsdale, AZ: Great Potential Press.

Goldberg, J., & Adderhold-Elliot, M. (1999). *Perfectionism: What's bad about being good?* Minneapolis, MN: Free Spirit.

Goodkin, S. (2005, December 7). *Leave no gifted child behind*. Retrieved March 3, 2008, from www.nagc.org/CMS400Min/index.aspx?id=1132

Graue, M. E., & DiPerna, J. (2000, Summer). Redshirting and early retention: Who gets the "gift of time" and what are its outcomes? *American Educational Research Journal, 37*(2), 509-534.

Helson, R. (1971). Women mathematicians and the creative personality. *Journal of Consulting and Clinical Psychology, 36*, 210-211, 217-220.

Hetherington, E. M., & Frankie, G.. (1967). Effects of parental dominance, warmth, and conflict on imitation in children. *Journal of Personality and Social Psychology, 6*, 119-125.

Horn, L., & Berger, R. (2004). *College persistence on the rise? Changes in 5-year degree completion and postsecondary persistence rates between 1994 and 2000*. Retrieved January 17, 2008, from http://nces.ed.gov/das/epubs/2005156/persistence3.asp

Irlen, H. (1991). *Reading by the colors*. Garden City Park, NY: Avery.

Kanevsky, L., & Keighley, T. (2003, Fall). To produce or not to produce? Understanding boredom and the honor in the underachievement. *Roeper Review, 26*(1).

Karnes, F., & Bean, S. (2005). *Methods and materials for teaching the gifted* (2nd ed.). Waco, TX: Prufrock Press.

Kinney, D. A. (1993). From nerds to normals: The recovery of identity among adolescents from middle school to high school. *Sociology of Education, 66*, 21-40.

Kristensen, P., & Bjerkedal, T. (2007, June). *Explaining the relation between birth order and intelligence*. Retrieved March 4, 2008, from www.sciencemag.org/cgi/content/full/316/5832/1717

Kulik, J. A. (1992). *An analysis of the research on ability grouping: Historical and contemporary perspectives*. Storrs, CT: National Research Center on the Gifted and Talented, University of Connecticut.

Laidig, P. (1991). The summer birthday dilemma: Outcomes of delayed school entry. *The Wisconsin School Psychologist 1*, 3.

Linn, M. C. (2007). Women in science: Can evidence inform the debate? *Science Magazine, 317*, 199-200.

McCoy, K. (2007). Studies track treatment outcomes for kids with ADHD. *HealthDay News*.

Monastersky, R. (2005). Primed for numbers? *Chronicle of Higher Education, 51*(26), A1

Mussen, P. H., & Rutherford, E. (1963). Parent-child relations and parental personality in relation to young children's sex-role preferences. *Child Development, 34*, 589-607.

Neumeister, K. L. (2005, Summer). Perfectionism and gifted children. *Indiana Association for the Gifted, 18*(3).

Reis, S. M., & Purcell, J. H. (1993). An analysis of content elimination and strategies used by elementary classroom teachers in the curriculum compacting process. *Journal for the Education of the Gifted, 16*(2), 147-170.

Renzulli, S. (2005, Fall/Winter). The irony of "twice-exceptional." *California Association for the Gifted,* 5-6.

Rimm, S. B. (1984a). Characteristics approach: Identification and beyond. *Gifted Child Quarterly, 28*(4), 181-187.

Rimm, S. B. (1984b, January/February). If God had meant gifted children to run our homes, she would have created them bigger. *Gifted Child Today,* 26-29.

Rimm, S. B. (1985). *AIM: Achievement identification measure.* Watertown, WI: Educational Assessment Service.

Rimm, S. B. (1986a). *GAIM: Group achievement identification measure.* Watertown, WI: Educational Assessment Service.

Rimm, S. B. (1986b).*Underachievement Syndrome: Causes and cures* (1st ed.). Watertown, WI: Apple.

Rimm, S. B. (1988). *AIM-TO: Achievement identification measure—teacher observation.* Watertown, WI: Educational Assessment Service.

Rimm, S. B. (1990). A theory of relativity. *Gifted Child Today, 13*(3), 32-36.

Rimm, S. B. (1992). A bicycle ride: Why we need grouping. *How to Stop Underachievement Newsletter, 1*(3), 1-3.

Rimm, S. B. (1994). Talk, talk, talk: How to talk to your kids. *How to Stop Underachievement Newsletter, 4*(4), 3.

Rimm, S. B. (2003a). *See Jane Win® for girls: A smart girl's guide to success.* Minneapolis, MN: Free Spirit.

Rimm, S. B. (2003b). Marching to the beat of a different drummer. *Sylvia Rimm On Raising Kids Newsletter, 14*(2), 2-3.

Rimm, S. B. (2005). *Growing up too fast: The Rimm report on the secret world of America's middle schoolers.* Emmaus, PA: Rodale.

Rimm, S. B. (2007a). How children feel about their changing families. *Sylvia Rimm On Raising Kids Newsletter, 17*(4), 5.

Rimm, S. B. (2007b, Fall). Listening for what gifted children don't say. *Duke Gifted Letter,* 3.

Rimm, S. B. (2008). What's the hurry? *Sylvia Rimm On Raising Kids Newsletter, 18*(3), 7.

Rimm, S. B., Cornale, M., Manos, R., & Behrend, J. (Eds.). (1990). *Guidebook— Underachievement Syndrome: Causes and cures.* Watertown WI: Apple.

Rimm, S. B., & Lovance, K. J. (1992). The use of subject and grade skipping for the prevention and reversal of underachievement. *Gifted Child Quarterly, 36,* 100-105.

Rimm, S. B., & Lowe, B. (1988). Family environments of underachieving gifted students. *Gifted Child Quarterly, 32*(4), 353-359.

Rimm, S. B., & Olenchak, F. R. (1991). How FPS helps underachieving gifted students. *Gifted Child Today, 14*(2), 19-22.

Rimm, S. B., & Rimm-Kaufman, S. (2001). *How Jane won: 55 successful women share how they grew from ordinary girls to extraordinary women.* New York: Crown.

Rimm, S. B., Rimm-Kaufman, S., & Rimm I. (1999). *See Jane Win®: The Rimm report on how 1,000 girls became successful women.* New York: Crown.

Rimm-Kaufman, S. (1996). *Infant predictors of kindergarten behavior: The contribution of inhibited and uninhibited temperament types.* Unpublished doctoral dissertation, Harvard University.

Rosenthal, R. J., & Jacobsen, L. (1968). *Pygmalion in the classroom.* New York: Holt.

Sapolsky, R. (2004).*Why zebras don't get ulcers* (3rd ed.). New York: Henry Holt.

Schultz, R. (2000). Flirting with underachievement: Hidden for a reason. *Highly Gifted Children, 13*(2), 42-48.

Sheehy, G. (1982). *Pathfinders.* New York: Bantam.

Shepard, L. A., & Smith, M. L. (Eds.). (1989). *Flunking grades: Research and policies on retention.* London, New York, Philadelphia: The Falmer Press.

Shorrs, T. (2006). Differences between the sexes: The mismeasure of woman. *The Economist, 380*(8489), 70-72.

Siegle, D., & McCoach, D. B. (2005). Motivating gifted students. In F. A. Karnes & K. R. Stephens (Series Eds.), *Practical strategies in gifted education.* Waco, TX: Prufrock Press.

Smutney, J. (2004, Winter). Creative underachievers...are they creative too? *Gifted Education Communicator, 34*(4), 41.

Stanley, J. C. (1997, September) *Letter to the editor, Johns Hopkins Magazine.* Retrieved March 5, 2008, from www.jhu.edu/~jhumag/0997web/letters.html

Steinberg, L., Dornbusch, S. M., & Brown, B. B. (1992). Ethnic differences in adolescent achievement—an ecological perspective. *American Psychologist, 47*, 723-729.

Tomlinson, C. (2004). *The differentiated classroom: Responding to the needs of all learners.* Upper Saddle River, NJ: Prentice Hall.

Tomlinson, C., Kaplan, S., Renzulli, J., Purcell, J., Leppien, J., & Burns, D. (2002). *The parallel curriculum.* Washington, DC: National Association for Gifted Children

Van Tassel-Baska, J. (2003). *Content-based curriculum for high ability learners.* Waco, TX: Prufrock Press.

Webb, J. T., Amend, E. R., Webb, N. E., Goerss, J., & Olenchak, F. R. (2005). *Misdiagnosis and dual diagnoses of gifted children and adults: ADHD, Bipolar, OCD, Asperger's, depression, and other disorders.* Scottsdale, AZ: Great Potential Press.

Webb, J. T., Gore, J. L., Amend, E. R., & DeVries, A. R. (2007). *A parent's guide to gifted children.* Scottsdale, AZ: Great Potential Press.

Williams, S. T., Conger, K. J., & Blozis, S. A. (2007). The development of interpersonal aggression during adolescence: The importance of parents, siblings, and family economics. *Child Development, 78*(5), 1526-1542.

Winebrenner, S. (2001). *Strategies and techniques every teacher can use to meet the academic needs of the gifted and talented.* Minneapolis, MN: Free Spirit.

Whitney, C. S., & Hirsch, G. (2007). *A love for learning: Motivation and the gifted child.* Scottsdale, AZ: Great Potential Press.

Endnotes

Chapter One

1 Horn & Berger (2004)
2 Many very bright children are incorrectly labeled as having a disorder. For an excellent discussion of this topic, refer to *Misdiagnosis and Dual Diagnoses of Gifted Children and Adults: ADHD, Bipolar, OCD, Asperger's, Depression, and Other Disorders* by Webb, Amend, Webb, Goerss, & Olenchak (2005).
3 Whitney & Hirsch (2007)
4 Rimm, Rimm-Kaufman, & Rimm (1999)
5 Sapolsky (2004)

Chapter Two

1 Benbow & Stanley (1983)
2 Stanley (1997)
3 Monastersky (2005)
4 Shorrs (2006)
5 Rimm-Kaufman (1996)
6 Rimm (2008)
7 Rimm (2005), p. 248
8 Linn (2007)
9 Kristensen & Bjerkedal (2007); Rimm, Rimm-Kaufman, & Rimm (1999)
10 Williams, Conger, & Blozis (2007)
11 Rimm & Lowe (1988); Rimm, Rimm-Kaufman, & Rimm (1999)
12 Goodkin (2005); Whitney & Hirsch (2007)
13 An excellent and very helpful book for parenting gifted children is *A Parent's Guide to Gifted Children* by Webb, Gore, Amend, & DeVries (2007).
14 Rimm (1990)

Chapter Three

1 Mussen & Rutherford (1963)
2 Hetherington & Frankie (1967)
3 Rimm (2007a)
4 Helson (1971); Rimm & Rimm-Kaufman (2001); Rimm, Rimm-Kaufman, & Rimm (1999)
5 Rimm, Rimm-Kaufman, & Rimm (1999)

Chapter Four

1   Bloom & Sosniak (1981)
2   Rimm (1984b)

Chapter Five

1   Davis & Rimm (2004)
2   (1968)
3   Davis & Rimm (2004)
4   Rimm (1984a)
5   Reis & Purcell (1993)
6   Brown & Steinberg (1990); Clasen & Clasen (1995); Kinney (1993); Rimm (2005)
7   Rimm (2005)

Chapter Six

1   Goertzel, Goertzel, Goertzel, & Hansen (2004); Rimm & Rimm-Kaufman (2001);
    Rimm, Rimm-Kaufman, & Rimm (1999)
2   Sheehy (1982)
3   Covington & Beery (1976); Whitney & Hirsch (2007)
4   Covington & Beery (1976)

Chapter Seven

1   Karnes & Bean (2005); Smutney (2004); Tomlinson (2004); Tomlinson, Kaplan,
    Renzulli, Purcell, Leppien, & Burns (2002); Van Tassel-Baska, J. (2003); Winebrenner
    (2001)
2   Baum (2004); Renzulli (2005); Schultz (2000)
3   Dweck (2006)
4   Baker (1996); Rimm (1986b); Rimm (2005)
5   Rimm (1992)
6   Kulik (1992)
7   Siegle & McCoach (2005)
8   Bloom & Sosniak (1981)
9   Emerick (1992); Kanevsky & Keighley (2003)
10 Rimm (2007b)
11 Rimm, Rimm-Kaufman, & Rimm (1999)

Chapter Eight

1   Rimm (1985)
2   Rimm (1986a)
3   Rimm, Cornale, Manos, & Behrend (1990)
4   Rimm (1988)
5   Cornale (1988)
6   Rimm (1990)

Chapter Ten

1   Dweck (2006)
2   Dweck (2006)
3   Davis & Rimm (2004)
4   Steinberg, Dornbusch, & Brown (1992)
5   Brown & Steinberg (1990)
6   Berg (1993)
7   Rimm (2005)
8   Rimm (2003a); Rimm & Rimm-Kaufman (2001); Rimm, Rimm-Kaufman, & Rimm (1999)
9   Irlen (1991)

Chapter Eleven

1   Rimm (2003b)
2   Glenday (2008)
3   Rimm & Olenchak (1991)
4   Rimm (2003a); Rimm, Rimm-Kaufman, & Rimm (1999)
5   Goldberg & Adderhold-Elliot (1999)
6   Neumeister (2005)
7   Rimm, Rimm-Kaufman, & Rimm (1999)
8   Rimm & Rimm-Kaufman (2001)
9   Davis (1992); Davis & Rimm (2004); Feldhusen (1993)
10 Graue & DiPerna (2000); Laidig (1991); Shepard & Smith (1989)
11 Dweck (2006)
12 Goertzel, Goertzel, Goertzel, & Hansen (2004)
13 Rimm & Rimm-Kaufman (2001); Rimm, Rimm-Kaufman, & Rimm (1999)
14 Siegle & McCoach (2005)
15 Rimm (2005)
16 Davis & Rimm (2004)

Chapter Twelve

1   Bloom (1985)
2   Sapolsky (2004)
3   Davis (2006); Davis & Rimm (2004)
4   Assouline, Colangelo, Lupkowski-Shoplik, Lipscomb, & Forstadt (2003)
5   Brody & Benbow (1987)
6   Dweck (1999)
7   Rimm & Rimm-Kaufman (2001); Rimm, Rimm-Kaufman, & Rimm (1999)

Chapter Thirteen

1   Rimm (1990)
2   American Psychiatric Association (2000)
3   McCoy (2007)
4   Rimm (1994)
5   Rimm & Lovance (1992)

Index